CAJETAN RESPONDS
A Reader in Reformation Controversy

CAJETAN RESPONDS
A Reader in Reformation Controversy

Edited and Translated
by
JARED WICKS, S.J.

WIPF & STOCK · Eugene, Oregon

Wipf and Stock Publishers
199 W 8th Ave, Suite 3
Eugene, OR 97401

Cajetan Responds
A Reader in Reformation Controversy
By Cajetan, Tommaso de Vio and Wicks, Jared, SJ
Copyright©1978 The Catholic University of America Press
ISBN 13: 978-1-61097-569-8
Publication date 5/23/2011
Previously published by The Catholic University of America Press, 1978

CONTENTS

EDITOR'S PREFACE

This book is intended to fill a need made evident by many English-language reading .lists on the Reformation. Teachers and students are presently oversupplied. with one-volume histories of the Reformation and with monographs on the life and thought of the principal Protestant Reformers. Numerous works of the Reformers are available in useful translations and *florilegia.* But the works of Catholic writers of the Reformation era are seldom represented in our bibliographies. Some important works of the Reformation Catholic controversialists have been edited in their original Latin or German in the series *Corpus Catholicorum,* but English translations from this genre of Reformation literature are rare.

The present work is an initial effort to fill this lacuna by making eleven controversial works of the Dominican theologian Cardinal Cajetan accessible in English translation. Such a collection can stand as a reminder to historians and students that the Reformation produced not only social upheaval in the wake of passionate religious protest, but also a series of closely argued theological debates.

In presenting Cajetan, I have sought to produce a workbook for study of the early Reformation argument. The footnote references can lead to parallel reading of Luther, Zwingli, and Melanchthon along with their Catholic critic Cardinal Cajetan. At times the notes point to further projects, for example (page 280, note 3), the instructive comparison between Cajetan's defense of *Exsurge Domine* and Luther's critique of it in works the Reformer wrote without knowledge of Cajetan's *Five Articles.* My introductory biography of Cajetan ends with an assessment, which however I have kept quite general, in order to open the way for the reader to engage in a more detailed reflection and evaluation as a step toward a mature understanding of the sixteenth century religious divisions.

I wish to express my gratitude to the following scholars for expert help on this book: Remigius Baumer (Paderborn), Robert Bireley (Loyola University, Chicago), Francis Gremovnik (DeAndreis Seminary, Lamont, Illinois), Peter Manns (Mainz), John W. O'Malley (University of Detroit), Robert W. Schmidt (Xavier University, Cincinnati), K. -V. Selge (Heidelberg), and J. A. Weisheipl (Toronto).

The translation and editorial work on this volume was completed with the support of a faculty fellowship grant from the Lilly Endowment administered by the American Association of Theological Schools.

INTRODUCTION

Historians of the Reformation regularly give prominence to three dramatic encounters between Martin Luther and leading representatives of the established order with which he found himself in conflict. In mid-October, 1518, at Augsburg, Luther stood before Cardinal Cajetan, Papal Legate to the Imperial Diet, and heard official charges that he had departed from orthodox teaching in published theological works. Eight months later Luther was in Leipzig, where he debated an able representative of traditional theology, Professor John Eck of Ingolstadt, on penance, indulgences, and – to the astonishment of many – the origins and rights of the papacy. Then in April, 1521, Luther faced the young Hapsburg Emperor, Charles V, in Worms. Charles, by birth Duke of Burgundy, had recently gained title over an impressive constellation of European territories: the Low Countries, Castile and Aragon, Sicily, Naples, Alsace, Styria, Austria, and the German Empire. Before his Christian Emperor Luther declared that he was bound in conscience to teach in accord with Scripture as he understood it and so could not recant the teachings the Pope had branded erroneous. On the next day, April 19, 1521, Charles responded with a ringing confession of allegiance to the faith and way of worship handed on by his Catholic ancestors and declared himself ready to take the indicated measures against any further influence of Luther's heretical ideas in the Holy Roman Empire of the German Nation.

Beginnings exercise a rightful fascination. In this case our attention fixes inevitably on the papal diplomat, Thomas de Vio, who from his birthplace Gaeta (in Latin, *Caieta*) was and is known to the world as *Caietanus* or Cajetan. What kind of man spoke for the Catholic Church in its first public censure of emerging Protestantism? How well did the Church's spokesman know Luther's theological vision? What were the human qualities and theological credentials of the man who confronted the young Wittenberg professor who had been laboring so intensely over the text of the Psalms, Romans, Galatians, and Hebrews?

A first glance at Cajetan's career impresses one with his remarkable versatility. He was "a man of many parts" in the Catholic world of the early sixteenth century. Cajetan remains to our day the classic commentator on the *Summa Theologiae* of Aquinas. Repeatedly, men of his own day sought Cajetan's judgment and advice on questions of personal and social morality. In the decade 1508-18 Cajetan was a reforming Master General of the Dominican order. While General, he found time to write a cogent defense of the papacy against the schismatic council of Pisa in 1511. In 1518 and 1523 he took on diplomatic missions as Papal Legate in Germany and Hungary. By the late 1520s Cajetan was deep into the labors of a critical exposition of the whole of Scripture. His biblical work was later judged to be a threat to Catholic belief, denounced by a fellow Dominican, and eventually censured by the faculty of theology of the University of Paris. In spite of this alleged radicalism, Cajetan spent the final years of his life in Rome (1529-34) serving Pope Clement VII as theological advisor. In this capacity he wrote a series of dignified rejoinders on theological issues raised in the early years of the Protestant Reformation.

The present collection presents, in translation or synopsis, the works in which Cajetan argued against the claims and teachings of the early Reformation. We begin with the painstaking analyses of Luther's published views on purgatory, penance, and indulgences written by Cajetan in preparation for the Augsburg meeting of 1518. We follow his work up to a belated appeal in 1534 begging King Henry VIII to correct the scandalous error of his divorce and remarriage. The genre, therefore, is controversial theology, where an author takes on the task of analyzing the position of a doctrinal adversary and marshalling arguments in refutation. Cajetan has been singled out as being no ordinary Reformation controversialist.[1] He placed a high premium on clarity of conception and avoided all polemic against personalities. While many early Catholic defenders attempted tiresome line-by-line rebuttals of Luther's tracts, Cajetan sought to isolate major dogmatic issues and cluster his theological arguments about a few central convictions. In his disciplined work, we will note a gradual concentration of effort on the development of cogent biblical arguments for his positions. But Cajetan was hardly heard above the din of the raucous pamphlet war of the early Reformation.[2] Still, his works deserve the attention of anyone seeking a clear grasp of the issues argued as the great confessional divide opened between Protestants and Catholics in the early sixteenth century.

The major portion of this introduction will sketch the life of Cardinal Cajetan, giving special attention to his meeting with Luther in 1518 and to the circumstances surrounding his composition of the eleven works in our collection. A concluding section will offer some considerations toward a just assessment of Cajetan's response to the Reformation.

Cajetan: a biographical essay[3]

The family of Francesco de Vio of Gaeta belonged to the lower nobility of the Kingdom of Naples. The fourth son, born in mid-February 1469, was christened Giacomo (James). In 1484, the year after Luther's birth, this son entered the Dominican order, receiving "Thomas" as his religious name. He was henceforth known as Thomas de Vio Cajetan.

After initial studies in Naples and Bologna, the young friar was sent in Spring 1491 to Padua to complete his training. The Paduan theological faculty had been formed in 1363 by the aggregation to the university of the already existing schools of four religious orders (Dominicans, Franciscans, Augustinians, and Carmelites). In March 1493 Cajetan was formally incorporated into the faculty, and in a short time became a respected exponent of Thomistic positions in the ongoing arguments with the other scholastic systems. Cajetan's principal early opponent was a Scotist, Antonio Trombetta, O.F.M., who had been teaching in Padua since 1477. Cajetan's earliest known works state and defend the fundamental notions of Thomistic metaphysics over against positions of the Scotist school.

Cajetan's Paduan lectures led to the preparation of a commentary (1494) on Peter Lombard's *Sentences* which is still extant in a

manuscript copy.[4] Two early printed works were an exposition of
Aquinas' *On Being and Essence* (1495) and a treatise, *The Analogy
of Names* (1498). Both of these works have been taken as standard
expressions of Thomist fundamentals in the revivals of scholastic
philosophy in the sixteenth and early twentieth centuries.[5] However, in recent decades Thomist philosophers have become acutely
aware of Cajetan's only partial reception of Aquinas and of his
perceptible modification of many of Aquinas' deepest insights.
Cajetan is found to be a reductionist and a rigid classifier, for
example, concerning the different kinds of analogical predication,
where Aquinas himself was supple and flexible.[6] Cajetan taught
many generations of Thomists a basically Aristotelian metaphysics
of essence and substance and was insensitive to Aquinas' ontology of
existence (*esse*) and participation.[7] Cajetan's Paduan debates with
Scotism appear to have caused his own articulation of Thomist
positions to be couched in concepts more closely approximating
certain views of his adversaries than the authentic thought of the
master he professed to follow.

A second formative influence on Cajetan in Padua came from
exposure to the distinctive tradition of Aristotelian philosophy
flourishing in the arts faculty of the university. Nicholas Vernia had
been professor of natural philosophy since 1466, continuing a
distinguished line of thinkers who interpreted Aristotle on the basis
of the commentaries of the twelfth century Arab philosopher
Averroes. During the years of Cajetan's teaching at Padua, two of
Vernia's protégés, Agostino Nifo and Pietro Pomponazzi, were junior
members of the arts faculty. Among the topics engaging the
attention of the Paduan Averroists in the 1490s was a cluster of
issues concerning the human soul: its unity or multiplicity, its
dependence on or independence of the body, and especially the
possibility or non-possibility of a rational demonstration of the
soul's immortality.[8]

Cajetan took up the challenge posed by the same Averroism
which Aquinas had opposed in the thirteenth century. In three years
(1496-98), he produced six commentaries on Aristotle which constituted a notable attempt to vindicate the Thomistic and Christian
interpretation of Aristotle's world view. A treatise of 1499, *The
Infinity of God*, was also intended to deal with problems posed by
the non-Thomist interpretations of Aristotle.[9]

The Paduan Averroists were also under attack by a circle of

humanists led by Almaro Barbarð in nearby Venice. The humanist contention was that Vernia and his colleagues were using woefully inadequate Latin translations of Aristotle and so were unable to criticize Averroes by comparing his views with Aristotle's original statements. In 1497 the Paduan arts faculty gave recognition to Barbarò's views by having a new teaching chair founded for the exposition of Aristotle from the Greek text.[10]

The humanist dimension of the Paduan world of thought had its eventual effect on Cajetan's philosophical work a decade later. He completed a commentary on Aristotle's *De anima* in 1509 (printed 1510), using a recent Latin translation rather than the Aristotle of the intervening commentaries.[11] Cajetan also conferred with humanists knowledgeable in Greek, a practice which will have a telling effect on Cajetan's work on Scripture in the 1520s and 1530s. In treating Book III of Aristotle's *De anima*, Cajetan moved confidently into the heated dispute over the soul-body relation and the demonstrability of the soul's immortality. His fresh access to Aristotle's text caused him to break with the Thomist tradition that found Aristotle proving immortality. Cajetan disengaged a more historical Aristotle who thought that the soul, as substantial form of the body, corrupted when it ceased its informing function. Cajetan made it clear in his commentary that he himself thought Aristotle was wrong in holding human mortality, but that he did this because of the certainties of Christian revelation and not because the philosophical arguments for immortality, even those offered by Aquinas, were completely satisfactory.[12]

Cajetan's exposition of the *De anima* was probably one influence in the development of Pietro Pomponazzi's thought toward his vigorous rejection of any philosophical proof for immortality in his *De immortalitate animae* (1516).[13] Pomponazzi was soon accused of heresy, and a Dominican critic, Bartholomew Spina, wrote in 1519 that Cajetan was responsible for the ideas of Pomponazzi and for the spread in Italy of intellectually disruptive and pastorally disturbing ideas suggesting an incompatibility between Aristotelian reason and Christian faith.[14] But by 1519 Cajetan had risen to such prominence in the church as to be well beyond the reach of Spina's angry and aggressive attacks.

Cajetan had been made Master of Sacred Theology by the Dominican Master General after a public disputation in 1494 against Pico della Mirandola. In 1497 Cajetan was called to take over the chair of Thomistic theology at Pavia, and in 1499 he moved to Milan for a period of teaching, which however was cut short by a call to Rome and appointment to higher administration in the Dominican order. His work as Procurator General beginning in 1501 did not, however, stifle his intellectual efforts. He made time for lectures at the Sapienza and continued a major project apparently begun in Pavia, a full commentary on the *Summa Theologiae* of Aquinas. The first part of this magisterial work was completed in 1507.

In writing the first complete commentary on St. Thomas' crowning work, Cajetan was putting his own talent for minute analysis at the service of students and teachers who would use the *Summa* as their theological textbook. Cajetan's comments show the place of each part, question, and article in the total vision of Aquinas, indicate the main divisions and steps in Aquinas' arguments, and take up the objections made against the Thomist position by intervening thinkers like Duns Scotus and Durandus of Saint-Pourcain. The significance of Cajetan's commentary for modern Scholasticism is indicated by the decision to republish it along with the *Summa* in Volumes IV-XII of the stately Leonine edition of Aquinas' works. But just as with Cajetan's philosophical work, so also his theological interpretations have come under fire in more recent work on Aquinas. One criticism, for example, is that Cajetan's commentary develops the distinction between the natural and supernatural orders to such a point that creation appears almost as a complete and self-sufficient sphere of reality to which God's gifts of grace and salvation in Christ are added on as a divine afterthought.[15]

While serving in Rome as Dominican Procurator Cajetan was called upon to take part in the liturgical life of the Renaissance papal court. On numerous occasions each year a carefully selected preacher would address pope and cardinals during mass at one of the stational churches. Dominicans regularly preached to this audience on the first Sundays of Lent and Advent.[16] Cajetan gave five such sermons before Popes Alexander VI and Julius II. Four of these were Advent sermons that show Cajetan's adeptness at working from lucid doctrinal explanations to themes of admonition and exhortation concerning sincere prayer, devoted longing for Christ and the resolute turning from dissipation in mundane affairs.[17]

During the years 1500-07 numerous prelates and Dominican confreres sought Cajetan's views on a host of ethical questions. His responses were usually in the form of short treatises in which evidence and arguments were evaluated as Cajetan moved toward delivering what he saw as a responsible application of moral principle to the case at hand. He treated such topics as the obligation of a Christian to give alms, problems concerning the seal of confession, the morality of demanding interest on money loaned, a new form of credit organization (*montes pietatis*) then developing in Italian cities, questions of marital morality, the obligations devolving on a priest when he takes a stipend for a mass to be offered, etc.[18] A modern student counted forty such topics in these works in which Cajetan sought to apply the principles of Thomistic ethics to the rapidly changing social and economic world of the Renaissance.[19]

In 1507 the newly elected Master General of the Dominicans died shortly after his term began. Pope Julius II appointed Cajetan Vicar General with the task of governing the order until an election could be held. The next year, at the age of thirty-nine, Cajetan was elected Master and entered the office he was to hold for an eventful decade (1508-18).[20] It does not appear that he became the highest Dominican superior on a wave of enthusiasm or much less by acclamation. In the order he was more respected than loved, being a small, severe man who was known for wasting little time in the pleasantries of small-talk. He did not share his age's concern for the elegant and erudite turn of phrase. Characteristic of a taciturn man, his first circular letter to the whole order after his election was a straightforward statement only nine lines long.

Cajetan's generalate began at a time when his order had experienced sixty years of weak leadership. The need for reform had been expressed by many. In 1498 a General Chapter had censured the laxness of the then Master General, Venetus, and issued statements of encouragement for the "observant" movements then promoting pristine religious discipline in Dominican houses of the German and Spanish provinces. Cajetan's predecessor, Bandellus, had tried to legislate renewal by multiplying decrees and threats of penalties for offenses against the rule. Cajetan accepted this grim diagnosis of the condition of the order, and a letter of his in 1513 spoke of the "*magnitudo ruinae illius*".[21] But among the first measures he took as General was the revocation of a number of Bandellus' ordinances. Cajetan's own activity in promoting reform was to be marked by a genial simplicity. Above all, communities must return to serious concern for the *vita communis*. Friars must have weighty reasons for living outside houses of the order; the provinces and communities must abhor the singularities and private incomes that ennervate the ideals of evangelical poverty.[22] Cajetan's second great theme as Master General was his insistence that Dominicans recapture their preaching and teaching mission in the Church. Practically, he raised the standards for the granting of theological degrees in the order, and instituted examinations to test the qualifications of men appointed to preach and hear confessions under less demanding regimes. Cajetan lived out what he sought to legislate for his order, spending two to three hours each day in study and theological writing. While Master General, he completed his expositions of Parts I-II and II-II of the *Summa* (1511, 1517).

The effectiveness of Cajetan's work for reform of his order lies beyond easy measurement, especially since most chroniclers of his day were far more interested in the dramatic *affaires* that troubled the Dominicans during Cajetan's decade as General. Ironically, this man of studious reflection had to contend with outbreaks of extraordinary and bizarre religious phenomena in the houses of his order.

Controversy still embroiled Florentine Dominicans in disputes over Savanarola, the fiery prior-preacher who had been executed in 1498. In Spain a furor erupted over the alleged visions of a Dominican lay-sister of Valladolid. In 1510 Master General Cajetan issued a severe prohibition against any promotion of the visionary by members of the order in Spain. In Germany, Dominicans became engaged in largely anti-Semitic polemics against the humanist scholar, Johannes Reuchlin. Cajetan would have had interviews in Rome with Reuchlin's accuser, Jakob von Hochstraten, O.P., but there is no evidence that Cajetan sought to exert strong influence on the order in this matter.

The most troublesome case broke out in Bern, Switzerland, where a young Dominican postulant, Johann Jetzer, gained sudden notoriety in 1507 for raptures, visions, and alleged stigmatization. Jetzer was clearly deluded, although it does not appear that he purposely sought to deceive. But the Dominican superiors tried to avoid an exposé and made no efforts to dampen the excitement of the Bernese people over Jetzer. In the midst of a first canonical investigation, Jetzer turned in accusation against four of the Dominican Fathers. The Pope appointed two ecclesiastical tribunals, whose hearings led to condemnation of the four for heresy, sorcery, and conspiracy to defraud the people. The Dominicans were delivered over to the secular arm and executed in Bern on May 31, 1509. As Master General, Cajetan wrote two appeals in 1507-08 calling for calm and careful examination of the alleged extraordinary events. But once the canonical trial began, he silently allowed justice to take the course that led to bitter disgrace for his order.

Cajetan's generalate is most remembered for his marshalling of Dominican opposition to the protest "council" of Pisa in 1511. French and Imperial enmity against Pope Julius II combined with a resurgent Parisian conciliarist theology to give Pisa its motive force.[23] In the underlying theology, Cajetan saw a notion of Church structure which, when judged in the light of the New Testament and the Council of Florence (1439), appeared heretical. The secular and ecclesiastical politics of Pisa seemed to a Roman observer like Cajetan to be verging toward another schism. The General immediately forbade all Dominican participation in or support for the council. He dispatched talented Dominican orators to Pisa to rouse resistance among local clergy and populace, and they may well have contributed to the council's decision to move after only three sessions (November 5-12, 1511) to the friendlier atmosphere of Milan.

On the Pisan side, Zacharias Ferrerius, Benedictine abbot of Subasio, wrote an apologia based on the older conciliarism of Pierre d'Ailly (died 1420) and Jean Gerson (died 1429). Ferrerius' main thesis was that a general council had the power to depose an unsatisfactory Pope for a list of specific faults or crimes. By October 1511, Cajetan had produced a comprehensive refutation, *A Comparison of the Authority of Pope and Council.*[24] He argued that the superiority of pope over a general council was divinely instituted by Christ in the words addressed to Peter in Matthew 16 and John 21 (*Comparison*, chapters I-III). One by one Cajetan turned back conciliarist views, whether based on Scripture (VII), declarations of the fifteenth-century councils of Constance and Basle (VIII), or rational argumentation (XI-XIV). Cajetan's Thomism served him well in his refutation of conciliarism, as he cited Aquinas eighty-two times in the treatise (but Augustine only fifteen times).

Cajetan is, of course, well known for his part in the growing accentuation of the papacy in the Catholic ecclesiology dominant from Eugenius IV to Pius XII, that is, from the decline of conciliarism (*ca.* 1440) to the eve of Vatican II.[25] Cajetan ranks with Juan de Torquemada and Robert Bellarmine as a leading exponent of the papal plenitude of power in the church, a fact acknowledged at Vatican I, when chapters IX and XI of Cajetan's *Comparison* were cited in the authoritative *relatio* of Archbishop Gasser preceding the definition of papal infallibility.[26] However, more recent work has rectified somewhat our understanding of Cajetan's total ecclesiology, especially by pointing out the themes he developed in his later biblical commentaries, such as that of the church as the mystical body in which Christ the head lives and works.[27]

Even the *Comparison* of 1511 was more than simply an affirmation of papal superiority in the church. In treating the favorite conciliarist issue of the deposition of a pope, Cajetan did say that the church can remove a convicted heretic from the papal office (Chapters XX-XXII) and he finally admitted that a general council would be the proper forum for such a deposition (XXIV).[28] The other cases which Gerson and Ferrerius listed as justifying deposition were according to Cajetan indeed abuses of papal power, but he held that they should be countered by forms of resistance that fall short of deposing the Pope from office. Cajetan wrote scornfully of slumbering prelates and indolent princes who allow abuses to compound themselves in the church but do not take upon themselves the onus of withholding flattery, arguing against a bad pope, refusing to obey his evil laws, and especially turning to prayer to beg God to deliver his church from an evil shepherd (XXVII).[28a]

An index of the incisiveness of Cajetan's anti-Pisan work is the vigorous reaction of his adversaries. In January 1512, the council, then at Milan, requested a theological censure against Cajetan from the theological faculty of the University of Paris. In February, copies of his *Comparison* were burned in Paris. King Louis XII intervened later to prevent a formal censure, since Julius II had finally convoked what was to be the Fifth Lateran Council. But a young Parisian professor, Jacques Almain, published a rebuttal against Cajetan in the Spring of 1512, to which Cajetan answered with a further treatise of November 1512. In the meantime Fifth Lateran had opened and at the second Session, May 17, 1512, Cajetan delivered a lengthy oration on the structure of the earthly church, developing an analogy with the heavenly church depicted in John's Apocalypse.[29]

In March 1513 Giovanni de' Medici succeeded Julius II, taking the name Leo X. Fifth Lateran continued with Cajetan in attendance by reason of his office of Master General of the Dominicans. In the eighth Session (December 19, 1513), the council turned to the issue raised by Averroist theories of the human soul. The declaration, *Apostolici regiminis,* was read to the assembly for its approval. The first part condemned as pernicious, false, and heretical the view then circulating that the human soul was mortal and that this was a datum of philosophical reasoning. A second part went on to command that university professors of philosophy were to refrain from treating philosophical ideas not in accord with the teaching of the faith. Furthermore, teachers of philosophy were to make every effort to show the truth of the Christian religion and to refute arguments made against it.[30] After the reading each of the one-hundred thirty council fathers was called upon to register his approval. There were only two dissenting votes, one of which was Cajetan's *non placet* to the second part, where he found an objectionable effort to compromise the distinctiveness and integrity of philosophical reflection.[31]

Fifth Lateran closed in the Spring of 1517, after speaking well enough on reform of the church — but to a church leadership devoid of any will to work for reform. Little did anyone suspect the torrent of events about to break over the church from Germany and Switzerland. Furthermore, the two doctrinal concerns of Fifth Lateran, papal supremacy over a council and the immortality of the individual human soul, were not such as to prepare the better minds among churchmen to deal with the issues of sin, forgiveness, faith, and grace, which Luther was to raise with such insistence in the first years of Reformation controversy. Cajetan was typical of those who were called from other parts of the theological terrain to attempt a response to the initial affirmations of Reformation theology. Cajetan completed his extensive commentary on Part II-II of the *Summa* in February 1517, and was included in Leo X's creation of thirty-one new cardinals on July 1, 1517. He received the church of St. Sixtus as his titular Roman church.

As Cajetan's generalate drew to a close in 1518, he was drawn into a project on which Leo X was expending considerable energy, the defense against the threat of Turkish conquest in the Balkans and eastern Mediterranean. In early 1518 Leo had legates fanning out over Western Europe to gain support from Christian rulers for a coordinated plan of battle. Five years of peace should be solemnly declared in the West, a fleet should be outfitted for the defense of Rhodes, troops should be sent to Croatia and Hungary, and all should levy a tax for financing the great crusade. Leo was convinced that three years would suffice to eliminate the Turkish fleet and secure the southeastern frontier of Christian Europe — if cooperation were forthcoming.

In February 1518 a diet of the German Empire was convoked for August in Augsburg to hear and ponder Leo's grand scheme. Cardinal Farnese was named Legate to the diet and charged with the uninviting task of facing this cumbersome assembly of princes, prince-bishops, barons, abbots, and civic councillors who would meet under the leadership of the aging Emperor Maximillian. The imperial diets had recently taken to issuing regular lists of *gravamina*, or complaints, principally against the ecclesiastical judiciary and Rome's financial projects — like the special indulgence then circulating for the building of St. Peter's Basilica, which many saw as nothing more than a device for hastening the flow of money southward out of Germany. Knowing something of the temper of his prospective audience, Cardinal Farnese pleaded ill-health, and on April 26, 1518, Cajetan was named Legate in his place. Cajetan named a vicar to fill out the closing months of his Dominican generalate and prepared himself for the journey to Augsburg and an unpromising exchange with the resentful estates of the Empire. The theologian and administrator was about to be tested for competency in the new field of papal-imperial diplomacy. And — a fact not realized by Pope or Cardinal — the way was opening for Cajetan's historic confrontation with Luther in October, three weeks after the close of the Diet of Augsburg.

Roman officials had begun hearing about Martin Luther, Augustinian and professor of Scripture at the new Saxon university of Wittenberg, in the first days of 1518.[32] The Archbishop of Mainz and Magdeburg had sent to Rome Luther's list of ninety-five disputation theses and his treatise, both treating the nature of indulgences and indicating proper priorities in preaching on the subject. Luther seemed to be offering a novel view, curtailing somewhat the effectiveness of papal grants of indulgences, and was clearly arguing that indulgences should have at best a peripheral place in the Christian life of penance and purification under grace.[33] The Archbishop asked for a doctrinal review of the works, since what Luther was saying could undercut successful preaching of the St. Peter's indulgence in territories under the Archbishop's jurisdiction.

It is not clear when Cajetan first heard of Luther's intervention on behalf of a reform of indulgence preaching. But, by an uncanny coincidence, Cajetan had himself been working out a theological account of indulgences in the late autumn of 1517. The result of his study and reflection was a treatise completed December 8 and dedicated to the Pope's cousin, Cardinal Guilio de' Medici, who held the office of Papal Vice-Chancellor at the time.[34] Cajetan's treatise shows no sign of any reading in the materials we know Luther had produced up to that time. He seems to have been simply attempting to lay down a competently drawn theoretical basis for indulgences, perhaps feeling the need for an alternative to the less critical articles on the subject in the recently published theological dictionaries of Sylvester Prierias (*Summa Sylvestrina,* 1516) and Johann Altenstaig (*Vocabularius theologiae,* 1517).

Whatever the immediate occasion, it is clear that Cajetan's moderate views would have made a difference if they had been translated into popular form in preaching on indulgences. In the treatise, Cajetan calmly charges that some indulgences have been issued for frivolous purposes and only serve in these cases to undermine Christian penance (Chapter VIII). Indulgences for the departed in purgatory are offered only as the Church's petition (*suffragium*) on their behalf, and not as an authoritative remission of punishment (V). On this basis, one could hardly claim that an indulgence automatically delivers a soul from purgatory. Also, the pious work of alms or prayer required for gaining an indulgence cannot be performed by a person cut off by sin from living communion with Christ and his members. Only the living members of Christ take part in the interior benefits distributed by indulgences (XI). Cajetan's treatise concludes with an expression of hope that by sane use of indulgences the faithful will be so encouraged that there will be a return of the "golden age" of Christian penance once experienced by the early Church. Unwittingly, Cajetan had prepared himself for a brief series of works on indulgences in the early years of Reformation debate.

As Cajetan travelled northward to the Diet of Augsburg in May 1518, he probably knew that some initial proceedings were underway in Rome against a Wittenberg Augustinian. Sylvester Prierias, a Dominican, held the post of official theologian to the papal court, an office that at times entailed the work of theological censorship. Prierias appears to have become involved in the "Luther case" in April, shortly before Cajetan's departure for Augsburg. It seems clear, however, that as he left Rome Cajetan had no reason to suspect he would become involved in the Holy See's measures against the Saxon professor.

The first step that Rome took against Luther was a directive given by Pope Leo X in February, 1518, that Luther's Augustinian superiors bring their overly articulate member under control. Some time later, probably in April, curia officials opened a canonical *processus ordinarius* against Luther as "suspect of heresy." Two steps initiated this procedure. The suspect's works were to be examined, in this case by Prierias, to see whether the suspicion rested on grounds justifying formal accusation and citation before an ecclesiastical court. At the same time, the suspect received a *monitio charitativa* informing him of the suspicion and calling for an immediate recantation to remove the suspicion. Otherwise, the suspect could expect citation to Rome for a trial in which the charges would be proven or disproven. The *monitio* appears to have been delivered by Luther's Augustinian superiors at the chapter of the order's German provinces held in Heidelberg in late April, 1518.

At this stage of the controversy, Luther began to receive influential support, not from his Augustinian superiors, but from the founder and proud patron of Wittenberg's university, Prince Friedrich the Wise, ruler of Electoral Saxony. Friedrich had earlier refused permission for the preaching of the St. Peter's indulgence in his lands, mainly as a measure against the ascending fortunes of his rivals, the Brandenburg house of Hohenzollern. Archbishop Albrecht of Mainz was a Hohenzollern and stood to profit considerably from the contributions to the St. Peter's building fund given to gain the indulgence. Also, Friedrich's university was in the process of introducing significant reforms of curriculum, as promoted by Luther and Andreas Carlstadt. Scholasticism was being relegated to the periphery so that biblical and patristic studies could hold the controlling place in the theological course. Friedrich knew well that the Leipzig and Cologne Dominicans were completely opposed to the new theological tack in Wittenberg.

Friedrich, therefore, did not hesitate to protect his talented professor of Scripture against opponents in the arenas of politics (Archbishop Albrecht) and education (the Dominicans), who were now suspected of using a heresy charge to discredit Wittenberg and its university. This animosity against the Dominicans, as the alleged initiators of the charges against Luther, is going to prejudice Luther's approach to Cajetan later in the year. The Dominican Johann Tetzel, however, will stoutly deny having caused Luther's denunciation before Roman authorities.[35]

As professor of the Wittenberg university, Luther had the status of a state official of Electoral Saxony. On this basis it was Friedrich who "allowed" him to attend the Heidelberg chapter of the German Augustinians, but with a strict injunction against the order's delivering Luther over for a Roman trial. In the coming months, Friedrich's influence will be crucial in saving Luther from a condemnation by Cajetan or by the curia, especially in early 1519, after the death of Emperor Maximillian, when Friedrich, as one of the seven imperial electors, began to play a key role in Leo X's calculations about the best choice as next Holy Roman Emperor.

For Luther, the Heidelberg chapter was an unadulterated triumph. In a public disputation on April 26, he made an impressive presentation of his Pauline-Augustinian "theology of the cross."[36] This is basically a deeply spiritual theology and experience of conversion of heart away from all sinful self-reliance (Thesis 17), by the annihilating self-accusation of sin (18, 23-24), eager seeking of God's healing grace (16), and no little confidence in the living Christ who brings forth our good works after infusing grace and faith at the crucial moment of conversion (26-27). The theological theses and concise proofs of Luther's Heidelberg Disputation remain to our day the best brief statement of his early theology of Christian conversion. It is most regretable that a short work of this quality was not circulating at the beginning of the Reformation. Since the modern student has this and other early works of Luther available, he can more easily grasp Luther's deeper intentions. Cajetan, as we will see, did not have access to works like the Heidelberg Disputation which would have given him a full account of Luther's theological program.

In Heidelberg, Luther also responded to the *monitio* addressed to him as suspect of heresy.[37] He held that he could not recant simply because some overly rash opponents thought they had detected a whiff of heresy in his works. He pointed out that no academic, civil, or ecclesiastical condemnation had been issued against him. So he would await a reputable judgment on his views, meanwhile paying no attention to the imagined charges conjured up by his enemies. The Prince Elector's hand stayed any further implementation of the canonical proceedings at that time. Nonetheless, Luther began to ponder thoughtfully what it might mean if he were condemned and excommunicated.

Back in Wittenberg, in the days Cajetan would be nearing the Alps, Luther gave a sermon on the subject of excommunication and its effects in the life of a Christian. He excoriated the excessive use of this censure by Church officials in his day, and then went on to maintain that the effect of excommunication was to sever only the external bonds of a person's communion with the Church as a visible body. In itself, it did not affect the bond of faith, hope, and charity by which a person could conceivably still be in interior living communion with Christ. In these days of May 1518, Luther's Wittenberg printer was straining his resources to bring out the *Explanations of the Ninety-five Theses* and there could be no thought of printing the sermon on excommunication. Consequently, instead of the actual text, a short list of "theses" drawn up by someone in Luther's audience began to circulate as the view Luther held on the Church's supreme canonical censure. These theses turned up in Augsburg in the late summer to prejudice some key figures against Luther.

In Rome, Sylvester Prierias completed his report on Luther's views on indulgences as found in the Ninety-five Theses. This served as grounds for formal indictment of Luther before an ecclesiastical judge. Consequently, the next step was to cite Luther as one "suspect of heresy" and call for him to appear in Rome within sixty days, where he would be answerable to the charges brought against him.

On August 7, 1518, in Wittenberg, Luther received the citation along with a printed copy of the *Dialogus* Prierias had composed to ground the charges brought. Luther reacted scornfully to Prierias' work as an inept conflation of bare words and random opinions of Thomas Aquinas. There was nothing of Scripture, nothing of the Fathers, nothing of Canon Law to show that Luther had deviated from Catholic teaching. Luther took only two days to dash off his *Responsio,* fully confident of having demolished the theological dwarf who had ventured against him.[38]

Instead of planning how he might be in Rome by October 7, Luther wrote immediately to Friedrich, who was in Augsburg where the Diet had begun on August 1.[39] Luther asked his Prince to intervene on his behalf with the Pope. The influential help of

Emperor Maximillian should be sought as well, to the end that the Pope remit the whole matter for settlement in Germany before an impartial judge. Luther does not name the appropriate judge he has in mind, but one can think of a German bishop or — more likely — a group of university theologians who would handle the matter as principally academic, as it was in its beginnings. The request for remission to a local judiciary would not be unique in the early sixteenth century, when rulers frequently showed concern that so many matters of ecclesiastical dispute were taken to higher courts for settlement far from the territorial scene of the dispute. Civil intervention on a doctrinal issue would be extraordinary, but Friedrich would certainly allege that academic matters were at stake, ultimately the good name of his Wittenberg university.

As we shall see, Emperor Maximillian would not be favorable to helping Luther, but in August, 1518, Friedrich could count on a sympathetic hearing from Leo X, for the members of the Diet were at that time pondering Leo's call for a mighty Christian effort — at great cost — against the Turk. After a two-month delay in the Tyrol, Cajetan had arrived in Augsburg for the opening of the Diet on August 1. Five days later he addressed the assembled estates on behalf of the Pope, assuring them that the future of religion and humanity itself hung in the balance. Germany itself would hardly be safe if Croatia and Hungary fell to the Turkish armies. The crucial measure was a graded tax of 5% to 20% on all revenues in the Empire to support military and naval operations for three years. The Emperor was favorable, but the estates were dourly suspicious of this appeal originating from a scion of the affluent Medici of Florence. On August 27 they drafted an evasive answer, pleading the need for time, since the consent of their subjects would have to be given. Maximillian expressed well-founded amazement at this novel idea, but conceded that the final answer would have to wait until another diet was held in early 1519.

Cajetan had therefore to report to Leo X that the imperial estates were showing a singular lack of enthusiasm for the project that was the principal goal of his legation. As a by-product of this appeal to the Diet, he became the butt of vicious satires authored by Ulrich von Hutten in 1519 and 1520. Hutten's dialogues cast Cajetan as a dissolute and supercilious Italian filled with contempt for things German. Cajetan came to Augsburg as a tool of Medici craftiness seeking to fleece Germany of its financial resources and to undercut any independent imperial policy-making in European affairs. Thus, Cajetan appeared as something of a stock character in a product of the often bitter anti-scholastic and anti-Italian polemics of German humanism.[40]

August and September then proved to be crucial months in the developing "Luther case", as Emperor, Curia, Cardinal Legate, and Prince Elector prepared the way for the October confrontation between Luther and Cajetan. The latter was to become for a short while the Church's delegated spokesman in the early assessment of Luther's teaching. At Augsburg the Turkish threat and the response of Christian Europe to Leo's crusade appeal gradually receded as the main topic. Conversations came to focus on the cluster of issues raised by Luther's protest and by the doctrinal and canonical response of Pope Leo and his curia.

In mid-August, the Pope received a remarkable communication signed by none other then Emperor Maximillian himself.[41] The Emperor reported that Luther's ill-founded and dangerous views — already judged heretical by the Pope's own court theologian — were finding further adherents and defenders in Germany. Luther was for Maximillian one of the tribe of disputatious theologians who were undermining doctrine and piety by the sophistries they were spinning out in theses and tracts. Significant in the Emperor's letter is his description of Luther as *pertinax* (obstinate) in his erroneous teaching. Maximillian did acknowledge that it was the Pope's responsibility to speak for the Church on Luther's theology of indulgences and excommunication, but the Emperor declared himself ready to take the indicated measures to prevent further undermining of Christian life in the Empire.

The Curia responded immediately to this new complaint about Luther's teachings. Two papal letters were completed in Rome on August 23. They show that the Curia had changed the canonical character of the proceedings against Luther in view of the most recent developments. A *processus summarius* was opened, whereby the earlier citation on suspicion of heresy, calling for appearance in Rome within sixty days, was simply set aside. Luther was now to be treated as a known and obstinate *(notorius et pertinax)* heretic. The accusation was taken as sufficiently proven and the accused was to be confronted with a simple alternative between recantation and acceptance of his condemnation. If he were condemned, there would certainly follow ecclesiastical penalties, such as excommunication and perhaps interdict on his supporters, and probably civil penalties as well, such as banishment from the Empire or even execution.

The first papal letter of August 23 gave Cajetan a series of instructions to be followed in implementing measures against Luther.[42] In accord with the *processus summarius*, Cajetan, with the aid of the Emperor and the estates, is to have Luther brought before himself and held in custody. If Luther responds with an abjuration and request for forgiveness, Cajetan is to reconcile him with the Church. But if Luther refuses to appear or escapes, Cajetan is authorized to issue wide-ranging penalties of excommunication against Luther and his protectors, even to the extent of placing under interdict cities or universities that might harbor the culprit.

The second papal letter was addressed to Prince Friedrich. It shows that the Curia had not lost sight of the need to deal carefully with this powerful member of the Diet which was then discussing Pope Leo's appeal for funds. The letter was couched in softer tones than appeared in Cajetan's instructions, and it applied the subtle pressures of a diplomatic request for assistance.[43] The Prince should think of the good name of his noble family. Ugly rumors report that Luther is attacking the Church under Friedrich's protection, but the Pope refuses to believe such calumny. The Prince is exhorted and ordered to bring about Luther's delivery over to the Church's judiciary as it is on hand in Augsburg in the person of the Cardinal Legate, Cajetan. Once Friedrich does this, he will be free of any taint of suspected misconduct, whatever may be the eventual judgment of the Apostolic See on Luther's doctrine.

The arrival of these two letters in Augsburg in the last days of August brought Friedrich to Cajetan for a long conversation on the matter at hand.[44] Friedrich's main request was that Rome remit the case for ultimate judgment by German bishops and/or theologians. Friedrich insisted that the papal letter he received indicated that no final judgment had been reached and that it was imperative that Luther be heard before impartial judges who would give him ample opportunity to disprove the accusations against him. Cajetan had learned enough in his brief diplomatic experience to prevent him from laying all the harsh facts about the *processus summarius* before Friedrich. This would endanger his first and basic responsibility for bringing about Luther's appearance in Augsburg. Cajetan had to answer that he could not ask the Pope to remit the case to a German judiciary, but he did expand on certain possibilities aimed at allaying

Friedrich's antagonism toward Roman canonical procedures. Cajetan
did have delegated faculties to reconcile a repentant Luther. He
assured Friedrich that he harbored no prejudice against Luther.
Cajetan could honestly plead that he was not a canon lawyer and
had no experience in the judiciary of the *camera apostolica*. He may
have spoken of his years as religious superior and his fatherly
relation to his Dominican subjects. Whatever was said, Cajetan and
Friedrich laid down certain definite conditions under which Luther
was to appear before the Cardinal Legate. There was to be full
examination and proof of charges; Luther would be given the
opportunity to defend himself; and no definitive judgment was to
issue from this hearing. As was frequently repeated later, Cajetan
was to proceed *paterne, non judicialiter*. On this basis Friedrich
agreed to have Luther come to Augsburg, promising that he would
himself never protect a condemned heretic and would, if eventually
necessary, carry out the indicated penalties laid down by the
Church.

Cajetan's small diplomatic success with Friedrich made it
urgent that he obtain modified instructions from Rome. This posed
no great difficulty, in part because this would fit well with the
Pope's desire to please the Prince Elector in view of the larger
European issues of the day. By September 11 another papal letter
addressed to Cajetan had been prepared.[45] No reference was made
to taking Luther into custody, and in effect the Pope suspended the
judgment of error, notoriety, and obstinacy underlying the *processus
summarius*. Cajetan was now commissioned to study the case
carefully in all its details and to arrive at a judgment on Luther's
orthodoxy. The Curia could be confident it was acting responsibly in
delivering the matter into the hands of a man with impeccable
theological credentials gained through a quarter-century of writing
and teaching. Someone may even have recalled that Cajetan had
been writing on indulgences less than a year ago. The letter made no
change in the prospective penalties that could be imposed on Luther
and his followers, if the Cardinal Legate arrived at an adverse
decision. But of course the Curia could later adapt itself in that area
as well, once it knew the outcome of Cajetan's investigation of
Luther's works and his hearing of the accused.

There were further letters from the Vice-Chancellor, Giulio de'
Medici, on October 3 and 7, urging Cajetan to restraint and prudence
in view of the positions taken by Friedrich, but these arrived well

after Cajetan had become convinced that this was not a matter that could simply be dropped so as not to offend Luther's patron and territorial overlord.[46]

In the city of Augsburg Cajetan was able to find copies of two of Luther's published works, the *Explanations of the Ninety-five Theses* (printed in August) and the *Sermo de poenitentia* (probably issued to aid the annual confessions made in Lent, 1518). While Luther was preparing for the trip from Wittenberg to Augsburg, Cajetan began a painstakingly careful study of these works. The results of his analysis, evaluation, and counterargument are the *Augsburg Treatises* (translated or synopsized below, pages 47-98).

These treatises, which Cajetan cast in the form of scholastic *quaestiones*, chart for us the emergence of the Cardinal's considered judgment that Luther had in fact departed from normative Catholic teaching. This was not a blanket judgment that led, in the style of a Prierias, to a wholesale condemnation of Luther's theological work. Among numerous points of detail argued in the treatises, Cajetan singled out just two views on which he called for a recantation if Luther wanted the *processus* to be halted. Cajetan knew the different degrees of doctrinal binding force, and he saw as well that a number of the points to which he objected could in fact be further refined and explained in an orthodox sense. As one informed person reported later, Cajetan repeatedly said to Luther, "Recant the two points. We can solve the rest by applying distinctions."[47] In the second and eighth of Cajetan's treatises we can watch the two pivotal issues taking shape in the exact form in which Cajetan understood them and marshalled evidence against them. Because of these two points, the "Luther case" was not settled in Augsburg through Cajetan's fatherly admonition and Luther's filial docility but underwent a new and dangerous escalation, as Luther found himself forced to ponder the validity of the norms by which Cajetan had judged the two points and called for him to submit to correction by the Church.[48]

The main events of mid-October in Augsburg have been recited in countless Reformation histories and Luther biographies. The following account focuses on the impact of divergent convictions on each other, with special attention to the reverberations of this impact in the minds of the two central figures.[49]

Luther arrived in Augsburg October 7, but refrained from approaching Cajetan immediately under advice from Saxon councillors, who suggested that an imperial document of safe conduct could be a prudent precaution against a sudden application of force by the Legate. Luther wrote on October 10 to Spalatin, Prince Friedrich's private secretary, that he was ready to submit to the teaching of the Roman Church and would recant upon demonstration that he had swerved from the Church's teaching. Luther admitted, though, that he was considering an appeal to a future ecumenical council if the Legate tried to apply coercion instead of sound argument. Luther's basic ecclesial docility was tempered in these days by suspicions which his own exchange with Prierias and the Diet's ambient anti-Roman resentment combined to engender.

On Tuesday, October 12, Luther came before Cajetan. He began by apologizing for making an issue of the safe conduct and proceeded to a very respectful expression of his docility under Church teaching. Cajetan responded that Scripture and the sacred canons were the norms governing their discussion and that he was going to proceed as instructed by Pope Leo X, whom he was representing. The method, however, would be more paternal than juridical. Accordingly, Luther should obey the requests the Pope was making that he recant his errors and promise never to disturb the Church by teaching such things in the future.

When Luther asked Cajetan for a specific indication of his errors, the Cardinal told him that one was in his *Explanations of the Ninety-five Theses*, Thesis 58, where Luther had contradicted the teaching of Pope Clement VI on the basic reality underlying indulgences. Luther had said that the basis for grants of indulgences was simply the power of the keys which Christ had conferred upon Peter and his successors, the popes. By the keys the popes imposed ecclesiastical penances and simply by the keys, Luther contended, they remitted these penances when they granted indulgences. Cajetan responded that Pope Clement VI, in the bull, *Unigenitus*, had taught that indulgences were based on the merits of Christ and his saints, which the popes applied in remitting penances. Thus Cajetan brought into the public forum the argument he had developed against Luther in the lengthy treatise he had completed a week before (translated below, pages 68-85).

The other error Cajetan indicated was in Luther's *Sermo de poenitentia* as well as in the *Explanations*, Thesis 7. In his treatise of September 26 (below, pages 49-55) Cajetan has organized his counter-arguments against what Luther had laid down as the proper way to receive forgiveness in the sacrament of Penance. Among these dispositions, Luther laid great stress on an attitude of faith. One receiving absolution must believe most certainly that his sins are in fact forgiven by the word of Christ. One not believing this, Luther taught, cannot be forgiven. But Cajetan maintained that this was to make a new and unacceptable style of faith into a salvific imperative in the Church.

It had been Cajetan's desire to avoid disputing with Luther, since a dispute would destroy the paternal-filial tone and would change his role from papal representative to theological opponent. In spite of this, a rapid exchange of arguments did follow. Luther maintained that both his points were supported by texts of Scripture that were more binding than the questionable authorities behind Cajetan's charges. Cajetan insisted that papal teaching had priority over councils and over Luther's interpretation of Scripture. Luther eventually sensed Cajetan's tenacity on the two points and requested a day for deliberation.

On Wednesday, October 13, Luther returned in the company of a notary, a group of witnesses, and the Augustinian Vicar for Germany, Johann Staupitz. In Cajetan's presence, Luther formally protested his adherence to the teachings of the Roman Church and declared that he was not conscious of going counter to Scripture or to the patristic and papal documents of the Catholic tradition. Luther declared that he was ready to submit to the lawful judgment of the Church, that he would gladly answer the two objections in writing, and that he would stand as judged by the universities of Basle, Freiburg, Louvain, or even Paris. Cajetan responded to the effect that the Church had spoken what was binding doctrine on indulgences in the bull of Clement VI. Staupitz broke the impasse of this meeting by asking Cajetan to agree to receive Luther's written response on the two points raised the day before. Cajetan agreed, and Luther left to work up the stand he would take on the foundation of indulgences and on faith in sacramental efficacy.

In the third meeting,[50] Cajetan accepted Luther's written statement on the two charges, but upon an initial reading the Cardinal did not find it sufficiently cogent to make him drop his demand for a retraction.[51] Luther was amazed at Cajetan's insensitivity to his biblical proofs. When the Cardinal urged him to retract, Luther tried to evade by referring to Pope Leo, who would give the binding verdict. Exasperated, Cajetan agreed to send the defense on to the Pope. The bull on indulgences came up again and Luther tripped up the Cardinal on a question of its exact wording. Luther further argued that Scripture was so filled with references to faith that he could not change his notion of sacramental forgiveness, while indulgences were such an open question that the theologians were free to argue their views until the Church spoke. Cajetan sensed the circular direction of the exchange and sent Luther away with instructions not to return until he was ready to retract his errors.

Two letters reveal Luther's attitude in the hours after he left Cajetan.[52] Because Cajetan was so adamant on the two points, Luther can see no hope of any good coming from the Legate — no matter how fatherly and friendly he may say he is. Luther is sure he has refuted Cajetan on the two points, but the Cardinal is obtuse when faced with biblical arguments. Luther will hold to his two views, especially faith in the sacramental word, since thereby he has himself become a Christian! In case Cajetan tries to have Luther taken into custody, Luther will have ready an appeal to the Pope that will take the matter over Cajetan's head. Another means of rendering the Cardinal ineffective will be the publication of the written defense against the charges. By this Luther is sure he can show the world what an incompetent judge he had in Augsburg. Luther asks for prayers, since a dire threat hangs over him as he does battle for faith in Christ and in God's grace. For us this evidence is clear: far from increasing Luther's respectful docility before Roman authority, Cajetan's charges wounded Luther in a sensitive area of his religious existence. Luther turned viciously upon the man who would do such a thing on grounds that Luther did not rate important.

On his side, Cajetan did not simply bide his time in the days after his meetings with Luther. First, he sought to enlist the help of Staupitz in persuading Luther to retract his two errors. Staupitz pleaded his own inability to keep step with Luther when biblical texts were being treated, but he did pass on Cajetan's assurance of good will toward Luther. Furthermore, Cajetan gave some time to reconsidering the exact cogency with which he could press his two charges. He seems to have sensed that on the second point, faith in the sacramental word, he did not stand on such firm ground as he had on the question of indulgences where he had the text of Clement VI. Therefore, a day or so later, through Luther's fellow Augustinian, Wenceslaus Link, Cajetan told Luther that the second point could at present remain open, since with refinement or slight re-definition Luther's view might well stand.[53] Now all he was asking was an expression of obedient agreement with the bull of Clement VI. If this were forthcoming, the *processus* against Luther would come to a halt. At any rate, Cajetan assured Luther, he was not about to level an exccmmunication against him for heresy.

On October 17 Luther wrote to Cajetan that he had received the messages sent by his two friends.[54] In response to Cajetan's good will, Luther expressed regret for having spoken harshly about the Pope's use of scripture. Apparently in response to Cajetan's reformulation of the required recantation, Luther did promise to observe a moratorium on the subject of indulgences, providing his opponents did the same. His conscience does not allow him to submit when proposed doctrines are founded only on Aquinas. Since so much is of doubtful certainty on indulgences, Pope Leo should judge the matter and determine what is Christian doctrine. Then Luther would feel justified in revoking or assenting.

Cajetan did not respond to Luther's partial concession, possibly because he had already set in motion a series of Roman reactions at a higher level. But three days without an answer were enough to disturb Luther's Saxon advisors. They had prepared Luther's appeal to the Pope, and they now urged the growing danger that a message from Rome could suddenly unleash stern measures against Luther and his friends. So Luther composed a second letter to bid Cajetan farewell and alert him to his formal appeal.[55] In it he reiterated his submissiveness to the Church's coming decision, and added his hope that Cajetan would be glad to be relieved of this troublesome matter as the case was laid in Pope Leo's hands.

Cajetan had not let the matter rest with his personal appeals to Luther. Immediately he grasped the handle offered by Luther's repeated promise to submit to an authentic decision by the Church. On October 15 Cajetan completed another treatise, his thirteenth in Augsburg, on the basis and efficacy of indulgences. Using sections of the treatise, he drafted a succinct statement which he then sent on to the Pope as a possible wording in which the clarifying decision could be issued. While waiting for an answer from Rome, he obtained a printed copy of Luther's sermon on excommunication and on October 29 he completed the last of his Augsburg treatises, a thoughtful rejoinder stressing aspects of the Church Luther had not considered in his account of the act of ecclesiastical excommunication. Leo X acceded almost immediately to Cajetan's request for a statement on indulgences, issuing the bull *Cum postquam* on November 9.[56] Using Cajetan's draft, Leo reinforced what Clement VI had taught and thereby gave Roman approval to Cajetan's compressed formulation of a minimal doctrine on indulgences. Cajetan also wrote to Rome asking for copies of documents issued under Pope Eugenius by the Council of Florence treating faith and the required disposition in one receiving a sacrament. The Cardinal, however, made no immediate use of the latter material.

Parallel with his theological activity, Cajetan made an initial effort on the diplomatic front. Keeping in mind the crucial place Friedrich of Saxony held in imperial politics, especially as Leo X wanted these to develop, Cajetan gave no thought to following the logic of the *processus summarius* by issuing a condemnation. He knew he had ample faculties for this, and he may even have had an approved draft of a bull of excommunication, but this was kept under lock and key. On October 25 he wrote to Friedrich to report in detail on his exchanges with Luther.[57] While underscoring how fatherly he had treated Luther, he dismissed Luther's written defense of the two teachings, maintaining that the document was disrespectful in treating the bull of Clement VI, a decree that was patently contrary to Luther's position on indulgences. Also, Luther cited Scripture quite ineptly in favor of his view of faith in the sacrament. After the inconclusive meetings, however, the contacts mediated by Staupitz and Link were showing promise of some kind of settlement. But when they left Augsburg and Luther followed, Cajetan's hope suddenly turned to frustration.

Cajetan pleaded with the Prince Elector not to bring the Saxon house into disrepute by extending further protection to one seeking to foist new dogmas on the Church. Cajetan assured Friedrich that the matter was much too serious to be dropped and that it would be far better if Luther were well away from Wittenberg when his errors were condemned. The best thing, however, would be for the Prince to send Luther in custody to Rome for completion of the canonical trial. Cajetan assured Friedrich that Luther's teachings were not authentically Catholic.

Back in Wittenberg, Luther drafted an appeal to a General Council and prepared his account of the Augsburg events for publication. The next weeks brought Luther into gloomy pits of uncertainty in the face of an imminent condemnation that would ruin the university work he had so enthusiastically begun and bring upon him serious ecclesiastical penalties and banishment from the Empire. As he pondered Cajetan's charges he became more deeply concerned about the way the papal decretals used — for him, abused — Scripture. Luther expressed this feeling in his *Acta Augustana* which he was sending out in printed form by mid-December.

Friedrich allowed Luther to read the letter from Cajetan and help draft the answer which was sent on December 8.[58] Friedrich refused to act as Cajetan requested, assuring the Cardinal that many learned men in the German principalities found no departures from orthodoxy in Luther's works. Friedrich again called for use of the disputation method and for recognition of the competency of the universities to bring judgment. Friedrich repeated his willingness to fulfil the duty of a Christian prince if Luther were shown to be teaching error.

Cajetan had hoped that the new papal bull, *Cum postquam*, would bring Luther to concede his error on indulgences. The document was promulgated in Linz, Austria, in December, and Cajetan was able to distribute copies as he moved westward in February and March 1519. Luther's response was one of amazement at the brevity of this alleged definition on the great issue being argued. He was deeply disappointed that the Pope, following Cajetan, simply repeated older doctrines, showing no concern about the pastoral problems raised by indulgence preaching. Worst of all, no single biblical text was given in support of what the bull declared as obligatory teaching. Luther thus found the papal statement utterly uncompelling.[59]

By the time Luther saw *Cum postquam* he was energetically preparing for his great debate with Johann Eck, scheduled for late June, 1519, in Leipzig. Luther's disappointment with the bull combined at this time with his researches into the historical origins and juridical rights of the Roman See. His criticism of the Papacy became more incisive as he moved toward his coming *contestation* of papal teaching authority in the name of *sola scriptura*. Thus the principal outcome of the clash over indulgences in Augsburg would seem to be that Luther found himself forced to reorder the system of norms for determining genuine Christian doctrine.

Another somewhat curious, yet symptomatic, result of Luther's brooding reflection on the Augsburg events was indicated by his remark in a letter to Karl von Miltitz, May 17, 1519.[60] Luther

wanted Cajetan kept out of any further discussion of his case.
Cajetan had proved so inept in the Augsburg meetings as to be
simply disqualified from further consideration. He had tempted
Luther to fall from Christian faith, and if Luther had the time he
would denounce the Cardinal to the Pope for the un-Christian errors
he had defended in Augsburg. This, Luther's considered judgment on
Cajetan, should be viewed in connection with Luther's statements
that the whole matter of indulgences pales into insignificance beside
the question of faith.[61] This evidence would indicate that the
critical moment in the Augsburg meetings had been Cajetan's
attempted critique of Luther's notion of justifying faith in proper
reception of a sacrament. In spite of Cajetan's eventual readiness to
drop his charge on this point, Luther reacted with outrage and with
dogged adherence to his view. This was certainly one of the pivotal
steps leading to the historically divisive Reformation, which was
soon to burst forth under the banner of "justification by faith
alone."

    Cajetan undertook no further canonical measures with regard to
Luther. The treatises he had drafted as he studied Luther's works
remained among his private notes for a decade, before they were
printed in the first collections of his shorter works. The Cardinal did
read Luther's *Acta Augustana* and was spurred on by Luther's attack
on the papal use of Scripture to write a brief rejoinder in Mainz,
March 22, 1519: *Misuse of Scripture–Response to Charges Against
the Holy See* (translated below, pages 99-104). In this work Cajetan
did not mention Luther's name, but he began by chiding the
originator of the charges for oracular self-confidence and lack of
reverence toward the supreme pastor of Christendom. In principle,
the Church might at times use Scripture texts in "a transferred
sense," since the Fathers did not keep to a narrow literalism. Still,
Cajetan did take up the charges in detail and showed that in these
cases the Pope had used texts in their literal meaning.

    January, 1519, brought the death of Emperor Maximillian, an
event that unleashed a spate of diplomatic maneuvers in preparation
for the election of the successor in Frankfurt in the summer. Cajetan
had to devote the last half of his legation to promoting Pope Leo's
designs and hopes among the seven imperial Electors.[62] From the
beginning, Cajetan had the task of opposing the candidacy of
Charles, the Hapsburg Prince and heir of Ferdinand and Isabella of
Spain. Maximillian had tried earlier to have Charles proclaimed King

of the Romans as a step toward the imperial throne, but for the Pope Charles was already in possession of more than enough power – in Spain, the Low Countries, and Naples. The Pope initially preferred that the Emperor be selected from the Electors themselves, among whom Friedrich of Saxony, Luther's lord and protector, was the likely choice. With the Pope inclined toward Friedrich, Luther gained considerable security from a papal condemnation in early 1519. As the summer drew near, Cajetan kept close to the Rhenish Electors, as Leo waited and watched the ineffective efforts of Francis I, King of France, to gain votes. Leo wanted an Emperor who would be strong enough to promote his plan for a crusade but not someone whose amassed power would upset the European political equilibrium. As Charles' agents began scoring successes with the Electors, Leo prudently instructed Cajetan to indicate his acquiescence in the election of Charles as German Emperor. This change of position occurred just before Charles' election took place on June 28, 1519.

Cajetan's legation ended with the imperial election, and he returned to Rome in September, 1519. His return was not triumphal, since the issues of defense against the Turk and a doctrinal clarification over Luther were both very much unsettled. Medici disfavor was evinced in Cajetan's having to give up title to the See of Palermo, to which he had been named in 1518. Instead, he had to content himself with the decidedly minor See of his birthplace, Gaeta. In the autumn of 1519 he received Pope Leo's permission to absent himself from all but the most important consistories of the cardinals resident in Rome. Cajetan's interests and lifestyle made him an outsider among the Renaissance men Leo had gathered around himself in the cardinalate. No one felt any urgency in taking up the Luther case again, and for the half-year after the election Roman policy-makers were more concerned with coping with Charles V's increasing power in Italy.

When proceedings against Luther were reopened in January, 1520, Cajetan resumed regular attendance at consistories. He co-chaired a first commission that took up the matter, and then, beginning in March, he found himself somewhat at cross-purposes with Johann Eck, who had arrived in Rome and was taking a leading hand in the second commission formed to recommend steps against Luther. Eck had himself drawn up a list of Luther's errors and was also circulating a set of Luther's teachings condemned by the university of Louvain. Cajetan maintained that it was imperative to discriminate between Luther's gauche formulations that could well disturb the faithful (*"piis auribus offensiva"*) and clear-cut matters of error or heresy. Cajetan was not intervening in defense of any of Luther's teachings but was calling for Pope and curia to demonstrate theological competence in the forthcoming document against Luther. This argument for discrimination was consistent with Cajetan's sharp focusing on just two issues at Augsburg. It is also in harmony with a remark he made in 1519 that the first university condemnations of Luther were inept in not distinguishing between scandalous formulations, errors, and heresy.[63]

By May 1520 another committee of only four members, including both Cajetan and Eck, was working over a draft condemnation of forty-one propositions in long meetings with the Pope. On the issue of specific censures, Cajetan was outvoted, probably because a global condemnation attracted Leo as the most expeditious solution.[64] The product of this work was the bull formally threatening Luther with excommunication, *Exsurge Domine*, issued June 15, 1520, which was followed by the declaration of Luther's condemnation in *Decet Romanum Pontificem* in January 1521.[65] It was the logic of this document that Charles V was following as he confronted Luther at Worms in April 1521 and signed the edict making Luther an outlaw of the German Empire.

Cajetan's intellectual vigor in no way abated during his forays into papal diplomacy and curial infighting. His commentary on Part III of Aquinas' *Summa* was growing during these years, and before completing it in 1522, he added a series of special questions on sacraments and indulgences. In early 1521 he wrote a detailed defense of the Roman Primacy as of divine institution (translated and synopsized below, pages 105-144). In this work he refuted one-by-one all the biblical and theological arguments marshalled in Luther's printed *Resolutio* of the thirteenth thesis he debated with Eck at Leipzig. Cajetan, of course, was well prepared to write on the papal primacy after his works against the Pisan council less than a decade before. What is remarkable in the work against Luther is Cajetan's assiduous concentration on the biblical witness to Peter's special role among the apostles. Cajetan did not at this time argue from Scripture exclusively but had the aim rather of interpreting texts in accord with the patristic and conciliar tradition, while showing that Luther had pressed the text into a shape that favored a wholly untraditional view. Cajetan's disciplined argument was praised by Erasmus,[66] but it met with stony silence on the Protestant side, in spite of the fact that this work was published immediately in Rome, Milan, and Cologne.[67]

In an effort to fill part of the painful lacuna in *Exsurge Domine*, Cajetan next took up five of its censured propositions and argued concisely for the justice of their condemnation in a work which appeared in June, 1521 (translated below, pages 145-152). He mentioned in his conclusion that, although he wrote while plagued with illness, he was still glad to fulfill Pope Leo's request for such a work. Cajetan's *Five Articles* is perhaps most significant for the indirect evidence it contains regarding the critical and dissenting voices raised in Rome itself over the condemnations in *Exsurge Domine*.

Both these works of 1521 document Cajetan's growing conviction that the Reformers must be met before all else by arguments from Scripture. His German contacts had impressed on him the deep antipathy felt by humanists and early Lutherans toward arguments in the scholastic or canonistic mode. Catholics were going to have to learn to use the weapons of the new adversary. For Cajetan himself, trained for more speculative and systematic thought, the need to search for the literal meaning of Scripture posed no small obstacle. Already in his fifties, he nonetheless began with a will the painful work of intellectual retraining. By the end of the decade he was well into a major exegetical project.

The highpoint of Cajetan's influence in the college of cardinals was the conclave that met in the first days of January 1522 after the death of Leo X. The first ballots revealed the existence of two strong groups among the cardinals, those favorable to a Medici successor and those under French-Imperial influence. However, neither group was strong enough to carry the election. Cardinal Giulio de' Medici finally suggested that the new pope would have to be an independent, perhaps someone not even at the conclave, although not one to whom Emperor Charles V would object. Cajetan saw immediately that Adrian of Utrecht met these specifications. Cajetan made an impassioned appeal on behalf of Adrian as one who would have the freedom and energy to initiate reform of the Church. The other cardinals acceded to Cajetan's exhortation and elected Adrian, who was at the time in Spain. Cajetan had the deep satisfaction of dedicating Part III of his commentary on the *Summa* to Pope Adrian

VI, the man he hoped would open a new age of renewal in the Church.

Adrian's arrival was awaited in Rome with mixed feelings, since many suspected that with him the era of the Renaissance popes was ending. In a consistory shortly after his arrival, Cajetan uttered the brutal truth with which Adrian would have to struggle, *"Peccaverunt valde praedecessores tui!"*[68] There is extant an Italian version of a memorandum on reform of the Church probably written by Cajetan at this time.[69] The document has only five points, but they embrace what could have been a thorough renewal of the Church's pastoral ministry. Residence in their dioceses is the first and greatest commandment for bishops, for only then can they feed their people with God's word and lead them in worship.[70] The cardinalate must be reduced in both size and income, lest it be coveted for perverse reasons. Clear norms are laid down for the training of the clergy. Local selection of bishops would aid the choice of better men. Finally, the religious orders must be exhorted, cajoled, and forced to undertake fundamental reforms if they are to spread a new spirit throughout the whole Church. In the light of incisive advice of this kind, the brevity of Adrian's pontificate is all the more lamentable. One observer has seen in Cajetan's work of 1522-23 the foreshadowing, some fifteen years before the fact, of the Cardinals' commission of 1537 that delivered the justly famous *Consilium de emendanda ecclesia* into the hands of Pope Paul III.[71]

In 1523 Adrian called on Cajetan to serve as Legate to threatened Hungary. Cajetan was again placed in an exposed position, perhaps as the result of efforts within the Curia to remove him from Rome and from close proximity to Adrian VI. While in Hungary Cajetan finished work on a handbook for confessors *Summula peccatorum*, (1523), in which he treated in refined detail the myriad sins encountered in hearing confessions.[72] While returning from Hungary he completed his first biblical work, *Jentaculum novi testamenti* (1524), an exposition of sixty-four problematical New Testament passages that might stump or embarass a busy pastor who had little time to think through a satisfactory explanation in answer to a question or in preparation for a sermon. The title indicated that the work was only a beginning, literally a "breakfast," and that Cajetan was soon to be offering more substantial biblical commentaries.[73]

Cajetan was saddened in September, 1523, by news that Pope Adrian had died and, following hard on this, that Giulio de' Medici had been elected Pope and taken the name Clement VII. Upon his recall from Hungary Cajetan, sensing again his isolation in the curia, went into semi-retirement and used the next three years principally for preparatory study of Scripture. He had begun to form plans for a complete commentary dedicated to a rigorous explanation of the literal sense of all the biblical books.

During this period, Clement VII called upon Cajetan once to serve as theological *peritus*. The need arose out of an exchange the Pope had in late 1525 with the canton of Zurich.[74] At first Zurich simply sent down to Rome a reminder that the Papacy was in arrears in its payments for the services of mercenary soldiers the canton had supplied for the Pope. But the cantonal secretary who delivered the request for payment also brought the news that a new doctrinal controversy was raging in Zurich, where Ulrich Zwingli had preached and written against the traditional belief in the presence of Christ in the Eucharist.

Clement VII wrote the Zurich council that he certainly could not deal with a Christian city that was falling away from the faith. The Pope offered to send a nuncio to Switzerland who could meet representatives of Zurich on neutral ground in Geneva or Lausanne to instruct them in the eucharistic faith of the Church. Zurich answered in January, 1526, that their preachers were quite well grounded in Scripture and needed no instruction in authentic Christian faith. Also, the disturbances of the time, the Peasant's Revolt and various Anabaptist movements, were so great that the leading men of Zurich would have to remain at home, where, however, they would be glad to welcome a Papal representative for further discussions.

As this correspondence began, Clement called upon Cajetan to draw up a handy sketch of the points the proposed nuncio might have to defend against the Zurich theologians. Cajetan was able to obtain a copy of Zwingli's *De vera et falsa religione commentarius* of 1525 and immediately began an analysis of its chapter on the Eucharist. He singled out twelve points of varying importance for criticism and rebuttal, each of which he then treated in a chapter of the tract *Errors on the Lord's Supper* (translated below, pages 153-173). Biblical arguments predominated in this work, as Cajetan was drawn into an extended consideration of Christ's discourse on the "bread of life" in John 6, especially on the pregnant saying, "Flesh profits nothing, it is the Spirit that gives life" (John 6:63).

Cajetan's longest chapter treated the words of institution, which Zwingli maintained should be construed, "This represents my body." Although no papal representative was eventually sent to Switzerland, Cajetan could take satisfaction in being early in the fray on another issue of Reformation controversy. For a moment he was unknowingly aligned with Luther, who in the next three years delivered a series of massive broadsides against the same Swiss eucharistic doctrine Cajetan had contested with disciplined biblical arguments in 1525.[75]

By 1527 Cajetan was ready to start publishing his biblical commentaries, beginning with the Psalter.[76] There followed in rapid succession expositions of the four gospels (1527-28), the Pauline epistles (1528-29), the Acts of the Apostles, and the Catholic epistles (1529). By early 1531 he was through the Pentateuch and had begun the other Old Testament historical books. In March, 1533, Cajetan completed Job, and in 1534, before his death in August, he wrote commentaries on Proverbs, Ecclesiastes, and chapters 1-3 of Isaiah.

Two basic principles underlay Cajetan's biblical work. First, he had what was for his day the still rare perception that the traditional Latin Vulgate was a quite fallible translation that needed to be checked against the original at every turn. For work on the Psalter and other Old Testament books, Cajetan obtained the services of two assistants knowledgeable in Hebrew. Their task was to explain to him word-by-word the exact meaning of the Hebrew original. Cajetan told how he needed at times to curtail their desire to interpret the words which in raw literal translation were often neither poetic nor even meaningful. With them Cajetan worked out a new Latin translation painfully faithful to the Hebrew of the Psalter. This inelegant and often obscure text was given in Cajetan's first commentary, in order that the reader would have both text and exposition before him. This critical view of the Vulgate, supported by expert assistance, permeated Cajetan's other commentaries, although not to the extent that he supplied an alternate Latin text.

For work on the New Testament, Cajetan found the ground prepared by Lefevre d'Etaples' recent publications and by Erasmus' edition of the Greek text of the New Testament with a new Latin translation (1516). Cajetan did take special care in checking the original Greek of the Fourth Gospel and of Romans, with the result that he offered emended Latin translations of numerous verses of these theologically significant books. Cajetan sensed that many would find abrasive his treatment of the Vulgate text, which was a fixed part of the liturgical and theological world of the early sixteenth century. One need only recall how steeped in the Vulgate were clerics, especially members of monastic and mendicant orders, whose round of prescribed prayer was little more than a tissue of Vulgate texts. Few Greek manuscripts were known in Western Europe and some viewed those that were known with suspicion, fearing tampering and adaptation to the traditions peculiar to the Greek Church.

In the introduction to his exposition of the Pentateuch, Cajetan pleaded that people take in stride his correction of flawed translations and the accompanying destruction of cherished interpretations. Cajetan added that it was silly to go on interpreting interpretations when with a little labor one could be expounding what Moses and the other biblical authors had in fact said. Again, the incensed reaction of the critics serves as an index that Cajetan had touched the nerve of a real problem in the Church of his day.

The second governing principle of Cajetan's biblical work was his strict adherence to explaining the literal sense of the text. Cajetan, who in many other ways was a medieval man, broke resolutely with the medieval tradition of "spiritual exegesis." As recently as 1513-15, Martin Luther had begun his own biblical professorship with lectures on the Psalter expanding at considerable length the Christological and "tropological" (individual, moral-spiritual) sense of the Psalm verses. For a complex of reasons Cajetan took care to avoid any mystical or "transferred" applications of the text. He held that such expositions were of quite restricted value, being applicable only in the realm of piety, not that of faith. Cajetan's work was wholly theological in intent, as he aimed, albeit indirectly, at countering the Reformers' appropriation of Scripture to their own doctrinal and ecclesiastical purposes.

The pressing theological needs of the Church in Cajetan's day were in the fields of doctrinal clarification and controversy – areas in which only the literal sense of Scripture carried weight. As a result, Cajetan's expositions at times offered little more than a simple paraphrase of the text. He had no great store of historical and philological knowledge to draw upon. There is evidence that he was well aware of his limitations, as when he explained that there would be no commentary on the Apocalypse, since this required more than human talent and perspicacity (*"exponat cui Deus concesserit"*).[77]

One result of Cajetan's rigor in attending to the literal sense is that his expositions are almost totally free of references to the controversies of the day. G. Hennig found only two passing references to Luther and one to Zwingli in Cajetan's gospel commentaries and a further mention of contemporary eucharistic disputes on 1 Corinthians 11:23.27.[78] He did however illustrate Matthew 5:13, on the salt that lost its savor being trodden under foot, by reference to the just punishment God allowed dissipated and irreligious Roman prelates to suffer in the sack of Rome. The merchants in the temple (John 2:4) prompted a reference to those selling candles and saints' pictures in churches, even on the steps of St. Peter's.[79]

Cajetan's passion for arriving at the literal sense of the text had deep roots in his view of the transmission of God's revelation. In his commentary on the *Summa* he had stated that the literal sense of Scripture contains all that is necessary for salvation. Obviously, more than a few points are only obscurely expressed in the biblical documents. Consequently, the theologian must first carefully compare obscure teachings with manifest teachings of Scripture and then be ready to submit his interpretation to the Church's authoritative clarification of what is revealed. Correlative with this guarded affirmation of the sufficiency of Scripture is a point Cajetan made in his 1511 work on the authority of Pope and General Council: our faith is not so directly correlated with single texts of Scripture that theologians are prevented from arguing for their own ideas on the basis of biblical interpretations. The truth of revelation, however, lies in an exposition of the text that accords with the tradition and the living judgment of the Pope on contemporary controversies.[80]

Cajetan's biblical commentaries occasioned no little *admiratio*. From Luther, there is a recorded remark, "Cajetan, in his later days, has become Lutheran."[81] Considerable zeal was expended by Ambrosius Catharinus, O.P., against the exegetical work of his retired Master General. Catharinus submitted a denunciation before the still acerbic faculty in Paris and proceedings began that could have led to another book-burning.[82] Clement VII intervened in a letter to the Parisian professors in September, 1533, to protect the man who was by then the Pope's regular source of valued theological advice. Proceedings were halted at this time in Paris, but not before an open letter of the Parisian theologians had begun to circulate listing the censurable propositions excerpted from the commentaries. The Sorbonne masters charged Cajetan with imprudently taking these notions from Erasmus or even Luther. The letter ended with a stinging rebuke of Cajetan's rashness in abandoning the long approved Vulgate text to base his work on new versions in no way guaranteed for their exactness. In 1534 a Wittenberg printer, no doubt with considerable glee over this discomfiture of Luther's old adversary, brought out the open letter in pamphlet form.[83] Catharinus published his criticisms of Cajetan's commentaries in 1535, revised and expanded them in 1542, and obtained a censure by the Paris faculty against Cajetan's biblical works in August, 1544.

The specific charges brought against Cajetan concerned the reservations and plain doubts he had expressed about the apostolic origin of the final eleven verses of Mark's gospel, the story of the adultress in John 8, and five whole epistles of the New Testament (Hebrews, James, Jude, and 1 and 2 John). These views were especially serious in Cajetan's case, since he had laid down the rule that apostolic authorship or direct approval by an apostle was normative for inclusion in the New Testament canon. Following Jerome, Cajetan also relegated the deuterocanonical books of the Old Testament to a secondary place where they could serve piety but not the teaching of revealed doctrine.

On points of detail, Cajetan drew fire for remarking in his exposition of 1 Corinthians 14 that vernacular languages could be used to good purpose in Catholic worship, for saying that James 5:14 was not about the sacrament of anointing of the sick, and voicing the opinion that Matthew 5:32 and 19:9 indicated that in divine law there was in fact some room made for divorce and remarriage.[84] His commentaries had also occasioned statements in which Cajetan stated categorically the non-demonstrability of the immortality of the human soul.[85]

As with Cajetan's Dominican generalate, so also with his biblical expositions it is not easy to gauge the effectiveness of his work. His commentaries did not have a long and complex printing history in the sixteenth century, as did his collected theological treatises. The Council of Trent did not reflect Cajetan's attitude to the Vulgate and to the canon of biblical books. The work of pre-Tridentine Catholic theologians has not been studied to an extent that would allow us to measure their usage of Cajetan's exegesis. He seems to have had more the role of solitary prophet among those of his day who identified themselves closely and explicitly with the hierarchical Church. Certainly Cajetan's commentaries deserved better treatment than they received at the hands of the fearful Catharinus and the censorious Parisian faculty. Cajetan's confident approach to the biblical text did not fit into the mentality of cautious defensiveness that began to predominate in the Catholic world less than a decade after his death. From our vantage point, it may well be that the most significant results of Cajetan's dedicated work on Scripture are to be found in the concise treatises he wrote in the final four years of his life.

A first problem Cajetan faced was the controversy over the validity of Henry VIII's marriage to Catherine of Aragon.[86] Beginning in 1527 the King spoke repeatedly of his conviction that he was living in a sinful union with Catherine, one expressly prohibited by the law of God in the Old Testament book of Leviticus. Catherine had been married to Henry's deceased elder brother, Arthur, but her marriage to Henry had been made possible by Pope Julius II's dispensation from the impediment of affinity in the first degree. Henry's Old Testament studies raised doubts in his mind whether the Pope could dispense from such a clear prohibition of marriage with a brother's widow as that found in Leviticus 20:21. Did not Catherine's failure to bear the longed-for male heir show God's disfavor on their marriage? In mid-1528 Clement VII appointed the curial cardinal, Lorenzo Campeggio, to preside with Henry's Chancellor, Thomas Wolsey, Cardinal-Archbishop of York, over a canonical hearing on the case in London.[87] Campeggio faithfully implemented Clement's strategy of delaying settlement of the case at every possible juncture. Catherine appealed to the Pope over the heads of the two cardinals, claiming that she was not receiving a fair hearing of her side of the case in England. Daughter of the strong-willed Isabella of Spain, she was not about to accept an unfounded declaration by suspect judges that would suddenly make her twenty-year marriage into concubinage and her daughter, Mary, into a royal bastard. Catherine's nephew, Emperor Charles V, had his ambassador to the Holy See act as advocate on behalf of Catherine's appeal.

In mid-1529 Clement revoked the matter to Rome and cited Henry to present his case before the papal matrimonial court, the Roman Rota.[88] At this stage Henry sought to marshal what he hoped would be an irresistible mass of learned opinion, precedents, exegesis, and university resolutions against the validity of his marriage. The beginning of the controversy coincided with the aftermath of the sack of Rome and Clement VII's humiliating imprisonment by the imperial troops of Charles V. Although Clement had regained his freedom of movement by 1529, he still showed at times a strained subservience to Charles. Nonetheless, a judgment delivering a blow to Charles' aunt was not entirely unthinkable. The problem was that on closer analysis Henry's experts, for all their number, made a singularly unconvincing case. Cajetan himself is a good witness to the way the argument inevitably boiled down to a discussion of the authority by which Julius II had acted in granting the original papal dispensation — a most neuralgic topic a decade after the outbreak of the Lutheran reformation.

Cajetan entered the controversy in early 1530 when Clement asked him to review some of the pamphlets and university judgments and deliver a report on the options open to the Pope. Cajetan's report was the treatise of March 13, 1530, *The King's Marriage* (translated below, pages 175-188). For this work Cajetan used to advantage the services of his Jewish linguistic assistants to clarify the literal meaning of the pertinent Old Testament texts. The result was more than a cogent defense of Julius' dispensation against the technical and substantive objections that had been raised. Cajetan found himself forced to turn the King's own weapon, the Old Testament, back on Henry with devastating force. His investigation showed that if any imperative arises from the Mosaic law it is that Henry was solemnly bound to take Catharine as his wife — just as he had done.[89]

Eight days after Cajetan finished his treatise, Clement issued an injunction against further public discussion of the case outside the Rota proceedings. On March 27 he wrote to Cajetan to thank him for expert aid in defense of Christian truth in a matter of such gravity.[90] The Rota hearings gave the dilatory Pope and the evasive King ample opportunity for further delay. Events in England easily overtook the Roman proceedings and Clement did not utter his definitive judgment upholding the validity of the marriage until March, 1534, five years after Catherine's appeal. By this time Henry's parliament was clearing the way for Royal supremacy over a national church in schism from Rome; a new Archbishop of Canterbury had declared Henry's marriage to Catherine null and void; and Anne Boleyn had successively become pregnant, married to Henry, and crowned Queen on June 1, 1533. Cajetan responded belatedly to this swift succession of events with a direct appeal to Henry to undo the damage done by all these actions stemming from an initial theological misconception. This letter is given in translation on pages 241-244 below, under the title *Marriage with a Brother's Widow—a Position*, as it is called in the later collections of Cajetan's shorter works.

In Summer, 1530, another imperial diet had met in Augsburg, a meeting at which Charles V and the estates tried to come to terms with the dissolving religious unity of the German Empire. The Protestant estates submitted their *Augsburg Confession*, authored by Luther's Wittenberg colleague, Philip Melanchthon, on June 25. Negotiations followed on both diplomatic and theological levels, as the Lutherans affirmed their fundamental Catholicity and pleaded for tolerance of their reforms of blatant abuses in worship and ecclesiastical structure. The clash of views soon focused on the terms of a possible *modus vivendi* for the Protestant cities and principalities within the Empire.

At the end of the inconclusive discussions, Rome faced the problem of charting a clear position in both the doctrinal and political areas. Clement VII was attracted by the prospect of a diplomatic settlement which would free him from having to give in to the frequent calls for a General Council. Cajetan himself tended to justify Clement's antipathy to a council in view of what he saw as the Protestant addiction to the bare text of Scripture.[91]

In mid-1531 Cajetan contributed to the discussion and reflection that the diet triggered in Rome.[92] He produced three short treatises aimed at clarifying the precise areas within the ambit of Catholic dogmatic conviction where flexibility could be shown in answering the positions taken by the Lutherans at Augsburg.

One point of eucharistic doctrine, the sacrificial character of the mass, was for Cajetan clearly beyond the limits of any compromise with Lutheran views. Cajetan expressed this with limpid clarity in his treatise, *The Sacrifice of the Mass — Against the Lutherans* (translated below, pages 189-200). True to principles by now almost second nature, Cajetan offered an exclusively biblical argument from the passages on the eucharist in the New Testament. He did not shy away from dealing with all the affirmations of the Epistle to the Hebrews on the unicity of Christian sacrifice. The insights of this short treatise have made it the most warmly appreciated of Cajetan's shorter doctrinal studies in our day. This appreciation is, of course, restricted to a very select group of Catholic theological scholars.[93]

Almost contemporary with *The Sacrifice of the Mass* is a brief treatise, *Guidelines for Concessions to the Lutherans*, written to assist the Pope and his Curia in discriminating between non-negotiable dogma and points on which concessions could well be made in an effort to reestablish Catholic unity (translated below, pages 201-203). Cajetan did not strive to be comprehensive, but kept to the actual topics of Melanchthon's memoranda of the previous summer, which had emphasized such things as clerical marriage and communion under both forms. Cajetan even sketched out a painless way Lutheran teachers could be honorably reincorporated into the Catholic communion. Most startling of all was his advice that all laws and practices not of divine but of ecclesiastical origin should be formally declared, for the whole Chruch, as not binding under pain of serious sin. To make clear what he meant, Cajetan appended a draft of a papal bull on the matter. Cajetan's recommendations were voted down, one suspects with an overwhelming majority, in consistory. Cajetan's final suggestion would, of course, have made a breathtaking difference in early modern Catholic life and practice by opening the door to full application of principles of local and individual adaptation and accommodation.[94]

In August, 1531, Cajetan wrote *Four Lutheran Errors*, a defense against Lutheran objections to Catholic worship and piety (translated below, pages 205-217). He apparently had the text of the *Augsburg Confession* before him as he wrote this rebuttal of arguments against communion under one form, integral confession of mortal sins, efforts of satisfaction after forgiveness of sins, and the inclusion of invocation of the saints in one's life of prayer. Although the Cardinal was ready to support concessions that allowed the Lutherans notable divergence from the externals of Catholic practice, he would not remain silent when their critical thrusts could be countered with arguments from parts of Scripture they had not reckoned with. A few months later, when copies of *The Sacrifice of the Mass* and *Four Lutheran Errors* reached Freiburg, Erasmus gave them a singular commendation and even spoke of having promoted a further edition of both works.[95]

Cajetan's final controversial work of major significance came in May 1532 after he had a chance to study Melanchthon's *Apology* of the *Augsburg Confession*. Cajetan, like Luther, saw the nub of the

Reformation argument in the doctrine of man's forgiveness, justification, and renewal by God's grace. The first half of the treatise, *Faith and Works — Against the Lutherans* (translated below, pages 219-239), takes up the controversy over the human response in faith to God's gracious action in the human heart. This continues the argument over justifying faith as certitude of forgiveness which Cajetan first raised as he read Luther's *Sermo de poenitentia* back in September, 1518. Compared with the second preparatory treatise he wrote in Augsburg (49-55, below), Cajetan's argument of 1532 includes some new and engaging developments on what it means to live in the love of mutual friendship with God. Cajetan's thinking had clearly been enriched through his exposition of Paul's epistles and 1 John. The second theme of *Faith and Works* is the meritorious character of the works of the man renewed by God's grace. Here Cajetan developed the Pauline theme of the believer's incorporation into Christ in a manner that manifested the narrowness of more than a few Reformation polemics against good works.[96]

In the early 1530s Cajetan's health began to fail. A man over sixty was for the sixteenth century well into old age, and the Cardinal had lived vigorously. Although others were talking about him as a candidate for the papacy to succeed Clement VII, Cajetan began in 1533 to prepare himself, both practically and spiritually, for death. He was beginning his exposition of the Old Testament prophets when he died August 10, 1534.

Cajetan and the Reformation

In assessing the importance of Cajetan's response to the Reformation, one could offer the image with which Garrett Mattingly began his *Catherine of Aragon.* Cajetan, too, was significant as one of those resisting rocks not moving with the current of events in his time. By not moving with the flow between 1518 and 1534, he seems only to have diverted the current momentarily as it swept by him toward the formation of a divided Christendom.[97]

This is, of course, a summary verdict that is justified only when one views Cajetan and the Reformation from some distance. Closer examination of the works in this volume shows that he did influence the early course of the Reformation and did make some contribution to shaping early modern Catholicism.

An important consideration in deriving a just assessment of Cajetan's role arises from closer study of the *Augsburg Treatises*. These fifteen *quaestiones* document Cajetan's conscientious and taxing labor of September and October, 1518, over Luther's texts and arguments then in public circulation. Pope and Church were well served by a man who expended so much energy in careful analysis and detailed rebuttal, for instance, of Luther's exposition of Thesis 58, on the *thesaurus* of indulgences (the eighth treatise). Reference has been made above to Cajetan's discrimination in selecting only two points in charging Luther with deviant teaching and then further reducing the charge to a single issue shortly after the third meeting.[98] One can question whether Cajetan's labor of preparation and his discretion in judgment have been justly portrayed in the standard historical works on Luther and the Reformation.

Lutheran observers of the Augsburg encounter of 1518 have on occasion expressed amazement at Cajetan's almost instantaneous recognition of the heart of Luther's newly-won understanding of man's justification under the Word of God.[99] They acknowledge Cajetan's perspicacity in judging, "*Hoc est novam construere ecclesiam*," toward the end of his second preparatory treatise, on Luther's notion of *fides sacramenti*. As suggested above, this treatise was of truly historic importance in the genesis of the Reformation.[100] Consequently, one must ponder carefully the charge which has been made that Cajetan's scholastic argument at this point caused him to misunderstand Luther's teaching on justification by faith.[101] A just assessment, however, must first take into account the quality of the works by Luther then available. Luther himself indicated that *Explanations*, Thesis 7, was tentative on absolution, humility, and faith.[102] The *Sermo de poenitentia* did not bear such a caveat, but a year later Luther produced a new *Sermon on the Sacrament of Penance*[103] that elaborated his central idea much better than the 1518 *Sermo* studied and criticized by Cajetan. Furthermore, some of Luther's central themes in portraying Christian conversion were expressed in works not published in early autumn 1518. Therefore, if there was any "misunderstanding" in Cajetan's 1518 critique of Luther's conception of justifying faith, it could well have been due to the imperfect quality of the works Luther had then released into the public domain.

Careful attention should also be given to the way Cajetan argued from the *sensus ecclesiae* in his second and sixth Augsburg treatises. His censure of Luther's views on absolution and faith was anchored in the lived understanding made manifest in the prayer and sacramental practice of devout Christians. Cajetan's principal norm was not scholastic or Thomistic when he argued for the primacy of contrition over the certitude of forgiveness proposed as essential by Luther.

One cannot overlook, however, the heavily analytical tone of large portions of Cajetan's treatment of Luther's arguments. His repeated use, for instance, of the distinction between merit and satisfaction in the eighth treatise stemmed from a sophisticated theological conceptuality, contrasting sharply with the pastoral and spiritual themes evident in Luther's approach to indulgences and grace. Luther's work on penance, and, even more, his arguments for *fides sacramenti*, resonate with themes from prayer, religious living, and pastoral care. The experiential tone does not mean that Luther's positions had necessarily to be accepted as true, but it does have consequences for an effective counter-argument. Luther's disputation (the *Explanations of the Ninety-five Theses*) was an affair of passionate religious conviction. But Cajetan sensed this too late or perhaps not at all. Hence he showed little concern for developing an engaging and compelling presentation of the positions he defended against Luther's protests and arguments. There was a tragic difference in the levels of discourse. This became even more apparent in Cajetan's summary dismissal of Luther's written defense of October 14, 1518. Against the background of Luther's pastoral concerns, this statement deserved careful study over at least a day or two and a discriminating judgment that would sift the elements of truth and error it contained.

This reflection on Cajetan's "cold correctness" is closely allied to the larger problematic of defensive theological writing by Catholics in the first years of Reformation controversy. Joseph Lortz has contrasted the vitality of Luther's consoling and liberating message with the aridity of the first Catholic rebuttals.[104] Cajetan's works of 1518-21 show that he was certainly a more able theological craftsman than the other early Catholic defenders. But he is one with most of them in touching only the tip of the iceberg as he dealt with the superstructure of Luther's argumentation. He made no attempt, for instance, in his work on the divine origin of the Roman primacy, to relate his thesis to Christian living, worship, and the whole realm of religious feeling. This work of 1521 was acutely argued and had long-range effects in Catholic ecclesiology. But one cannot conceive of it causing people to cherish lovingly their bond of communion with the Roman See.

We must not underestimate the difficulty of responding to Luther, who himself once admitted being very much a moving target in these early years of controversy.[105] The explosive shifts of Luther's polemic combined with his uncanny mastery of both his biblical source and the rhetorical means to play on the moods of his unsettled German audience to make counter-arguments doubly difficult. Cajetan, however, for all his unstinting work and obvious competence, was in these early days ill-equipped to make an attractive presentation from the Catholic side that would win loyalties and compel agreement by displaying Christian values in full force.

If Cajetan's early responses to the Reformation are judged as having significant limitations, his works of 1531-32 embody values far outweighing any lack of popular appeal. Four significant impulses issued from Cajetan's writings of the early 1530s.

First, his biblical commentaries evinced a commitment to the text and to its literal sense that met the Reformation in its chosen arena of discussion. Clearly, his work on Scripture could have contributed much to the renewal of Catholic preaching so needed in the early sixteenth century. Cajetan laid a foundation for developing a biblical theology that could have offset the Scholastic dominance of Catholic theology in the later sixteenth century. But Cajetan's work was rendered suspect by the criticism it met from Catharinus and the Sorbonne. Hence no one appeared to cultivate vigorously the ground broken by Cajetan's biblical commentaries.[106]

Second, a work like *Four Lutheran Errors* (1531) was a solid contribution to the defense of the external practices that became for so many people intimately connected with their sense of Catholic identity. A defense of this kind served to strengthen Catholic self-awareness and prevented a collapse of confidence that would have made later renewal impossible.

Third, in *The Sacrifice of the Mass* (1531) and *Faith and Works* (1532), Cajetan produced genuinely biblical statements articulating Catholic convictions on two of the major theological issues of the day. In these works, Cajetan broke loose from the control of the attacking adversary, a factor dulling the effect of his earlier work on the primacy. These two works were eminently positive expositions that related specific doctrines with central Christian convictions about the living Christ and the work of the Holy Spirit. These are both model works of controversy that rank among the very best products of pre-Tridentine Catholic answers to the Reformation. Measured against these two works, many other works of this genre appear in all their superficiality.

Fourth, there was Cajetan's memorandum of 1531 to Pope Clement VII on concessions that could be made in working out a plan of union with the Lutherans. In this work Cajetan's own sense of confidence, courage, and freedom cannot but impress. Knowing clearly his own doctrinal standpoint, and having a sense of the hierarchy of truths and values, he could counsel wide-ranging changes without threatening his own sense of identity in the Church. Again, the Church was not ready to move with this courage and freedom. Only in the late twentieth century is Catholic consciousness coming to be significantly shaped by the acute awareness of the distinction between divine, or foundational, elements in the Church, and the many human, historical, and contingent developments. But this distinction underlay Cajetan's suggested *Guidelines* for ecumenical accommodation in 1531.

Thus, in spite of Cajetan's lack of immediate impact through his works of 1531-32, their enduring significance seems apparent. This small, severe man left a monument that stands out as an impressive part of the Catholic landscape at that time.

I

AUGSBURG TREATISES 1518

1
CERTAINTY OF SALVATION IN PURGATORY

We ask whether all the souls in purgatory are certain they will attain their eternal salvation. The following are the arguments proposed against this certainty. First, since the pains of hell and purgatory are identical, some of these souls experience such terror and fright that they cannot tell in what state they are.[1] Second, many of the souls of the departed have appeared, but they did not know their state, as if God, although he had passed judgment on them, had suspended promulgation of his decision.[2] Third, no argument from reason and no text of Scripture or Church teaching can be found that says all the souls in purgatory are certain they will attain their eternal salvation.[3]

But in fact the common teaching of the Church is contrary to this conclusion.

The reason for this position is that when a soul is separated from the body it has a direct intuition of itself that is no longer impeded by the body as was the case in this life. The soul sees itself and all aspects of its being. Consequently, a soul in purgatory sees the charity or habitual grace had within itself and thus, knowing it is in the state of grace, it is certain of attaining its eternal salvation.

This is confirmed by the fact that in every separated soul undergoing purgation faith remains. But this entails the certainty had on earth that all those in purgatory are among the elect. Since the soul knows it is in purgatory, it is consequently certain of its salvation. We give the following proof that it knows it is in purgatory. The soul retains the certainties of faith held in this life. But among these is that the departed souls of the baptized are in one of three states immediately after death: beatitude, damnation, or purgation. There is no fourth possibility. But a soul knows it is baptized, that it has left this bodily life, and that it is neither blessed nor damned. Thus it must be undergoing purgation for eternal salvation.

The same conclusion can be confirmed by arguing from the nature of hope. For all the souls in purgatory retain not only charity and faith, but hope as well. But the latter is not dormant, but ardently longs for its object, eternal happiness. But since hope is the certain expectation of future happiness, and thus is impossible in the damned, the same conclusion follows as in our previous argument.

In answer to the first argument to the contrary, we first say that although some pains are the same in hell and purgatory, still the experience of those in pain is different. Clearly those suffering in hell are disposed much differently from those suffering in purgatory. Those undergoing purgation have an upright will conformed to the will of God. They love God's righteousness and trust in God and in the salvation won by Jesus Christ. But the dispositions of the damned are opposed to these. Consequently the fire common to hell and purgatory is experienced differently by those damned and those being purified. The mistake lies in not sensing this difference. The horror experienced in hell arises from fear of divine justice and the flight of a perverse will from punishment. The punishment of purgatory is painful but there is no fright, because the souls love the justice of God and gladly undergo the punishment divine justice requires. Second, just as the extreme terror experienced by the damned does not prevent them from sensing their own state, far less would those undergoing purgation be hindered from sensing their state. For the terror of purgatory is not greater than that experienced in hell.

In answer to the second argument to the contrary, we maintain that the teaching of the Church does not rest on the uncertainties of visions. This is what you have in visions the Church has not approved. Perhaps they were dreams, or ecstatic states, or hallucinations, or illusions caused by demons for the purpose of raising new dogmas.

In answer to the third argument, we have shown that one can frame a cogent argument that all the souls in purgatory are certain of attaining their eternal salvation.

Augsburg, September 25, 1518.

2

FAITH IN THE SACRAMENT AS
CERTAINTY OF FORGIVENESS

It is asked whether for fruitful reception of absolution in the sacrament of penance one must have that faith by which the penitent believes with full certitude that he is absolved by God. A number of arguments are given in support of this view.

First, one must have faith in Christ's words, "Whatever you loose on earth . . ." [Matthew 16:19].[4] Second, if the impossible were to occur, that is, if one confessing were not contrite, or if the priest were to give absolution in jest and not seriously, and one still believed he was absolved, then he would most truly be absolved — so powerful is faith in the word of Christ. Church history proves this, because St. Athanasius, while playing with other children, baptized them as he had seen the priests do, and Bishop Saint Alexander judged them to be truly baptized. Similarly with an actor who was baptized in a mock baptism to entertain the Emperor.[5]

Third, it is not the sacrament but faith in the sacrament that justifies. As Augustine said, "The sacrament cleanses, not because it is performed, but because it is believed."[6] Fourth, one should more urgently inquire of the penitent whether he believes he is absolved than whether he is truly contrite. For contrition is never really adequate. If it is genuine, still it is not certain. If certain, it still would not be sufficient. But faith and the word of Christ are supremely certain, wholly genuine, and utterly sufficient.[7]

Fifth, not only one approaching the sacrament with attrition and placing no obstacle of actual sin or of the intent to sin, but even a person approaching fully contrite, will not attain the grace sought unless he believes in the absolution. Sacraments so received would lead to death and damnation, even for a contrite person.[8] Sixth, a person approaching the sacrament of penance is asking for the forgiveness of sins from God. But it is written, "Whatever you ask in prayer, believe you will receive it, and so you will" [Mark 11:24]. And James said, "One should ask in faith, with no doubting" [James 1:6].[9] Therefore such faith is required.

But against this is the ordinary understanding of the Church.

In order to gain clarity on this issue, one must first grasp that a novel idea has been introduced, namely, requiring this kind of faith to such an extent that it is more necessary than contrition. Also, those are damned who do not incline to believe they are absolved until they are certain they are sufficiently contrite. This fanciful notion is based, first of all, on the well-known biblical texts on faith and trust in the word of God, such as, "Remember your word, in which you granted hope," [Psalm 119:49],[10] and countless other texts like this. A second type of argument proceeds from the ordinary beliefs concerning the efficacy of the sacraments, namely, that faith is operative in the sacraments.[11] Third, it is argued from the utterly certain efficacy of one specific saying of Christ pertaining to this topic, that is, "Whatever you loose on earth . . . " [Matthew 16:19].[12] This certain indication of efficacy leads then to the conclusion that the penitent must believe he is absolved when the priest absolves him. It makes no difference whether the priest is mistaken or not, just as one is certain he is baptized even if a priest mistakenly baptizes him. They add that in saying, "Whatever you loose," Christ conferred the power, and in saying, "shall be loosed," he meant to rouse our faith in this effect.[13]

The fact that this novel view is alien to Church teaching will readily become evident if we distinguish between the two kinds of faith we can have, namely, acquired faith or infused faith.

Infused faith is one of the theological virtues, and is mentioned all through Holy Scripture. Without it one cannot please God, and by it the saints conquered kingdoms and brought about righteousness [Hebrews 11:6.33]. If it is a question of this infused faith, clearly it must be had in receiving the sacrament of penance. After all, only baptized believers in Christ are capable of receiving this sacrament. But even though faith of this kind extends to the sacraments, as is clear from the Creed, it does not extend to such particular facts as, for instance, that this event is a sacrament and that the effect of a sacrament is had in this individual instance.

For example, we must believe "in one Baptism for the forgiveness of sins," but we are not bound to believe that when a given priest pours water over Joseph, a Jewish adult, saying, "I baptize you in the name of the Father, and of the Son, and of the Holy Spirit," then Joseph actually receives God's grace and the baptismal character. For we cannot tell whether the baptizing priest or the person baptized only intended to simulate baptism. The priest may not have intended to do what the Church does, and Joseph may not have intended to receive baptism. In our own day a certain Jewish man admitted before me that this had happened to him. This holds with regard to the baptismal character. Regarding the reception of grace, Joseph may receive baptism while deliberately intending to commit the sin of fornication, thus placing an obstacle in the way of the grace of God. A similar example could be given regarding the Eucharist. Although we must believe by faith that a rightly consecrated host contains the true body of Christ, it is not part of infused faith to believe that a given host is rightly consecrated. There could be various human defects intervening, as in the intention of the minister or in the use of uncertain matter.

The all-embracing principle excluding particular facts of this kind from the ambit of infused faith is that infused faith cannot embrace error. Its ground is divine truth. Its object is truth, no less than any acquired knowledge concerns only what is true. But if infused faith were extended to include these particulars, it would at times be embracing error, as is evident from the countless further examples we could cite. Consequently it is not part of infused faith to believe in the effect of absolution in this particular person, that is, in myself. What is of infused faith is rather the belief that absolution rightly given by the Church's minister is efficacious in granting grace to a worthy recipient. This latter faith entails no error, but I can err if I believe in the effect in myself or in this particular individual, since in either of us there could be some obstacle. In the other sacraments we believe in the word of God and in the sacraments themselves. Especially, we believe in the utterly certain efficacy of the words, "Whatever you loose on earth," for a disposed recipient. But we do not have infused faith that the effect takes place in me or that I am a disposed recipient, since there could be an unknown obstacle in me. Since the ambit of faith must not include error, but only most certain truths, we do conclude that infused faith is roused and in fact rendered certain about the effect of absolution by the words, " . . . will be loosed in heaven," as applied to a disposed recipient. But this does not apply to me, since I am perhaps not disposed and hence faith would be believing error. Since it would lead to infused faith embracing error, the view we described is wrong when understood of infused faith.

If the view we described is understood as an aspect of acquired faith, it is also wrong. Although acquired faith has to do with particulars of this kind, since by it we believe that this host is rightly consecrated, this person rightly baptized, and the like, still it is not by this faith that we place our trust in the word of Christ at work in the sacraments. It is not by this faith that we believe in the effectiveness of Christ's words, "Whatever you loose on earth," and in the other objects of Christian faith. Hence those texts referring to infused faith cannot form the basis for acquired faith, nor do they enable such faith to be infallibly certain of its object, namely, that I am absolved in a manner effective before God. On this everyone remains in doubt in this life, in accord with the ordinary norm that one does not know whether he is in God's grace or not. Nor is anyone certain he is sufficiently disposed through the grace of God granted through absolution. According to Job 9 [:21, Vulgate], "And if my heart is undivided, my soul will not know it."[14]

Furthermore, a schismatic or heretic who in other respects confesses correctly could have faith of this kind. It would follow that he would be thereby truly absolved, if a priest mistakenly absolved him. He would consequently be simultaneously in God's grace (because truly absolved before God) and in mortal sin (because he is heretical or schismatic). But this is impossible. Furthermore, if this is the faith by which, "as much as you believe, so much you have,"[15] then a conclusion follows that is alien to Christian truth. For this faith, because acquired, is a human work, and it would follow that confidence in penance would consist in one's own work of believing. Lastly, we argue that since the necessity of such a disposition for the sacrament of penance is derived neither from Holy Scripture, nor the sacred canons, nor Church tradition, nor the sainted teachers, and furthermore since it is opposed to reason, it cannot be exculpated of either presumption or ignorance.

In responding to the countless objections concerning faith, one should distinguish between the sacraments in themselves, and the person who receives the sacrament. Now, concerning the sacrament itself, faith is utterly certain, and should be so even with reference to the specific effect of the sacrament in my case. But when faith regards me as recipient, there may well be some doubt about the effect of the sacrament on me. The Church teaches this when in the prayers after Communion the priest begs that the sacrament received not lead to a debt of punishment and to condemnation, and the like. Hence the Church also teaches every single believer to say after confession and absolution, "Lord, I am not worthy. . ." As I see it, the failure to take notice of this distinction is the cause of this novel teaching.

To the first argument for this view, we say that one has sufficient faith in the word of God and of Christ when he accepts all the articles of faith. Infused faith, by which we believe in God, does not include belief in the effect of these words in my case, as we explained.

We say that the second argument, in its treatment of baptism, is faulty in taking something as a cause that is not such. The persons are not thereby truly baptized because they believe they were baptized. In fact they may have believed they were receiving no grace. A baptism performed in jest can be true baptism if the jest consists in baptizing in these circumstances and not in simulation of baptism. Similarly, if one baptizes and the other is baptized for a motive of pleasure, or out of avarice, in both cases the baptism is genuine. The pleasure or avarice is not an element in baptism itself but would be the cause why one administers or receives baptism. It would be different if the intended jest went so far as to consist not in baptism but in administering or receiving a simulated baptism. Then the jest or avarice is the reason for an act that is no baptism at all.

The second argument also assumes the impossible, that is, that one not contrite is truly absolved if he believes he is absolved. This could only be true if one has the kind of attrition that some hold is converted into contrition by the power of the keys. But on the basis of this assumption one who is neither contrite nor whose attrition is changed to contrition by the keys would either be justified by his own acquired faith (which would be wrong), or he must be simultaneously uncontrite and absolved before God (which is impossible).

In answering the third argument, we say that the sacrament cleanses, not because it is performed, that is, not because of the action in itself, but because it is believed, that is, because of the power believed to be in the sacrament. It is not effective, however, because the recipient believes with all certainty in the effect on himself on a particular occasion. Note that Augustine did not say, "because the minister or recipient believes," but said impersonally, "because it is believed," referring to what is believed. Unless one intends to do what the Church does, he does not baptize. In imitating the Church in performing the act, the reality believed is included, even if not by the faith of the recipient nor of the one baptizing, as is clear in the case of a non-believer who baptizes an infant or an adult who has said, "Let it effect whatever it can."

In the fourth argument what is assumed is not only false but involves arrogant presumption in going against the rite of the universal Church. For contrition is necessary above all else, while this acquired faith in the effect of the sacrament is impossible in itself, since it involves and must always involve an element of uncertainty. There is no need to inquire whether the penitent so believes, since if a person did not believe himself forgiven he would not submit to absolution. There is no problem in contrition being uncertain, for God himself has commanded us to approach the sacraments in just this kind of uncertainty. The argument is wrong in stating that contrition is never adequate, as we know from the many people who come to confession with contrition which — although to themselves uncertain — is still genuine and adequate.

The objection adds that faith in Christ is "supremely certain, wholly genuine, and utterly sufficient." One must answer that this is so concerning matters in the ambit of infused faith, but not so concerning matters outside this ambit, such as the particular effects of the sacraments in individual cases concerning ourselves. About these latter, infused faith is neither certain nor uncertain, since it is not about them. Infused faith believes that the sacraments most certainly confer grace on worthy recipients, as was defined by the Council of Florence under Pope Eugenius IV.[16] This derives from the Apostle's words, "Whoever eats and drinks unworthily, eats and drinks unto judgment" [1 Corinthians 11:27]. Here the Apostle also says, "Let a man examine himself, and so eat of this bread" [11:28], to show that one ought to ascertain whether he is worthy or unworthy. He then said, "If we judge ourselves, we will not be judged by the Lord" [11:31], to make it evident that examining oneself means judging oneself and punishing oneself. In the ordinary language of the Church and its theologians this latter is called "contrition."

Hence it is evidently both wrong and irresponsible to say it is more important to inquire whether a penitent is convinced about the effect of the sacrament he is to receive than to inquire about his contrition. The Apostle prescribes self-examination (that is, contrition), just as the Church and all confessors ordinarily require. But for the penitent to believe in the effect in his own case — this requires a hitherto unknown dogma.

The fifth argument maintained, first, that one with attrition who places no obstacle will not receive the grace of absolution unless he believes in the way described. This is an arbitrary assertion of an unheard of and irrelevant quality in place of the disposition necessary for receiving God's grace through sacramental absolution.

It was maintained secondly, that even for the contrite person sacraments lead to damnation unless one believes he is forgiven. This is not deserving of an answer but of a correction. This asserts that the sacrament of penance, which the Church administers with the requirement of confession, contrition, and satisfaction, leads to damnation without a fourth element, namely, certain belief in the effect in the recipient. This is to construct a new Church.[1 7]

The sixth argument concerned prayer, but diverged into treating a peripheral aspect outside the essence of the sacrament. Prayer is obviously distinct from the sacrament itself and, in fact, comes under the heading of satisfaction, the third part of the sacrament of penance. Nonetheless, one must also say about prayer that faith in its effect can be had in two manners. In view of God's mercy, grace, power, providence, and promises, and the like, the faith with which one prays must be free of any doubt. But in view of the one praying, or of that for which one prays, there must at times be a pious doubt about the effect sought. Otherwise, faith would often prove to be mistaken. This is evident in the prayer of Paul, who surely followed Our Lord's teaching that one is to believe without doubt that he will receive what he seeks. He sought three times that the thorn in his flesh be taken from him, but he did not receive what he requested, as we read in 2 Corinthians 12 [:8f].

We see that our belief that we will receive whatever we request does not refer simply and without qualification to receiving what we request, but to this in the context of God's mercy and His other attributes. Otherwise this faith would at times be mistaken. Paul's faith would have been mistaken. For it can occur, for some other reason pertaining to ourselves, that we do not receive what we seek. For this reason, when Our Lord was teaching this, he first said, "Have faith in God" [Mark 11:22], and then began, "Amen, I say to you..." [11:24]. This was to show that our firm faith about specific effects should look to them as concerns God and not as concerns ourselves.

Augsburg, September 26, 1518.

3
INDULGENCES AND PUNISHMENTS
REQUIRED BY GOD'S JUSTICE

The question is posed whether when an indulgence absolves one from imposed sacramental penances it also remits the punishment for sin owed before God's justice. The following arguments appear to lead to a negative answer. First, just as the penances imposed by the confessor are binding only in the external forum of the Church, so also absolution from them pertains only to this forum.[18] Second, the voluntary penance, about which Christ said, "Do penance" [Matthew 4:16], is required by Christ's teaching, is essential in spiritual penance, and is wholly necessary for salvation. Hence, no priest has authority to remit this penance, which consists in mortifying our passions and following Christ in bearing the cross.[19] Third, the powers to bind and loose are on the same plane. But the Pope can bind one only to canonical penance. Consequently his absolution extends only to canonical penance.[20] Fourth, sacramental satisfaction is not called "satisfaction" because it satisfies simply for guilt, but because it satisfies in accord with the norms of the Church. Consequently, remission of this satisfaction is not absolution from satisfaction simply and in itself. The premise holds, because when one speaks of satisfying for guilt, this is properly by means of the punishment of mortification and the like.[21]

But the ordinary understanding of the Church is opposed to this view.

To gain clarity on this topic one must grasp the interrelation between canonical punishment imposed by the priest in sacramental confession and satisfactory punishment for our guilt before the divine justice. These are not two different punishments, but are determinate and indeterminate forms of the same punishment. The same interrelation holds between the precept to confess sins as issued by God and by the Church. It is not that two confessions are commanded, but the Church's precept is rather the determinate form of the indeterminate divine precept. The Church commands the same thing God commands, but while God's command does not prescribe when, the Church specifies this as each year. But still it is one and the same confession prescribed by God and the Church, and undoubtedly a single confession fulfils both the precept of God and of the Church. It would be silly to confess once to obey God and once to obey the Church. We see the same thing in the topic under discussion here. If someone commits a sin, perjury for example, he is held by God's command to make satisfaction, but the penalty is not specified. For the penitent can make satisfaction by alms, fasting, or prayer. Now for the identical sin the confessor will oblige him to satisfaction by imposing a specific penance, such as fasting for seven years. This penitent is not obliged to perform two penances, one to satisfy before God and the other to satisfy in the eyes of the Church. But as he carries out the penance imposed by the Church he is making satisfaction before God and the Church together. He will either make all that is due for the sin, if what the priest imposed equalled that due according to divine justice, or that part corresponding to the imposed penance, if this imposed penance was less than that required in accord with divine justice.

We have not made this up arbitrarily, but it can be shown as evident by reviewing all those acts commanded by both God and the Church. It is clear regarding the precept to observe both feasts and fasts. God and the Church prescribe one and the same thing, with God's command being indeterminate and the Church's determinate. When one has obeyed the Church, he does not still remain obligated to fulfill the corresponding divine command. The same thing holds in other cases, namely, that where God and the Church command the same thing, we are obliged to one and the same act by a twofold obligation, that is, to God and to the Church.

Consequently, one could conceive a remission of imposed penance by an indulgence not remitting the satisfactory penance simply and without qualification. Conceivably it could be removed as obliged by the Church and remain as an obligation before the justice of God. Just as when the Pope remits a fast imposed on someone, he does not excuse him from the divine and natural requirement of fasting, but simply relieves him of the obligation to fast arising from Church law. Similarly just as the priest binds a person by a new obligation to a penalty by imposing penance of a specific type and extent, so he would remit by an indulgence that removes the obligation to the Church and the specification of this particular penance.

But the view alleged here is wrong in not discerning the difference between remission by way of an indulgence and remission by way of permission. The latter is given by all rulers, both ecclesiastical and civil. All rulers can loose what they have bound by granting permission not to fulfil what they have commanded. This is the kind of remission granted in the case of fasting and the like. But it is not this kind of remission that is granted by indulgences, since they are founded on the privilege given by Christ, "Whatever you loose on earth. . ." [Matthew 16:19]. The remission granted in view of this privilege is certainly not of the kind granted by all rulers, since they act in virtue of their office as ruler, not needing a privilege. Furthermore, remission granted by way of permission embraces all positive prescriptions of law in the same manner. One prescription can be remitted as well as another. But the power to remit which Christ gave Peter by a privilege has as its object matters relevant to the kingdom of heaven. As Christ said, "I will give you the keys of the kingdom of heaven" [Matthew 16:19]. The privilege is specially relevant to sins, as we well know from Christ's words, "Whose sins you shall forgive, they are forgiven" [John 20:23], and to punishment for guilt, as indicated by Christ's words in Matthew 18[:17f], where after saying, "If he will not listen to the Church, let him be to you as a gentile," he said, "Amen I say to you, whatever you bind on earth. . . ."

From another viewpoint, if indulgences were no more than exemptions from the obligation imposed by the priest or the canons, then the whole body of the faithful would be deceived in their belief that not only the obligation but the punishments themselves are remitted. Here is convincing proof that indulgences grant another kind of remission, for it is the ordinary understanding of the Church and her theologians that a person truly gaining an indulgence has made satisfaction just as if he had carried out the penance corresponding to the indulgence.

It evidently follows that when indulgences absolve from imposed penances, they not only remit the obligation imposed by the confessor or the canons but remit as well the temporal punishment due for sin in view of divine justice, to the extent that this corresponds to the indulgence gained. Further, the argument derived from the ordinary understanding of the Church and her sacred teachers is not of minor importance. It is sufficiently authoritative that it is irresponsible to hold an opposing view. This position on indulgences is then confirmed by the way one finds reflected in it the exercise of the privilege granted to Peter in "Whatever you loose on earth. . . ." Remitting punishment for sin due in the forum of divine justice is not the act of a ruler following human laws, but the act of the divine power Christ granted to Peter.

In addition Pope Clement VI taught explicitly that an indulgence remits the temporal punishment due for sin, as we read in the *Extravagans* received by the whole world during the Jubilees held every fifty years.[22] This is now published in the *Extravagantes Communes,* under the title, *De poenitentiis et remissionibus,* in the chapter, *Unigenitus.*[23] But one is not permitted to hold a view opposed to the teaching of the Apostolic See.

In answer to the first argument, we say that humanly or canonically imposed penance is of two kinds. Some are wholly from man or the canons, such as excommunication, or imprisonment, or things of this order. These bind solely in the ecclesiastical forum. In other cases, the obligation of punishment is presupposed by man or the canons and then imposed by them solely as to extent and kind of penance. Thus people are able to complete the punishments they are presumed to owe. The latter penances oblige in part only in the ecclesiastical forum, since one is only held to complete this kind of penance in this life. But they also oblige in part before God in an unqualified way, since if one does not satisfy in accord with the specified kind of penance, he is held by the divine justice to satisfaction in the next life for the complete penance he would have completed, had he carried out what was imposed. Hence, in the same way that sacramental penance obliges before God, so also is remission valid before God.

Responding to the second argument, we say that the Church does have power to remit by indulgences punishments obliging under divine command and obligation. The Church does not do this on human authority but on the basis of the divine authority conferred with the privilege, "Whatever you bind. . . ." Peter, as the vicar and minister of Christ, acts with the authority of Christ. One should not wonder that he can remit punishment required by Christ's precept and entailed in interior penance as necessary for salvation. After all, he can remit guilt, which is so much greater than punishment that the Jews exclaimed [Mark 2:7], " Who can forgive sins but God alone?" A priest acts ministerially in absolving from guilt and forgiving the sins of those who confess to him, in accord with Christ's words, "Whose sins you shall forgive, they are forgiven" [John 20:23]. The minister of Christ can much more surely absolve from punishment, since guilt and punishment both hinder one from entering the kingdom of heaven, for "nothing defiled will enter it" [Revelation 21:27] and "God will wipe away every tear and there will be no more pain" [Revelation 21:24]. The removal of the hindrances of both guilt and punishment must fall under the power of the keys; otherwise, they would not suffice to open the kingdom of heaven for the faithful. But they clearly do suffice, given a disposed recipient and the fulfillment of the other requirements.

Hence by an indulgence a person does in fact receive by absolution the remission of the penance to which he as a sinner was obliged by divine precept, which the interior virtue of penance was to elicit for his sin, and which was necessary for his eternal salvation. When so absolved, a person is no longer obliged to this penance— neither by divine precept, nor from interior penance, nor in view of the goal of eternal salvation. He has already satisfied in another way, namely, through remission received in a rightly adminstered indulgence given by one Christ has endowed with his own authority.

What is further said, namely that the penance obliging the sinner is the cross of Christ and the mortification of his passions, has already been solved by theologians. For they say that indulgences do not substitute for penance insofar as this is curative of our passions. Consequently, even after obtaining indulgences we should continue to do penance for the healing of our passions. But indulgences do substitute, insofar as they make satisfaction for sins committed. The same distinction should be applied regarding the following of Christ in bearing the cross, and regarding things of this kind.

The third argument assumes that the powers of binding and loosing are on the same plane. We answer that this is to be taken with a grain of salt. They are the same in the ambit they embrace, since regarding both Our Lord said "Whatever . . . ," that is, "Whatever you loose," and "Whatever you bind." But they are not the same in the manner of operation. For the priest takes away sins by exercising an authoritative ministry, in virtue of which his absolution makes a sinner righteous. But he cannot by this ministry so bind a person as to make a righteous person a sinner. This makes it clear that with regard to sins Peter looses in a different manner than he binds. Similarly with regard to punishment the Pontiff binds and looses differently. He absolves ministerially both by sacramental absolution and by indulgences which remit the punishments due according to divine justice. But he binds one to both punishment and guilt in an indirect way. He binds to guilt by not remitting or by issuing a prescription by the transgression of which one is made a sinner. So also he binds to punishment by not remitting or by doing that which makes a person by himself incur a debt of punishment before the justice of God.

Using this distinction, we reply to the minor premise that if one is speaking of Papal power without regard for its manner of operation, then the Pope can bind to both canonical and non-canonical punishments and can similarly absolve in an unqualified manner before God, as we have explained. But if one is speaking of a power exercised in a specific manner, that is, directly imposing or removing, then the premise is false. The powers of binding and loosing are not the same with regard to the power of the keys. For he can directly absolve what he cannot directly impose, as was shown regarding guilt.

Still, there is another possible response to the minor premise, namely that the canonical penance imposed as satisfaction in the forum of penance does include the punishment due before divine justice. As we explained above, one and the same punishment is presupposed and is specified by the confessor or the canon. Consequently, when the priest binds one to canonical penance, he is simply binding to penance garbed in the qualifications added by himself or a canon. And in the same way, when he absolves from canonical punishment he is simply absolving from punishment. By absolving from a punishment specified by the confessor or a canon, he absolves from the punishment and from the specification. This must be, since absolution from the whole involves absolution from each part included in the whole. Thus, even granting that he binds and looses only canonical punishments, one still concludes that he binds and looses the punishment simply due as satisfaction for sin.

A third possible approach to the same argument is to apply the ontological distinction between act and potency, which is applicable to every kind of being. Since a potential man and an actual man, and something potentially white and actually white, are of the same respective genus, so also canonical penance is also divided between actual and potential, although both are of the same genus, that is, canonical penance. The Church has authority over canonical penance in act and over canonical penance in potency. In fact through the canons of penance and the judgment of confessors the Church only makes actual, according to set canonical form (as, so many days fasting), the punishments due for sin which were potentially canonical. And since the Church has this authority over canonical penances both actual and potential, it has authority over all temporal punishment due in satisfaction for sin. For all such punishments are canonical either in act or in potency, that is, they are either canonically determined already or determinable, either actually imposed by a confessor or able to be imposed. Hence, although the Church's grants of indulgence ordinarily speak of remitting only imposed penances, she can also remit those not imposed. This follows from the proofs given here, and is supported by the authority of St. Thomas and other theologians.[24]

The fourth argument spoke of satisfaction "simply," a notion that can have two meanings. It can be equivalent to "totally" or it can rule out some additional specification. In the latter sense an Ethiopian is not called white simply but with the additional specification that it is his teeth that are white. But we are called white "simply" because we are so called without any addition. Now concerning the topic of sacramental satisfaction, if "simply" means "totally," then sacramental satisfaction is at times simply satisfactory and sometimes not simply so because only partial. Obviously it is at times equivalent to the punishment due for sin and at times not equivalent. But if "simply" means "without additional specification," then sacramental satisfaction does satisfy simply, as long as the penitent is rightly disposed as he performs it. For he satisfies both the Church and God for as much punishment for sin as corresponds to the sacramental satisfaction. What we say here is not arbitrary but was effectively proven above.

Augsburg, September 29, 1518.

4

INTEGRAL CONFESSION

SYNOPSIS: Also on September 29, 1518, Cajetan dealt with the section of the *Sermo de poenitentia* in which Luther argued that integral confession of all one's mortal and venial sins was impossible and an act of presumption.[25] Cajetan responded that confession of all one's mortal sins, instead of being presumptuous, is an act of integral submission to Christ's minister that corresponds to the integral sorrow by which the penitent submits to God. Since integral confession is taught by the decree *Omnis utriusque sexus* of IV Lateran, and further qualified as "all the sins one recalls" by the Council of Florence,[26] it is rash for one to teach the contrary without the backing of reason and authority. The confession of venial sins is to be commended as an act of humility and mortification, as the practice of devout persons shows. There is presumption in arguing against a customary way religious persons strengthen themselves in God's grace. In response to Luther's arguments, Cajetan contended that mortal sins can be known because they are voluntary acts; that Luther's texts from the primitive Church were not about confession and therefore beside the point; and that all our works are not sins, since some of them arise from God's grace working in us to bring forth works meritorious of eternal life (2 Timothy 4:8).[27]

5
PENANCES REMAINING AFTER DEATH

SYNOPSIS: On September 30, 1518, Cajetan treated Luther's contention that canonical penances imposed by a confessor and not completed in this life cease to bind after one's death.[28] Cajetan made the distinction elaborated in the third treatise between the indeterminate debt of satisfaction owed for sin before the divine justice and the determinate form this debt is given by the confessor. Two extremes must be avoided in speaking of penance due after death. One should not deny the existence of any obligation, but on the other hand one should not say that the determinate form given by the confessor must still be completed. The substantial debt will remain, at least in part, if it has not been worked off in this life. Both arguments urged by Luther refer to the determinate forms canonical penances are given in this life.

6
SACRAMENTAL ABSOLUTION

It is asked whether the effect of sacramental absolution is the remission of guilt. A first argument for a negative answer is the confession of the whole of Scripture and the Church that God alone remits guilt.[29] A second argument is that prior to the priest's absolution of the penitent God remits guilt when the person decides to confess. As Scripture says, "I said, 'I will confess the unrighteousness of which I am guilty,' and you forgave the guilt of my sin" [Psalm 31:5, Vulgate].[30]

But this is contrary to the common teaching of the Church that the sacraments of the New Law grant grace.

To gain understanding of this matter, recall that the question was raised earlier and was treated in Book IV of the *Sentences,*

Distinction 18.[31] Because of the obscurity of the texts cited on this
point from ancient teachers, the Master of the *Sentences* held the
view that the priest of the Gospel gave an absolution that declared
one had been absolved by God and so readmitted the person to
ecclesiastical communion. The new theory now advanced adds to
this the conferral of peace of soul, since before absolution the soul is
disturbed over forgiveness of its sins, but when absolution is received
in the belief that one is truly absolved, then the soul becomes secure
in the conviction that forgiveness has been granted and it comes to
experience peace. This faith in the presence of grace derived from
the ministry of the priest is claimed to be so important that sin
would remain unless one believed it forgiven. Remission of sin and
the gift of grace do not suffice, since one must also believe that his
sin has been forgiven.[32]

However a different view emerges when one ponders diligently
the words Our Lord spoke when he gave this sacramental power. He
did not say, "Whose sins you shall declare forgiven. . .," but rather,
"Whose sins you shall forgive. . ." [John 20:23], and, in the same
vein, "Whatever you loose. . ." [Matthew 16:19]. Neither did he
say, "They are forgiven before the Church," or, "It will be loosed in
respect to the Church," but instead, "It will be loosed in heaven"
[Matthew 16:19], and, "They are forgiven" [John 20:23], simply
and without qualification. Hence if the words of Our Lord are to be
taken in their proper sense, they prove that the ministers of the
Church have the power to forgive sins by the authority of Christ.

The reasons are as cogent for accepting these words of Our Lord
about the sacrament of penance as true in their literal sense as for
taking his words about the sacrament of the Eucharist ("This is my
body") as true in their literal sense. There is no reason why we
should believe the latter are literally true but then accept the former
words in a non-literal sense, especially since the greater miracle is
that by the ministry of the priest bread becomes the body of Christ.
Hence if the words spoken by the priest over the Eucharist compel
us to believe that what is beneath these species is "my body," that
is, Christ's, then the other words of Our Lord ("Whose sins you shall
forgive, they are forgiven" and "Whatever you loose on earth will be
loosed in heaven") equally call for our belief in their literal sense,
that is, that by the ministry of the priest sins are forgiven and sinners
are absolved from their guilt. The effect of the word of Christ
spoken by the priest, "I absolve you of your sins," should be no less

than what is brought about by the priest speaking the words of the same Christ, "This is my body." Both bring about what they express, providing the conditions are fulfilled, for instance, that the minister has authority and the penitent the proper disposition. For not anyone can give sacramental absolution, but only a priest with ordinary or delegated authority. Also the recipient must be worthy of absolution; otherwise, we fall back into that extreme error condemned by St. Jerome, namely, arbitrarily condemning the innocent and absolving hardened sinners.[33] The sacrament of the altar is similar, for we believe it pertains to the ministry of priests, not deacons, to consecrate by speaking these words only over unleavened bread, and not over just any kind of matter.

As a sign of this, when Our Lord conferred the power to forgive and retain sins, he began, "Receive the Holy Spirit," and then went on, "Whose sins you shall forgive. . ." [John 20:22f] , as if to say, "Whose sins you shall forgive under the guidance of the Holy Spirit, they are forgiven, not those at the urging of your own spirit." For undoubtedly the Holy Spirit moves and guides toward absolving or binding, providing all the conditions are fulfilled, as the minister of Christ absolves or binds. A correct conferral of absolution is by the proper minister following the required form over rightly disposed matter, namely, a penitent who confesses sins and is worthy of absolution. In this case we must believe and confess that the effect of sacramental absolution is the forgiveness of sins, granted albeit authoritatively by God alone but ministerially by the priest though Christ's sacrament.

This then fulfils literally the words, "Whose sins you shall forgive, they are forgiven." The Church does not forgive before God forgives, as if God followed after the judgment of the Church. He did not say, "Whose sins you shall forgive, they will be forgiven," referring to the future, but, ". . .they are forgiven," in the present. This indicates that forgiveness by the minister is one and the same with the forgiveness granted by God. The forgiveness of sin is one and the same, conferred ministerially by the priest and authoritatively granted by God. So also in the conversion of the bread into the body of Christ, what the word of Christ brings about when spoken by the priest, this God effects authoritatively.

Earlier the solution to this question may have been doubtful, but now it has been definitely given by the Council of Florence under Pope Eugenius IV, where it is said, "The effect of this sacrament is absolution from sin."[34] It does not speak of a declaration or of peace, but of absolution as the effect, not of God alone, but of this sacrament. Consequently, when the required conditions are fulfilled, the priest by his absolution truly absolves from sins and only consequently declares the penitent absolved, and — as far as human conjecture goes — makes the sinner certain his sins are forgiven. According to the ordinary norm the sinner will always remain uncertain that his sins are forgiven before God, since it always remains unclear whether or not we receive the sacrament of penance out of, or with, infused charity.

Hence, the recent view we have described is not an admissible opinion but an error, since it leaves the sacrament of penance bereft of efficacy unless one is convinced of its effect in oneself. It says that the priest's remission only grants forgiveness to one believing he is forgiven. Even worse, since unintelligible, is what it holds about sin remaining after forgiveness and the conferral of grace, unless the penitent believes his sin is forgiven. Such views are unworthy of a hearing not only by the learned but even by ordinary Christians. As to opposing these ideas, we can well observe the advice of the Philosopher, that it is foolish to be concerned about answering anybody proposing contradictions.[35] Obviously baptism remits sins for a recipient not having this conviction, as in the case of infants. Clearly almost all come to the sacraments of penance and the Eucharist in reverent fear of the Lord and uncertain of being in grace. In fact theologians praise their continuing uncertainty and ordinarily attribute its opposite to presumption or ignorance.[36]

In answer to the first argument we say that the texts in question refer to a different manner of forgiveness. God alone forgives sins authoritatively, which does not exclude the minister of the Gospel having power granted him by God to forgive sins ministerially, by means of the sacrament Christ himself instituted for this purpose.

We answer the second argument by recalling that sacramental absolution is said to bring about forgiveness of sins in two ways, either in desire or by actual conferral. One who gains forgiveness before confession receives this from sacramental absolution in desire, according to the text, "I said, 'I will confess. . . ,' and you forgave" [Psalm 31:5]. In the words, "I said, 'I will confess,' " the person is tending toward confession, and undoubtedly he is thereby absolved. Otherwise there would have been no need to say, "I said, 'I will confess,' " but it would have been sufficient to say, "I admitted to the Lord the unrighteousness of which I am guilty."

If the penitent receives forgiveness of sins before absolution, then this grace of forgiveness of sins is increased by the subsequent absolution. If he is not forgiven beforehand he attains it by absolution, if, as we have said, he is then worthy of receiving absolution. This is not an opinion we have developed on our own, but we have received this from the universal Church, which confesses "one baptism for the forgiveness of sins." The Church understands all this consistently. As we explained above, by actual conferral baptism forgives the sins of one whose sins have not been forgiven in desire and who approaches baptism worthily. In the person already forgiven by the sacrament in desire, actual conferral increases grace. It is not any defect in the sacraments that produces this diversity but rather the diverse dispositions of those receiving the sacraments.

Augsburg, October 1, 1518.

7
IMPERFECTION IN GAINING INDULGENCES?

SYNOPSIS: On October 2, 1518, Cajetan responded to Luther's statements on the gaining of indulgences being morally defective, since they are an escape from the penances which the best Christians willingly embrace.[37] Against this, Cajetan points out the main purpose of indulgences, which is the satisfaction of divine justice out of the merits of Christ and the saints. Also, indulgences are only gained by those acting in love. Hence he finds no disorder in using such means, but judges them appropriate for virtuous people who thus remove obstacles on their road to the heavenly homeland. The petition, "Forgive us our trespasses (*debita nostra*)," confirms this, since if one may so pray, it is certainly morally good to seek release from *debita* remaining from sin. In fact, gaining an indulgence, if motivated by the desire to enter eternal life, can be a meritorious act. Still, Cajetan admits it is a greater good to satisfy as well by actual performance of the penance, since this adds the element of healing to that of satisfaction. He adds a reference to Treatise 3 on the relevance of indulgences for penances due before divine justice, thus showing that all can profit from indulgences, even those upon whom no canonical penance has been imposed.

8

THE "TREASURY" OF INDULGENCES

We ask whether the indulgences of the Church are granted out of the treasury of the merits of Christ and the saints. A series of arguments appear to call for a negative answer.

First, such indulgences would not be indulgences or remissions of anything, but rather satisfaction and complete payment to the last penny through the works of others.[38] It further follows that the one granting the indulgence would take on the burden of satisfaction. All deny this, because then the Pope would not remit, but would satisfy through others.[39]

Second, such indulgences would be a transferral of merit by the power of the keys, not an act of absolution. But this would contradict the word of Christ, "Whatever you loose. . ." [Matthew 16:19]. Further the keys would only be effecting something that is actually taking place. For if there are works of the saints in a treasury of the Church, then the Holy Spirit does not leave them dormant but brings them to the aid of people they can help.[40]

Third, no works of the saints are left unrewarded. For one thing, "the sufferings of the present time are not to be compared to the glory to come" [Romans 8:18]. Also, by such indulgences the saints would not be rewarded for their works of supererogation but we would be instead, thus giving the reward on a lower level but not on a higher level. If one says the saints are also rewarded for these works, then he is doing away with their unrewarded works for the treasury.[41]

Fourth, no saint adequately fulfils the commandments of God in this life, and therefore there are no superabundant works remaining for conferral by indulgences. A first proof of this is the word of Christ, "When you have done all that is written, say, 'We are unprofitable servants'" [Luke 17:10]. But an unprofitable servant has not acted over and beyond but below the standard set. Another proof comes from Matthew 25[:9], where the wise virgins refused to share their oil out of fear of having none. Further, every saint is bound to love God as much as possible, if not more. But none of them did this or could have done it. Even those who become saints through the supreme work, martyrdom, do no more than they ought, and hardly do even this. Consequently, their other works were much less than was called for.[42]

Fifth, the affirmation of the treasury is made without any backing of Scripture, theologians, or argumentation.[43]

The denial of the treasury is grounded as well on the texts of the saints. First, Augustine says that all the saints pray, "Forgive us our trespasses." But one admitting trespasses has no superabundance.[44]

Second, there is a text of Jerome against Pelagius on [Psalm 31], "Blessed the man to whom the Lord imputes no sin." Jerome cites verse 6, "Every saint prays for this at opportune times," and urges the question of how one can be a saint, if he prays over his iniquity.[45]

Third, in Augustine's *Retractions*, Book I, Chapter 19, we read, "One fulfils all the commandments when what he has not done is forgiven." Thus he denies that the saints fulfill perfectly the commandments of God, by saying that more comes from God's forgiving than from man's fulfilling.[46]

Fourth, a text from Book 9 of Augustine's *Confessions*: "Woe to men judged in the absence of mercy, no matter how laudable their lives may have been." As Job said, "Even if I have some righteousness, I will beseech my judge" [Job 9:15].[47]

Fifth, according to Augustine no saint is without sins in this life. For we read in 1 John 1[:8], "If we say we have no sin . . ." Therefore, there are no superabundant works of the saints.[48]

And if it is argued that the saints committed only venial sins and could still have done more than was required, one can answer that the very best work is a venial sin. Hence they always did less than was required, and so they committed sin. The premise rests on Augustine, as cited above in the third argument.[49]

One could also argue that even if there were superabundant merits of the saints, they would be of no benefit, since each one will receive his reward according to his own labor and not according to another's, as we read in Romans 3[= 2:6]. It would not be right for the Church to distribute these merits, since remission of punishment is the least valuable of the Church's gifts. Nor would the Church be seeking the best for her own by lessening penance, since it pertains more to genuine religion to inflict punishment than to remit it.[50]

Proof is then offered that the merits of Christ do not constitute the treasury of indulgences. First this assertion has no basis in Scripture. If one appeals to the authority of the Roman Church, then we would not be able to give an account for the faith, or the hope, that is in us [1 Peter 3:15].[51]

Second, on this point one can also apply the arguments cited above, namely, that indulgences would not be indulgences but satisfactions through another. Nonetheless, the canon says that indulgences diminish satisfaction (*"Cum ex eo,"* in the section on penance and remission). It does not say satisfaction is changed from one to another, but that it is diminished. Similarly, the keys would not be applied to loose, but to transfer to another, and to deny that they loose is sacrilegious. If they do loose, they take away the whole, and do not transfer. The merits of Christ, since they are not dormant, would be applied to do what they are actually doing already.[52]

Third, it does horrible irreverence to the merits of Christ, if they are only applied to reducing punishments. Such a paltry gift is far beneath him who is the exemplar of all the martyrs.[53]

Fourth, St. Thomas and St. Bonaventure say that our good works are better than indulgences. But they also say that the merits of Christ are conferred through indulgences. However, since the merits of Christ are obviously better by far than our good works, indulgences must be better than our good works — which contradicts the first statement. Consequently, it must either be true that indulgences are not the merits of Christ or that they are and should therefore as the merits of Christ be sought after to the exclusion of all else.[54]

Fifth, theologians ordinarily advise people who have gained indulgences to fast nonetheless, since "no one knows whether he is deserving of love or hatred" [Ecclesiastes 9:1]. But then it follows either that this opinion is an insult to God and to the Church or that the merits of Christ do not constitute the treasury of indulgences. For if theologians are right, then the keys of the Church have no certain effect, which is a blasphemous idea, making indulgences confer an uncertain gift, and making the Church thereby guilty of an unholy deception. Or, if indulgences do depend on the merits of Christ and the saints, then one should cease performing one's own works. Again, if the merits of Christ are conferred through indulgences and I am still uncertain about the forgiveness of sins, then I either believe in the sufficiency of the works of Christ granted to me and applied to my forgiveness, or I doubt their sufficiency. If I believe, then there is no further need of fasting, since I should not consider my own works as better than the works of Christ. If I doubt — what is more detestable! Confirming this is the argument that the goodness of the merits of Christ exceeds our works beyond all proportion. Hence either they are not the treasury of indulgences or else to avoid insult to the merits of Christ indulgences have to be ranked ahead of all other works commanded by God.[55]

Sixth, the addition of the merits of the saints is inappropriate, implying as it does that the merits of Christ are not enough.[56]

Seventh, the grace of contrition is granted no one except along with a gift of the merits of Christ. Hence, independently of indulgences a person shares in the treasury of merits.[57]

Eighth, if the merit of Christ is the treasury of indulgences, then it should free from death and its pains. This must follow, because otherwise the merit of Christ would be proven inadequate. Also it is powerful enough to free from eternal death.[58]

Finally, if the absolution granted in indulgences confers the treasury of Christ, then other absolutions as well will confer the treasury of Christ, especially absolution from excommunication when one is made a sharer in the merits of Christ and the Church.[59] Furthermore, if the absolution granted in indulgences is a distribution of the treasury of Christ, then the act of binding closes or restricts the treasury of Christ. But the latter is not part of the power of the keys, since it is done independently of any operation of indulgences.[60]

But against all these arguments there stands the position taken by theologians.

To clarify this question we must demonstrate that the merits of Christ and the saints do constitute the treasury of indulgences, how we come to know this, what occurs in an indulgence, and to what end this occurs.

Indeed, we have it on apostolic authority that the merits of Christ and the saints are the treasury of indulgences, since Pope Clement VI said the following about the treasury of the merits of Christ in *Unigenitus*:

> Christ entrusted this treasury for distribution to the faithful by St. Peter, the bearer of the keys of heaven, and by his successors, his vicars on earth, a distribution to be made for pious and reasonable causes, for the remission in whole or in part of the temporal punishment due for sin. It is to be generally and individually applied out of mercy, as this seems right before God, upon those who are truly repentant and have confessed. The aggregate of this treasury is known

to be increased by the merits of the Mother of God and of
all the elect.

These words of the Pope come after a long passage on the
superabundance of merits, as now found in the section *De
poenitentiis et remissionibus* of the *Extravagantes.*[61]

The binding power of this decretal arises from two sources. First,
there is the principle that recognizes the letters and decrees of the
Roman Pontiffs as ranking in authority next to Holy Scripture. This
is enunciated both in *In canonicis* in Distinction 19[62] and in the
defense of the apostolic *Extravagantes* in canon 1 of the same
Distinction.[63] Second, *Unigentus* teaches about one part of the
sacrament of penance, namely satisfaction. However, the chapter *Ad
abolendam* in the decretals *De haereticis* lays it down that on
questions of sacramental doctrine no one is allowed to dissent from
the teaching and practice of the Roman Church.[64] Hence we believe
that one must not treat such teaching as a doubtful opinion. For the
Roman Church did not dream up the notion of this treasury of
indulgences or just imagine it, for it is convincingly derived from
texts of Holy Scripture and rests on cogent arguments developed by
theologians.

For a clearer understanding of this topic, one should begin by
pondering the difference between merit and satisfaction. A condign
merit (this is what we refer to) is a work by which one becomes
deserving of eternal happiness as due to him. As the Apostle said, "I
have fought the good fight . . . . There is laid up for me the crown of
righteousness which the Lord, the just judge, will award to me on
that day" [2 Timothy 4:7f]. On the other hand, satisfaction is the
voluntary performance of a punishment by which one bound to
punishment satisfies the requirement of justice. When he completes
the punishment, he doubtless satisfies for what was owed.

Merit and satisfaction are not so far apart that they are not often
aspects of one and the same work. For in works done out of love,
the merit is proportionate to the positive goodness of each work and
the satisfaction is proportionate to the negative element of
punishment. For instance, fasting as a good work is meritorious; but
as a punishment it is also satisfactory. Here we have been treating
the formal difference between merit and satisfaction.

Another difference between them pertains to their efficacy or
benefit. Except in the case of Christ, merit goes no further than the

person meriting. No one is able to merit eternal happiness for another, but only for himself, except Christ who merited it for his elect. The reason for this difference is that Christ was given the grace of headship, a universal grace, while others are given a partial grace. Hence the merit of Christ, not of others, is granted us through the sacraments for our salvation. Paul therefore asked [1 Corinthians 1:13], "Was Paul crucified for you? Or were you baptized in the name of Paul?" But one person can satisfy for another, as is clear when one does a sacramental penance in place of another.

Because of this difference, the saints themselves have received the reward for their own works, in so far as these were meritorious. As such they benefit only themselves. But in so far as they were satisfactory, they first paid the debt of punishment for their own sins, and then if they had more of a penal element than was required as due for the person's own sins, that excessive amount remains as superfluous to the saints' own needs. This excess is what some call the unrewarded works of the saints, which is not due to a defect either in God's generosity or in the work or person of the saint, but is due to the excellence of the person who has willingly suffered in this excessive manner. Because the person who suffered owed no more punishment for sins, the excess satisfactions could not be rewarded in themselves, or, to speak more exactly, the satisfactions could not serve as payment on their own behalf.

Because many saints suffered far more than was due for their own sins, there is consequently a great deal of excess satisfaction remaining from them. It is evident that the saints performed much more satisfaction than was due for their sins. The Blessed Virgin, as sinless, needed no satisfaction for her own sins, and underwent much that was satisfactory. Her life is the beacon light for many churches, and we read with reference to the pain she suffered, "Your own soul a sword will pierce" [Luke 2:35]. Job bears witness, "Would that the sins by which I deserve wrath were weighed in the balance with the tragedies I suffer, since the latter seem greater than the sands of the ocean" [6:2f]. And who is so empty-headed to say that Lawrence, Vincent, and the other martyrs who endured so much deserved all these pains as satisfaction due for their own sins? Hence there are many satisfactory works of the saints over and beyond the ocean of Christ's excessive satisfaction for the sins of the whole world, to which John the Evangelist refers[1 John 2:2]. Why, if after all conceivable sins, every member of humanity were baptized, then by the satisfactory merits of Christ everyone would go immediately to heaven! But the great multitude of the lost have made themselves unworthy of benefitting from Christ's satisfaction, and so out of that which sufficed for all there is an excess left. Hence to avoid error you must understand that the treasury of indulgences is made up of the excess merits of Christ and the saints in so far as these are satisfactory in nature.

We have shown that such satisfactory works of Christ and the saints do remain in excess; now we must show that they are left for our benefit and for distribution by the Church militant. Three considerations show that the satisfactory works of this kind were left to be shared with us to make satisfaction on our behalf, just as if the saints had done these works in their lifetime for the purpose of completing the punishments due for our sins. First, satisfactions of this kind should not be useless or without purpose. But they would be fruitless as satisfactions, if they did not attain their proper end of making satisfaction. This would not be an extrinsic defect, as if persons were lacking whom they could benefit, but an essential defect because of their specific character as satisfactory works of supererogation. As such they would be fruitless, since neither the person performing them nor others could benefit from them as satisfactory works of supererogation.

Second, the unity of the Church requires that whatever its members do that can be of benefit to the Christian community be in fact directed by the Holy Spirit, the ruler of the Church, to the benefit of those in the Church. Clearly the satisfactory works of supererogation can benefit the Church, since the saints could have by their own intention applied them as satisfactions for this or that member of the Church who was bound to make satisfaction for his own sins. Hence it is reasonable to suppose that the saints' satisfactory works of supererogation have been ordered to the benefit of other members of the Church. Since they cannot satisfy for those who have done them, their specific usefulness lies in satisfying for others. I said, "specific usefulness," since we should not judge in general terms, but look to what is specific to the matter being treated.

Third, and most important, Paul bore witness concerning his own works of satisfaction in Colossians 1 [:24], "I rejoice in my sufferings for your sake, and I fill up in my own flesh what is lacking in the suffering of Christ for his body, the Church." Here you can see this intention of completing in one's own flesh the afflictions lacking to the suffering of Christ for completing the full measure determined by God for the Church. Clearly the other saints were of the same mind as Paul, as Augustine pointed out when he cited this view of the Apostle, in commenting on Psalm 68.[65]

Finally, it is easy to show that the treasury of merits, as satisfactory, is to be distributed by the Supreme Pontiff. In all states the ruler is the one who distributes the common goods to the state. It stands beyond contradiction that the one entrusted with the care of the state is also entrusted with dispensing things promoting the common good of the state. Now the satisfactory works are clearly on the order of benefits common to the Church, since they were done for her benefit and left over for this purpose, as we explained. Hence the distribution of this treasury pertains to him who has care of the whole Church. Since only the successor of Peter is over the whole Church, the Roman Pontiff alone is to distribute this treasury, and not give it out arbitrarily. Since, as *Unigenitus* says, indulgences remit the temporal punishment due as satisfaction for sins, and since the Pope can only grant this remission in connection with the Church's sacrament, that is, by applying the satisfactions of others to the one granted the remission, hence both the Apostolic See in the above mentioned decree, and theologians enlightened by the Holy Spirit, come to the quite reasonable conclusion that this treasury is dispensed by indulgences granted the faithful who are by charity living members of Christ. Hence it obviously follows that when an indulgence grants a person absolution of a specified punishment due for his sins, it applies to him from the treasury an amount of satisfaction equivalent to the punishment remitted. At one and the same time, this is a work of mercy freeing the person from punishment, and a work of justice applying to his benefit the satisfaction of others. So the earthly Jerusalem descends from heaven through our invitation, since all the ways of the Lord are both mercy and truth. – This, then, renders evident the position taken.

In response to the first argument for the contrary we point to the different kinds of actions that make up an indulgence. As an absolution and remission of punishment it is and is called the act of a judge. As the application of satisfaction for a person's benefit, it is and is called an act of distribution. As something completing punishment required before the justice of God by the applied satisfaction it is and is called a work of justice. Hence we offer this brief answer: with reference to the one gaining the indulgence, it is an act of remission and reduction of punishment; but with reference to divine justice, it is a payment to the last penny. It is a payment, but not by myself. This is an act of great grace that my debt is paid by one other than myself.

This is not extraordinary nor something new amid the mysteries of the Church, since we admit that in the same way all is given us by grace in baptism, with all being settled not by baptism itself but by the merits of Christ in which one comes to share by baptism. I say even more readily that God has so linked mercy and justice that he was willing to forgive our sins, and in the manner that his own only-begotten Son satisfied divine justice for us. This was a work of such abundant grace as not only to remit what was due but also to provide the one to make satisfaction. Hence the fact that according to divine wisdom indulgences make payment through the merits of Christ and the saints is in no way detrimental to his grace and mercy. The argument proceeds as if these things were mutually exclusive which take place according to the order of the divine plan. The further argument lacks even a semblance of truth when it states the consequence that one granting an indulgence obligates himself to the satisfaction. The alleged proof is given that one satisfies through others. We answer that one must grasp what is meant by the Pope satisfying by others in granting an indulgence, namely, that he applies the satisfaction of others. There are no even apparent grounds for conluding that the Pope therefore binds himself to make satisfaction. It is one thing to apply to a person the satisfaction of another and quite another to oblige oneself to make satisfaction for the person. These are as different as flying and remaining seated.

In answer to the second argument we deny that nothing occurs by the power of the keys. There is both the application of the works of the saints to the person, and his absolution from the punishment due for his sins. So the words of Christ, "Whatever you loose...," are literally fulfilled. In the same manner we also deny that the power of the keys only brings about what is actually taking place. The proof offered was that if there are merits of the saints the Holy Spirit does not leave them dormant. We answer that since these satisfactory merits of the saints were done for the Church, and not specifically for one or the other member, they are therefore not operative for this or that specific person unless God or his vicar applies them to this person or that. Without such application they are not in fact operative, for they are common to all. Neither are they dormant, for by their nature they are ordered and applied in this manner so as not to be otherwise operative.

The third argument concerned the unrewarded works of the saints. This involves a misuse of words, since those saying this take "unrewarded" to refer to the fruit of these works in the saints themselves. If this is meant, one must answer that the good works of the saints can be taken in two ways. As meritorious, they are all rewarded in the saints themselves; but as satisfactory, those which are supererogatory are not rewarded in the saints themselves but are left to be rewarded in us. The reasons offered do not disprove this explanation. The first reason ("The sufferings of the present time are not to be compared . . . " [Romans 8:18]) speaks of our sufferings according to the substance of the work, that is, as they proceed from free choice. But the reward considers our works and sufferings specifically as they are done out of love or the grace of God. The second reason was that God rewards beyond our deserts. This is no proof, since what is said must be understood of the reward for our works taken specifically as meritorious. Also the fact that the saints' works, as satisfactory, are not rewarded in the saints themselves is not caused by a defect in the one granting the reward but by the excellence of the saint doing the work. Since he is not bound to any punishment to be satisfied, he cannot satisfy for himself. The third reason was that works of supererogation would not be rewarded in the saints themselves but in us. But this does not hold, since works of supererogation, specifically as meritorious, are rewarded in the saints themselves. As the Samaritan said, "Whatever you give out in excess, I will repay to you upon my return" [Luke 10:35]. But in so far as punishments are left in excess, they cannot be rewarded in the saints themselves because of their excellence. Hence there is nothing out of order, since all the aspects fit together quite well. It accords with the order of right reason that one first makes satisfaction on his own behalf and then if punishment remains in excess which he does not owe for himself it can pay for another. Nor does it follow from our saying that the same works are rewarded in both the saints and ourselves that thereby no works of the saints are unrewarded in themselves. When it is said here that some merits of the saints remain unrewarded, we are not distinguishing between two sets of works with some being rewarded and others unrewarded. This is to interpret our argument wrongly. Our distinction is between different aspects of one and the same work. Our meaning is that as meritorious the works of the saints are rewarded in the saints themselves, while as satisfactory they are left unrewarded in so far as that element of punishment is left in excess. Thus it cannot be contested that all aspects fit together harmoniously.

To the fourth argument we say that a holy man can be judged in two ways. First, in so far as he acts on the basis of his own free choice, it is true that no saint adequately fulfils the commandments of God in this life. But in so far as his actions proceed from divine grace dwelling within to aid him, any saint does adequately fulfil the commandments of God in those things for which we praise them. If one tries to refute this by urging the arguments given before, we will answer them. To the first we answer that if Our Lord's words are cited in full they demonstrate the opposing view. He said, "When you have done all things I command you, say, 'We have done what we ought. We are unprofitable servants'" [Luke 17:10]. You see, by including, "We have done what we ought," he shows they did fulfil the commandments adequately. Otherwise they would not have done what they ought, since what they ought to do is to adequately fulfil the commandments. It is not true that a servant who does what he ought would be unprofitable if he had done less. If he had done less, he would not have done what he ought. But it is true that such a servant does no supererogation and hence is called unprofitable. For one who does only what he ought is called unprofitable. Hence all this text proves is that the saints in fulfilling the commandments of Christ did nothing of supererogation. This accords with the fact that they were able sufficiently to fulfil the commandments of Christ and to do works of supererogation, in order both to do what they ought and be profitable servants in the house of the Lord. On the second text, we answer that the oil the wise virgins feared would not suffice pertains to the awareness of merit and not to punishments. To the third point, we answer that it is wrong to say that the command to love God binds man to do more than he is able. As Jerome said, "Cursed be he who says God commanded the impossible."[66] It is also wrong to say that the command to love God entails loving as much as possible, if this means that one sins by omitting some possible act of love. This is evident, since many acts of love look to works of supererogation, for instance, wishing enemies well and doing good for them in a specific instance outside a case of need. This is a matter of perfection, not of precept. But it is commanded that one love God with his whole heart and with all his strength, which means that he must admit nothing contrary to the love of God into his heart and mind and strength. Augustine shows that if we understand this command as meaning actual love, then it does not indicate what we are bound to do here and now but the goal toward which we are bound to tend.[67] In this way the saints have fulfilled this command and so have performed works of supererogation. Fourthly, concerning martyrdom, we say that the saints whose martyrdom was outside extreme necessity did more than they ought, since this is of supererogation. And in the case where martyrdom was necessary in confessing the faith, the saints often made supererogatory satisfaction, since they willingly suffered more than was required for their sins.

We answer to the fifth argument that this teaching rests on Scripture, reason, normative texts of the Roman Church, and on the theologians. Asserting the contrary is rash and presumptions, indeed it is an undisciplined mind which will not agree with so much evidence over and beyond the authority of Saints Thomas and Bonaventure and the vast number of theologians following their lead. A docile person will not demand mathematical certitude in moral questions of both philosophy and theology. Total confusion will result, unless we hold those things for certain in moral questions which conform to reason and at the same time are held as proven by consensus of theologians.[68]

We can now take up the texts cited from the saints. In response we say that all the saints did have some debt for sin over which they could pray as long as they lived. This does not mean that they were always sinning, but at times they were free of all sin while at other times they did sin. But at the same time they performed many meritorious and satisfactory works of supererogation. They admit their debt when they pray for the forgiveness of their trespasses. This holds for the whole of life in so far as depends on ourselves, however different it might be if the saints be judged in view of the grace God gives them.

Let us avoid repetition of this same point. One can distinguish between two ways of judging the saints and their works. First, in themselves and proportionate to their own powers, they are always debtors deserving condemnation. They do not fulfil God's commandments. As Isaiah said, "All our righteous deeds are like a filthy rag"

[64:6]. But judged in view of the grace of the Holy Spirit that dwells in them and assists their works, the saints do observe the commandments and are not debtors. They are rather creditors, deserving of eternal life by reason of their holy works, and do not face condemnation. As 1 John 3 [:9] says, "No one born of God commits sin, since the seed of God abides in him and because born of God he cannot sin." And the Apostle says in Romans 8 [:1], "There is no condemnation for those who are in Christ Jesus." He also wrote to Timothy, "I have fought the good fight, I have finished the course, I have kept the faith. For the rest there is laid up for me the crown of righteousness which the Lord, the just judge, will award to me on that day" [2 Timothy 4:7f].

Hence the discerning reader will sense when Scripture or the teaching of the saints speaks of us or of our works as they are our own and of them as they proceed from divine grace. All possible evil is truly predicated of us and of our works in so far as they are ours. But on the other hand infinite good is truly found in the same works as products of divine mercy and grace, as is evident in the Scripture texts just cited and many others that could be cited.

With such a principle, this and all the following similar objections are solved. The fact that all the saints are of themselves debtors does not exclude the fact that by the work of divine grace they perform works of supererogation. Similarly they are of themselves iniquitous, but by prayer arising from divine grace they merit not having their iniquity imputed to them. Likewise, in forgiving their sin, God gives them grace so that they thereby fulfil the commandments, which is not a case of man fulfilling them on his own. All the commandments are fulfilled when whatever we do not fulfil of ourselves is fulfilled through grace. Also, woe to the man of laudable life if he be judged in the absence of grace, the result of divine mercy. In the same way, if I have any righteousness according to human norms, I will beseech my judge. Similarly, every good and well-done work, as done by our powers, is a sin and like a filthy rag. But as proceeding from the grace of God it is no sin but is meritorious and a good work of supererogation.

If therefore the fifth argument intends to refer to our good works simply and without qualification and to say that they are venial sins, not thereby specifying that this is only in so far as they proceed from us and does not hold in so far as they proceed from charity — then the objector does not require an answer, but rather a censure,

or even the fire. If he means this, then the Blessed Virgin sinned
venially in all she did. But Augustine says she was granted the grace
of conquering sin totally.[69] Then it would follow, contrary to the
Apostle, that his works were undeserving of the crown according to
divine justice. It would also follow, contrary to John the Evangelist,
that even one born of God commits sin.—This suffices to solve all
the objections brought by texts of the saints.

Objections were brought against the beneficial character of the
excessive merits of the saints. In answer to the first, that everyone
receives the reward due for his own labor, we say that this obviously
refers to the reward which does correspond to a person's merit. We
also admitted that each person gains merit for himself alone. But on
our present topic, the remission of punishment, we say that one
person can make satisfaction through another.

The second objection stated that it would be improper for the
Church to distribute these. We answer that the Church most
appropriately distributes satisfactory works on behalf of one making
satisfaction. Nothing could be more worthy than such a distribution.
Although the remission of temporal punishment is a low-ranking gift
in comparison with gifts of spiritual grace, it is nonetheless an
appropriate gift because proportionate to the merits of the saints
specifically as satisfactory. As such, all these merits can do is
complete temporal punishments.

Third, it was said that the Church would not be seeking the best.
Rather, the Church, as a mother, is seeking the very best in these
remissions granted her sons. God has judged it right to adopt them as
sons, and a mother should not constantly inflict punishment on a
son. All things have their appointed time.

Now we turn to the arguments against the treasury of indulgences
deriving from the merits of Christ. The response to the first point is
evident from what we have said, since this teaching is affirmed on
the authority not only of the Roman Church, but of Sacred
Scripture, the saints, and theologians as well. Even if it were
affirmed as a definition backed by the Roman Church alone, this
would suffice for giving an account of the faith we hold, no less than
if it were affirmed on the authority of a general council. Heretics can
refute a council just as easily as they can the Roman Church. I have
not dreamed up what I say. Jerome wrote to Pope Damasus, "If this
is approved by your apostolic decision, one contradicting it knows
he is a heretic."[70] The Council of Florence, under Pope Eugenius

IV, accepts this in the confession of the Armenians, "We approve what the Roman Church approves and we repudiate whatever the Roman Church rejects."[71]

We have already answered the second argument. We add only that its citation from the authoritative canon is ineptly made, since that text was not teaching about indulgences. It spoke of indiscrete indulgences being weakened by lack of discretion. Similarly the third argument has been answered conclusively, that is, that no irreverence is involved.

On the fourth objection, we note that when good works are said to be better than indulgences this refers to the effects of indulgences and not to the merits of Christ and the saints. The latter are not identical with indulgences, but rather their supererogatory satisfaction is the source of indulgences' efficacy. This line of argument makes so many false assumptions, and takes its true ones in a merely causal manner and not formally, that it is no wonder it destroys itself.

To the fifth argument we answer that this advice is for the best, since the keys of the Church are like the other sacraments. There are two manners in which they are said to bring about a certain or uncertain effect. Simply of themselves, their effect is certain, and to deny this is sacrilegious. But in some circumstances, if for instance the matter or recipient is not disposed, we say of the keys of the Church, and of baptism as well, that their effect is not certain. For example if water is poured over one whose hidden intention is not to receive baptism, then he does not even receive the baptismal character. And if one approaching the sacrament intends to sin mortally, he receives the character but not the grace of baptism. This is the case in the present topic, where uncertainty about disposition of the recipient causes doubt about the effect of the keys in his case. Still, we are certain that the keys produce a certain effect in a recipient well disposed for that effect, and so an indulgence is a certain grant to one so disposed. There is no deception when an indulgence is applied to one truly repentant. It is not because of some defect in the merits of Christ and the saints that we do not rest from doing penance after gaining indulgences, but because we have doubts about the disposition of the recipient, which is not the work of man alone but of God who shows mercy by bestowing true contrition.

When the fifth argument then adds that I either believe that the merits of Christ applied in my case by an indulgence are sufficient or I doubt this, one can answer that one thing more should be added, namely how I received them or shared in them. I believe without any doubt that the indulgence applies the merits of Christ to me, and when I share in them by accepting them they adequately complete the temporal punishments due for my sins. But I doubt whether I share in them, because I doubt about my own disposition for receiving them, and this is a holy doubt.

If indeed I believe I have shared in them, I also want to add my own satisfactions, not ranking them above the satisfactions of Christ, but because it is better to satisfy in two ways than by one alone. Christ's and my satisfaction are together a multiplication of goods over Christ's satisfaction alone. In confirmation of this we repeat that the merits of Christ are not the indulgences but are the cause of the efficacy of indulgences. The indulgences Christ's faithful receive are nothing other than remissions of their punishments through the merits of Christ. Just as remissions of punishments are not to be put ahead of the merits of Christ, nor ahead of the commandments of Christ or the Church, so also neither should indulgences. But with this it remains true that remissions are granted by the merits of Christ.

We answer the sixth argument by saying that the addition of the merits of the saints fits well in the divine plan, not because the merits of Christ are inadequate, but in order to multiply the sources of satisfaction in the mystical body of Christ. The Apostle taught this: "I fill up in my flesh what is lacking in the passion of Christ for his body the Church" [Colossians 1:24].

To the seventh point we say that the Church does not teach that the treasury of the merits of Christ and the saints has been entrusted to herself for dispensation through indulgences in such a way that Christ, the high priest, ceases to distribute these on his own. It simply does not follow that since one can partake of this treasury independently of indulgences, one therefore does not partake through indulgences. The members of Christ can in fact partake of this in many ways.

We simply deny the line of argument in the eighth objection. No inadequacy in the merits of Christ prevents the treasury of the Church from remitting the punishment of death. On God's part this results from the plan of divine wisdom; on our part there is the disparity in punishments. Some of the punishments we undergo are natural and some are personal. That is, some beset us because of the sin of nature, original sin, while others are due to us because of our own actual sins. The punishments we incur because of our infected nature continue in force until nature is renewed which will take place also by merit of the passion of Christ at the time of the general resurrection. For by his death he destroyed the deaths we face in both soul and body. These then are not remitted by indulgences, since they pertain to the whole period of infected nature.

Indulgences do remit the punishments to which we are bound in this life for our own actual sins. For this life is a time of purification of our persons, not of human nature. Even Baptism heals the person, not our nature. Since death with its penal aspects is a punishment of nature, consequently the merits of Christ as applied through indulgences do not extend to the punishment of death. It is thus evident that the fact the punishment of death is not remitted in this life through indulgences is not a result of inadequacy in Christ's merits, but follows from the character of the punishments and the conditions of our present life.

The fact that the merits of Christ do remit the punishment of eternal death does not mean that they should therefore remit the punishment of temporal death. The eternal pain of sense is one of the personal punishments, but death is a natural punishment. Also, it is one thing to speak of satisfactory merits of Christ without qualification and another thing to say that those not distributed by the sacraments are left for distribution through indulgences. They work in an absolute manner in the sacraments to remove the punishment of eternal condemnation and pain of sense. This is less a work of satisfaction than the concomitant effect of reconciling an enemy of God as his adopted child. Eternal punishment is removed, because one's child is never punished out of enmity. Only enemies deserve destructive punishment, while one's children are afflicted and purified in accord with nature. The treasury of indulgences offers the merits of Christ as satisfactions.

The final argument attacked the conferral of the treasury of Christ's and the saints' merits by the absolution given in indulgences. We answer first that the act of absolving in indulgences is not the same as in other absolutions, whether those from censures or those in other cases outside the sacrament. Also, this absolution pertains to the third part of the sacrament of penance, since it takes the place of penitential satisfaction, while the merits of Christ pertain directly to the sacrament itself. The other absolutions have no reference to any part of the sacrament. Also this absolution remits punishment due before divine justice in this or the future life. But since the other absolutions remit punishments binding only in this life, the sole authority of the Pope suffices to effectively remit them. But the absolution of indulgences requires over and above Papal authority both the disposition of true repentance in the recipient and an application of the merits of Christ. The latter is not done by a simple act of will, since a minister only remits punishments owed to his superior by an act of dispensation. As the Apostle said, "Let a man count us as ministers of Christ and dispensers of the mysteries of God" [1 Corinthians 4:1].

We answer the second argument by indicating the parallels between the sacrament of penance and indulgences. In the sacrament the keys act positively to loose from sins, but only negatively in binding. This refers to the key of authority, since the key of knowledge refers positively to both binding and loosing. So in indulgences the key of knowledge discerns in a positive act both the loosing and the binding. But while the key of authority does loose by positive absolution, it binds only negatively. This binding is the same regarding sins, that is, only the refraining from absolution based on the discernment and power of the key of knowledge. Hence if you speak without qualification of not loosing, this does not refer to an act of the keys, that is, to an act of binding. The act of the keys is to bind on the basis of a judgment of the keys. This makes it clear that although these effects, binding and loosing, can occur independently of the keys, this binding and loosing does not take place in the Church militant except by exercise of the keys.

Augsburg, October 7, 1518.

9

ALMSGIVING AND INDULGENCES

SYNOPSIS: Cajetan argued on October 7, 1518, against the position affirmed in Luther's forty-fifth thesis: one offends God by omitting an act of almsgiving in order to use the money for obtaining indulgences.[72] Cajetan denies that omission of a greater good is adequate reason for branding another act sinful, since sinfulness must arise from a disorder in the act itself. Almsgiving is a greater good, but it is not commanded under sin in every case where it is possible; in the circumstances in which one is obligated, refusal is sinful, whatever be the alternative preferred. But almsgiving can give way to other actions, as is clear from Matthew 26:6-12, where Our Lord commends the woman who anointed him in place of selling the oil so that alms could be given. Luther had argued from 1 John 3:17, "If anyone sees his brother in need and closes his heart to him, how does God's love abide in him?" Cajetan's response offers a calculus of degrees of obligation to give alms and of sinfulness in refusing. He contends that Luther caricatures the teaching on extreme necessity (as source of serious obligation) since this is not reached when the man is dying, but when aid would still be meaningful. There is also a middle area in which refusal is venially sinful, when the need is considerable and help can be given without notable inconvenience.

10

UNFORCED WILLINGNESS TO CONFESS

SYNOPSIS: On October 8, 1518, Cajetan dealt with Luther's instruction that those coming to confess their sins should consider especially whether they would willingly confess if not obliged by precept. If this willingness be lacking, their disposition is, according to Luther, inadequate because not rooted in love but in fear.[73] Cajetan brands this self-inflicted reflection on an unreal condition a dangerous temptation having no redeeming features. The perfect have no need of it, since they cannot be separated from the love of Christ (Romans 8:35f), while the imperfect need only the disposition of loving God above all things. Proposal of unreal conditions can give rise to many sinful desires. Further, the precept to confess is a positive ordination of the sacramental dispensation and would not oblige (as would the prohibitions of the Decalogue) if the precept were rescinded. With the conditions Luther gave, there would be no evil in not wanting to confess. Luther's argument neglects the role of filial love in carrying out God's positive commands. There would be no sense in considering how one would feel if such commands were not given, and, besides, Scripture does not teach us to engage in such a reflection.

11

SIN IN FEARING PUNISHMENT?

SYNOPSIS: Writing on October 12, 1518, Cajetan answers Luther's contention that in righteous persons fear of God's punishment is sinful, because it arises from self-love and lack of trust in God.[74] Cajetan finds no evidence that such fear is intrinsically evil and uses the example of Christ's distress and fear in Gethsemanie (Mark 14:33f) to drive home his point that fear can at times be appropriate. One must discern between sinful self-love and a natural and reasonable concern for one's own welfare. The latter can give rise to fear of punishment and continue to co-exist with a fundamental submission to God's will. Lack of trust does intensify fear, but Christ's example shows that defective trust is not always at the origin of fear.

12

IMPERFECT LOVE AND FEAR

SYNOPSIS: On October 14, 1518, Cajetan treated Luther's view that imperfect love at the time of death necessarily results in dread of punishment, since only perfect love casts out all fear of punishment (1 John 4:18).[75] Cajetan's first argument rests on the teaching of the Council of Florence that upon dying a person who has not sinned after baptism passes immediately into the heavenly vision of God. Since such a person may well not love God perfectly, there cannot be anything in imperfect love that keeps one from the vision of God. Cajetan argues that all servile fear is overcome by God's outpouring of the Spirit of adoption (Romans 8:15). Also, dread of punishment arises only when the punishment actually threatens. However, when one dies even in imperfect love he does not therefore face punishment and consequently experience dread. After offering some traditional interpretations of 1 John 4:18, Cajetan concludes that it is not death that makes love perfect, but that God does this, when one comes to him without debt of punishment, by infusing the light of glory and admitting one to the vision and enjoyment of his own majesty.

13
THE POWER OF THE KEYS AND PURGATORY

It is asked whether the Pope exercises the power of the keys in granting an indulgence to souls in purgatory.[76] Three arguments lead to a negative answer. First, the power given Peter was restricted to matters on this earth, when Our Lord spoke about whatever you bind or loose on earth.[77] Second, the wording of grants of indulgences for the departed expressly speaks of giving indulgences to them by way of suffrage. But a suffrage clearly does not pertain to the power of the keys but to help offered by intercessors.[78] Third, such a power is not attested by Sacred Scripture nor by the holy canons.[79]

But against these arguments there appears to stand the normative teaching of papal writings.

For understanding this matter one must grasp that since keys are used for opening, the use of the keys of the kingdom of heaven granted to Peter is consequently to open the kingdom of heaven, undoubtedly to those who are to enter it from among the members of Christ. But opening a kingdom is nothing else than removing obstacles to entry into it. And since the obstacles are of two kinds, so the act of opening takes on two forms. Some obstacles are lodged in our nature, as results of original sin. With reference to these obstacles, Christ himself has opened the kingdom of heaven both by his passion and death (by which the doors were removed, never more to be shut) and by baptism, by which heaven is opened. Other obstacles are personal, resulting from our actual sins, with the obstacle consisting in guilt and in the punishment due for actual sins. Peter has been appointed to open the kingdom of heaven by removing these obstacles. He removes personal guilt by use of the power of his keys in the sacrament of penance, in accord with Our Lord's words, "Whose sins you shall forgive, they are forgiven" [John 20:23]. Personal punishment, due for actual sin, Peter also removes by the power of the keys.

Both kinds of obstacles prevent one from entering the kingdom of heaven, and the keys would not adequately open, if they did not suffice to take away both kinds of personal obstacles preventing entry into the kingdom of heaven. This would curtail the universality of power Our Lord granted: "Whatever you loose on earth . . ." [Matthew 16:19]. If this does not extend to the punishment due for actual sin, then the exercise of the keys does not extend to loosing "whatever," as the words indicate. Therefore since Peter's keys are for opening the kingdom of heaven for the members of Christ by removing the obstacles of personal guilt and punishment, it must follow that the indulgences granted by ecclesiastical authority under the requisite conditions pertain to the power of the keys, since they remove the punishment due for actual sins.

If we add to these considerations the fact that all indulgences are of the same character in respect to their cause and effect, we must also conclude that indulgences are given to the departed by the same power of the keys by which they are given to the living. All indulgences proceed from the ecclesiastical authority to distribute the treasury of satisfactory merits of Christ and the saints, and they all have the effect of removing a certain temporal punishment due according to divine justice for actual sins.

These arguments are confirmed by the manner of expression in the documents of the Roman Church granting indulgences for the departed. They state first that an indulgence is granted by apostolic authority for the souls in purgatory; and second that this indulgence aids the souls toward the remission of punishment by way of suffrage. By this the Roman Church teaches that the Apostolic See distributes the treasury of Christ's and the saints' merits for the benefit of the souls in purgatory by the power of the keys. It is only by the power of the keys that there is apostolic authority for opening the kingdom of heaven by applying the merits of Christ and the saints in order to remit the punishments by which the souls in purgatory are prevented from entering the kingdom of heaven.

The documents also teach that indulgences are applied to the remission of the punishments of the souls in purgatory by way of suffrage and not by way of absolution. Absolution is the manner in which indulgences are granted to the living, as is taught in the *Decretals* in the section *De poenitentiis et remissionibus,* chapter *Quod autem.*[80] This indicates that while indulgences granted to the living and the dead have the common features that both are granted by the power of the keys distributing the treasury of penal merits of Christ and the saints and that both are granted for the remission of temporal punishment due for actual sins, they differ in the manner in which the indulgence comes to their aid: the living who truly gain an indulgence are aided by way of absolution, while the departed who truly gain an indulgence are freed by way of suffrage.[81]

We answer the first argument by granting that the Pope cannot authoritatively absolve the souls in purgatory. It is one thing to absolve them authoritatively and another to distribute authoritatively the treasury of Christ and the saints for their benefit. The latter takes place when they are loosed by way of suffrage, and in doing this the Pope does not act beyond the limits of his jurisdiction, since he does not thereby authoritatively absolve those under the earth.

The second argument was from the wording of papal documents "by way of suffrage." But this is not all they say. They also speak of an authoritative grant of an indulgence. Thus by these two expressions they indicate both their power to distribute and the manner of suffrage by which they come to the aid of the souls in purgatory.

We can answer the third argument since this power is sufficiently grounded in Holy Scripture, since we know of Peter's keys from Scripture. And the Roman Church, in laying down the canons, has explained the different manners in which the keys open the kingdom of heaven to the living and departed members of Christ, as we showed.

Augsburg, October 15, 1518.

14

GROWTH OF LOVE IN PURGATORY?

SYNOPSIS: Cajetan's work of October 17, 1518, countered the view Luther favored in explaining Thesis 18 of the *Ninety-five Theses,* namely, that the souls in purgatory continue to increase in merit and love during their purification.[82] In approaching a solution, Cajetan finds it necessary to determine the precise sense in which purgatory is an intermediate state between this life and heaven. He then derives this from the teaching of the Council of Florence that the one purpose of purgatory is that of satisfaction of temporal punishment due for actual sins.[83] There is no ground here for the other purposes Luther asserted, and these also go against the teaching of St. Augustine.[84] Purgatory removes the debt of punishment, which is an obstacle preventing the soul's entry into heaven, but the soul's level of merit and love remain what they were at the moment of death. In responding to Luther's arguments, Cajetan holds that charity is not the only way fear is diminished, since this also takes place by removing the cause of fear. The one sense in which the souls in purgatory are *in via* is with regard to satisfaction.

15

THE EFFECT OF EXCOMMUNICATION

The question is posed whether excommunication excludes a person from interior sharing with the faithful.[85] The following arguments lead to a negative answer. First, excommunication does not take away any more than the Church's power of jurisdiction can confer. Excommunication is an act of authority, that is, of jurisdiction and not of sacred orders. Christ, who is more inclined to confer blessings than evil, did not leave the Church an authority more effective in taking away blessings than in conferring them. Since the ecclesiastical power of jurisdiction cannot confer faith, hope, and love, the gifts by which each believer shares interiorily in the blessings granted other believers, the same power cannot take away this kind of interior sharing.[86]

Second, a just and an unjust excommunication are fundamentally the same, since both are effective acts of binding. Gregory indicated this in words now had in Part II of the *Decretum,* question 3, "The decision of one's pastor, whether just or unjust, is to be revered." But an unjust excommunication does not exclude one from interior but only from external communion. Therefore excommunication as such deprives one only of an external communion with the faithful.[87] This is confirmed from Scripture, where excommunication is had only in the sense of exclusion from external actions. It is an extrinsic punishment only, which you can easily see by reading through the letters of John and Paul. All they forbid is external communion. When one is handed over to Satan, he is to be extrinsically harassed, as is clear from what is said, ". . . that his spirit may be saved" [1Corinthians 5:5]. Consequently it is arbitrary to assert that excommunication deprives one of spiritual help from the prayers of the Church.[88]

But there stands against these arguments the opinion of the

Master of the Sentences in Book IV, distinction 8, which theologians appear to follow almost unanimously on this point.[89]

In seeking a right understanding of this topic, we will only escape error by avoiding two extremes. Precisely as believers, people are joined in a communion that has three aspects. One is the external communion of praying at the same time, as when they gather in church for mass and other solemn rites of worship. This is one extreme. The other is the "communion of saints", consisting in the love that joins Christ's members, through faith informed by love, both to Christ and to the other members of Christ who are so gifted. This is another extreme. The third aspect is the communion of the faithful in the common suffrages instituted by the Church, such as occur in the Church's prayers and masses. This is an intermediate aspect of communion. One mistake, then, would be to say that excommunication takes away only the external communion, and the other would be that its direct effect is the removal of all aspects of communion. Both of these extremes are clearly wrong.

The truth is that excommunication excludes a person from external communion, and from the interior communion in the ordinary suffrages of the faithful, while it presupposes that the communion of saints in love has already been ruptured. Our explanation of this need not treat external communion, since no one has doubts about it. Rather we must first grasp the difference between the two kinds of interior communion, and then we must demonstrate that excommunication takes away both of them.

Since the communion between believers consists in both giving and receiving, their interior communion will entail both sides of this exchange. They give of their merits, prayers, and suffrages before God as intercession and aid for the benefit of others. They receive by the help of others gifts of grace and increase of grace, and the protection of God sheltering them from evil and increasing the good things in their lives. There is a twofold cause at the origin of these spiritual aids. At times they arise directly from an individual's loving concern, as when a person living in charity prays according to his individual intention on another's behalf, or does a good work or some penance for this person, and so obtains for him the gift of grace, increase of grace, protection against temptation, or the like. But at other times help is given by way of an institution or action of the Church, as when by masses and by other official forms of worship people are helped toward doing good or avoiding evil. Here love has been given institutional forms by holy mother Church ordering our actions to the common good of the Church and of each member according to the faith and devotion motivating each one's contribution. The sacraments conferred on Christ's faithful belong to this latter kind of giving by way of the action of the Church.

Hence, concerning what a person receives there is no fundamental difference between the interior communion of direct sharing in love and the interior communion by way of the action and institution of the Church. There is only a difference in degree, with the one exception of sacramental graces. All the spiritual gifts I can receive from the one type of interior communion I can also receive from the other. We must only except sacramental graces such as the characters imprinted by confirmation or orders. One cannot receive such sacramental gifts solely through the communion of charity, but there must be actual reception in the communion of the Church's sacraments. A sacramental communion in desire is not outside the communion in charity, but actual sacramental communion pertains to communion resting on the Church's action. What is received differs consequently in degree, since clearly one receives greater grace from actual reception of the sacraments than from reception only in desire.

On the side of conferral there is a major and fundamental difference, since the interior communion rooted directly in the charity of individuals entails the giving of individual merits, prayers, and suffrages. But the communion in love that affects one's interior life by way of the action or the institution of the Church, that is, through its sacraments and sacramentals, entails the giving of merits, prayers, and suffrages held in common in the church. Undoubtedly the Church prays, offers suffrages and merits, and confers the sacraments and sacramentals out of love, and before God these bring it about that the Church and we the faithful receive blessings of grace, increase of grace, protection, and the like, providing only that we pose no obstacle to the gift.

The text, "I share with all who revere you" [Psalm 118:63, Vulgate], refers to the first type of interior communion. And the communion of saints, as an article of faith, refers at once to both inner communions, since it includes sacramental communion. The first communion is restricted to those actually in charity, while the second also embraces Christians who are in mortal sin, since the Church prays for sinners, even hardened sinners, and her prayers are often heard. After all we celebrate mass for the conversion of sinners. — What we have said here is quite well known and needs no detailed proof, since its truth is manifest from the Church's liturgy.

From what we have said, it is evident that excommunication separates a person from the actions entailed in the communion of ecclesiastical charity. By being placed outside the communion of the Church, he is also excluded from receiving the blessings deriving from these same actions. But many interior gifts are included among these blessings. Consequently excommunication excludes the excommunicated person from sharing in many interior blessings. The exclusion from the Church's communion by excommunication becomes manifest in the fact that the Church does not pray for the excommunicated. One is thus excluded from the actions on which the other aspects depend. For instance, one is not allowed to celebrate mass for excommunicated persons. Bernard pointed to the dire character of excommunication, in that the Church prays on Good Friday for Jews and pagans, but not for the excommunicated.[90] There is a rudimentary kind of proof of this in the gospels, since the ordinary practice of the Church is that we pray only for our brethren. But the fact that excommunicated persons are not of our brethren is clear from what our Savior said about excommunication in Matthew 18, where he gave the Church the power to excommunicate. Regarding one excommunicated, he said, "Let him be to you like a foreigner" [Matthew 18:17], that is, like a Gentile. This makes it clear that excommunication makes one of our brethren become like a Gentile. Hence Augustine said, "Count him no longer in the number of your brethren."[91]

Another argument is that if excommunication brought only external rupture with the Church, there would be no need for it to rest on the authority of Christ. After all, every ruler, every city, and every community can expel someone from its outward communion. But Matthew 18 makes it clear that excommunication rests on the authority of Christ, where he said, "Whatever you bind on earth" [Matthew 18:18], to which the Gloss adds the explanation, "by the bond of anathema."[92] Chrysostom comments, "Note how he binds him with a double affliction, both a punishment on earth by exclusion from the Church ('Let him be to you like a foreigner'), and a punishment to come ('shall be bound in heaven')."[93]

Another proof is that when the Church expels the excommunicated person, she excludes him from all that she confers upon her members. This means therefore that by excommunication she takes away the prayers, suffrages, and the like, that she by her actions and institution confers on her ordinary members. It is to these that she readmits by reconciliation. Excommunication is supposed to be the Church's supreme penalty. But it would not be such if it did not take away all that the Church confers.

There would still remain a greater penalty, if the excommunicated person was still not excluded from something the Church gave and continually gives its members. The fact of expulsion is clear from the way masses are offered not only for the common benefit of the Church, but also for individual members. This is clear in the Canon of the mass where we first pray, "for your holy Catholic Church," and then in the second place, "for all orthodox holders of the catholic and apostolic faith." The Church also has us pray for certain individuals in the Memento, and has instituted the canonical hours and other prayers for the faithful. It would be nonsense to doubt that these are suffrages offered by the Church and in the name of the Church.

Thus it is evident that the excommunicated person is excluded from the communal actions by which the Church grants blessings on its faithful members. He is therefore excluded from these blessings which derive from the communal actions. This means that excommunication separates from many interior blessings, since among the benefits of these actions are the help and increase of grace for doing good, turning from evil, warding off the devil, and the like.

These arguments are confirmed by the normative view of Augustine, who commented on the words of the Apostle [1 Corinthians 5:5] in Sermon 68: "Every Christian whom the priests excommunicate is handed over to Satan. Why is this? It is because outside the Church the devil reigns, just as Christ within the Church. Therefore exclusion from ecclesiastical communion means that one is in a certain way given over to the devil."[94] Here you see how Augustine understands being outside the Church. It is not exclusion from a building, nor from external communion, but being outside of Christ. In answering he speaks of the person being given over to the devil in a certain way, since he is not given over to be possessed, but to be corrected.[95] Jerome says the same thing in commenting on "Whose sins you shall retain..." [John 20:23]: "That is, those whom you exclude by interdict from the church are, unless they be reconciled by doing satisfaction, among those to whom the gates of the kingdom of heaven will be shut."[96] Both texts are given in Part II of the *Decretum*, question 3.[97] They make it clear that excommunication excludes a person from sharing in interior blessings which open the gates of the kingdom of heaven. An excommunicated person is deprived of the Church's suffrages, through which interior blessings descend upon us from the divine mercy arranging all things appropriately.

In answer to the first objection, we say that even though all suffrages proceed from love, they do not all arise ordered in the same way from love. Some proceed directly by the individual intentions and actions of the faithful alone. Communion in them stems from charity, and excommunication itself does not directly exclude from this communion. Rather, excommunication presupposes that this communion has been ruptured, since one does not incur excommunication except by a mortal sin entailing the loss of charity and hence of this first bond of communion.

But other suffrages proceed from love by the action of the Church in the communal suffrages made in the name of the Church. All the faithful not cut off from the Church share in these, since they are common to all the faithful even those in mortal sin, as we proved above. There is then this difference between a believer in mortal sin who is not excommunicated and one who is excommunicated. The one not excommunicated is helped by the communal suffrages of his loving mother, the Church, while the excommunicated person is not helped by these suffrages but is left to himself as a Gentile, in accord with Our Lord's precept. Still, mother Church does not totally desert them, since she calls on them to repent and she does not omit working for their salvation, just as she does not omit this with regard to the pagans, a fact to which Augustine referred to in the text cited above. Entailed in the Church's sollicitude, over and above the personal burden, are such things as obligating excommunicated clerics to say the canonical hours and binding all the excommunicated to the fasts instituted by the Church.

Consequently, we admit that it is only by way of presupposition that excommunication takes away communion in charity. But along with this, it directly removes communion in the communal suffrages of the Church and thereby communion in the interior blessings given as the fruit of these suffrages. This latter communion is included in the immediate communion of charity, about which was said, "I share with all who revere you" [Psalm 118:63, Vulgate]. However these words are more appropriately applied to a person who is a true member of the Church and not cut off from it. Such a person says in all truth, "I share," since he is sharing in all things without qualification.

The second argument proceeded from the nature of an unjust excommunication, that is, one based on no real crime. But strictly speaking this is not an excommunication simply and without restriction, but only in one aspect, that of its binding power in the judicial forum. The fact that it is not an excommunication in the full sense becomes apparent by application of the principle that an unjust judgment is no judgment. This is easily proven, since in excommunication there is the act of a judge declaring the law. But declaring wrongly is not to declare the law. Just as excommunication is an act of declaring a particular law to hold, an unjust excommunication is the declaration of something unjust. Hence, if unjust, it is not in substance an act of excommunication.

The case would be different if the injustice lay in the motive. I could be dealing with one whose crime could rightly lead to excommunication, but then if I declared the excommunication solely out of ill feeling it would be just in itself, although unjust as regards motive. Hence it is a true excommunication and brings with it all the effects of excommunication.

But an excommunication that is in itself unjust does not bring about the effects of excommunication, except in the external forum. One so excommunicated is not truly deprived of the suffrages of the Church. He is not excommunicated in heaven. He is not one who refused to listen to the Church and he does not thereby become like a Gentile [Matthew 18:17]. Hence Augustine commented on Our Lord's words: "You have begun to treat your brother as a publican and you bind him on earth. Take care that you bind him justly, since justice breaks unjust bonds."[98]

The one who is unjustly excommunicated must obey it in avoiding external communion, since he is bound in the external forum. This is what Gregory was teaching when he said that the decision of one's pastor, whether just or unjust, is to be revered.[99] As is ordinarily said, and well said, this would not be the case if the decision were simply null and void even in the external forum. The difference between an unjust excommunication and no excommunication at all is not that the former is an excommunication and the latter none at all, but that the former binds in the external forum and the latter in no forum. Neither are excommunications without restriction, and the latter is none at all. Cases of the latter would be excommunications based on an intolerable error of fact, say if one were excommunicated who was not actually living in concubinage, or an error in law, as when one is excommunicated after making a legitimate appeal. You have this in the Gloss.[100] Therefore just and unjust excommunications are not fundamentally the same. Injustice is a condition that in part inauthenticates an excommunication. In the same way, an actual man and a portrait are not fundamentally the same. Consequently, the nature of an excommunication is not to be determined by the minimal effect of an unjust excommunication, but simply and without restriction as it is in its fulness and efficacy. This alone is called an excommunication in the proper and formal sense of an act in which a judge declares the law.

This is confirmed by Scripture's view of the excommunicated person as one excluded from spritual blessings and from the kingdom of heaven (Matthew 18). Since the Church treats him as a Gentile, he is deprived of the Church's suffrages, just as a Gentile would be deprived of them. Since he is bound in heaven, he is deprived of the blessings that loose heavenly bonds. The same thing is expressed by the very form excommunication takes, since external actions of the Church are signs of what occurs within, provided no mistake has been made.

Hence the fact that the Church excludes the excommunicated person from the Church's outward communion indicates that he is excluded from an interior communion with the Church. As a sign of this, the primitive Church imposed upon them only external penalties. Over and above interior penalties, it added the external punishments of the devil. Similarly, in the primitive Church besides interior blessings the good experienced visible manifestations of the Holy Spirit, such as speaking in tongues and the like. The argument referred to the purpose, ". . . that his spirit may be saved" [1 Corinthians 5:5]. But this is not to the point, since excommunication clearly excludes one from the suffrages of the Church, leaving the person by himself so that he may be converted and so his spirit may be saved. Excommunication is on the order of a medicine, as is stated in the chapter *Quum medicinalis* of the section on excommunication in the *Decretals.*[101]

Augsburg, October 29, 1518.

II

MISUSE OF SCRIPTURE —
RESPONSE TO CHARGES
AGAINST THE HOLY SEE
1519

We are impelled by the love of Jesus Christ to investigate whether the Apostolic See twists the meaning of Holy Scripture in its sacred canons.

This appears to be so, first, because [Pope] Clement VI, in the *Extravagans, Unigenitus*, in the section, *De poenitentiis et remissionibus*, wrongly applied Proverbs 7 [= Wisdom 7:14] to the treasury from which indulgences are derived, by saying that by use of this treasury people come to share in the friendship of God. It is, however, evident that the grace of indulgences does not grant us a share in God's friendship, but pertains solely to making satisfaction for punishments to which we are bound.[1]

Second, Pope Pelagius, cited in the *Decretum*, Distinction 21, canon *Quamvis*, proved that the Apostolic See had a prelacy over all other churches by citing Matthew 16[:18], "You are Peter ... Whatever your bind ..." But another statement of Our Lord makes it clear that Peter was not prelate over the others. Also these words were addressed to Peter in the person of all, just as Peter had spoken on behalf of all. Consequently the holy doctors understand the words, "Whatever you bind ...," to have been addressed not to one person but to a unified group in which all were equal. Our Lord himself used the plural when he repeated this in Matthew 18[:18], "Whatever you bind ..." Our Lord also said, "What I say to one, I say to all."[2]

Third, in the *Decretals, De constitutionibus*, in the chapter

Translato, the words of the Apostle, "When there is a change in the priesthood, there must also be a change in the law" [Hebrews 7:12], are cited in proof. The view of the decretal is that the priesthood was transferred first from Moses to Christ and then from Christ to Peter. For the canon lawyers make this interpretation and the Pope permits or approves it. Obviously, however, it is perverse to say that the priesthood was transferred from Christ to Peter. One must conclude therefore that the Apostolic See misuses and does violence to Holy Scripture in its decretals.[3]

In opposition to this conclusion there stands the dignity of the Apostolic authority itself.

Impelled by love, we have raised this question lest people of lesser education might think true what they read in these insults and attacks against the Apostolic See. Perhaps even those attempting to spread these innovations will be brought to their senses, or at least to restraining their tongues.

It is improper to disparage the pastor and teacher of all Christians, the Roman Pontiff, and to heap abuse on him by writing openly that he twists and does violence to Holy Scripture. This should not be done, even if he at times applies a text of Scripture in a transferred sense, since the holy doctors also often do this. We never hear such insults from Augustine, Jerome, Ambrose, and the other most holy doctors. James the Apostle said, "If anyone thinks he is religious and does not restrain his tongue . . . , this man's religion is vain" [1:26]. Instead one's mind and tongue should be made obediently subject to Christ in his Vicar when his words seem to us inappropriate, providing the teaching of the faith remains unsullied. We should not speak out as oracles, especially since human judgment is frequently deceived, and what one person judges a misuse of a text another understands as the proper meaning. This is the case in the present matter, for none of the texts referred to is misused by the sacred canons, but each of them is used in its proper sense, which can be demonstrated in each case, as I have taken a little effort to do.

First, Clement VI did not misuse the text of Scripture but used it properly. The treasury Scripture refers to is the treasury of divine wisdom, which however is the treasury of the merits of Christ, who is himself divine wisdom and the fount of wisdom. In fact, whoever uses this treasury by actually gaining indulgences, if he has that perseverence without which any treasury is used in vain, will be made to share in a perfect friendship with God. No one can share in this friendship while he is still bound to undergo punishment for sin, since this perfect friendship is had only in the heavenly homeland which no one bound to punishment can enter. Indulgences therefore take away from a person hindrances to the ultimate divine friendship, and consequently the treasury of indulgences can in a true and proper sense be said to be a means to sharing in the friendship of God.

The argument carries no weight that the treasury of divine wisdom existed before there were any indulgences and that anyone may benefit from it without gaining indulgences.[4] Some conclude that indulgences have no connection with this treasury of divine wisdom, because what it contains is the many works of divine wisdom, such as acts of thinking the things of God, the merits of Christ taken as both meritorious and satisfactory, and many other things. Since this treasury existed before there were indulgences, its content does not depend on indulgences, but rather indulgences depend on it. But one can avail himself of this treasury in different manners, either by gaining indulgences or independently of them. Similarly one can come to share in perfect divine friendship either by gaining indulgences or by other means. The Roman Church does not teach that indulgences are the unique means of attaining the ultimate divine friendship, but they are one means leading to its attainment by removing obstacles to it, as was said above.

The second objection concerned a text from the gospel [Matthew 16:18f]. But if this text is carefully considered, one will see that it obviously supports what Pope Pelagius meant. There was no misuse, for many facts indicate that the words of Our Lord were addressed to Peter alone.[5]

First, the promise would have been made to the same person on whom the promised reality was then conferred. But clearly Peter alone was made by Our Lord head of the Church, as the last chapter of John shows. After his resurrection, Our Lord singled out Peter from the other Apostles and said to him, "Feed my sheep" [21:17]. He made a comparison between Peter and the others by asking [21:15], "Do you love me more than these?" Immediately he began speaking, not of the martyrdom of Peter and the others, but of the martyrdom Peter was to meet as the result of his pastoral office: "When you were young..." [21:18]. Chrysostom confirms this interpretation, writing, "the Lord passed over the other Apostles to ask Peter, 'Do you love me?' "[6]

Second, since Our Lord said, "Blessed are you Simon Barjonah for flesh and blood . . ." [Matthew 16:17], it is certain he was not declaring all the Apostles blessed and that the Father had not revealed to each what was revealed to Peter. Confirming this is the fact that Judas was then among the disciples who was blessed neither in reality nor in hope, since he was a thief, as the evangelist John bore witness [John 12:6].

Third, Our Lord began this utterance by addressing Peter as distinguished from the others, saying, "I say to you that you are Peter and on this . . ." [Matthew 16:18]. Evidently, "You are Peter" is not true of Andrew, nor of John, nor of James and the others. Consequently, the words of the Gospel text show that Our Lord addressed Peter singly when he said, "I will give you the keys of the kingdom of heaven" [Matthew 16:19].

Thus Pope Pelagius did not misuse that text but used it in its proper sense to show that the see of Peter has by Our Lord's word and intention a prelacy over the others. Pelagius was not the first to use this text to demonstrate this, since Anacletus, a martyr under Trajan said the same thing, as one reads in the *Decretum*, Distinction 22, canon *Sacrosancta.*[7]

I can answer the first argument alleged for this view. Peter is said to have answered for all, because Our Lord asked generally of them [Matthew 16:15], "Who do you say that I am?" But since according to Our Lord's witness the revelation was given to Peter alone, clearly the answer did not arise from advice given by the others, but from God's revelation to Peter alone. Because all were then satisfied with his answer, it is said to be the answer of all. It repeatedly happens that when a number of colleagues are together the well-said word of one is taken as if said by all. But he alone deserves praise who answered wisely. The holy doctors who take these words as said not for one but for the single group are affirming a truth that is not opposed to our view. There is no opposition, because ecclesiastical unity, of which they speak, is a unity of order, having one head. In fact, their interpretation confirms the view of Pope Pelagius, because when their words refer to the unity of the Church they imply reference to one head. Through the head the unity of the Church has the keys of the kingdom of heaven, as the power of loosing and binding is derived from Peter by the others who become associated with him and share in his concerns.

Therefore the keys were received, not by Peter alone in his own person, but in the person of all his successors. Neither were they received by Peter alone and his successors so that they might keep them to themselves. Rather, the unity of the Church received them through one man, since Peter took them to be shared with the unity of the Church. What the argument said about a unified group of equals is false. The saints do not refer to the unity of equals, but to the unity of the Church, which is clearly a unity of order. Not only the *Glossa Ordinaria* says this;[8] but also Cyril, the greatest of the early eastern Fathers, understands this of Peter and his successors in the Roman church in the book, *Thesaurus*, as cited in the *Catena*, on Matthew 16.[9]

One can answer the second argument by pointing out that Our Lord did not repeat his words concerning the keys of the kingdom of heaven when he said to all, "Whatever you bind . . ." [Matthew 18:18]. He thereby left a clear indication of the superiority of Peter over the others. Also, the order of the passages, that is, first words addressed to Peter alone, and then words addressed generally to the others, suggests that the power of binding and loosing should pertain first to Peter and then to the other bishops.

The third argument rested on the text, "What I say to one, I say to all."[10] But Our Lord did not say, "What I give to one, I give to all." He did not give all his disciples the dignity of apostleship, nor did he give to all the dignity of the seventy-two. The issue here is not what he said, but what he gave. For he said, "To you I will give the keys . . ." [Matthew 16:16]. Thus, "What I say to one, I say to all," is simply not to the point, since it was meant by our heavenly teacher to refer literally to doctrinal discourse, so that instructions he was giving to one person might then be proclaimed openly to all.

The third principal objection concerned the text of Paul the Apostle [Hebrews 7:12]. But the decretal in question never dreamed of saying that the priesthood was transferred from Christ to Peter, since Peter is only the minister of Christ's priesthood. The decretals constantly say he is the vicar of Christ. It is therefore no fault of the Pope if the canon lawyers understand this incorrectly, unless one is so disturbed in mind as to impute to the Pope all the errors of teachers, simply because he does not correct them. One can only wonder when these objectors force upon the Pope's decretal a meaning alien to it. Could it be that such an obvious mistake is evidence they do it maliciously?

They then add that for more than eight hundred years the Christians of the whole Orient and of Africa were not under the

Roman Pontiff.[11] But if they had only examined the Council of Chalcedon, one of the four Councils Gregory received like the holy gospel, and if they had pondered what the Fathers decreed and did, they would have seen a consecutive series of testimonies from all ages witnessing to the primacy of the Roman Church.

It is absolutely false that Christians of Africa and the Orient were not subject to the Roman Church. To show this, we need only cite two witnesses from approximately a thousand years ago. The first is a Greek, Cyril, cited in the *Catena* on Matthew 16, from the *Thesaurus*, "According to this promise of Our Lord, the apostolic church of Peter has remained unsullied by every error and heretical group, having in its pontiffs superiority over all bishops and heads of churches and peoples by reason of its fullness of faith and authority from Peter."[12] A second witness is a Latin Father, Gregory, who wrote in a letter to Bishop John of Syracuse, "Who doubts that the church of Constantinople is subject to the Apostolic See?"[13] This is found in the *Decretum*, Distinction 22, canon *De Constantinopolitana.*

Mainz, March 22, 1519.

III

THE DIVINE INSTITUTION OF THE PONTIFICAL OFFICE OVER THE WHOLE CHURCH IN THE PERSON OF THE APOSTLE PETER 1521

To the Supreme Pontiff, Pope Leo X:

When some fail to discriminate between matters obvious in themselves and matters learned indirectly, and thus invent difficulties where none exist and blindly stumble in the full light of day, then, most blessed Father, truths evident to the learned must also be presented to a wider audience. Some persons not content with their own lot have felt so free as to obscure the clarity of the Gospel and thereby disturb the otherwise most serene countenance of the Church under the guise of new ideas, because they set out to call what is certain into question and make evident matters appear difficult for others. Consequently we take up the subject of the rightful primacy of Peter and his successors, the Roman Pontiffs, a primacy held in peaceful possession for untold ages in the resplendent light of the Gospel but now assailed by arguments upsetting those less grounded in Holy Scripture. This primacy we intend to defend against attack, clear of all darkness, and so present to everyone that this truth may illuminate all men and reach with its splendor the farthest corner of creation. May therefore the Catholic Church, entrusted to you, most blessed Father, accept this small work for the benefit of the simple, lest they be overcome by darkness.

1
SUBJECT, METHOD, AND ORDER
OF TREATMENT

Although the supremacy of the Roman Pontiff over all the churches of Christ has been assailed on many fronts, it is our intention to treat this matter in a single investigation. In the present case it is not questioned that the Roman Pontiff is actually the head of the Church,[1] nor that he has this authority from God in the manner spoken of by the Apostle in Romans 13[:1], "there is no authority except from God, and those instituted are from God."[2] The many adversaries would also admit a papal authority from God like that of the Old Testament kings, referred to in 1 Samuel 8[:22], "Hear their voices and institute over them a king." Many of the adversaries admit all of this. What they call in question is that Christ instituted the primacy of the Roman Pontiff over all the churches in Saint Peter in such a way that Christ made Peter along with his successors his vicar in governing all the churches of Christ.[3]

Hence we have put aside as not to our purpose the arguments from reason and from authorities affirming that Peter or the Roman Pontiff was or is the head of all the churches. We will present only those arguments showing that Christ Our Lord conferred such a supremacy on Peter alone. The true answer to this question is to be found wholly in Scripture in two principal passages, Matthew 16 and the final chapter of John, both of which treat of this mystery explicitly.[4] We must therefore first examine whether the words of Christ in both these passages are spoken to Peter alone. Second, we must ask whether by these words Christ entrusted to Peter alone primacy over the whole church. Third, was this primacy over the whole church which Christ entrusted to Peter given as well by Our Lord to Peter's successors? Fourth, was this primacy given by Christ to the Roman Pontiff as Peter's successor?

To obtain a clear resolution of the first point, we will initially deal with the passage in Matthew, treating in turn the following views: first, that the words of Christ were not addressed to Peter, but to a certain qualified person; second, not to Peter, but to to the Church; third, to Peter and to the other Apostles; finally, not to Peter alone, because to the Church.

They have made many different attempts to obfuscate Our Lord's promise recorded in Matthew 16[:19], "I will give you the keys . . ."

Some restrict these words so much that the person of Peter is not addressed but solely a divine gift found in Peter.[5] Others also restrict the words, excluding Peter's person, and have them directed to the Church alone, which Peter symbolizes.[6] Many extend Our Lord's promise to the other Apostles, understanding the words as being addressed to Peter in the person of all the Apostles.[7] Some others admit the words addressed only to Peter, but deny that a unique supremacy was granted him, since we read that a similar authority was given by Christ to the other Apostles, for instance, in Matthew 18[:18], "Whatever you bind on earth . . . ," and in other texts.[8] Finally, some have doubts about how the keys were truly given to Peter alone, though we all accept that the keys were given to the Church.[9] We will therefore take up one after another each of these five interpretations, presenting in each case the contrary arguments alleged, so that the conclusions will be clarified by juxtaposition with opposing views.

2
KEYS PROMISED TO PETER AS A PERSON, NOT TO
A GIFT OF REVELATION OR BEATITUDE

SYNOPSIS: Cajetan counters an interpretation of Matthew 16 that has Christ's promises addressed specifically to the virtuous qualities, such as simplicity and firmness of faith, which were given Peter and then manifested in his confession of Jesus as Christ and Son of God. What was promised would accordingly not be had when these qualities were not flourishing in Peter.[10] Cajetan first responds that this revives the Donatist heresy which judges invalid the official actions of sinful prelates or priests. He then takes up three points in detail: the blessing and approbation that Jesus spoke (Matthew 16:17) in response to Peter's confession; the first promise, that the Church would be built on Peter as on the rock of true faith (16:18); and the second promise, of a different kind, by which Christ was to grant the keys to Peter, as the individual who was to be pastor of Christ's flock (16:19).

3
KEYS PROMISED TO PETER PERSONALLY, NOT ONLY TO THE CHURCH

SYNOPSIS: Cajetan refutes the view that Christ promised the keys to the Church, of which Peter was a figure or symbol, giving six arguments for this view from Luther's *Resolutio*, and adding four confirmations which Luther had given, principally texts in which Augustine stated that Peter represented the Church as recipient of the keys.[11] Cajetan then argues from the methodological principle that the literal and historical sense of Scripture is prior to any mystical or figurative sense. Only the literal sense carries weight in disputing a truth of faith, while the figurative sense serves edification or devotion. In the present case, the literal sense relates the history of the promises made to Peter in person. A figurative interpretation can be added, in which Peter is seen as a symbol for the Church. The latter is justified, but to deny the literal sense because of it is to turn the passage into a mere parable. Cajetan then responds to each of the initial arguments. For instance, he specifies that by his denial of Christ Peter did not fall from office but was still to strengthen his brothers. The keys were not a gift of interior grace which is often not perceptible in others, but a gift of official authority for Church governance. The texts Luther cited from the Fathers are all true as figurative interpretations, but this does not deny the underlying history.

4
CHRIST SPOKE TO PETER, BUT NOT AS REPRESENTING ALL THE APOSTLES

SYNOPSIS: Cajetan answers the contention that the keys were promised to Peter in the name of all the Apostles. He lists four arguments in favor of a representative role of Peter in Matthew 16.[12] Cajetan answers that a close examination of the text shows that this is unwarranted. The blessing Jesus spoke over Peter would not apply to all the Apostles, since Judas was there, who, Jesus knew, did not believe. Neither is there evidence for a revelation by the Father made to the others. Jesus' words were in the singular, "*Tu es Petrus*," and, "*Tibi dabo* ..." In countering Luther's

arguments, Cajetan notes that at 16:20 Matthew records Jesus' shift
from Peter alone to all the disciples. A text Luther cited from
Chrysostom, saying Peter spoke, *"Tanquam os apostolorum,"* is
granted in the sense that the others subsequently approved his
confession and let it stand for themselves. Also, Cajetan underscores
the difference between the plurals in John 6:67-69, where Peter
answered for all, and the singulars in Matthew 16:17-19, where Peter
spoke for himself and received a personal promise.

5
OTHER APOSTLES NOT GRANTED THE SAME AS PETER

SYNOPSIS: Cajetan presents a lengthy rejoinder to the view that the
other apostles were equal to Peter in what they received from Christ,
namely the power to bind or loose (Matthew 18:18) and to forgive
or retain sins (John 20:23). Further New Testament texts show
Peter acting as the equal of the others (Acts 8:14, 15:6-22; Galatians
2:7-9), a fact confirmed by patristic interpreters, such as Cyprian
and Jerome.[13] Cajetan responds that the promise to Peter was
unique in referring to Christ's building the Church and giving the
keys. The powers of binding or loosing and forgiving or retaining
sins, as given to the other Apostles, were but parts of the much
wider power of the keys of the kingdom of heaven given Peter in the
Church built upon him. Cajetan constructs a further set of objections to his own answer, e.g., that Christ is the one foundation (1
Corinthians 3:11) and that the common theological understanding
of the keys sees their exercise by all the ordained as binding and
loosing in ecclesial Penance. He then responds that Peter is the
foundation as pastor on earth of Christ's church, and that what
theologians say about the power of orders in the Church touches
only a part of what Our Lord conferred on Peter. In answering the
initial arguments of this chapter, Cajetan points to Peter's humility
in working in the early mission as the equal of the other Apostles,
not exercising the power given him. Cajetan fends off the patristic
arguments by citing other texts of Cyprian and Jerome on Peter's
pre-eminence as source of unity and bulwark against schism.

6
COMPATIBILITY OF CONFERRAL
ON PETER ALONE AND ON THE CHURCH

SYNOPSIS: Cajetan counters Luther's statement that conferral of the keys on Peter alone and on the Church are mutually exclusive.[14] He explains that the two gifts go together quite well, since the gift to the church is dependent in two ways on the historical gift to Peter. The gift to Peter signifies a gift to the whole Church, and through the gift to Peter the keys come to the Church by derivation — a view having support in both Cyprian and Augustine. Cajetan responds briefly to the ancient contention that Catholics make of the Church a two-headed monster: Christ in heaven is simply and absolutely head, while Peter is *vicecaput* on earth. After summarizing the five arguments treated so far, Cajetan warns his readers to keep their eyes open, so as to detect the traps set to ensnare them.

7
THE PROMISE: PETER TO BECOME
PONTIFF OVER THE WHOLE CHURCH

In the words we have been treating Matthew the evangelist relates that Our Lord promised Peter four things, the last two of which (the powers to bind and to loose) he also conferred upon the other apostles. But the first two remain proper to Peter: "On this rock I will build my Church," and "I will give you the keys of the kingdom of heaven" [Matthew 16:18f]. After treating at some length the promises concerning binding and loosing, we must now show that the first two promises refer to Peter's pontifical office over the whole church.

There are six aspects to be noted in the first promise: first, the significant point that he said "my Church," and not "my churches"; second, simply "my Church," not "a certain church of mine"; third, "my Church," not "every church of mine"; fourth, "my Church," not in the indefinite; fifth, "my Church," in the singular, referring to a unique reality; sixth, "my Church" without any addition. You should take note of each of these.

He did not say "my churches" but "my church," to indicate the one Church, which although embracing many partial churches, is not thereby a Church rent, divided, or multiplied, but is numerically one with many parts, just as one body has many members. The Apostle pointed this out in Colossians 1[:18], "He is the head of the body, the Church," and the Canticle 6[:8] says, "My dove . . . is my only one."

He did not refer to a certain church, but said, "my Church," that one might know that he was speaking of the whole Church in its entirety, not of a part of the Church nor of one particular church. It would not accord with divine wisdom to build one church on the one person of Peter and another not on him, for God's works are perfect.

Neither did he speak of "every Church of mine," since a multitude of Churches would be implied by the distributive modifier. Against this is the statement of Our Lord in John 10[:16], "I have other sheep, who are not of this fold; I must bring them also . . . so there will be one fold and one shepherd." It is contradictory for a singular to be applied to a plurality in a distributive manner, unless it is applied universally as to the integral parts of the whole – which is not claimed in this case. Further on, he will nonetheless indicate how the parts of the Church are to be built "upon this rock."

He said, "my Church," not in an indefinite way that would leave the mind confused as to which church of Christ was to be built "on this rock". He did leave uncertainty of this kind when he said at the Last Supper, "One of you is to betray me" [Matthew 26:21]. His words thus assure us that Christ's only Church is built in its entirety "on this rock" and they leave us no room for uncertainty.

He said, "my Church," so one might understand he was speaking of the whole Church which is singular and unique and alone is his Church. This is what we mean in the Creed, "one catholic Church."

By the simple pronoun "my," he spoke in a determinate manner, so that we might perceive that he spoke of that one Church which is – without any additional modifier – the Church of Christ. Each of the particular churches is termed the church of Christ only with an added modifier, such as, "of Rome," "at Antioch," "in Constantinople," and so on. This is not only a modern usage, but is scriptural, as is evident at the beginning of both epistles to the Corinthians, where we read, "To the Church at Corinth." The same thing is at the beginning of Galatians ("To the churches of Galatia") and Thessalonians ("To the church of the Thessalonians"). Hence, by "my Church" one must understand the same as "one catholic Church."

Nonetheless, certain sophist objectors still argue from the fact that each particular church is truly a church of Christ. They say that Christ referred to that church of which it is verified that it is his Church, that is, Christ's. But since this is true of each particular church, that is, that it is his church, consequently Christ was referring to each particular church when he said, "On this rock I will build my Church."[15]

The fallacy in this argument is easy to spot, if one only attends closely and speaks to the precise point. One must indeed say that each particular church is church of Christ, but is not the whole Church, nor is it "church" without qualification, but is church as the "church of Milan". The only way it is church is by being part of the Church. But Christ was speaking of the entire Church, which is not this church or that Church, but is his Church without qualification.

Nonetheless, just as each church is "my Church," that is, Christ's, in that very manner it is true that is is built "on this rock." To understand this more adequately, one should note the difference in the way the Catholic Church is Christ's and the way each particular church is Christ's. All the particular churches have in common with the Catholic Church that they are Christ's, since each partial church is church of Christ and the Catholic Church is Church of Christ. But they differ in the manner in which this is true. The Catholic Church is Christ's as a whole, while each church is Christ's as a part. Hence the Catholic Church is built "on this rock" as a whole, while each particular church is built "on this rock" as a part. In the very way a particular church is his church, in just that way is it true that it is built "on this rock". Because it is his church as a part, it is consequently built "on this rock" as a part. But since the Catholic Church is his Church as a whole, it is also built "on this rock" as a whole. Since the whole embraces every part and is related to the parts as the complete to the incomplete, and since the unity and wholeness of the Church go hand in hand, consequently Christ's words are to be understood as literally referring to the one catholic Church by reason of which each particular church is understood as a part of the one Catholic Church built on Peter. Similarly, by reason of the one Catholic Church each partial church could be called by Christ "my church," only because it is part of the Catholic Church, and this would not be true if it were separated from the unity of the Church and thus were not church of Christ.

It is no argument against this when the holy canons or certain sayings of the saints seem to speak of the church of Rome as being built by Christ "on this rock". Many interpret in this sense the words of the Council of Constance condemning the articles of John Wyclif.[16] For the Catholic Church is at times spoken of as "the Roman Church," but in our discussion this is nothing more than a question of a name. This sense is not identical with the meaning intended by those who refer to the church of Rome as to one particular church distinct from the other particular churches. In the latter case, it is not true in the strict sense that the Roman Church is built by Christ "on this rock," but this is said only by appropriation. This becomes evident if one considers what the Roman church and the other churches have in common and in what they differ. In common is that as particular churches they are parts. Hence in the strict sense it is not true of any particular church, but only of the Catholic Church that it is built "on this rock." Only of the latter was Christ speaking literally when he said, "On this rock I will build my Church." All the particular churches were nonetheless included in this as parts in the whole.

The Roman church differs from the other particular churches by its nearness to the head of the Catholic Church, since its own head is not just near to, but is identical with, the head of the Catholic Church, since one and the same Peter was made Pontiff over the church of Rome and over the Catholic Church. The Roman church, taken by itself, is immediately united to the pontiff of the Catholic Church. But no other particular church is itself immediately united to the pastor of the Catholic Church nor is its head identical with the head of the Catholic Church. Because of this nearness and identity between the church of Rome and the pastor of the Catholic Church the words of Christ are applied by appropriation to the Roman Church rather than to the others, though they are not proper to it, but to the Catholic Church, as we said. – By the first promise, "On this rock I will build my Church," Our Lord therefore promised to Peter that he would be the foundation of the Catholic Church.

In the second promise, "I will give you the keys of the kingdom of heaven," Christ promised the fullness of ecclesiastical authority, as can be shown in three ways.

First, there is what the keys of the kingdom of heaven signify, namely, authority to open and shut the kingdom of heaven, not just to certain persons but unrestrictedly in a manner embracing all men who have not reached their final goal. To them the kingdom of heaven may be closed or opened. Such authority embraces a fourfold power. There is, first, a judicial power for exercise both in the forum of sacramental penance and in the forum of the Church. Every ecclesiastical judge by loosing or binding in both fora opens or closes the kingdom of heaven to the person loosed or bound. Second, there is the governing power over the Catholic Church, since arranging, governing, appointing, disposing, and other acts of this kind, are the way the kingdom of heaven is opened or closed.

This authority, thirdly, also extends to purgatory. Note that Christ did not give Peter a judicial power over purgatory, even though he did give him the keys of the kingdom of heaven for opening or closing on behalf of those in purgatory. Speaking of judicial power, he specified the place, as "on earth," when he said, "Whatever you loose on earth . . . ; Whatever you bind on earth . . . " [Matthew 16:19]. He thereby excepted those who are no longer on earth from the judicial power granted Peter. But with reference to the keys of the kingdom of heaven, he excepted no one short of his final destiny from the Church's ability to open or close the kingdom of heaven, but said absolutely and without restriction, "I will give you the keys of the kingdom of heaven." Thereby Peter was made able by a positive act to open and − at least by not acting − to shut the kingdom of heaven to everyone short of his final destiny. By saying this we in no way mean to oppose Augustine and the sacred canons, where these hold that Peter was given power even to excommunicate deceased persons.[17] Rather, what we said agrees with their view, for an ecclesiastical censure against a deceased person only looses or binds with reference to what is still on earth, that is, the living who are either bound in order to prevent their union with the deceased or loosed for such union. But opening or closing the kingdom of heaven does pertain to the deceased for whom the kingdom is thereby truly opened or closed. While therefore judicial power is limited to those on earth, the keys of the kingdom of heaven extend to all short of their final destiny.

Finally, there is the power to command all who pertain in any way to the Church. Of course this is only in relation to the kingdom of heaven. Right reason demands that the power ordered to the ultimate end is able to command all others in relation to that ultimate end, as is evident in the crafts and in the cases of men holding offices of commander, general, or prince. Every artisan, commander, general, or prince assigned a higher end is able to order other artisans, commanders, generals, and princes to his end and thus give them commands in so far as they are directed to his end. Clearly the kingdom of heaven is the supreme end, the one corresponding to the power of the keys promised to Peter. All other matters of a temporal character must at some time be ordered to this end. Consequently, this power given Peter entails the power of commanding all kings and princes with reference to the kingdom of heaven. Such power or rule is simply to open and shut the kingdom of heaven, as is obvious. Consequently, what was promised by the keys of the kingdom of heaven makes it evident that in saying, "I will give you the keys of the kingdom of heaven," Christ promised Peter the fullness of ecclesiastical authority.

The same point can be shown from the way Holy Scripture speaks, as in Isaiah, of the full authority of the High Priest Eliakim: "I will place on his shoulder the key of the house of David and he shall open and none shall shut and he shall shut and none shall open" [22:22]. In the New Testament, we read in Revelation 3[:7], "He who has the key of David opens and no one shall shut, shuts and no one shall open." It is no objection that the text of the Gospel does not say that if Peter opens none shall shut and if he shuts none shall open. Though these words do not occur, the meaning is there. For the Gospel does refer to the lesser actions included in the power of the keys: "Whatever you bind on earth shall be bound in heaven, and whatever you loose on earth shall be loosed in heaven" [Matthew 16:19]. Obviously, this means that what Peter binds no one looses and what he looses no one binds. For what is bound on earth is also bound in heaven, that is, it is so bound that no one shall loose. Similarly, what is loosed on earth is also loosed in heaven, that is, it is so loosed that no one shall bind.

This suffices to show that Peter opens the kingdom of heaven in such a way that no one shall shut, and so shuts that no one shall open. For it follows that the keys given Peter will carry out their proper actions in a higher and not a lower manner that holds for the lower actions. Note also that the words of Isaiah 22 speak of Eliakim with reference to Christ, as the Gloss on this verse says.[18] As a further sign of this John the Evangelist repeats the same thing about Christ [Revelation 3:7], so as to show he was prefigured in Eliakim. Isaiah himself wrote of Christ in 9[:6], "And the rule will be upon his shoulder," to show that the key on his shoulder is the rule on his shoulder. Hence we also understand that "the keys of the kingdom of heaven" refer to the fullness of authority. In addition to these testimonies there is the custom that the keys of the realm are presented to a king as a sign of his supreme authority.

If we link together the two promises, it becomes evident that in these words Peter was promised the pontifical office over the Catholic Church. From the first promise, Peter is to be the foundation of the Catholic Church. This promise establishes Peter's office of supporting the Catholic Church in firmness of faith and at the same time imposes on the Catholic Church the necessity of adhering to Peter its foundation. If a building is to be built up, it must necessarily adhere to the rock on which it is founded. In the second promise, the fulness of authority in the Church is promised Peter. Clearly these two are the principal elements in the pontifical office over the whole Christian Church.

Hence, from the words of Matthew beginning, "You are Peter . . . ," by comparing them with the other gospels and discussing them in themselves, we believe we have shown that Christ promised to Peter alone the pontifical office over the Catholic Church.

8

"FEED MY SHEEP" ADDRESSED
TO THE PERSON OF PETER

SYNOPSIS: Cajetan announces the four steps of his treatment of John 21:15-17: the words were addressed to the person of Peter, and to him alone (Chapter 9); granting him care of the whole Church (Chapter 10); and thus conferring a pontifical office over the whole Church (Chapter 11).

Cajetan then fends off the view that Peter was addressed specifically as loving Christ, and that therefore he loses his commisssion when his love fails.[19] Cajetan grants that right use of pastoral office does require charity, but insists against Donatism that office itself endures even in a sinful minister. He underscores the personal indications in John 21, for example, the three uses of Peter's proper name and the reference to Peter's sorrow.

9

"FEED MY SHEEP" ADDRESSED TO PETER ALONE

The fact that Christ said, "Feed my sheep," only to Peter is obvious from the text itself, both from the threefold repetition of Peter's and his father's name, and from the comparison with the others in, "Do you love me more than these?" [John 21:15]. The comparative shows the diversity between him and the other apostles then present, with whom he is being compared. Further, there is Peter's own emotion of sadness at the third interrogation, as he recalls his denial of Christ which was foretold as he earlier professed himself ready to die with Christ. Hence, there is no possible ground for doubting. Since these words were addressed to Peter after Our Lord's resurrection, and since nothing like this was said to the other apostles before or afterwards, it can only be that "Feed my sheep" was addressed uniquely to Peter.

It is no objection that the Church calls all the apostles the pastors of the Lord's flock in the Preface that refers to "those whom you appointed to be vicars in your work and pastors over you flock". This clearly speaks of the apostolic office, and so they are called pastors of the Lord's flock in the way that pastoral care pertains to the apostolic office. As the name "apostle" indicates, pastoral work pertains to the apostles as to the legates of Christ, and so they are called pastors of the Lord's flock precisely as legates of Christ. But it is evident from what we have said (and what we will say) that Peter was appointed as ordinary pastor even over the apostles themselves. This is what Christ meant by the words, "Feed my sheep."

10

"FEED MY SHEEP" ENTRUSTED THE WHOLE CHURCH TO PETER'S CARE

SYNOPSIS: Cajetan demonstrates that Christ's reference to "my sheep" includes the whole Church, both because there is no limiting qualification added and because of the parallel with "my church" in Matthew 16:19. Six objections are offered from Luther, arguing that the text is not explicit and, from a number of perspectives, that

Peter could not and did not feed all the sheep of Christ.[20] Cajetan responds that the text did not need to say "all" explicitly in view of Jesus' words about his sheep in John 10:14ff. Peter was not required to feed all personally, since as head he had the help of others who aided in the work of feeding and directing the flock.

11
"FEED MY SHEEP" APPOINTED PETER TO A PONTIFICAL OFFICE OVER THE WHOLE CHURCH

There are some who deny that by these words Peter was granted a pontifical office over the whole Church. First, "feed" is said not to mean "rule" or "have primacy over."[21] Second, this word of Christ is either an exhortation or a command to feed, not to subject the sheep.[22] And to what point is the claim that only a superior can feed? Find a text where the words grant Peter authority over the Church. Here he is only appointed to feed.[23]

It is in fact not difficult to show that by these words a pontifical office was conferred. For to feed the sheep of Christ is an act of authority by the one feeding, an act benefitting the sheep, having its ultimate purpose in Christ. By committing his followers to Peter as sheep to be fed, he made it absolutely clear that he set Peter over the others as a shepherd is over the sheep. There is no need to find another text where Peter is given authority over the Church, because this text bears witness to this gift. One could only mistake this by stupidly believing "Feed my sheep" was said to Peter as to a hired worker and not a shepherd. This stupidity is disproven by the threefold question about Peter's love for Christ, since one is surely no hired worker to whom the sheep are committed for feeding with reference to love for Christ.

Therefore, even though "feed" does not mean "rule", it does indicate the act of an ecclesiastical ruler. Also, if it does not mean "rule", it does presuppose ruling, because it presupposes a shepherd. So, the answer is to the point that only a superior can feed. When this is dismissed as not to the point, I answer that it is very much to the point, in view of the context. When this is considered, one can understand the rest. If it is true that only a superior can feed, then one told to feed is also told to be superior. So this point makes it evident that one need not find another text of Scripture where Peter is placed over the Church, since it is clear in this text.

We admit that Christ's words are a command. In fact if the Apostle Paul can say, "woe to me if I do not proclaim the gospel" [1 Corinthians 9:16], there is a far greater woe upon Peter if he does not feed the sheep of Christ. But the words of Christ are not simply a command, but an appointment. If in the first part of creation the word of God appointed the most important creatures and at the same time commanded their proper works, as the Psalm says, "He established them in eternity and forever, giving a command that will not pass away" [Psalm 148:6], then it rightly follows that in founding the Christian Church he would establish its first member by the same word that both commands the supreme pontifical function and appoints one to the pontifical office.

In the same act in which Peter is committed the task of feeding the sheep of Christ, the Christian people is ordered to be related to Peter as his sheep. For it would be pointless for them to be entrusted to Peter as the sheep he is to feed unless the same Lord should present them to him as sheep. The words of Our Lord, "Feed my sheep," therefore indicate both feeding and subordination. Augustine bore witness to this by interpreting feeding as both teaching and ruling: "He entrusted his sheep to be fed, that is, to be taught and ruled."[24] Chrysostom agreed that feeding my sheep meant taking over care of one's brethren.[25] In the Gloss of Alcuin feeding the sheep means strengthening believers in Christ so that their faith does not fail, arranging earthly support for one's subjects if needed, offering both the preached word and the example of virtue, defending against foes, and correcting wayward subjects.[26]

Hence, although feeding does not mean ruling, it does mean directing the sheep of Christ, which entails ruling. Though it does not mean ruling, it implies this, just as it implies seeking out, leading back, binding up, strengthening, protecting, and healing, as the Lord says in Ezechiel 34[:4.16]. Consequently, Peter is said to be appointed prince of the Apostles and ruler over Christ's people. According to Gregory's words to Mauritius, "Care and rule over the whole Church was entrusted to him."[27]

One could ask why Our Lord entrusted the pontifical office to Peter by referring to feeding his sheep and not by words referring to prelacy, authority, or dignity. The answer lies near at hand in the matter itself, because one is a prelate or has authority in order to feed the sheep of Christ, and not vice versa. Another purpose was to check ambition, since what one seeks in pontifical office is not a high position, not dignity or authority, but the feeding of the sheep of Christ. As the Apostle later said, "If one aspires to be a bishop, he desires an excellent task" [1 Timothy 3:1]. Another reason was the fulfillment of Scripture, since he had said before his passion, "the kings of the gentiles hold rule over them, and those exercising authority are called benefactors; but not so with you, since the greater among you should become like the lesser" [Luke 22:25f]. Consequently in the ministerial act of feeding the sheep of Christ there is a tacit reference to the pontifical office as to an added element which is to be valued only for the benefit of the sheep of Christ, in contrast to gentile kings and lords who regulate all things to promote their own rule and lordship.

Furthermore, the work commissioned shows what is primary in Peter's office, where feeding the elect is to be the primary pontifical act. The supreme work of God's providence is caring for the elect, since it was for their happiness that he not only ordered the movements of the heavens, as John gives witness in Revelation 6[:11], "They were told to rest a while longer, until the number of their fellow servants should be completed," but he also came down from heaven, became man, and was crucified, died and was buried, enduring all this for the elect. Similarly, the supreme part of ecclesiastical care, called "pontifical", must also be feeding the elect. Clearly, he was referring only to the elect when he said, "Feed my sheep," as Our Lord himself showed in John 10[:27f], "My sheep hear my voice and I know them and they follow me; I give them eternal life, and they shall not perish for eternity, and no one can snatch them from my hand." It is not that Peter's pontifical office is thereby restricted to the elect alone, but rather that every pontifical act for the others is subordinate to the feeding of the elect. Similarly in the order of the universe though the movement of the heavens is for fulfilling the number of the elect, it also extends to bringing forth the non-elect. And in the order of grace, although Christ, the good shepherd, "laid down his life for his sheep" [John 10:15], that is, for the elect, still that same death was for the life of the whole world. Thus in the sacred mysteries the supreme pontifical office is for feeding the elect, but also embraces the non-elect.

This is not improper since the concern for an end rules the arranging of the means. In this case the life of the elect is the end of governance over the others. In 2 Timothy 2[:10], the Apostle said, "I endure everything for the sake of the elect," and in Romans 8[:32] he said that all things are given over to the elect, and in

Matthew 23[=24:47] the elect are said to be "set over all the Lord's possessions".

I would not say that the foreknown non-elect are passed over in silence, since some of them could well be included under the reference to the lambs [John 21:15]. There are many imperfect Christians, "always learning but never coming to the perfection of the sheep" [2 Timothy 3:7], whom Our Lord entrusts to Peter for feeding along with the sheep, that is, the elect.[28] He twice entrusted the lambs, and only in the third place the sheep, not only because the imperfect require greater care, but also so that the number might hint at the differences among his sheep. For among those living the same Christian life, some are reprobate and others are elect. The sheep are entrusted only once, and in the last place, since all Christ's sheep are among the elect. The ascending order ends on the highest level.

When all are entrusted to Peter's pastoral care, only the lambs and the sheep are given to be fed. The wolves, lions, and bears are entrusted, we are to understand, but to be warded off, fled, or wiped out. Hence no one would be excepted from Peter's pontifical office, even if he had only been told, "Feed my sheep." It is for them that he does all things, for those for whom "everything works together for their good," as the Apostle bears witness in Romans 8[:28].

The excellence of this entrusted work becomes yet more evident when one goes through the pastoral and pontifical tasks, namely, "seeking out the lost, leading back the fallen away, binding up the injured, strengthening the weak, healing the sick, and watching over the fat and strong" [Ezechiel 34:16.4]. The Lord attests that these six pastoral actions pertain to feeding the sheep when he accuses the shepherds, "Woe to the shepherds of Israel who have been feeding themselves. Should not shepherds feed the sheep? But you drink the milk and cover yourselves with the wool" [Ezechiel 34:2f]. The reason he gives for their neglect is clearly that the evil shepherds feed themselves, not the sheep, and the reason for performing all these tasks is to feed the same sheep.

No doubt even judicial acts, whether in the Church's forum of penance or in the external forum, are ordered to the feeding of Christ's sheep. Opening and closing the kingdom of heaven also pertain to feeding the sheep, since opening the kingdom of heaven is an act of feeding the sheep of Christ, and closing is ordered to feeding them, since it is referred to the good of the elect, for whom "everything works together for their good" [Romans 8:28].

Consequently, if we bring together every aspect of meaning entailed in "Feed my sheep", it is evident that Peter was entrusted with a pontifical office over the whole Church. This concludion we have not forged anew but only presented as we learned it from the Fathers. We have sought only to confirm their testimony to Peter's pontifical office, as will become evident in our final chapter.

12
BY CHRIST'S INSTITUTION PETER HAS
SUCCESSORS IN HIS PONTIFICAL OFFICE

After our demonstration of Peter's pontifical office over the Catholic Church, we must treat of his successors. To make quite clear the differences between Catholics and schismatics, let us note beforehand our points of agreement and disagreement.

We agree that Peter was head of the apostles, and was Roman pontiff just as the apostle James was pontiff of Jerusalem. Consequently we agree that each bishop of Rome succeeds Peter as Roman pontiff, just as each bishop of Jerusalem succeeds James as pontiff in the Jerusalem church. We further agree that a bishop of Jerusalem only succeeds James in the episcopal office over the church of Jerusalem. He does not succeed James in the authority of the apostolic office.

But disagreement erupts when they strive to show that the Roman pontiff succeeds Peter only in an episcopal office over the Roman church. As Catholics we hold that the Roman pontiff succeeds Peter not only as bishop of the church of Rome but also in his pontifical office over the Catholic Church.

Hence careful examination reveals two questions still to be treated: whether by divine right Peter has successors in the pontifical office over the Catholic Church, and whether the Roman pontiffs are these successors. The schismatics deny that the Roman pontiff is bishop over the Catholic Church, and they further deny that by divine institution a single person is to succeed Peter in governing the whole Church. But prior to these issues, they deny that Peter was appointed by Christ to a pontifical office over the Catholic Church. Since we have already treated the last point concerning Peter's pontifical office, we must now ask whether he has successors, and then whether these are the Roman pontiffs.

Following the method used so far, I wish first to present arguments against there being successors to Peter in the pontifical office over the Catholic Church. A first argument proceeds from the contexts of Christ's words to Peter, "I will give you the keys of the kingdom of heaven" [Matthew 16:19], and, "Feed my sheep" [John 21:17]. If these are extended to successors, then the antecedent, concomitant, and subsequent words addressed by Christ to Peter should also be understood not of Peter alone but as well of his successors.[29] But this conclusion is clearly false, as is evident from examination of each point. In Matthew, Our Lord began, "You are Peter" [16:18], and later admonished Peter, "Get behind me, Satan, for you do not think the things of God." In John, he began [21:15], "Do you love me more than these?" Similar questions are interspersed with Peter's answers. Later he added, "When you were younger you girded yourself . . ." [John 21:18]. But none of these sayings refer in their literal sense to Peter's successors.[30] Consequently, neither do the words, "To you I will give the keys . . . ," nor, "Feed my sheep." They are not literally about Peter and his successors, but are — just as the other sayings — mystically applied to the successors.

A second argument would be similar. Since the words of Christ in Luke 22[:32], "I prayed for you . . . ," were not addressed in their literal sense both to Peter and to his successors, therefore neither were the words, "I will give you the keys," and, "Feed my sheep," addressed to Peter for both himself and his successors. The parallel makes the conclusion necessary, especially since the former text is cited by the holy doctors to show the firmness in faith of Peter's successors. The basis of proof is clear from the fact that he said, "When you have once turned back, strengthen your brethren" [Luke 22:32]. If these words apply to each successor, then the successors would have at some time to turn away, so they could truly turn back, just as Peter turned away by denying Christ with an oath and later turned back to strengthen his brethren.[31]

A third argument could be made from other sayings of Our Lord to Peter, for example, "Before the cock crows, you will deny me three times," (Matthew 26[:34]) or "Go to the sea and cast a hook . . ." (Matthew 17[:26]). Why are sayings like these interpreted as addressed to the person of Peter alone and not to his successors, while the others, "I will give . . ." and "Feed . . ." are applied to the successors? This application thus seems arbitrary.

A fourth argument proceeds from an omission, since Christ nowhere said his words were addressed to Peter both for himself and for his successors. But he should have done this, since this is presented as one of the necessary articles of belief in the Church. In Isaiah 5[:4] he said of the synagogue of the Jews, "What more should I have done for my vineyard that I did not do for it?" If he did all that he should for the synagogue, it is far more certain that he did everything for the Christian Church. This argument is strengthened by what Our Lord said in Matthew 28[:20], "Behold I am with you all days even to the end of the age." To impress on us that he would be with the Church through the whole of this time, he said, "Behold I am with you even to the end of the age." This was evidently spoken to his disciples concerning both themselves and their successors. From this, one can argue that if he intended to address both Peter and his successors, he would have been explicit or have suggested the successors, as there he suggested the successors of his disciples.[32]

A fifth argument is from the fellow apostles. Why does no other apostle have successors in the apostolic office, but only Peter? Further, why are the successors of the apostles the bishops, who are evidently equal, calling each other "brother", but one bishop is successor of Peter over the whole Church?[33] Again, as was said earlier, why does the bishop of Jerusalem succeed James in the episcopal office in that city, but not in the apostolic office, while the successor of Peter succeeds him in both apostolic and pontifical offices over the whole Church? Since scriptural authority is lacking, the latter must then rest solely on human arguments or a human decision.

Lastly, they argue by showing many untoward consequences. First, if Christ's words refer to Peter alone, then it is not about any successor, and it must further be that the keys come and go with Peter. The conclusion is proven by the principle that what is said to only one cannot pertain to a plurality.[34] Second, if Christ's words extend to successors, they must necessarily refer as well to the other apostles, since they were then present, and as yet there were no successors of Peter.[35] Third, it would be nonsensical for all churches to have the same baptism, the same Eucharist, the same confirmation, the same word of God, the same priesthood, the same faith, hope, charity, grace, death, life, and glory, but for earthly authority to be granted by the word of God (which all have in common) to just one, the successor of Peter.[36] Fourth, if one bishop ranks ahead of the other bishops by divine right, then Jerome was openly teaching heresy in his letter to Evandrus (cited in Distinction 93, canon *Legimus*), and not only he, but also Peter, Paul, John, and Luke, whom he cites as unshakeable authorities. For Jerome says openly that bishops were the same as priests and that bishops are of equal dignity.[37] Fifth, the same Jerome comments on Titus (as cited in Distinction 95, canon *Olim*), "Just as priests know that by the customary practice of the church they are under the one presiding over them, so bishops know that it is more through custom than through Our Lord's institution both that they are over priests and that they should act in common in ruling the Church."[38] For these reasons, there is not by divine right a bishop who succeeds Peter in being over the others.

To make this matter evident, there is a threefold way of showing that the words of Christ repeatedly addressed to Peter were not only said concerning Peter himself but concerning his successors as well.

The first way is from Our Lord's words themselves, "Feed my sheep." By saying "Feed my sheep" he appointed a single shepherd of his sheep, as the words indicate without need of further proof. But "shepherd" stands for the ordinary ruler over the sheep, as is clear both from the terms "shepherd" and "sheep" and from the purpose, which is feeding. Also, one with ordinary care over the sheep is either a hired worker or a shepherd. But John 10[:12f] rules out the hired worker, since the hired worker "sees the wolf coming and flees, since as a hired worker he cares nothing for the sheep." Consequently, the one with ordinary care of the sheep is the shepherd. However the shepherd, as an ordinary official, obviously cannot cease with the death of the one holding the office of shepherd, but must continue through successors. Hence, the appointment of a shepherd is the founding of a perpetual office, and what is granted the shepherd in the initial appointment must thereby be given to each successor in the office. Consequently, since in saying "Feed my sheep," Our Lord appointed a shepherd over the whole Church, he was founding a pastoral office over the whole Church from that moment to the end of the ages and, as a result, what he gave then to Peter he meant to give in Peter to each of Peter's successors.

His words "Feed my sheep" show on another count that the

perpetuity of the shepherd was meant. He knew that his sheep were to endure, as he said, "unto the end of the age" [Matthew 28:20], in one fold in the present time of trial. Consequently by the very fact that in saying to Peter, "Feed my sheep," he arranged for a single shepherd for the sheep who were to endure in the one fold to the end of the age, by the same fact he indicated he was arranging for a single shepherd "unto the end of the age." It is therefore shown by two aspects of the gospel words themselves that in Peter Our Lord was appointing each successor of Peter as pastor over the whole Church.

The second way of demonstration is by arguments founded on Holy Scripture. It would be ridiculous to think that Christ arranged for a shepherd of his sheep for only the least segment of time, namely, Peter's lifetime, and not for the long period "unto the end of the age," through which his sheep were to continue to live. Also it makes good sense to join temporal universality to local universality, that is, to conclude from the way he included his sheep all over the world in "Feed my sheep" to the inclusion of the same sheep for all future time. Furthermore Christ said to the synagogue, "What more should I have done for my vineyard that I did not do for it?" [Isaiah 5:4]. But he would have inadequately provided for the Christian Church, if he had founded it as one fold without a shepherd of the same duration as the fold. He must have dealt with his sheep "agreeably," that is, meaningfully and according to the needs they have both for a spiritual life and for earthly existence as well. Of him it is written, "He reaches mightily from one end of the world to the other, and orders all things agreeably" [Wisdom 8:1].

The third way of proof is the best and most certain, proceeding as it does from an explicit divine revelation made to his holy Church. Later we will present the normative texts in exact citation. This will make it evident that innumerable saints and all the sacred councils have so understood Christ's founding of Peter's pontifical office over the whole Church. An interpretation of Scripture is beyond all doubt the true one if we receive it handed on as the consensus of the saints and it is then defined by an ecumenical council. We therefore profess without any doubt that each successor of Peter was in Peter appointed pastor over the whole Church.

We therefore respond to the first contrary argument, which proceeded from the Gospel contexts, that two things are found in the antecedent, concomitant, and subsequent words, namely, things relevant to the pastoral office and things not relevant to it. Concerning things not relevant to the pastoral office, there should be no concern about their pertaining to the successors. An example of this is the saying, "Get behind me, Satan" [Matthew 16:23], as is evident from the Gospel text itself. But concerning what is relevant to the pastoral office, one must say that they pertain to the successors in the same manner they belong to the pastoral office. Let us descend to particulars. Since the initial words in Matthew, "Blessed are you, Simon Bar-Jonah . . . ," have no reference to the pontifical office, but to Peter's confession (as we showed), they therefore have no reference to the successors. But since the words, "You are Peter and on this rock . . . ," necessarily refer to the pontifical office over the whole Church, they must also pertain to the successors. A successor of Peter must needs be the rock, that is, firm in faith, so Christ may build his Church "on this rock". The difficulties that are had with this will be treated in the next chapter. The two questions in John, "Do you love me?" [John 21:15f], pertain in one way to the pastoral office, but in another way do not. For right exercise of the pastoral office demands love of Christ, even though one can have and exercise office without love of Christ. Consequently, love of Christ pertains to the successors with reference to right exercise of their pastoral office, but not with reference to having or exercising this pastoral office. A similar distinction can be applied to the words that follow, "when you were young" [John 21:18], for with the fulfillment of the prophecy it no longer pertains to Peter, but by suggesting both the pastor's attitude of readiness to lay down his life for the sheep of Christ, and the frequent occurrence in the experience of the good pastor of persecutions and death for Christ's sheep, the words are relevant to the uprightness and courage of the successors.

In response to the second objection, we also distinguish between things related to the pastoral office and things not related. Christ's words about strengthening one's brethren do pertain to the pastoral office and so are to be understood as said to Peter for himself and for his successors. Theophilus commented here: "He said this to Peter, since Peter could grow proud over what Christ had promised him . . . . After you have wept and repented of denying me, strengthen the rest, since I appointed you ruler of the apostles. This is fitting for you, who with me are the strength and rock of the church."[39] Cyril commented on this passage, "Passing by the rest, he came to Peter, the prelate over the rest."[40] This does not therefore mean that each successor to Peter has to fall from love of Christ, since Our Lord's words do not entail the necessity of one's turning away, but point out the possibility of failing in love while continuing always in faith. If therefore one does fall, when he turns back he will strengthen his brethren. The text consequently affirms the indefectibility in faith gained by Christ's prayer for Peter and his successors. It obligated them to strengthening the brethren. It also shows a fall can occur, but it foretells a conversion to follow. The adverb "once" [Luke 22:32] suggests the latter, for just as conversion is foretold as happening "once" and not always, the falling away is also suggested as coming at one time. For this to come true, it must not necessarily be that each successor fall away but it is enough — or even too much — that at some time a successor fall away from love of Christ.

Our solution to the third objection is already clear. Only those things are said to Peter with reference in the literal sense both to himself and to his successors which pertain to the pastoral office. The literal sense of the rest pertains to him alone.

It is also evident how one responds to the fourth argument, which was presented with such force. Christ himself showed that in addressing Peter he spoke to each of his successors, by the very fact that he appointed him shepherd of his sheep. We showed this both on the basis of the pastoral office, and from the perpetuity of the sheep. Here [John 21], as he dealt with Peter, there was no less reference to his successors than in Matthew [28:18-20] where he dealt with his disciples and referred to their successors. In the latter passage he indicated the succession by one aspect, namely, the continuity in time. In the former passage, there are two such aspects, the pastoral office, and the perpetuity of the sheep, as we showed.[41]

We respond to the fifth objection by pointing out that succession in apostolic office differs from succession in pontifical office. As the name itself shows, an apostle is an ambassador or one sent by another. The Apostle spoke of this in 2 Corinthians 5[:20], "We serve as ambassadors for Christ," and Ephesians 6[:20], "I serve as ambassador even in these chains." But an ambassador only has a successor if the Lord sends another. Otherwise the mission ends when the ambassador departs. A pastor, however, has an ordinary office in which a successor follows. The Church therefore does not have apostles successively exercising the office Christ gave the apostles. Instead, bishops succeed the apostles, not in apostolic authority, but in the episcopal dignity and authority. If one were to speak with complete precision, it is not true that Peter has successors in the apostolic office, since he shared the apostolic office with the other apostles, and all of them were equal in this office. Concerning succession in the apostolic office all were equal. We know well that the writings, however holy, of no successor of Peter are included in Holy Scripture. Even a brief recommendation of a single slave, that is, Paul's letter to Philemon, is reckoned as a part of Sacred Scripture. Still, because the successor of Peter comes after him in pastoral office over the sheep of Christ, which is a pontifical office over the world, he does succeed to the principal part of the apostolic office, which is, as St. Thomas says, governance over the Catholic Church.[42] Christ delegated this in common to all the apostles, but conferred it uniquely on Peter as a pastoral office. Therefore only the successor of Peter inherits this governance, by the fact that he succeeds Peter in the pontifical office over the Catholic Church. Hence only the see of Peter's successor is called and is the Apostolic See, since the authority for governing the Catholic Church resides in it alone. The latter is the highest power delegated to the apostles, and thus the successor of Peter is apostolic, his rank or office is apostolic, and his authority is termed apostolic since it includes the highest authority granted to the apostles. This makes evident the answer to all the problems posed: it shows why Peter is the one apostle to have successors in apostolic authority, why Christ appointed only him as shepherd of his sheep, and how one can without contradiction say that all the bishops succeed the apostles in the episcopal dignity and authority with the bishops being equal among themselves. The latter is in no way contrary to the truth we have affirmed. We further see why the bishop of Jerusalem does not succeed James in apostolic authority. For Peter had apostolic authority even as ordinary shepherd appointed by Christ over his whole fold, but James had this authority only as an apostle. This was not done on the basis of human argument or decision, but, as we have shown, it was so arranged by the founding act of Christ, true God, when he appointed Peter as the sole shepherd of his flock by the words, "Feed my sheep."

We can now answer the final objection, which was based on the untoward consequences. In the first, the conclusion is of no weight.

Where it was argued that what is said to only one cannot pertain to a plurality, we answer that what is said in appointing only one to an official position can in fact pertain to his countless successors. What is said to him is understood as addressed to each successor, and consequently what was said to Peter appointing him the first shepherd of Christ's sheep was also said to each one succeeding him in this pastoral office. The same holds for the promises made to him.

Similarly we say that in the second point the conclusion is not valid. We deny that there are equal or even greater grounds for extending these words to the other apostles then present than to Peter's successors. Although each successor was not there himself at that time, he was in fact in Peter under the form of the office he was to bear. In this manner the other apostles were not present in Peter, since none of them was then bearing or was to bear the form of office he received.

The third consequence is not nonsensical, but rather conforms to the divine plan. All the churches do share in the same sacraments, and so on. But since the word of God founded the one fold to which all belong, so the same word of God which all have in common appointed one shepherd over this one fold. Upon thoughtful examination this does not appear to be to the advantage of a particular church or individual, but instead looks to the unity of the fold. Just as all the particular churches share in the unity of the fold, so the oneness of the shepherd is beneficial to all the churches. This fulfills quite well Paul's words in 1 Corinthians 3 [:22], "All things are yours, whether Paul, Apollo, or Cephas."

Neither the fourth nor the fifth consequence holds since both are derived from irrelevant premises. What Jerome said on both points, that is, on the equality of bishops and priests as such, is not to the point. The question whether by divine right bishops and priests are or are not equal, or even identical, has nothing to do with the question of there being one pastor over the whole Church. One person is not pastor over the whole Church because bishops are above priests; rather, he is this because he is the successor of Peter, whatever might be the order of rank between priesthood and episcopate in the Church.

There is no need to prove that by divine right bishops are as such equal to each other. We affirm this, but maintain it is not to the point. All bishops are equal in the episcopal order and the successor of Peter is in no way more a bishop than any other bishop. Neither is he more a priest than any other priest. One person is not therefore pastor over the whole Church because one bishop is more sacred than another, but because one person is successor of Peter. This same one is the one pastor over the whole church and prelate over bishops and priests. Consequently from the fact that by a divine right instituted by Christ one priest or bishop as successor of Peter is over the other bishops and priests, and even over the whole Church, it does not follow that Jerome and those he cited (Peter, Paul, John, and Luke) were teaching heresy, as the objectors dared to conclude. The perceptive reader will grasp that their words were not to the point for which they were cited on this topic.

13

THE ROMAN PONTIFF SUCCEEDS PETER IN THE PONTIFICAL OFFICE OVER THE WHOLE CHURCH

Once it is established that Peter is to have successors, one must show who then succeeds Peter in the pastoral care for the whole Church. Certain specific problems arise concerning whether this is the Roman bishop.

A first difficulty concerns the question of time, since the Roman pontiff arose many years after Peter received the pontifical office. Peter's first see was Antioch, and for many years before coming to Antioch he had no particular see.[43] A confirmation of this point derives from the Apostle's argument in Romans 4[:9-11], where he showed by the sequence of time that Abraham was not justified by circumcision but by faith, simply by showing that before he was circumcised he was righteous before God by faith. If this argument of the Apostle is valid, so must the following be valid: when Christ granted the keys to Peter, he was not yet bishop of the city of Rome, but was simply one of the Apostles, and consequently the keys were conferred on him only as apostle and not as something he became later by a change of place or office. For Abraham was not accounted righteous because of anything he became after believing.[44]

A second difficulty is that the words of Christ relating necessarily to Peter's successors would have to be true of each Roman Pontiff, if in fact the Roman pontiff is Peter's successor in caring for the whole Church. We need not repeat that we will always be speaking of this latter succession, unless we make it explicit at some time that we are discussing succession only as bishop of Rome. But certain words need not be true of each Roman Pontiff, and so the Roman Pontiff is not the successor of Peter. The antecedent is proven by the fact that à Roman Pontiff can fall into heresy, and thus Christ's words would not be true of him, "You are Peter," that is, one solid in faith, nor would it be true that "On this rock I will build my Church," for the firmness of faith on which the Church must be built would not be present. Further it would not be true that "I have prayed for you, that your faith fail not." But it was shown that all of these were addressed to Peter's successors.[45]

Third, not every Roman pontiff is marked by love of Christ, which Christ three times sought as he founded the pastoral office. Hence one who does not succeed to the love Christ sought in Peter is not Peter's successor.[46]

Fourth, not every Roman Pontiff feeds the sheep of Christ, because many of them feed their own sheep by exercising their pontifical office for the sake of their own glory, rank, benefit, and the like. When Our Lord said, "Feed my sheep," he indicated that Peter's successors must either be shepherds of the sheep of Christ, loving him and feeding them with teaching, righteousness, and the like, or, if they do not so love and teach, this word does not pertain to them and they are therefore not Peter's successors.[47]

Fifth, the early Roman Pontiffs refused to be called universal bishops. When Gregory was old he objected to this in his letters and said that his predecessors had refused this title.[48] But if Gregory and others did not want to be called universal bishop, it follows that they were not, or did not believe themselves to be, universal bishops. The same would hold for a universal pontifical office over the whole Church. Hence the Roman Pontiff did not succeed Peter as pontiff over the whole Church.

Sixth, we read in Eusebius' *Ecclesiastical History*, Book X, chapter 6, that the Council of Nicaea made this statute: "Both in Alexandria and in Rome the ancient custom is to be maintained, so that the former is to bear the concerns of the churches of Egypt, as the latter is to do for the churches in the vicinity of Rome." But if the Roman pontiff were Peter's successor in a pontifical office over the whole Church, the Council of Nicaea would not have presumed to limit the ambit of his concern to the churches of his immediate vicinity.[49]

Seventh, if the Roman Pontiff is by Christ's appointment over the whole Church as the universal vicar of Christ, then all who were not or are not under obedience to the Roman Pontiff were and are guilty of sin. Hence it follows that the whole primitive Church was in error, since then there was as yet no Roman Pontiff. Also, a great many saints and martyrs were in error for four hundred years after Christ, since in that period the Roman Pontiff was not acknowledged as pastor over the whole Church.[50] In a later period, Asia, Africa, and Greece are to be condemned for not acknowledging the Roman Pontiff as head over all.[51] Finally, the Christians who today are in Persia, India, Scythia, and throughout the Orient are to be damned for not being subject to the Roman Pontiff. The latter obviously do not acknowledge the Roman Pontiff, since neither their bishops are appointed by him or by his authority nor are their councils held under him.[52]

Eighth, Jerome wrote in *De viris illustribus* that Bishop Acacius of Caesarea, a disciple of Eusebius of Pamphilia, at the command of Constantius deposed Pope Liberius and appointed Felix. This obviously does not fit with the primacy of the Roman Pontiff, if he is to preside over the whole Church.[53]

Ninth, if any church is first because it was founded directly by Christ Our Lord as the mother of all the churches, this can only be the church of Jerusalem. It existed many years before the Roman church, and from it all apostles and bishops went out into the whole world. As a sign of this, collections for the church of Jerusalem were made by all the churches, including the Church of Rome.[54]

For a satisfactory treatment of this topic two distinct issues must be taken up: first, whence it comes that the Roman Pontiff succeeds Peter, and second, how this is known.

Regarding the first issue, one must distinguish two things, namely the manner of succession and the fact that there are successors. The manner of succession is not something found in the Gospel, but in the later action of Peter, by which he firmly associated with himself as his own the Roman church. I will now treat each of these points, but first I ask the reader to note carefully that it is one thing to succeed Peter and another for this person, the Roman Pontiff, to succeed Peter. The reason why Peter has successors lies in the Gospel, in Our Lord's founding in Peter a pastoral office over the whole world, as has already been made clear. But the reason why this person, that is, the Roman Pontiff, succeeds Peter does not lie in the Gospel. The text of the Gospel does not entrust the Church of Rome to Peter as his own, but it does entrust the whole Church, by the words, "Feed my sheep." If Peter had therefore lived to the end of his life as he began, that is, without taking a particular church as his own, then the successor of Peter would have been neither the Roman Pontiff nor any other local bishop. At the death of Peter, someone would have been chosen as bishop over the Catholic Church and so as successor of Peter. If Peter had lived out his life in the see of Antioch, which he first took to himself, then the successor of Peter would not have been the Roman Pontiff but the Bishop of Antioch. If Peter had left Rome and relinquished the see in order to choose a see elsewhere, the Roman Pontiff would not have succeeded Peter, just as the Bishop of Antioch does not succeed Peter, since Peter left Antioch and relinquished its see. It thus becomes evident that the fact the Roman Pontiff succeeds Peter is not of evangelical origin and institution. The Gospel did not concern itself with these changes, but left the matter to be arranged through later events.

Consequently the fact that Peter took the church of Rome to himself for the exercise of his pontifical office, and that this fact was confirmed, is at the origin of the Roman Pontiff's succession in Peter's office. We say this was confirmed, both because Peter's death settled the matter and because Christ's authority gave it firm confirmation. For as Peter wanted to leave Rome, Christ met him and commanded him to undergo death in Rome by saying to him, "I come to Rome to be crucified again." The Church sings of this event, and Ambrose spoke of it in his discourse against Auxentius treating the handing over of churches (now in Book V of Ambrose's letters, after Letter 32).[55] Before Ambrose, Hegisippus told of Peter's vision in Book III of *De excidio urbis Hierosolymitanae*.[56] Hence not just the fact of Peter's death in Rome but death in Rome at the command of Christ confirms the Roman see for succession after Peter.

If one therefore considers the source and beginning of the Roman Pontiff's succession in the place of Peter, the reason for succession is the fact that Peter took to himself the Roman church for exercise of his pontifical office, a fact then confirmed by Peter's death and Christ's command. When we therefore speak of Peter as both Roman Pontiff and pontiff over the Catholic Church, we do not understand two pontifical offices, since they are not actually but only potentially two. They could have been two, as we explained. They are therefore not related as two episcopal offices joined in one person, for there was no episcopal office in Rome before Peter. It was Peter who elevated the Roman Church to the pontifical office, that is, to none other than the office he bore with himself. So as Peter took the Roman church as his own, he brought to it the pontifical office Christ had conferred on him for the Catholic Church. The unity of the pontifical office adds considerably to the oneness of the Roman Pontiff with the pontiff over the Catholic Church, since it is both oneness of person and identity of pontifical office. A sign of this is that the Roman Pontiff has only one pallium, not two, whereas those holding more than one archbishopric receive more than one pallium.

Concerning the fact that there are successors, we come back to evangelical institution. The Roman Pontiff, as successor of Peter, has apostolic authority from the word of Christ in the Gospel, "Feed my sheep." Consequently, even though the union between the Apostolic See and the Roman Pontiff began when Peter took the Roman church to himself, still this event establishes that by the fact a person is truly the Roman Pontiff, he holds the pontifical office over the Catholic Church which Christ founded in Saint Peter. This then explains why the Roman Pontiff is Peter's successor and pastor over the whole Church.

This fact is known by divine revelation made to the universal Church, to countless holy teachers, and to the sacred councils. No Christian is allowed to doubt that divine revelation is the source of something attested by these witnesses as pertaining to the content of Christian faith. That this matter so pertains is clear from the decree *Unam sanctam.*[57] The common confession of Christians was, is, and always will be that only the see of the Roman Pontiff is the Apostolic See. But this is simply to profess that the Roman Pontiff as successor of Peter has governance over the Catholic Church. Anyone grasping the meaning of the word knows that the Apostolic See has apostolic authority. One well grounded in Christian sources knows that apostolic authority embraces power to govern the whole Church. This is so evident that everyone agrees that Christ put the world under apostolic authority, so that each apostle could, wherever he might be, found churches, appoint bishops, and perform other actions of this kind. The apostles' deeds bear witness to this, and in 1 Corinthians we read, "In the Church God appointed apostles in the first place" [12:28], to which the interlinear gloss adds, "rulers and judges over everything,"[58] thus explaining that apostolic authority is power to rule and judge all else. This intention is evident from the fact that we only confess the see of the successor of Peter as apostolic.

The see of Jerusalem still exists, where the apostle James once ruled, and the Bishop of Jerusalem is now his successor. Why then is not this see also an apostolic see, in which the apostle James ruled and which was prior in time to any other local see? The one reason is that apostolic authority does not reside there, while it does reside in Rome. If the Christian faithful confessed an apostolic see solely on the basis of succession after an apostle, then no doubt there would be many apostolic sees, with both Jerusalem and Rome being apostolic sees. But since the Christian people at present know of only one Apostolic See, and loudly confess this to be the see of the Roman pontiff, one can only conclude that an apostolic see is a see with apostolic authority. This is confirmed by parallels, for an episcopal see entails pontifical authority, an archiepiscopal see archiepiscopal authority, and a patriarchical see patriarchical authority. Similarly, the Apostolic See entails apostolic authority. When Christian people have recourse to the former sees they are seeking out the corresponding authorities. Similarly in having recourse to the Apostolic See, or in any way venerating it, the people are acknowledging apostolic authority.

Furthermore acknowledgment of the Apostolic See entails confession of its divine institution, since an apostolic see and apostolic authority can in truth only derive from Christ alone. He alone could make men apostles, and founding an apostolic see or apostolic authority does not rank below this, just as institution of episcopal authority and an episcopal see does not rank below appointing a bishop. Hence one confessing an apostolic see must necessarily admit that its authority is immediately from Jesus Christ and that it is consequently founded by divine right. Hence you see why the teachers who profess that the Apostolic See of the Roman Pontiff is apostolic or has apostolic authority also admit that the Roman Pontiff has governance over the whole Church. This should be examined most attentively as an argument in its own right, and it then will not need to be repeated frequently as we cite later the texts of the saints. But before we present these texts, we must respond to the objections recounted above.

One can answer the first difficulty, since the fact that Peter became Roman Pontiff after receiving the keys in no way hinders the Roman Pontiff from succeeding Peter. For this succession it suffices that the one succeeded became this before his death. We respond to the argument from the parallel reasoning of the Apostle Paul on the justification of Abraham by showing that this does not disprove our view but instead disproves the view of the objectors. This is evident if one distinguishes the accounting of Abraham as righteous from the righteousness that was accounted, just as one can similarly distinguish in the case of Peter the reception of the keys from the keys received. Just as Abraham was accounted righteous because of faith and not because of his subsequent circumcision, similarly Peter received the keys because of his pontifical office over the Catholic Church and not because of the church of Rome or the subsequent pontifical office in Rome. Peter was given the keys when he was made shepherd of the Christian fold. Just as the righteousness accounted in Abraham was not restricted to the time before circumcision but extended to the subsequent time of circumcision, in the same way the keys Peter received extended to his subsequent pontifical office in Rome. As the Apostle said, "It is consequently by faith, so the promise is firmly based on grace for the benefit of all his descendants, and not only to those under the Law . . ." [Romans 4:16].

Further, the righteousness accounted in Abraham was then attached to the subsequent circumcision, that is, to Abraham himself when he later became father of the circumcised, so that his offspring in circumcision might be before all in the fulness of righteousness promised as the blessing on Abraham. As the Apostle said in Galatians 3[:16] "The promises were made to Abraham and his offspring . . ., which is Christ," who clearly was born of circumcision. Similarly the keys received were then attached to the Roman Church, that is, to Peter, as he later became Roman Pontiff, so that it might open the kingdom of heaven to all related to it over the face of the earth. Consequently, although it does follow from an argument of this type that Peter received the keys just as he then was, that is, as an apostle and shepherd of the sheep of Christ, it does not follow that the keys then received were exclusively restricted only to that state. For if we follow out the analogy with Abraham, it follows that the keys received were extended and attached to the Roman pontifical office in accord with the action by which Peter came to Rome and officially took its church to himself.

In answering the second difficulty one should take note that there are two senses in which one can hold that the successor of Peter, the Roman Pontiff, cannot fall into unbelief or heresy. This can be held concerning his person as related to the Catholic Church, or simply concerning his own person as such. Both senses are true, for Our Lord referred to both in the Gospel. He indicated the firm faith of Peter and his successors in their own persons in the sayings, "You are Peter," and, "I have prayed for you, that your faith not fail." The former concerned the present while the latter looked to the future. Our Lord referred to their faith as related to the Church in the sayings, "On this rock I will build my Church," and, "Strengthen your brethren." The fact that the person himself can become heretical does not tell against the truth of what we have said about the faith of the Roman Pontiff in his own person. For as soon as his faith fails, he immediately ceases to be Peter's successor in actual fact before God. In God's judgment, "he who does not believe is condemned already," as we read in John 3 [:18], however it might be in the external order of the Church. In this latter order the same situation obtains, for by the fact that a man called the successor of Peter is even unwillingly subjected to the judgment of the Church for falling from faith, it becomes obvious that in actual fact he is no longer the successor of Peter. For if he were in fact Peter's successor, he would be judge over the whole Church, not one brought in unwilling submission to the Church.

Because of the firmness of the Roman Pontiff's faith as related to the Church, he consequently cannot err in solemnly defining the Christian Faith, since the faith of the whole Church is fashioned by such a definition and by it Christ himself is building his own Church on the rock of the Apostolic See. Obviously the whole Church cannot err in faith.[59] One can ponder how persuasively Scripture commends such a definition of faith. By faith the Church is formed, since according to Hebrews 10 [=11:1], faith is "the substance of things hoped for." Faith corresponds to the acts of building and solidifying, both of which concern the basic structure of the building. Since faith is a gift of God, Christ therefore attributed to himself the building up of the Church upon the Apostolic See, as he said, "On this rock I will build my Church" [Matthew 16:18]. The ministerial service of Peter and his successors is to strengthen the faithful amid the turbulence of uncertainty and questioning about the faith. Hence Our Lord said to Peter, and his successors, "Strengthen your brethren" [Luke 22:32].

Every action of the Apostolic See in defining the faith does nothing more than declare what pertains to the content of the faith given by Christ. In doing this he strengthens his brethren. The Fathers of the Council of Chalcedon affirmed that those gathered at the Council of Constantinople had handed on the doctrine of the Holy Spirit. This did not imply that those gathered earlier in Nicaea were of lower rank but was meant to oppose certain heretics. From this it follows that even the Roman Pontiff himself is subject to definitions of faith by the Apostolic See, just as he is subject to the faith. The Roman Pontiff does not therefore subject anyone anew, since what a person implicitly believed before must be believed when made explicit, for faith is made sufficiently explicit with regard to things previously not explicit as pertaining to the truth of faith. If someone finds this response astonishing, let him recall that it is written, "Marvellous are your testimonies" [Psalm 118:129]. Jesus Christ has given testimony on these matters. Why should the faithful be astonished at such a great help given by divine grace to Christ's vicar on earth? Grace aided Caiaphas when he held pontifical office over the synagogue, as it was losing its rightful character and was persecuting Christ himself. By reason of his pontifical office he was given prophetic speech, as John the Evangelist bore witness: "He did not say this on his own, but being high priest for that year, he prophesied that Jesus would die for the people" [John 11:51]. Why else did John teach and reveal this, if not to reveal the special divine assistance given one in pontifical office?

We respond to the third objection that the love Christ sought three times of Peter pertains to the right exercise of the pastoral office. One therefore not succeeding Peter in love for Christ in no way succeeds him in the upright quality of his pastoral work, but such a one still has the name and office of pastor, even though he is in intent and in actual exercise a hireling.

To the fourth point one should say that loving and feeding the sheep of Christ pertains to the successors of Peter as their commission and obligation. Christ entrusted to him the feeding of his sheep, and to this the successor is bound. He takes on this obligation when he accepts the pontifical office. Hence if he neither loves nor feeds, this text does not therefore cease to pertain to him. Rather feeding the sheep of Christ is highly pertinent, since he is bound to it by command and by office. This text requires that he feed and love, and imposes feeding and loving as his duty. Although one failing to love and feed is unworthy of pastoral office and deserves to be deprived of it, he is not thereby deprived of office. Both testaments bear witness to this. In Ezechiel 34[:2-10], the evil shepherds were condemned for feeding themselves and not God's flock. Prophetic threats were made that God himself would deprive them of the shepherd's office, but they still remained shepherds. In Matthew 23[:2], Our Lord said, "The scribes and Pharisees have sat on the seat of Moses; and so observe and do whatever they say to you, but do not act according to their deeds."

I answer the fifth objection by saying that Gregory was following in the footsteps of his predecessors when he refused the title universal bishop. As he said many times, if one person were called universal bishop, he would appear to be the only bishop and the rest would seem to be deprived of their episcopal office. It was not that the authority of the Roman pontiff was limited and did not extend over the whole Church, but that Gregory abhorred any arrogant words that might be detrimental to the other bishops. He did not reject the fact of apostolic authority extending over the whole Church. We will cite below a passage of Gregory's on Peter's authority over the whole Church. This came in a letter to Emperor Mauritius, in which he said this about Peter: "Care and rule over the whole Church was granted him, although he was not called 'universal apostle'."[60] Gregory was clearly convinced about his care over the whole Church, and also about avoiding the word "universal". Later Roman Pontiffs have agreed and not departed from Gregory's path of humility, for they shift the word "universal" from direct to oblique reference and even today affix their signature as, "I, N., bishop of the Catholic Church."

We answer the sixth objection by recalling that authority is one thing while exercise of authority is something else. By praiseworthy custom, although the Roman Pontiff has authority over the whole Church, he does not exercise authority in particular matters of concern in the other churches, except when some case demands this. Thus it is cutomary that bishops are confirmed by archbishops, pastors are appointed by bishops, and countless things of this kind are done. This is the "ancient custom" of which the Council of Nicaea spoke as it decreed the observance of this "ancient custom". The Roman Pontiff, present through legates, accepted this decree. But this does not mean that the decree touched or diminished the authority of the Roman Pontiff, just as today the authority of the Roman Pontiff is neither diminished or injured when in many places under obedience to the Roman Pontiff authority of this kind is exercised by local officials.

One can say to the seventh point that there are two ways one can understand Christ's appointment of the Roman Pontiff as a prelate over the others. In terms of its inception, this is not so, as we explained above. But in terms of Peter's taking the Roman Church to himself, it is completely true, and in this sense we grant the conclusion that all not acknowledging him as prelate were and are guilty of sin. However we deny the first inference, that is, that the primitive Church was in error, because then Peter had not yet taken the Roman Church to himself, which must occur if the Roman Pontiff is to be over all. At that time it sufficed for the whole Church to acknowledge Peter as pastor of the whole Church. After he took the Roman Church as his own, one must acknowledge the Roman Pontiff, Peter's successor, as pastor of the whole Church, not strictly speaking because he is the Roman Pontiff, but because he is the successor of Peter.

Then it was claimed that a great many martyrs and saints for four hundred years were in sin because they did not acknowledge the Roman Pontiff. But it is not true that these martyrs and saints did not acknowledge the Roman Pontiff, for Peter was acknowledged from the very beginning of the Church, and then the series of Roman Pontiffs who succeeded him, as the saints' texts to follow will make manifest. When it is likewise claimed that Asia, Africa, and Greece erred by not submitting to the Roman Church, this is obviously wrong and based on erroneous evidence and reasoning. Evidence for the contrary can be found in the collected letters of Gregory, which are filled with the concerns of Asia, Africa, and Greece.

The final inference about oriental Christians of today not being under the Roman Church is wrong, providing one is not speaking of the schismatics. This is evident from the Council of Florence held under Eugenius IV, where the Jacobites, Armenians, and Greeks confessed and acknowledged the Roman Pontiff as pastor over the whole Church. Thus, the answer is evident concerning the added argument that their bishops are not appointed by the Pope nor are their Councils held under the Pope's authority. The custom that authority should be exercised in this manner in some places neither diminishes nor injures the Pope's authority. Nonetheless the oriental Christians of our time have often deemed it right to seek from the

Roman Pontiff the appointment of a bishop or the confirmation of one newly chosen. This occurred in the time of both Alexander VI and Julius II.

To the eighth objection we answer that we are speaking of what is by divine right while the objectors allege a condemned deed of violence. Jerome himself testified to this, saying, "Achacius was so influential, that he replaced Liberius with the Arian Felix."[61] Consequently this Felix is not named in the list of Pontiffs, as Augustine bears witness in a letter to Generosus, that is, in Letter 165. When Augustine recounts the Roman Pontiffs from Peter down to his contemporary, Anastasius, he lists Damasus, not Felix, as successor of Liberius.[62]

To the ninth argument we say that the term "Roman Church" can be taken as referring either to the body of the church of Rome in itself or to the head. We grant that the Roman Church in its other members was neither first among the churches nor mother of all, nor was it immediately founded by Christ. Nonetheless, this same Roman Church, in terms of his head, Peter, and of Peter's successors, is first and is mother and teacher of all the churches with authority and solidity granted directly by Christ's word in the Gospel, as we explained above. Hence when decrees and writings of the saints hold that the Roman Church is first and is mother and teacher of all the churches, or that it was founded and made firm by Christ Our Lord's word in the Gospel, then this is true in terms of its head. It is clear that these writings mean just this, from the fact that their views rest on Our Lord's words to Peter, who in himself and in his successors was and is head of the Roman Church. What is said about the church of Jerusalem is not contrary to this primacy, since this church did not come before Peter, and submitted itself to Peter. The others took up collections for the church of Jerusalem because it was in need, not because it was over them, as is clear in Galatians 2[:10]. Thus the last argument is beside the point.

14

TEXTS OF EARLY SAINTS AND COUNCILS ON PETER'S AND THE ROMAN PONTIFF'S PONTIFICAL OFFICE OVER THE WHOLE CHURCH

SYNOPSIS: The aim of Cajetan's final chapter is to demonstrate that the Roman Pontiff was respected as one who by divine right

governed the whole Church as its pastor. The texts selected by
Cajetan fall into four sections. First, he cites the Greek Fathers:
John Chrysostom, Theophylact, Cyril of Alexandria, Maximus the
Confessor and Cyril of Jerusalem. Second, there are texts from early
synods and canonical collections. Third, six Latin Fathers appear,
Cyprian, Ambrose, Jerome, Augustine, Gregory the Great, and Pope
Leo I. Fourth, there are medieval citations on the Roman primacy
from Bede, Bernard of Clairvaux, Thomas Aquinas, and the Councils
of Constance and Florence.[63] Cajetan then concludes his treatise as
follows:

I am passing over a great mass of countless canons and doctors
who hold the same view. Those we have cited make it so obvious
that there is no further room for doubt that in Peter Christ
appointed the Roman Pontiff, Peter's successor, as pastor over the
whole Church. After what we have said, any one still doubting this is
either ignorant and foolish, or aligned with the herectics and
schismatics, or perhaps not even a Christian. Philosophy tells us that
one lacks all training and docility if he demands mathematical
certitude in all areas.[64]

Heretics and schismatics always cite Scripture, but in a sense they
have forced from the text. Truly Catholic Christians wisely grasp the
teaching of Scripture according to the interpretation of the holy
doctors and of the sacred councils bearing apostolic authority.
Whoever rejects this way of knowing Christian truth is no Christian.
Whoever leaves this path falls from faith. For if deviation from this
way be allowed, one may well join Arius in doubting that the triune
God is one substance, one may doubt with the ancients that the
Holy Spirit proceeds from the Son, and one will question whether in
the Sacrament of the Altar bread is changed into the body of Christ.
All these truths are made certain for Christians and defined as
matters of certain faith by no other method or authority than the
interpretations of Sacred Scripture in accord with the teaching of
the saints and the definitions of holy councils on the basis of
apostolic authority.

In the present case, we have relevant texts from the gospels, with
which the teaching of the saints has proven to be without exception
in full agreement. There are moreover the definitions of sacred
councils bearing apostolic authority. Further, every Christian age
from Peter's time down to our own in the holy Catholic Church has

confessed this truth. All this, along with countless testimonies of the other teachers, makes it so certain that the Roman Pontiff, as Peter's successor, was in Peter appointed by Christ pastor of the whole Church, that a more certain article of faith could not be found. Amen.

Rome, in the year of Christian salvation, 1521, the fifty-second year of my life, February 18th.

IV

FIVE ARTICLES OF LUTHER — JUSTIFICATION FOR THEIR CONDEMNATION 1521

[For Pope Leo X:]

Following in the footsteps of Peter the Apostle, we stand ready to given an account to all who ask concerning the faith that is in us [1 Peter 3:15]. Five articles among those condemned in the apostolic letter against Martin Luther have caused alarm to certain outstanding persons. These we wish to enlighten by explaining why the articles were rightly condemned, taking up each article in turn along with the objections we hear are raised by those who are disturbed. Thus we will give a satisfactory account of each article.

1

TRUE PENANCE

The first article reads, "It is a valid maxim, and a teaching ranking ahead of what everyone has up to now said on contrition, that an excellent penance is to sin no more, and the best penance is a new life."[1] It is therefore objected that on this article all the holy Fathers appear to agree with Luther, and consequently there can be no error or heresy in the article.

We answer that the article was rightly condemned both according to its meaning in itself and according to the sense intended by Luther.

If the maxim is taken according to the literal sense of the words, it turns out to be false, since neither an excellent nor the best penance is one in which there is no forgiveness of sins. For our Savior declared in the last chapter of Luke that Christian penance entails forgiveness of sins, as he said that penance for the forgiveness of sins should be preached [Luke 24:47]. But the two elements mentioned in the article, not sinning again and a new life, clearly do not suffice as penance for the forgiveness of sins, since in addition there must be sorrow over one's past sin, as Peter wept bitterly after the sin he committed [Luke 22:62], and one must also have recourse to the divine mercy, praying with the publican, "God, be merciful to me a sinner" [Luke 18:13]. Hence we read in Ecclesiasticus 21[:1], "Have you sinned, son? Then do so no more, but pray over your sins that they may be forgiven." Augustine noted, in commenting on this verse, that it was not sufficient to say, "Do so no more," but that prayer for forgiveness of previous sins was explicitly added.[2]

It is therefore not excellent penance to sin no more, nor is the best penance a new life, if these do not include sorrow for one's sins and prayer over them. See how the article would lead to overly hasty penance, since according to it the most excellent and best penance of an avaricious person would be to cease from acts of avarice and to live a life of generosity. Similarly an intemperate person would cease following his unruly passions and would live continently from then on. This would hold for other cases, since this is the meaning of sinning no more and living a new life. But if this constitutes the most excellent and very best penance, then there is no point to what we believe about the need for remorse over one's sins and having recourse to God for forgiveness. The article was as a consequence rightly condemned according to the meaning it has in itself.

If the same article is taken in the sense in which it emanated from Luther, the condemnation will also appear well-founded. He offered this kind of maxim in his denial of two parts of penance, namely, contrition and satisfaction. The intention for which the maxim was used was the removal of any need for contrition, which consists principally in sorrow for sins, and for satisfaction. This much is clear in his books and in the other condemned articles.[3]

Hence the article cited does not agree with the holy Fathers, either in its literal sense or as it comes from Martin. If, however, an opinion like this were to be found in the holy Fathers, then it should be benignly interpreted and taken in a good sense.

2

BELIEF ONE IS FORGIVEN

The second article reads, "No one's sins are forgiven, unless he believes they are forgiven when the priest forgives . . . ."[4] The objection is that this article seems to enunciate the unvarnished truth, resting as it does on a firm foundation in faith.

We answer that there are two manners in which one can believe his sins are forgiven when the priest absolves. This can rest on the sacrament, or on the person who is absolved.

Believing in the first manner is necessary for forgiveness of sins, since such belief is an act of infused faith, without which one cannot please God. But believing in the second manner is not necessary for forgiveness of sins, since the penitent who is absolved may piously doubt whether his own disposition is sufficient for worthy reception of the sacrament. Job said, "I fear concerning all my works" [Job 9:28, Vulgate]. Isaiah 64[:6] says, "All our righteousness is like a filthy rag." And even having this pious doubt, he can receive the sacrament of absolution worthily and attain forgiveness of his sins, since a pious doubt of this kind is not contrary to the firm foundation of infused faith, but is contrary rather to the firmness of acquired faith. Clearly it is a matter of acquired faith to believe that one is himself sufficiently or not sufficiently disposed.

Consequently the article is established as false, since a person's sins can be forgiven if he does not believe, but piously doubts because of his own disposition, that his sins are forgiven. This does not detract from the firm foundation of Christian faith, which does not include the fact that my sins are forgiven, but that they are forgiven when I worthily receive the sacrament of penance. Similarly it is not a matter of Christian faith that the body of Christ is in this particular host. Our faith is rather that, given the fulfillment of all requirements for the sacrament of the Eucharist, the body of Christ is in this host. This article therefore does not contain the unvarnished truth, but was rightly condemned as false.

3

RIGHTLY APPROACHING HOLY COMMUNION

The third article is this: "They are greatly mistaken who confidently approach the sacrament of Communion because they have confessed, because they know they are without mortal sin, and because of their prayers and preparations."[5]

It is objected that this article also rests firmly on our faith and consequently appears neither erroneous nor heretical.

We answer by first granting that it would be a great error to approach the sacrament of Communion with such confidence if this were understood as a means of justification. This would be contrary to the apostolic teaching found in the saying, "I am not aware of anything against me, but I am not thereby justified" [1 Corinthians 4:4]. But it is no error to approach using this same confidence as a preservative against the sin of unworthy reception of the sacrament of the Eucharist. This latter is an apostolic counsel. When the same Apostle teaches how one avoids unworthy reception of the sacrament and escapes eating and drinking judgment upon himself, he says, "Let a man examine himself, and so eat of the bread and drink of the cup." [1 Corinthians 11:28]. Here he shows that one who examines himself approaches the sacrament securely, because he is not guilty of profaning the body and blood of the Lord, nor does he eat and drink judgment upon himself.

Now the Christian people frequently hear both teachings of the Apostle, namely, that each one can attest for himself by examining himself before reception of the sacrament of Communion as to his contrition, confession, prayer, and the like, and then he may use this confidence as a preservative against unworthy reception, but not as a means of justification. Because this is true, this Lutheran article was condemned as destructive of the holy confidence of the Christian people, as scandalous, and as inimical to apostolic teaching.

4

THE TREASURY OF INDULGENCES

The fourth article reads as follows: "The treasury of the Church from which the Pope grants indulgences is not the merits of Christ . . ."[6]

It is objected that since Luther cannot be refuted on this point by any normative text, the censure simply constructs a decree and asserts the bull.[7]

We preface our answer by noting that all matters of Church teaching cannot be demonstrated for Christians to the same degree nor in the same manner. Although some matters are more explicit in Holy Scripture and others less so, we still say that in all questions authority suffices to prove. Take an example from the sacraments: everything is proven concerning baptism by authority because both its matter and form are explicit in Holy Scripture; but regarding the sacrament of confirmation, even though neither the matter, nor form, nor institution is explicit in Holy Scripture, one attains proof by the authority with which the Apostles imposed hands and by which the Church uses this. This is true in many other cases.

It is true that on the matter of the treasury of indulgences Luther cannot be refuted by any normative text because this is not as explicit in Holy Scripture as is baptism. But it is inane to seek the same degree of certitude in every matter taught by the Church. If one asks respectfully by what authority Luther can be refuted concerning the treasury of indulgences, the answer is not difficult. Luther can find proof radically in Holy Scripture, implicitly in the universal Church, and explicitly in the Roman church and many holy doctors.

Scripture refers to the treasury of the superabundant sufferings of Christ and the saints and indicates their satisfactory value. The fact that by his sufferings Christ satisfied to a greater extent than is required by all those to whom his passion is applied, is both apparent in itself and taught by John the Evangelist: "He is the expiation for our sins and not for ours only but for the sins of the whole world" [1 John 2:2]. But in actual effect the passion of Christ is not applied as satisfaction for the sins of the whole world. Consequently the whole amount of satisfaction which could satisfy for the lost, is now left in excess. The fact that many of the saints have suffered more than was required to satisfy for their own sins, is attested by holy Job, when he said, "Would that the calamities I suffer were weighed in the balance against the sins by which I merited wrath. Now my calamities outweigh the sands of the ocean" [Job 6:2f, Vulgate]. The same is true of many other saints, especially the martyrs, who like Job endured so much. Especially the most blessed Virgin, who had to satisfy for no sin of her own but still suffered, as Simeon said, the piercing of her soul by the sword of Christ [Luke 2:35], and so is held to be more than a martyr.

Scripture does not just teach the existence of this treasury, but also that it has been constituted by Christ and the saints for the purpose of being of benefit to the Church. The Apostle bore witness to this in Colossians 1 [:24] when he said, "I fill up in my flesh what is lacking in the sufferings of Christ for his body, that is, the Church." The same thing could be said both of Paul and of the other saints who suffer more than is required as satisfaction for their sins.

This most devout conclusion is not disproven by the other statement of the Apostle, "The sufferings of this present time are not to be compared to the glory that is to come" [Romans 8:18].[8] For the sufferings of the saints, specifically as meritorious of a coming reward, are without a doubt not of comparable value with this. God rewards them beyond what they deserve, as this verse indicates in saying they are not comparable to the glory that is to come. But these same sufferings of the saints, specifically as satisfactory, are frequently superabundant, that is, as often as the saints suffer more for Christ than is due as punishment for their own actual sins. Since they are not in a position to apply these precisely as satisfactions to themselves (since they have no sins for which to satisfy), there remain superabundant satisfactions, which therefore, as the Apostle taught, are left over for the body of Christ, that is, the Church.

Hence Luther can be refuted by the authority of Holy Scripture which shows that in the Church of God there is a treasury of the merits of Christ and the saints, in so far as these are superabundant satisfactions, and that this treasury exists for the benefit of the body of Christ, that is, the Church.

One should then add to this that the whole Church approves indulgences as grants of holy Mother Church replacing the penitential satisfaction which is the third part of the sacrament of penance. It thereby becomes evident that indulgences are means of satisfaction before the divine justice for punishment due to our actual sins which otherwise would be carried out before the same divine justice in penitential satisfaction. On the basis of this approbation by the whole Church, one must conclude one of two things: either indulgences have this satisfactory value as acts of pure authority, or that they derive from the treasury we have described.[9] Since the first alternative is absurd and inadmissable, we must conclude that indulgences have their satisfactory value from the treasury described above. This has in fact been frequently expressed authoritatively by the Roman church, the teacher of all the churches. And one could add the authority of saints like Thomas, Bonaventure, and others.

The perceptive person will consequently understand that it is false that Luther could not be refuted by an authoritative proof for the treasury of indulgences.

5

PAPAL AUTHORITY IN QUESTIONS OF FAITH

The fifth article is this: "If the Pope along with a great part of the Church holds a certain view, even if it is not erroneous, it is nonetheless neither sin nor heresy to hold the opposite view, especially in a matter not related to the salvation of one's soul, until one or other view has been condemned or approved by a general council."[10]

The objection is that those condemning this article hold the superiority of the Pope over a general council, a position that can never be proven on the authority of Scripture, as the Patriarch of Antioch declared in his book comparing the Supreme Pontiff to a sacred council.[11]

We answer that the objectors are wrong in thinking the condemnation of this article rests on the opinion that the Pope is superior to a council. The condemnation takes no account of this dispute, since it rests on another basis, namely, that the Supreme Pontiff has authority to judge questions of faith. The sacred canons teach often that the Supreme Pontiff has such authority, and Jerome attested to it in writing to Damasus, "If this my confession finds approval in your apostolic judgment, then whoever ventures to accuse me will not show that I am a heretic but will rather prove that he himself is inept or evil-minded, or even not a Catholic."[12] Our Lord disclosed this authority when he said to Peter, "I have prayed for you that your faith not fail; when you have turned, strengthen your brethren" [Luke 22:32].

The article was condemned because of the hidden poison in the words, "until one or other view . . . by a general council." This asserts that a definitive judgment rendered by the Supreme Pontiff in a question of faith does not bind and that to hold the opposite view is neither sin nor heresy. This is entailed in the words, "until it has been approved or condemned by a general council." Since experience, our teacher in practical matters, attests that many heresies have been condemned by the Apostolic See without any general council, this article was therefore justly condemned.

This then, most blessed Father, is what in the midst of many illnesses I have gladly written out of obedience to you, and submit to your apostolic judgment. With the objectors brought to silence, and no one accused, may the truth find free access into the hearts of each.

Rome, June 6, 1521.

V

ERRORS IN A BOOKLET ON THE LORD'S SUPPER — INSTRUCTION FOR THE NUNTIO 1525

1
THE EUCHARIST IN JOHN 6

The first position to be answered is that in John 6 Our Lord did not speak of the Eucharist, both because the subject of his discourse was man's faith and trust in Christ, and because he said in this chapter, "He who eats my flesh and drinks my blood abides in me and I in him" [John 6:56]. But it is obvious that many partake of the sacrament of the Eucharist and then do not abide in Christ through faith informed by love.[1]

The learned reader should note both the truth and the error in what is said here. It is true that in John 6 Our Lord spoke of the need of faith in himself that is informed by love. He spoke first of faith in his divinity and then of faith in his death for the life of the world. But it is false to say that this therefore ruled out a reference to faith in the sacrament of the Eucharist in that discourse.

This will be clear if one recalls the three different aspects of the Eucharist. First, there is the sacrament itself, which we adore. Second, there is a sacramental eating which is the same for good and evil men alike. The Apostle says in 1 Corinthians 11[:27], "Whoever eats and drinks unworthily . . . , " which obviously means that the unworthy eat and drink sacramentally. They receive the sacred Host as a sacrament and not merely as bread, since they receive in the belief that it is the sacrament of the body of Christ. Third, proper to the good, there is spiritual eating through faith informed by love. This is a refreshment of the soul's spiritual life, namely, that life spoken of in Galatians 2[:20], "I live, now not I, but Christ lives in me."

Since there are these three aspects of the Eucharist, the fact that in John 6 Our Lord did not speak of one of these ways, namely, of sacramental eating, does not justify the conclusion that the other two were excluded. In fact he did speak of them, that is, of the sacrament itself and of spiritual eating of the sacrament. His words referred clearly to spiritual eating when he said, "Whoever eats my flesh and drinks my blood abides in me and I in him" [John 6:56]. Spiritual eating of the Eucharistic sacrament is to abide in Christ through faith informed by love and conversely for Christ to abide in oneself. The fact that he spoke as well of the sacrament itself is clear from the future tense when he said, "The bread which I will give . . ." [6:51]. He had not instituted the sacrament of the Eucharist when he said this in the Capernaum synagogue. We know that the sacrament of the Eucharist was instituted in Jerusalem on the night he was betrayed. Reference to the sacrament itself is also found in the distinction he made between eating and drinking: "Unless you eat the flesh of the Son of Man and drink his blood, you will not have life in you" [6:53]. If he were speaking of faith only in his death for the life of the world, it would have sufficed to refer to his death for the life of the world by speaking of the separation of his flesh and blood that occurred on the cross. But he not only indicated the separation of his flesh and blood for the life of the world, but also commanded that if we desire to have life in us we should eat his flesh and drink his blood. Thereby he made known that he was going to institute the sacrament of his body and blood in the form of food and drink. His flesh and blood is both immolated on the cross and contained in the sacrament. Only if we spiritually eat and drink his flesh and blood will we have life in us. It is thereby indicated that it is necessary for salvation to believe as well in the sacrament of the Eucharist.

Furthermore, it was John the Evangelist's purpose to treat the more sublime mysteries of Christ which the other evangelists had treated less fully. But in John's account of the Last Supper there is nothing about the Eucharist. Because the other evangelists had expressed the sacramental reception of the Eucharist, John set out to describe its spiritual reception and effect, as in the words, "He who eats my flesh and drinks my blood has eternal life" [6:54]. If John had not been concerned about this spiritual aspect of the sacrament, he would not have taken so much care to distinguish the acts of eating and drinking and to affirm that together they now lead to our abiding in Christ and Christ's abiding in us. He also taught the future unending effect, eternal life, and spoke of the necessity of both ("Unless you eat . . . "[6:53]). What is here drawn together shows that the Evangelist wrote about a spiritual eating and drinking not only of the death of Christ, but as well of the sacrament of Christ's death under the form of food and drink.[2]

If all this is compared with the text of the Gospel, the learned reader can easily see, first, that it is true that John 6 does speak of informed faith in Christ the Son of God and in his death for the life of the world. Also, admittedly, the chapter does not treat sacramental eating. But it is not true that this chapter excludes the informed faith which is spiritual eating of the sacrament of the Eucharist.

This much concerns the first position.

2

THE MEANING OF JOHN 6:63

The second position is that Our Lord's words in John 6 [:63], "The flesh avails nothing," exclude his true flesh from the sacrament of the Eucharist. The proper sense of this verse is that the eating of flesh is in itself of no benefit. The fact that the Jews had just asked, "How can this man give us his flesh to eat?" [6:52] is said to show this is the natural meaning of Our Lord's words, "The flesh avails nothing." Since both the question and the discourse concerned eating, the answer that the flesh avails nothing must refer to flesh in connection with eating, meaning equivalently, "Eaten flesh avails nothing." It thus follows that flesh is not eaten in this sacrament, and that there is no flesh present, because it avails nothing. Since flesh avails nothing, there should be no question about flesh in reference to this sacrament.[3]

This constantly repeated position is alleged as the unshakeable foundation of all the errors proposed. But one should first take note that interpreting "The flesh avails nothing" as "Eaten flesh avails nothing" is not in accord with the literal sense of the words, since it

explicitly contradicts the context in the Gospel. In this same context
Our Lord said that his eaten flesh gives eternal life. "He who eats my
flesh and drinks my blood has eternal life" [6:54]. Thus the gloss,
"Eaten flesh avails nothing," is contrary to both the meaning and
the words of Our Lord.

If one were to defend this interpretation by saying that the
interpreter's intention is to refer not to spiritual but to carnal eating,
then you would have the sense of the text, because the words of Our
Lord would not be interpreted as excluding his flesh from the
sacrament. For the Church does not teach that the flesh of Christ is
eaten carnally in this sacrament. Ruling out carnally eaten flesh from
this sacrament is quite correct, but this does not therefore mean that
the true flesh of Christ is therefore ruled out of the sacrament.
Rather, the true flesh of Christ is to be eaten spiritually in this
sacrament, and when eaten spiritually it gives eternal life. In fact,
spiritual eating is of such great importance that we say of any
reception of the flesh of Christ in this sacrament that, unless it is a
spiritual eating, it avails nothing.

Second, take note that the genuine sense of this verse can be
explained in two ways, both of which lead to one and the same
understanding of the truth affirmed. One explanation begins from
the fact that in this verse Christ did not refer any more to his own
than to another's flesh, but spoke simply of flesh in an absolute
sense. He did not say, "My flesh avails nothing," but, "Flesh avails
nothing." Here Christ spoke of the flesh as distinct from the Spirit.
The Gospel context bears witness to this sense in the words, "It is
the Spirit that gives life, the flesh avails nothing" [John 6:63]. The
flesh is undoubtedly unavailing in giving life.

A second way of understanding the verse would be, "The flesh
alone avails nothing," with "alone" excluding the Spirit. It is as if it
read, "The flesh without the Spirit avails nothing toward eternal life,
since it is the Spirit that gives life." This interpretation has a twofold
foundation: first, the absolute sense of "flesh" (since it is clear that
flesh taken simply in itself without the Spirit gives nothing toward
eternal life) and, second, the distinction Our Lord made between
flesh and Spirit. The interpretation is confirmed by the way it
squares with the purpose at hand. The flesh of Christ had just been
described as giving eternal life when eaten, and now it is shown that
without the Spirit this avails nothing toward eternal life. This is true,

since however much the flesh of Christ was crucified for us, it avails nothing without the Spirit of adoption as sons of God.

Another confirmation is that in this way the verse is a direct answer to the Jews who asked [John 6:52], "How can this man give us his flesh to eat?" Christ was not speaking of flesh alone when he said, "My flesh is truly food," and "Unless you eat the flesh of the son of man . . . " [6:55.53], for flesh alone is of no avail toward eternal life. Rather, he was speaking of his flesh accompanied by the Spirit, for it is the Spirit that gives life, and thus they could grasp that his flesh is indeed to be eaten, but under the action of the Spirit bringing about the eating. If the Spirit does bring about the eating of his flesh, then what he said will be true: "Whoever eats my flesh has eternal life" [John 6:54].

Another way of interpreting the verse is to take "flesh" not as a substantive but as referring to a fleshly function. Thus, the meaning is that fleshly food avails nothing. This meaning is derived from the same source as in the case above where "flesh" was taken in an absolute sense and not as referring to Our Lord's own flesh in the words, "The flesh avails nothing." He distinguished flesh from Spirit, and with reference to eating said that it is the Spirit who gives life while the flesh is of no avail. The meaning is that fleshly food avails nothing, but spiritual food gives life. This was a direct answer to the question posed by the Jews who asked not about the substance of what was promised but about the way it would be given [John 6:52]: "How can this man give us his flesh to eat?" Presupposing the gift of flesh, they asked how it would be given. Our Lord answered that the manner is not fleshly but spiritual. Flesh, that is , fleshly food, is of no avail toward eternal life, but spiritual food gives life to the soul.

The fact that in Holy Scripture "flesh" can refer not to the substance of flesh but to a fleshly function is clear from the Apostle in 1 Corinthians 15[:50], "Flesh and blood cannot inherit the kingdom of God." It is clear that the fleshly function, not the substance of flesh and blood, is not excluded from the kingdom of God. For when we rise, we like Christ will have flesh and bones.

The context of John 6 shows that in this passage "flesh" does not refer to the substance of flesh, for Our Lord said of the substance of his flesh, "He who eats my flesh and drinks my blood has eternal life" [6:54]. Clearly the substance of his flesh, when eaten spiritually avails greatly and gives life, that is, eternal life. Therefore, the saying, "The flesh avails nothing," is not about flesh as a substance, but refers literally to the fleshly function, as is clear from the carnal-minded question of the Jews ("How can this man give us his flesh to eat?" [6:52]) to which they are a direct answer. "Flesh," that is, fleshly food, profits nothing, while spiritual food gives eternal life. They were thereby given to understand what he meant by claiming, "Unless you eat the flesh of the Son of Man . . .", and "My flesh is truly food" [6:53.55]. He was speaking here of spiritual, not carnal food.

Similarly Our Lord spoke to Nicodemus about spiritual birth: "Unless one is reborn of water and the Spirit, he cannot enter the kingdom of God" [John 3:5]. To rule out carnal birth, he added immediately, "That which is born of flesh is flesh, and that which is born of the Spirit is spirit" [3:6]. Thus, when the Jews asked [John 6:52], "How can this man give us his flesh to eat?" he answered, "It is the Spirit that gives life, the flesh avails nothing" [6:63]. His meaning is that fleshly food profits only the flesh, while it is spiritual food that gives life. If you wish to draw both interpretations into one statement, you have this: Flesh received in a fleshly manner is of no avail for the life of the soul, but when endowed with the Spirit it gives life.

From all this the learned reader will understand that while Our Lord did speak of flesh with reference to eating ("Flesh avails nothing" [6:63]), it is false to apply this to the flesh eaten. He was speaking of flesh as fleshly food. It is also wrong to conclude from these words to the exclusion of the true flesh of Christ from the Eucharist. So, if you want to convince these men made bold by the words of the Gospels, ask them whether the flesh of Christ eaten spiritually profits toward eternal life. If it does so profit, then the true flesh of Christ when eaten is of profit. Thus we conclude that Our Lord's words, "The flesh profits nothing," do not rule out a spiritual eating being of profit. If it does not help because flesh avails nothing, then Our Lord's words spoken in the same place would be false: "He who eats my flesh and drinks my blood has eternal life."

This suffices on the second position.

3

CORPOREAL RECEPTION OF THE EUCHARIST?

The third argument is that theologians themselves allege that in the Eucharist the body of Christ is received corporeally and perceptibly. This conclusion is said to follow from the confession of faith demanded of Berengar found in the Section *De consecratione*, Distinction 2, beginning *"Ego Berengarius."*[4]

This argument is utterly false. Theologians do not say that the body of Christ is received corporeally and perceptibly, but rather that it is received spiritually and not grasped perceptibly either by the senses or the mind. They say that the body of Christ is received in the Eucharist in faith, while it is the sacramental species that are received corporeally and perceptibly.

One should interpret the words of Berengar's confession on the basis of what it intended. Berengar held the error this man is seeking to revive, namely, that the flesh of Christ was in the sacrament only as in a sign. But the Catholic Church confesses that the flesh of Christ is not simply signified but really contained in this sacrament. The Fathers of the Synod decreed out of detestation of this error that Berengar was to confess that the body of Christ is received sensibly, is taken by the priests' hands, and is torn by our teeth. By these words Christians were given to understand that in receiving the Eucharist they receive not merely the sacrament, that is, a holy sign, of the flesh of Christ, but receive as well the species containing the flesh of Christ. Heretics had denied and attacked this truth. But the Fathers did not think nor want others to understand that the flesh of Christ is itself felt, touched, and torn by our teeth. Christ's faithful would not even dream of saying this. The difference lies in the fact that Berengar first said Christ is eaten in a sign alone and then was forced by the Catholic faith to confess that the flesh of Christ is eaten not only as in a sign but as contained in the Eucharistic sacrament.

This is enough on the third argument.

4

THE FREEDOM AND OBJECT OF FAITH

The fourth view is that theologians err on two points. First, they think that faith comes from man's judgment and choice. Second, they hold that faith has to do with sensibly perceptible realities. The latter is judged wrong, since no one believes something he senses or sees.[5]

The learned reader will easily grasp the mistake on the first point, since theologians will agree with Paul the Apostle in Ephesians 2 [:8] that faith is the gift of God. But this gift is not granted to one who is unwilling. Rather one must be willing and disposed for the gift by voluntarily choosing Christianity. Thus, regarding this disposition it is true that faith depends on man's choice.

The second proposition can be both right and wrong. If one understands that faith extends to sensibly perceptible realities as to what is believed, this is wrong. It is clear that what is believed is not perceived. But theologians do not mean this when they say that faith extends to things perceived by the senses. They agree with Paul in Hebrews 11 [:1] that faith grasps things not seen.

If one understands that faith extends to sensibly perceptible things as the outward extensions of what is believed, this is correct. It is quite wrong to object to this, since many things in which we believe involve a union between visible and invisible realities. Since one must believe in this union it follows then that faith does have to do with sensibly perceptible reality as one member in the union in which we believe. Regarding the mystery of the Incarnation this is clear, since we say that the Word was made flesh. The mystery lies in the union of the Word with sensibly perceptible flesh. This union cannot be believed if faith does not extend to flesh. If we were to see Christ present before us, we would not believe in the flesh, which we would see, but in the union of divinity with his flesh. Thus our faith would extend to the flesh we see, not specifically as seen, but as the outer extension of an invisible union with the Deity. Clearly one who denies that faith has to do with sensibly perceived reality must deny the Christian belief in the mystery of the Incarnate Word. It is the same in the position under discussion here. Our faith does not direct itself to the species of the Eucharistic sacrament, since we see them. But we believe in the presence of the body of Christ under these species. Faith grasps the marvelous union of the species with the body of Christ, not the species itself which we see and feel.

Let this suffice on the fourth view.

5

THE TRUE BODY, BUT EATEN SPIRITUALLY

The fifth error is that these two are mutually exclusive: the true body of Christ being in the sacrament of the Eucharist, and this body being eaten spiritually. Spirit and body are said to be so opposed that one cannot be the other. The identity of the two is seen as implied in the claim that corporeal flesh is eaten spiritually.[6]

The perceptive reader will readily see how ridiculous this argument becomes, simply by confusing the thing itself with the manner of its existence. No one is so foolish to say that a spirit is a body. We say, rather, that the body of Christ has a spiritual manner of existence in this sacrament. The true body is present in the sacrament, but not in a corporeal manner. It is present corporeally in heaven, but not so in the sacrament. In the sacrament the body does not exist occupying space, but is present in a spiritual manner that the human mind cannot grasp. In the same way we cannot grasp how the Word is united with the assumed humanity, nor how the one God is three persons. But we believe these, in spite of our lack of understanding. Similarly the true body of Christ is eaten in the sacrament, not in a corporeal manner, but spiritually. Thus we say that Christ's body is not chewed by a physical eating, although the sacramental species of his body are chewed. The true flesh of Christ is contained beneath these species, and the soul's spiritual eating attains to this flesh of Christ present in the sacrament.

This is our response to the fifth error.

6

A CHARGE OF OBSCURANTISM

The sixth topic is the allegation that theologians forbid Christians to think about the mysteries of the Eucharist, lest the truth come to light.[7]

One feels silly responding to such an allegation. Clearly theologians temper their advice according to the abilities of the people they address. They urge retarded and uneducated persons to simply believe in what is taught about the Trinity, about this sacrament, about predestination, and the like. They follow the saying, "Seek not among things exalted above you" [Sirach 3:22, Vulgate]. But persons capable of grasping the mysteries of faith are urged to ponder them and through Holy Scripture to come to know the mysteries of faith, including the sacrament of the Eucharist.

No more is needed on the sixth topic.

7

"THIS IS MY BODY"

The seventh contention is that in the words of consecration, "This is my body," the word "is" is not to be understood in its literal meaning, but in a non-literal way, as meaning "signifies". The sense of the words would be "This signifies my body." Thus the body of Christ is present in this sacrament only as in a sign.

Four arguments are given. First, "is" often occurs in Holy Scripture with the meaning "signifies", as in Genesis 41[:26f] Matthew 13[:38f], and Luke 8[:12.14f].[8] Second, they argue that we must understand "signifies" for "is" in the words of consecration, since we face the alternative between charging Christ with error in saying, "Flesh avails nothing" [John 6:63] — which is sacrilegious — and taking "is" as "signifies". The implication is clear: if "is" is taken literally, the true flesh of Christ would be present in this sacrament as availing toward eternal life and Christ would be wrong in saying, "Flesh avails nothing."[9] Third, the same conclusion is urged from the nature of faith. Since a body can be perceived and touched, it is in no way related to faith.[10] Fourth, they argue that taking "is" as "signifies" fits well with everything else concerning this sacrament. It fits with Our Lord's words, "Do this in remembrance of me" [1 Corinthians 11:24], and with Paul's statement, "As often as you eat this bread and drink this cup, you proclaim the death of the Lord" [1 Corinthians 11:26]. Also this interpretation fits with the description in 1 Corinthians 11[:18] of the way the primitive Church assembled for the Lord's Supper.[11]

In response, each argument can be taken separately. The first point is true in stating that in Holy Scripture "is" sometimes means "signifies". But it is wrong in not discerning between the different manners of speaking found in Scripture. At times Scripture speaks metaphorically, and at times literally. When the language is metaphorical, "is" can mean "signify", as in "the rock was Christ" [1 Corinthians 10:4], "I am the true vine" [John 15:1], "I am the door" [John 10:7], and other similar statements. In these cases the law of figurative speech forces us to understand "to be", "it is", "he was", "I am", and "I was" not literally but as expressing a similarity. Obviously, all the texts he gives in the first argument are of this kind. But when Scripture is not speaking figuratively but literally, then "it is", "to be", "he was", and "it was" are never taken in a sense other than their literal meaning, but according to this literal meaning. In the present case it is clear that Christ did not speak figuratively of his body, but referred to his own true body when he said, "This is my body." Even the adversaries admit this. Therefore those are wrong who take "is" as "signifies" merely because this must be done in figurative and metaphorical language.

The second argument, that is, that flesh avails nothing, does not require extensive refutation. It was shown in our second chapter that in the words, "The flesh avails nothing" [John 6:63], Our Lord merely meant that flesh alone, or fleshly food, is unavailing toward eternal life. This truth fits together perfectly with the other truth that "this", the substance beneath these accidents, "is my body." For the body of Christ contained in this sacrament is not carnal food, nor does it avail without the Spirit.

It is amazing that so patent an error would be urged as is contained in the third argument from the nature of faith, namely, that corporeal reality in no way pertains to faith. The Creed is filled with references to Christ crucified, dead, and buried, to his ascension into heaven, and to the resurrection of the body. These are all corporeal. How can one say that whatever is corporeal in no way pertains to faith?

In the fourth point, namely, that everything fits together that is said about this sacrament, you must beware of poison. It is certainly true that this sacrament is a memorial and recollection of the death of Christ, and, what is greater, it is a sign of the body of Christ. We know how often theologians treat the teaching of Book IV of the *Sentences* that the sacramental species are the sign of a twofold reality, namely, of the natural body of Christ as therein both contained and signified, and of the mystical body of Christ which is not contained but is signified.[12] We agree that all this is true. But now this man argues from statements about sign, memorial, and the like, to a denial that the flesh of Christ is contained. As if the two cannot go together, that is, that both sign and what is signified cannot be in the sacrament. The fact is, both do most truly go together, but this man argues from one partial truth to the exclusion of the other truth. Clearly, the assembly of the Corinthians for the Lord's Supper, the proclamation of the death of Christ, and whatever else of this kind that is said, are all true in what they affirm. However, they do not deny the other truth, the presence of the body of Christ in the same sacrament.

We can see that the assembly of the Corinthians for the Lord's Supper, as the Apostle Paul indicated, was not an assembly merely for giving thanks, or only for bread taken as a sign, but for sacramentally receiving the true body of Christ. Otherwise Paul would not have said, "whoever eats and drinks unworthily, eats and drinks judgment upon himself" [1 Corinthians 11:27]. Why did he add, ". . . not discerning the body of the Lord" [11:29]? If they assembled to receive only a sign of the body of Our Lord, one would not be guilty of unworthily receiving the body and blood of the Lord. Clearly one is not guilty of profaning the body and blood of the Lord if he unworthily receives bread in the Church, if he eats blessed bread (as is done in many Churches), or if he as a Christian is present at divine services.

Nonetheless by assembling in the Church for these actions, we profess we are Christians and that as Christians we belong to the mystical body of Christ. Similarly when the heretics assemble for the Lord's Supper, they too profess they belong to the mystical body of Christ. From the Apostle's teaching concerning that assembly, we learn therefore that the assembly for the Lord's Supper entails more than bread taken as a sign, since we are instructed that one is guilty of profaning the body and blood of the Lord, if he receives unworthily.

We must ask our adversaries, what other words should the Apostle have used to indicate the true body of Christ, if these are not sufficiently clear? What words should Christ have used, if it is not enough to say, "This is my body." One should then refute them by asking, if these words of Christ and Paul do not sufficiently teach the presence of the true body of Christ in the Sacrament of the

Eucharist, then will you please say what they should have said to express the presence of the true body of Christ in the sacrament? These words, "This is my body," in their most literal sense signify that the substance indicated beneath the accidents of bread is the body of Christ. If these words, spoken literally, do not suffice, then no words would suffice. If he had used metaphorical language, the meaning would be ambiguous. If he had used a circumlocution, our certainty would be reduced and the truth of our explanation would be less. Every sense other than the literal is less than the literal.

Tell us also how else Paul should have explained the sacramental eating of the true body of Christ, if he did not do this by saying, "Whoever eats and drinks unworthily, eats and drinks judgment upon himself because he does not discern the body of the Lord," and then by explaining, "He is guilty of profaning the body and blood of the Lord" [1 Corinthians 11:27]. These words express it so clearly, that it cannot be more clearly expressed. He says one will be guilty of profaning not a sign of the body and blood but the body and blood themselves. The adversaries should be ashamed of themselves.

In order to understand clearly the words of consecration, "This is my body," you should first recall that it is only when they are completely said that their truth is decided. This is not specific to this sentence but holds for it and for all declaratory statements. The reason is that the truth of a declaratory statement accompanies the meaning of the statement. A declaratory statement is not true before it means something. Before its meaning is complete, it is neither true nor false. It is also evident that the meaning of a statement is not complete before it is completely said. Hence before this, it is neither true nor false. Consequently if the priest does not finish saying the words, the sacrament is not confected.

Recall secondly that these words not only express the truth, but also bring about the truth they express. They express that this is the body of Christ, which is utterly true once these words have been said in the person of Christ, in whose person it is clear the priest affirms, "This is my body." They also bring about that this is the body of Christ. The meaning is expressed by the words themselves, but their effectiveness is confessed by Christian faith. We believe these words transform the bread into the body of Christ. Faith alone suffices to grasp this.

Consequently you can join two things as verified together at the end of the saying of these words, namely, both being and becoming. For this has become and is the body of Christ. Being corresponds to the true meaning of "This is my body." Becoming corresponds to true effectiveness, that is, to this becoming the body of Christ. Together and in the very same instance, it is verified that this has become and is the body of Christ. If one untrained in natural philosophy finds it amazing that something becomes and is in the same instant, he should consult the philosophical rule on instantaneous effects in which the same thing both becomes and is such in the same instant. This is true of the air which by instantaneous illumination both is and becomes actually diaphanous in the same instant.

Proceeding from these points, it is first clear that in the words, "This is my body," the pronoun "this" indicates neither the bread nor the body of Christ, since an indication of the bread would go against the truth of what is. Then the sense would be that this, this bread, is my body — which is patently false. This bread is not the body of Christ, neither at the end of the words, nor afterwards, nor before, since bread is never the body of Christ. However, once the sacrament is confected and while it continues to be, it is true that what was bread is the body of Christ. Nonetheless it is never true that bread is the body of Christ. An indication referring to the body of Christ would go against true becoming or the truth of what is brought about, since the body of Christ is not made the body of Christ. If the pronoun "this" were indicating the body of Christ, this would mean that this, my body, is my body. This would not be brought about by the words, but would be quite true before the words were said.

Consequently referring the pronoun "this" to the bread goes against the true meaning of the words, because bread is never the body of Christ. Referring the pronoun "this" to the body of Christ goes against the effectiveness of the same words because the body of Christ is not made the body of Christ nor is it transformed into the body of Christ.

Consequently the pronoun "this" must refer to that which pertains to both being and becoming, that is, that which is indicated uniquely as becoming and being the body of Christ. As the ancient Fathers have taught, this is an individual substance independent of the determinate nature of bread or the body of Christ. This is not an arbitrary assertion, since the pronoun "this" is undoubtedly demonstrative of a single substance. Thus they speak of it as referring to an individual substance. The grammarians also teach that "this" means the substance independent of the quality giving it a determinate nature. Since the reference of the pronoun is to no more than this, and this kind of indication fits well with both becoming and being, they therefore conclude that in these words the pronoun "this" indicates the substance beneath these accidents but without specifying its nature as bread or as the body of Christ.

Obviously this explanation squares as much with the becoming as with the being. Through these words, when they are completed, the substance contained beneath these accidents becomes the body of Christ. Also it is fully true when they are completed that the substance contained beneath these accidents is the body of Christ. You can easily see that this interpretation brings out both the true meaning of the words and their true effectiveness. By these words spoken in the person of Christ, namely, "This (that is, this substance) is my body," this substance becomes and is the body of Christ.

This has been detailed and extended, since this interpretation entails no wrenching of the words, no improper sense, no untruth, but remains within the literal meaning of the words and within the confession of the Christian faith.

This is adequate treatment of the seventh contention.

8

SINS DESTROYED BY THE SACRAMENT

The eighth error holds that it is wrong to believe that this sacrament destroys sins, since Christ's death alone destroys sins.[13]

You will easily detect the error on this point if you examine the reason given. From the fact that Christ's death alone destroys sins, it does not follow that the application to us of Christ's death does not destroy sins. Just as the fact that a craftsman alone makes a sphere does not rule out the craftsman's tools used in making the sphere, so the fact that Christ's death alone destroys sins does not rule out the sacraments of the Chruch, which are the instruments by which Christ's death is applied to us. Otherwise, one should delete from the Creed the confession of one baptism for the forgiveness of sins. If the fact that Christ's death alone destroys our sins would rule out the sacraments, then baptism also is ruled out from destroying sins. As in truth baptism is not ruled out, neither are the other sacraments ruled out from destroying sins. The reason given is therefore of no value.

This is sufficient on the eighth error.

9

THE EUCHARISTIC SACRIFICE

The ninth position says it is false to believe that the Eucharist is a sacrifice. The sacrifice of Christ offered once on the cross suffices for eternity, as is taught by Paul the Apostle in Hebrews 10[:14], "By a single work of sanctification he has made perfect for all time those he sanctified." Also, in Hebrews 9[:12], "By his own blood he entered once for all into the holy place, gaining an eternal redemption." Also it is false that Christ is offered in the Eucharist, since he would only be offered in sacrifice if he died and blood were involved. Paul the Apostle also teaches this in Hebrews 9[:25f], "nor was it to repeatedly offer himself, for then he would have had to repeatedly die from the founding of the world." Clearly Christ does not die, nor could he die. Another point is that the Mass was instituted neither by Christ nor by the apostles.[14]

Take note of the error in this position, where it judges that the sacrifice of the altar is a different sacrifice from the sacrifice Christ offered on the cross. In matter of fact, it is the same sacrifice, just as it is the same body of Christ and the same blood of Christ – on the altar, on the cross, and now in heaven. The difference is in the manner of offering, since then it was offered corporeally, but now it is offered spiritually. Then it was offered in actual death, now in a mystery of death. This you should understand in reference to the offering, both as to what is contained and to what is signified in this sacrifice. I say this, because if one refers to the sacramental species, then the corporeal and perceptible offering is obvious. But this spiritual offering does not therefore render the sacrifice of Christ insufficient, but in it as in a holy mystery Christ and his sacrifice are constantly recalled, as Christ commanded, "Do this in commemoration of me" [Luke 22:19; 1 Corinthians 11:24f].[15]

The arguments made from Paul's teaching in Hebrews lead to an equivocal use of terms. Paul the Apostle was speaking of the corporeal offering of Christ, which we profess as one and all-sufficient for eternity. But to speak of the eucharistic sacrifice is to shift to a spiritual offering. Note well that we are not saying that a spiritual body of Christ is offered in the sacrifice of the altar, but that the natural body of Christ is offered in a spiritual oblation in the sacrifice of the altar. The knowledgeable reader should understand this with reference to the reality contained in this sacrifice, namely the body and blood of Christ. For when one refers the sacrifice of the altar to the death of Christ, a sign is involved and not the reality, since neither the death of Christ nor Christ in death is present in itself. Since Christ lives and reigns in heaven, his death is consequently not contained in this sacrifice but is rather signified.

Two things must be rightly understood: Christ himself is both signified and contained, while his death is indeed signified but not contained. There is no need therefore that Christ die each time this sacrifice is offered, as it must be true that he be present in the sacrifice, be contained in it, and be offered as what is contained and offered. Christ's death is signified in this sacrifice, not only because the words of consecration express it, in saying, ". . . which will be shed for you and for many," but also because the blood is consecrated in separation from the body. This sacramental separation signifies the real separation of his blood from his body in his death.

With reference to the objection that the sacrifice of the altar was not instituted by Christ nor by the apostles, you should recall that evidence is derived from the words of Paul the Apostle in 1 Corinthians both that Christ instituted this sacrifice, and that in the time of the Apostles it was celebrated not only as a sacrament but as a sacrifice as well. The Apostle says, "I accepted from the Lord what I handed on to you, that the Lord Jesus on the night he was betrayed . . . "[11:23]. From the fact that Paul says he had handed on to the Corinthians before he wrote them his first epistle what he had received from the Lord, we derive two points.

First, the Apostles handed on many things to be observed by the churches which were not written by the Apostles in the books of Holy Scripture. You see in this case that unless this letter had in fact followed we would not know that Paul handed on to the Corinthians what he received from the Lord concerning the Eucharist. Nonetheless he had in fact handed on to the Corinthians the teaching on the Eucharist he had received from the Lord, as he bears witness.

Second, what he received from the Lord and handed on to the

Corinthians concerning the Eucharist is the same thing he recalled as
a rite already observed in the Corinthian church, saying, "Flee the
worship of idols . . . . The cup of blessing which we bless, is it not a
sharing in the blood of Christ? The bread which we break, is it not a
sharing in the body of Christ? Because the bread is one, we though
many are one body, since we all share in the one bread. Consider
Israel according to the flesh; are not those who eat the offerings
sharers in the altar? What do I mean? That an idol is anything, or
that what is offered to an idol is anything? I mean rather that the
offerings of the pagans are to demons and not to God. I do not want
you to become sharers with demons. You cannot drink the cup of
the Lord and the cup of demons. You cannot share at the table of
the Lord and at the table of demons." [1 Corinthians 10:14.16-21].

In these words, both in their meaning and context, the Apostle is
obviously supposing the rite of the Church observed both then and
now, namely, that those partaking of the Eucharist receive from the
sacrifice of the altar. Since they receive from a sacrifice, from things
offered to God, he warns the Corinthians to flee the worship of
idols, alleging from the rite of the old law that those who eat the
victims are sharers in the altar. He also argued that the gentiles who
offered to demons were sharers at the table of demons.

This striking text shows that in the time of the Apostles the cup
and bread of the Lord were treated as a sacrifice. One should not be
so foolish as to think that the Apostle's accurate references to these
things were beside the point. When this text is linked with the
Apostle's saying, "I received from the Lord what I handed on to
you" [1 Corinthians 11:23], then one has ample evidence that
Christ instituted not only this sacrament but this sacrifice as well,
and that the Apostles taught by Christ handed on this sacrifice to
the Church.

If one relies on writers outside Holy Scripture, we find that
James, the brother of the Lord, added the celebration of Mass, as the
sixth Council relates (Section *De Consecratione,* Distinction 1,
canon *Iacobus*). In the time of Pope Telesphorus, the eighth after St.
Peter, Masses were celebrated on the night of Our Lord's Nativity
(*De Consecratione,* Distinction 1, canon *Nocte*).[16] Note that the
former text does not relate the institution of Mass by the sixth
Council, but is rather the witness of the Council to an addition made
by James, the brother of the Lord, concerning the Mass. It was not
the Roman Pontiff, not the Latin Church, but the Eastern, or Greek,

Church that testifies to an ordinance concerning the Mass by James the Apostle, as this Church gathered in the person of the one hundred and fifty Fathers at Constantinople in the time of Pope Agatho and the Emperor Constantine the Younger. If one accepts the word of a single historian, certainly unhesitating trust should be given the witness of the one hundred and fifty Fathers. I will pass over what was said about the Roman Church offering the sacrifice of the Mass on the night of Our Lord's Nativity in the time of Pope Telesphorus, eighth after St. Peter, at a time when the Roman Church gloried in no temporal prowess but solely in the triumph of the martyrs. You can easily find this in *De consecratione,* distinction 1, in canon *Nocte.*

If these persons trust the authentic records kept by the Church concerning the martyrs, then you have evidence that the sacrifice of the Eucharist flourished before the time of Constantine, when the Roman Church had no earthly glory but abounded in martyrs. This is clear in the words of Lawrence to Xistus, "Where are you, a holy priest, rushing without a deacon? You have been accustomed never to offer the sacrifice without an assisting minister." See, Xistus was accustomed to offer sacrifice, undoubtedly the Eucharist. Hence Lawrence added, referring to himself (a deacon), "Try to choose a worthy minister to whom you can entrust the distribution of the blood of the Lord."[17]

Finally, you should notice that even if nothing were written, still sufficient witness that this sacrifice was instituted by Christ and handed on by the Apostles is found in the continuous tradition, not of just one part of the world, but of the universal Church spread over the whole world. This is evident, if only from the fact that the authority of the Church is competent to do even greater things, since it is by the authority of the Church that we have all the books of Holy Scripture. I would not know that the Gospel of John ranks ahead of the Gospel of Bartholomew, unless the authority of the Church apprised me of this. This is true of other matters as well.

If the Latin Church alone had this sacrifice, or if it were introduced anew into the Church of God, then grounds would exist for suspecting it as a Roman invention. But when the Greek, Latin, and other Churches have had it from earliest times, without some beginning at a later time, this should suffice. How much more, then, when written evidence abounds.

This is enough on the ninth position.

10

ADORATION OF THE EUCHARIST

The tenth error is that it is idolatry to adore the sacrament of the Eucharist. This is alleged, first, because Christ's humanity is in itself not to be adored. Second, while only God, whom no one sees, is to be adored, the adorers of the Eucharist adore what they see. Third, we do not read that the Apostles adored the Eucharist at the Last Supper.[18]

The error of the first argument for this view is obvious. In this sacrament, one does not adore Christ's humanity in itself, but Christ, true God, who has assumed true human flesh. The second reason is wrong on the same point, since we do not adore the accidents of bread and wine which we see, but Christ contained beneath these accidents.

Two things can be said concerning the third reason given, namely, that we do not read that the Apostles adored the Eucharist at the Last Supper. First, since in fact nothing is said of their adoring Christ present at the Supper, then why wonder that nothing is said about their adoring the sacrament of the same Christ. If the argument that we do not read about the Apostles adoring Christ at the Supper leads anywhere, it is to the conclusion that we then should not adore Christ. Secondly, this argument as universalized carries no weight in this form, that is, one does not read the Apostles did X, and so X is not to be done. We never read in Holy Scripture that they instituted a confession of faith, yet they did this. We never read in Holy Scripture that they approved the Gospels of Luke and Mark, yet we believe these were approved by them.

This is sufficient on the tenth error.

11

PATRISTIC VIEWS ON CHRIST'S PRESENCE

The eleventh point is that Tertullian, Augustine, Origen, and Hilary promote the view that the body of Christ is in the Eucharist as in a sign.[19]

On this topic, this man says many things that an intelligent person can show on the basis of our foregoing chapters to be irrelevant to the conclusion. One should, however, note that whenever these ancient writers say that the sacrament is a sign or figure of the body of Christ, or something to this effect, they do speak the truth. But they do not therefore go on to deny that with this sign there is present also what is figured, signified, and indeed contained, that is, the flesh of Christ. By reason of the sacramental species, theologians have called, and continue to call, this sacrament the sign, the figure, and the like, but have not as a consequence denied the reality contained beneath the figure.

Note also that the holy doctors wisely rank the virtues ahead of frequent reception of the sacraments, since the virtues are proper to good men, while the sacraments are common to good and evil alike.

No more need be said on the eleventh point.

12

ANOTHER WAY OF FAITH?

The twelfth view is that if we were to believe in the Eucharist, then there would be two ways of salvation, the one being faith in Christ, the other faith in the sacrament.[20]

As a knowledgeable person, the reader will see this is ridiculous. There are not two arts in the goldsmith, one by which he works on gold and the other by which he uses his tools to produce golden objects. So there are not two faiths, one in Christ, the other in the instruments which mediate and apply his saving power to us. The sacraments of the Church are the instruments of Christ, instituted by him for our salvation. Whoever denies faith in the sacraments expunges from the Gospel the words, "Unless one is born again by water and the Spirit, he cannot enter the kingdom of God" [John 3:5].

This covers the twelfth view.

Completed in the year 1525.

This, most blessed Father, is what I in obedience to your command think should be written to instruct the learned Nuntio. I submit it to your apostolic judgment. Amen.

VI

THE KING'S MARRIAGE 1530

1

PREFACE
AND INTRODUCTION

To the Supreme Pontiff, Clement:

Most blessed and deeply revered Father: Greetings.

Upon delivery to me of a group of tracts dealing with the marriage of the King and Queen of England, you commanded me to study them carefully and to set out in detail whatever judgment and counsel I would have on the whole question at issue. In an effort to obey as quickly as the matter would allow, and to do what I could to relieve your Holiness of these troubles, I have read the tracts on both sides and noted the many questions they raise. They speak of the different kinds of divine law and of the respective durations of these laws, of the different laws of nature, of the limits of judicial precepts, of the different manners of dispensation, and of the authority of the Pope regarding matters of divine or natural law.

If one were obliged to treat all these matters, he would have to write many volumes and traverse a vast literary battlefield, and he would still not reach the desired goal. I have consequently focused on the specific issues of this case and sought to come to its central point. I decided I should first set forth that which is being called in question, so that all may then grasp the topic of which I speak. Then we can turn to investigate what the laws of God and nature require. When this is grasped, the truth now being sought will become apparent.

2

CIRCUMSTANCES OF THE MARRIAGE

When the present King of England was a youth, his father, then the King of England, arranged that he should be joined in marriage with her who is at present Queen of England. She was at that time not Queen, but the widow of the present King's elder brother, who was first-born of his family but who had died without having offspring. She was also the daughter of the King and Queen of Spain. The marriage was made possible by authoritative intervention of the Roman Pontiff, with the purpose of maintaining peace and friendship between these same rulers. The marriage was consummated, offspring have been born, and the King has lived many years united in conjugal affection with the Queen. But the King now requests dissolution of the marriage as being invalid, because it is contrary to the divine law and to the natural law as both have been confirmed by sacred councils, Roman Pontiffs, and theologians. This then is the matter we must take up in terms of its specific issues.

We begin by setting forth the content of the apostolic dispensation.[1]

> Julius . . . , to our dearest Henry, son of our beloved son, Henry, the illustrious King of England, and to our dearest Catherine, daughter of our beloved son Ferdinand and our beloved daughter Isabella, the Catholic King and Queen of Spain and Sicily: Greetings to Your Highnesses.
>
> The Roman Pontiff exercises the pre-eminent authority conferred on him from above in accord with what his considered judgment of persons, times, and affairs shows to be conducive in the Lord for the welfare of mankind.
>
> The petition recently submitted to us on your behalf states that you, Catherine, our daughter in Christ, had at one time contracted lawful marriage with Arthur, who was then the eldest living son of our beloved son in Christ, Henry, the illustrious King of England. This marriage was for the maintenance of bonds of peace and friendship between our beloved son in Christ, Ferdinand, and our beloved daughter in Christ, Isabella, the Catholic King and Queen of Spain and Sicily, and the aforementioned King

and Queen of England. That marriage being perhaps consummated by carnal union, the aforementioned Arthur died, without any offspring being born of this marriage.

The same petition goes on to state that to further preserve this same bond of peace and friendship between the aforementioned Kings and Queens you desire to contract a lawful marriage between yourselves. You have therefore supplicated us to deign out of our apostolic concern to grant you the appropriate dispensation in view of the foregoing. Therefore, since we ardently desire that peace and harmony flourish between individual Christians and especially between Catholic Kings and Princes, we now absolve you and any of your retainers from any bond of excommunication .... Accepting your present supplication, we grant you a gift of special favor, and by apostolic authority, in accord with what is here set forth, dispense you, so that you may contract lawful marriage between yourselves, notwithstanding either the impediment of affinity deriving from the aforementioned, or any apostolic constitution or ordinance, or whatever else may be to the contrary. You may lawfully remain in such a marriage once contracted, even if perchance you have already so contracted in public or in secret and have consummated this by carnal union. We by the same apostolic authority absolve you and any of your retainers, in the event you have so contracted, from this transgression and from the sentence of excommunication you would thereby have incurred. We further declare legitimate any offspring whether conceived perchance already or to be conceived of this marriage, whether it is contracted already or still to be contracted, providing only that you, Catherine, our daughter in Christ, were not subjected to force in this matter. If you have already contracted such a marriage, our will is that you choose or have chosen a confessor who will impose a salutary penance for this, which you are bound to carry out ....

Given at Rome, December 26, 1503, in the first year of our pontificate.

3

DIVINE LAW ON LEVIRATE MARRIAGE

The Mosaic law lays down three precepts concerning marriage between a man and his sister-in-law. Leviticus 18[:16] says, "You shall not uncover the nakedness of your brother's wife, since it is your brother's nakedness." The same book says in chapter 20[:21], "If a man takes his brother's wife, it is an alien deed (that is, unlawful), since he has uncovered his brother's nakedness, and he will be without offspring." The third text is Deuteronomy 25[:5-10] and reads as follows:

> When brothers dwell together and one them dies without offspring, the wife of the deceased may not marry another, but her husband's brother shall take her and he shall raise up offspring for his brother. The first son she bears shall have the name of him who died, so that his name be not blotted out in Israel. But if the man refuses to take his brother's wife, whom the law has bound to him, she shall go to the city gates and shall address the elders, 'My husband's brother does not want to raise up offspring in Israel for his brother. He will not take me as wife.' The elders shall summon him forthwith and question him. If he responds, 'I do not want her as wife,' the woman shall in the presence of the elders come before him, pull his sandal from his foot, spit in his face, and say, 'So shall it be done to a man who does not build up his brother's house.' His name in Israel shall then be called, One De-sandaled.

I have given this text as it stands in the Vulgate. Although this should be adequate for determining the true answer to the present problem, I have made the effort to obtain an exact translation of the text from the original Hebrew.[2] Some have argued from differences in the Hebrew in order to call in question whether the law of Deuteronomy refers to what we would call blood-brothers. They object that it does not say, "Her husband's brother shall take her," but, "His relative . . ." They also say the text repeatedly speaks of a female relative, not a sister-in-law, with "relative" obviously implying blood relationship. The Hebrew text is as follows:

When brothers reside together and one of them dies
without having a son, the wife of the dead man shall not go
out to a man not of the family, but her brother-in-law shall
lie with her and in fulfilment of his levirate duty shall take
her as wife. The first-born son she shall bear shall rise up in
the name of the dead brother and his name will not be
blotted out from Israel. If the brother-in-law does not want
to take his sister-in-law, she shall go up to the gates and
address the elders: 'My brother-in-law refuses to make
offspring rise up for his brother in Israel. He will not
perform his levirate duty to me.' The elders of the city will
call him and speak to him. He will stand before them and
say, 'I did not want to take her,' and his sister-in-law shall
approach him in sight of the elders and take his sandal from
his foot and spit in his face. She will answer and say, 'So
shall it happen to a man who did not build up his brother's
house.' His name in Israel shall then be called, House of
One Unsandaled.

Here it is evident that the law treats of brothers whom we would
call blood-brothers. The recent interpretation which spoke of the
man and woman as "relatives" has imposed the veracular Italian
upon the Latin by calling him a "male relative" where the Latin has
"brother-in-law" [*levir*], and her a "female relative" where the Latin
has "sister-in-law" [*fratria*]. The Hebrew even uses the specific word
for brother-in-law [*levir*], so that from it a new Latin verb had to be
derived (*leviro, —as*) and used twice in this law to indicate
observance of what the law requires of the brother-in-law regarding
his sister-in-law. It is strange that anyone should doubt that his law
refers to blood-brothers, since in the Gospel the Sadducees bore
witness to this meaning when they presented to Christ the case of
the wife of the seven brothers according to the law of Moses
[Matthew 22:23-33]. Also the words of Naomi in Ruth 1[:11],
indicate that this was well known among the women of Israel. As
well, the frequent repetition of the word "brother" in the law itself
makes it clear. Each time these laws speak of "brother" [*frater*] the
Hebrew uses exactly the same expression. The same word for
"brother" is used in the laws of Leviticus and in Deuteronomy, so
that if ambiguity may be introduced in one passage, the same
ambiguity must hold for the other passage as well.

Hence if anyone stubbornly maintains that the law of Deuteronomy refers to men who are not blood-brothers, he should refrain from the further argument, since by the same argument the laws of Leviticus can be interpreted as referring to men who are not blood-brothers. If this be done, then we simply do not have any written divine or natural law pertaining to marriage between brother-in-law and sister-in-law. In this case, the present question ceases to be an issue based on written divine or natural law, which has been the foundation on which the whole structure of the controversy has rested. Consequently, one should raise no question about whether these laws refer to men whom we call blood-brothers.

4

EXCEPTIONS TO THE PROHIBITION OF LEVIRATE MARRIAGE IN DIVINE LAW

The laws of Leviticus and Deuteronomy agree in that they both treat of blood-brothers. The evident difference between them is that while the Levitical law is generic the Deuteronomic law is specific. Leviticus rules for the case of the brother's wife, without specifying whether he be living or dead, while Deuteronomy speaks of the wife of a deceased brother. Leviticus does not specify whether he had a son or not, while Deuteronomy legislates for the case in which the deceased brother had no son. Leviticus prohibits carnal knowledge of one's brother's wife without specifying whether it is for raising up offspring for one's own or the brother's name, while Deuteronomy speaks of union with the wife of a childless deceased brother for the purpose of raising up offspring in the brother's name. A fourth specification must also be understood in addition to these, namely that Leviticus does not specify whether the brother's widow is advanced in age or whether she can still bear children. Deuteronomy is obviously legislating for the brother's widow young enough to bear children, since it commands that she be wed in order to raise up offspring for the brother.

This evident series of differences between the two laws makes it clear beyond question that not every marriage between a man and his brother's widow is forbidden by divine law. One must discern between the unqualified marriage of brother-in-law and sister-in-law and the marriage modified by so many specifications as in the law of Deuteronomy. One must conclude that in general, without any further specification, a marriage between a man and his sister-in-law is condemned by divine law. But another marriage between a man and his sister-in-law, when a number of certain conditions are present, is not only allowed, but is required by a precept of divine law. This, then, is what God has obviously determined concerning marriage between a man and his sister-in-law.

The question whether these divine laws of the Old Testament are binding on New Testament believers, or whether they have expired, is of little importance in the case under discussion. This fact must not be passed over in silence, since the two laws in fact agree in many aspects. The matter is basically the same: a marriage between a man and his sister-in-law. The moral act is the same: an act of piety, based on reverence and an obligation between men related by blood. The moral basis is the same: the moral obligation of natural piety that binds all of us. The type of precept is the same: both are precepts which are partially judicial and partially moral. The law-giver is the same: since all these laws were issued by Moses with divine authority. Hence any argument supporting the binding power of the Levitical law as a divine law will also support the continuing authority of the Deuteronomic law as a divine law. Also any reasons given for the expiration of Deuteronomy will also argue to the expiration of Leviticus with the coming of grace and truth through Jesus Christ. I said "as a divine law", since we are not at present treating these as moral laws, but as laws given on divine authority by Moses.

5

EXCEPTIONS TO THE PROHIBITION
OF LEVIRATE MARRIAGE BY NATURAL LAW

From what has been said so far, there is no difficulty deriving what the natural law prescribes about marriage between a man and his sister-in-law. If one takes away the bond imposed by both divine and human positive law, leaving only their witness, it is evident, first, that simply and in itself the marriage of brother-in-law and sister-in-law is evil. For there is in such a union a moral baseness that stands opposed to the goodness of the reverence due by natural piety to one's sister-in-law. The basis for this is one's own brother, as the law of Leviticus indicated in saying, "You shall not uncover the nakedness of your brother's wife since it is your brother's nakedness" [Leviticus 18:16]. Second, a marriage between brother-in-law and sister-in-law when it is modified by the conditions described above is morally good. From the fact that simply and in itself a marriage between brother-in-law and sister-in-law is base, one can argue that the baseness is not present in a marriage between the same two persons when so many conditions modify the case. If this were not so, then a marriage modified by so many conditions would also be morally base, and hence illicit — which goes against the witness of divine law.

Since moral baseness is only removed by moral good, consequently there must be a moral good entailed in the convergence of so many conditions in a specific marriage of brother-in-law with sister-in-law, that removes the baseness which would qualify the same marriage without these conditions. Hence a marriage between brother-in-law and sister-in-law, when rendered virtuous by so many conditions is morally good. If you consider the matter more at length, you will find that the moral good in a levirate marriage rendered virtuous in this manner is greater than the baseness in such a marriage without the modifying conditions. The good of the former must overcome the baseness of the latter, or else the precept given for the former in a specific case would not overcome the prohibition of the latter as a general norm. The fact that divine law commands the one marriage while the prohibition of the other is still in force shows that the goodness of the former is greater than the baseness attendant on intercourse between brother-in-law and sister-in-law. The goodness is of such character as to remove the base aspect from such intercourse and make it virtuous and honorable. Consequently if a brother-in-law and sister-in-law are in this manner freed from the prohibition of both divine and human law and then contract a marriage rendered virtuous by these conditions, they are beyond doubt united in a virtuous and honorable marriage. This same fact is shown by the marriage between Tamar and the sons of Judah in the period before the law was given, as in Genesis 38.

6

OTHER CONDITIONS RENDERING A LEVIRATE MARRIAGE LICIT IN DIVINE AND NATURAL LAW

From what we have so far shown to be of divine and natural law, one must conclude that it is utterly reasonable that a levirate marriage would undoubtedly also be honorable if there were some good calling for it that ranks ahead of all the conditions given in the law of Deuteronomy. This would be so, in terms of divine law and natural law, omitting for the present any consideration of human laws. This argument would evidently hold according to the law of nature, since it is a requirement of right reason that if a lesser good suffices for taking away the baseness of a marriage between brother-in-law and sister-in-law, then a greater good is all the more adequate to remove the same baseness. The argument would also hold in divine law, since laws are never multiplied in view of a mere multitude of cases that can occur. If this were true we would need an infinite number of laws, according to all possible events. In any commonwealth, the laws laid down are so understood that from one case in a decree one can understand all similar cases under the same decree. If a lesser good is decreed to be adequate for removing some baseness, one is to understand that it is decreed as well that a much greater good also suffices to remove every element of baseness.

I believe these points are so clear that no proof of them is required. All that is needed is to point out what is specific to the case under discussion. We need not digress to treat an unspecified greater good, but only the greater good accruing to the deceased brother. The reason for this is that the baseness of a levirate marriage consists in the dishonor shown to the deceased brother. In the marriage prescribed by Deuteronomy this irreverence to the deceased brother is overcome by the good accruing to him, that is, as his name is carried on and offspring are brought into the world in the family of the first-born son by his wife and his brother. She had been one flesh with him and he had been the dead man's closest relative in the flesh. In spite of this, the brother as it were substituted for the deceased in bringing forth a family for the departed one.

We have not discussed this last point because we think that the marriage between the illustrious King and Queen of England was contracted for the purpose of carrying on the name of the deceased brother. This was clearly not the case, but we wish to show how in the natural law, as confirmed by divine authority, there is not just one circumstance in which levirate marriage is rendered virtuous. Rather, this holds in every case where the good accruing to the deceased brother ranks ahead of the minimal good of his name continuing through a son. The latter is itself uncertain, since no one knows for certain that a child will be conceived.

7

LEVIRATE MARRIAGE RENDERED
LICIT BY THE COMMON GOOD

We should consider carefully and ponder well what the law of nature, as expressed in these Levitical laws, is indicating. The irreverence to one's deceased brother is outweighed by such a minimal and precarious benefit, which comes to him by merely human actions that cannot affect himself for good or ill but only affect his standing in the estimate of others. This indicates as well that the common good of a city or nation, something consisting in reality and not just in human opinion, would suffice to render virtuous a marriage between brother-in-law and sister-in-law. It is itself a much greater good, and of its own nature and purpose is the goal to which external goods of individuals are ordered. Hence according to both natural and divine law, a marriage of this kind if contracted for the common good of one's country would be morally good. The common good of one's country is more effective in removing the dishonor to the deceased brother than is the minimal and precarious benefit to this deceased brother alone. The latter is an external good affecting only his name, and not even because of an outstanding deed done by him. It is so little, that it results from nothing he does, but is the work of another, if in fact the brother is able to beget offspring.

This argument does not entail digressing from the specific topic of our discussion. Moving from an external benefit accruing to one person to consider the common good is not to digress but to advance from the part to the whole, from a partial good to the total good, from something ordered to an end to the reality of the end itself. This is so obvious and so accords with all laws that it would be detrimental to the law to discuss the topic further.

8

THE MARRIAGE OF THE KING AND QUEEN OF ENGLAND

The witness, therefore, of divine law about a lesser benefit shows that the common good of one's country is adequate for removing the baseness in a levirate marriage. The natural law indicates the same about a lesser good. Consequently, one can only conclude that the marriage of the illustrious King and Queen is not contrary to divine law nor to the natural law. They entered marriage to maintain the blessing of peace between the kings of Spain and England, as the apostolic document stated clearly, and this made their marriage honorable and consonant with both laws. So much so, that if human laws were put aside, this marriage would have needed no dispensation, since it promotes the common good of peace between such illustrious kings. This is a condition which according to divine and natural law is adequate to render honorable a marriage between brother-in-law and sister-in-law.

The ecclesiastical dispensation was only required to remove an impediment from human laws and to authorize the honorable character this unique marriage took on for the promotion of the common good of peace. The marriage was rendered honorable in itself by its relation to the common good of peace. Theologians only add a doctrinal declaration of this, and the apostolic dispensation gives authorization.

Hence Pope Julius in no way encroached on divine law by his dispensation. Neither did he infringe on natural law, but he only removed an impediment from human law that prevented this unique union. He declared it to be legitimate and added his customary authorization that the marriage was in accord with divine and natural law for the reasons given. These are the effects of a dispensation given by reason of the common good of peace. It would be utterly alien to Christianity for the Pope to abrogate in whole or in part even the least requirement of divine or natural law. Doing this is reserved to the divine lawgiver and Creator. But it is not alien to Christianity for the Pope to interpret in case of doubt and thus define the law of God and nature.

Hence that dispensation produced different effects in accord with the different objects it dealt with. Dealing with human law, it rendered permissible what human law forbade. Dealing with divine and natural law, it declared and authorized as permissible what was doubtful under these laws. It made clear something that could have been doubted or even thought to be forbidden.

Also two further benefits to the deceased brother add to the honorable character of the marriage. First, his widow, who was one flesh with him, was by this marriage exalted to become the future Queen of England, so that at least she who was of his flesh took possession of the kingdom he was not able in himself to rule because of death. Second, by this marriage his own brother gained full immunity from the vast number of evils brought on kingdoms by war. The Gospel showed that evils threatening a person are of concern to his deceased brother, when the rich man deep in hell asked Abraham to keep his brothers from coming into the place of torment [Luke 16:27f]. Hence this marriage was also rendered honorable by a benefit accruing to the deceased brother which was in no way less than what Deuteronomy described, a benefit in fact and not only in name, one that was certain and not doubtful. But the honorableness especially arose from the great common good of peace, as was authorized by apostolic authority.

9

AN HONORABLE MARRIAGE, WHETHER THE OLD TESTAMENT BINDS OR NOT

From our review of the whole of divine law, it is quite apparent that this marriage between the illustrious rulers of England was permitted as an honorable union. This is the case, whether the divine laws legislating for levirate marriage are still binding or whether they have expired. If God's prescriptions in the Old Testament have expired then nothing can be argued against their marriage from the

Old Testament. If these prescriptions are still in force in our time, then there is no argument against the marriage, since we must follow the same divine law where it prescribes in Deuteronomy 17[:8-13] that the High-Priest is to determine the law of the Lord in ambiguous and difficult cases. Hence even if the expected benefit was not totally evident as one adequate to render honorable this marriage between brother-in-law and sister-in-law, it became clear once the High-Priest was presented the case for judgment. This was evidently the reason for submitting the petition to the Supreme Pontiff, and for his pondering both the apparent impediments to the marriage from the laws of God, nature, and man and the expected benefit of maintaining peace. Julius, who then was High-Priest, gave his dispensation, thus authorizing the levirate marriage between this illustrious couple, and rendered it permissible and honorable by reason of the blessing of peace it was to bring.

The Pope, by the divine authority conferred on him under the law of God, freed this marriage from every impediment, whether of divine natural, or human law. For although no one would go so far as to utter this, one might — if free rein were given to the imagination — conceive an objection against the marriage because of an uncertainty in the light of divine and natural law, that is, whether the blessing of peace was in fact adequate to render a levirate marriage honorable. But the determination of such a question pertained to the then High-Priest, and he did determine that the goal of the common good of peace was consonant with the divine law, since nothing promotes human welfare as much as the blessing of peace. I have not expanded on this because the matter itself was doubtful. For we concluded already that the blessing of peace was quite adequate to render this marriage honorable under the laws of God and nature. I wanted to show that if the matter were ambiguous or difficult, the authority of the High-Priest sufficed to determine, in accord with arguments fitting perfectly with the laws of God and nature, that this marriage was permissible, honorable, and legitimate. Thus he was competent to render the marriage permissible, honorable, and legitimate, even if it be the case that Christians are bound by the moral laws of Leviticus as by divine laws.

10

THE MARRIAGE NOT QUESTIONABLE
BY COUNCILS, POPES, OR THEOLOGIANS

The fact that sacred Councils, Supreme Pontiffs, and theologians have condemned marriages between brother-in-law and sister-in-law as contrary to the divine and natural laws, is however, in light of what we said above, not an argument against this marriage.[3] In fact it was contracted with apostolic authority in accord with the divine and natural laws. What these authorities condemned were simple levirate marriages bereft of the conditions consonant with the law of God and nature. This is clear from the fact that they base their condemnations on the divine and natural law. We have already brought to light that the laws of God and nature prohibit levirate marriages in general or without further modifications. But when a marriage between brother-in-law and sister-in-law is modified by a considerable number of honorable elements, such as benefits to the deceased brother or promotion of the common good, then it is in accord with both laws.

Consequently, Julius did not act contrary to the teaching of sacred Councils, Popes, or theologians, nor did he even go against those theologians who say — and rightly so — that the Pope has no power to dispense matters of divine law or natural law. For he cannot make licit a matter clearly forbidden by divine or natural law. As is clear from what we said above, a levirate marriage contracted for promoting peace as a common good is not forbidden by the laws of God or nature. In fact it accords well with both these laws. The Pope, then, acted in virtue of his ordinary power by which he lawfully determines Church law, in declaring and authorizing this marriage as honorable in view of the common good of peace. This he did to clear away any possible doubt arising from these two laws.

This, Holy Father, is my judgment on this matter. As far as counsel is concerned, I can think of nothing better than that we surely have as inspired by the Holy Spirit: "Love justice, you who rule the earth" [Wisdom 1:1].

May your holiness remain blessed forever.

Rome, March 13, 1530.

VII

THE SACRIFICE OF THE MASS AND ITS RITE — AGAINST THE LUTHERANS 1531

From Thomas de Vio Cardinal Cajetan, to the Supreme Pontiff, Clement VII: Greetings.

Earlier, most blessed Father, you commanded me to write an instruction for your Nuncio in response to the booklet on the Lord's Supper which asserted that the body and blood of Christ were only signified in the Eucharist.[1] Recently a Lutheran writing was given me, which, although it affirms the true body and blood of Christ in the Eucharist, denies the sacrifice of the Mass,[2] thus going against all the churches, even those of the schismatics. I judged it my duty not to wait for a command but to elucidate immediately the causes of error in this new heresy. May you accept my work and in your Apostolic Office be pleased to judge this small essay of mine. My best wishes accompany it.

1

PURPOSE OF THE TREATISE

The sole teacher of all men, Our Lord Jesus, refuted the Sadducees by arguing exclusively from the books of Moses, the only books of Scripture recognized by the Sadducees [Matthew 22:23-33]. Our Lord's example teaches us not to counter the heretics with authorities they do not acknowledge, but to argue from the same sacred witnesses they urge against us. Therefore, against the heretics now named "Lutherans", who base their teaching solely on texts of Holy Scripture, I will present arguments and teaching on the sacrifice of the Mass derived exclusively from Scripture. Thus they will be prevented from boasting that their denial of the sacrifice of the Mass has a solid foundation in Scripture. Neither will they ignorantly think that the sacrifice of the Mass rests on the determination of the Church and not on the authority of Scripture. Finally those Lutherans who err because of lack of instruction will be given reasons for changing their views.

Seeking to make the truth shine forth for all to see, I will proceed by treating the following: first, the points of agreement and difference between Lutherans and Catholics; then, the biblical teaching on the sacrifice of the Mass; finally, a discussion of the Lutheran objections.

2

AGREEMENTS AND DIFFERENCES BETWEEN LUTHERANS AND CATHOLICS ON THE SACRIFICE OF THE MASS

The Lutherans agree that the Mass can be called a commemorative sacrifice, since the true body and blood of Christ are consecrated, venerated, and received in commemoration of the sacrifice offered on the cross. As Our Lord said, "Do this in commemoration of me."[3]

But the Lutherans then make two denials. They say first that the body and blood of Christ are not offered to God. Although they affirm that the true body of Christ is on the altar, they deny that Christ's true body is offered to God.[4] They also deny that there is on the altar a victim or sacrifice for the expiation of the sins of either the living or the dead.[5]

They base both denials on the clear teaching of the Epistle to the Hebrews that the offering of the body of Christ made once and for all on the cross was sufficient expiation for the sins of the whole world.[6] They conclude from this that while the worship of the body of Christ was instituted in commemoration of Christ's passion and death, any offering of the body of Christ as a victim for sins must be a human invention that is contrary to the teaching of Holy Scripture.

3

CHRIST'S INSTITUTION OF THE OFFERING OF THE EUCHARIST

As Catholics we recognize that the institution of an offering of the Eucharist is recorded in Holy Scripture. In Luke, chapter 22, and especially in Paul's letter to the Corinthians, chapter 11, we read that after the many things the Lord Jesus did during the Last Supper he gave this precept: "Do this in commemoration of me" [Luke 22:19; 1 Corinthians 11:24]. Since these are the words of Jesus Christ, they must be pondered intently, taking up first the pronoun "this", then the verb "do", and then the phrase "in commemoration of me".

To understand what is indicated by the pronoun "this" we must review what went before. Previously Jesus took bread, gave thanks, broke the bread, gave it, and said, "Take, eat, this is my body which is broken (in Luke, given) for you." Then he immediately added, "Do this in commemoration of me." The pronoun "this" is not restricted to indicating any single action that went before, nor does it mean to exclude any of the previous actions. Consequently it must be an indication extending to all that went before.

The verb "do" is freighted with mysteries. He did not say, "Say this," but, "Do this." This shows that he was commanding something consisting in an action and not merely in words. When words are said, the purpose does not lie in the words but in the action. Thus we are to understand that the words of consecration are effective in bringing about what they signify. When he added "in commemoration of me", he thereby distinguished the action from the commemoration. Looking closely, we note that he did not say, "Commemorate this," but, "*Do* this in commemoration of me." Our Lord's command therefore is to do "this", namely, all that went before, in commemoration of himself. The action, doing this, is commanded for the purpose of recalling the Lord Jesus.

"Doing this" entails not simply making the body of Christ present but making that body present which was broken (or, given) for our sake. Consequently the Lord Jesus' precept is to make present "my body which is broken and given for you." His words about the body "broken and given for you" are equivalent to speaking about the body "offered for you". The body was broken and given by being crucified and given over (that is, offered) for you. Therefore, to make present "my body offered for you" in just this manner, is consequently to make present my body precisely as offered for you.

To grasp this point more deeply, note that if the Lord Jesus added "broken (or, given) for you" simply to indicate it was his true body, it would in fact have sufficed to say, "my body as you see me personally," or something else like this. But it would be alien to Our Lord Jesus Christ to use imprecise speech. If he had so spoken, we would be left to wander about amid infinite possibilities bereft of all certainty. But by saying, "my body broken (or, given) for you," he made his intention quite specific: make present my body precisely as offered for you, and do this action in commemoration of me.

Further, "doing this" in commemoration of Christ is more than simply by consecration to make the body of Christ present, because the "doing this" is making present the body of Christ given and broken for you. "Doing this" is also more than simply recalling Christ to mind, because it is making present the body of Christ given and broken for us and thereby recalling Christ to mind. Its being given and broken for us is its offering for us, since "being given" is a generic term for "being offered" and "being broken" refers specifically to the manner of offering, namely through being broken. On the cross Christ gave himself to God by having his hands, feet, and side broken open for us.

Consequently when the Lord Jesus commanded, "Do this in commemoration of me," he ordered that it be done in the manner of offering in commemoration of him. Making present the body of Christ which is offered is to do this by offering or in the manner of an offering. Only in this manner is the body of Christ made present precisely as offered. We do not make the body of Christ present precisely as offered unless we carry out both aspects: by consecration making the body of Christ present, and by offering making it present as given and broken for our sake. The third aspect is then the commemoration of Jesus Christ.

The perceptive reader will note and consider regarding the Last Supper how one institution corresponded to another institution, an action to another action, and an offering to another offering. The supper, with the eating of the Paschal Lamb, was instituted in commemoration of the exodus from Egypt. It consisted in an act of offering, since the supper was an offering of the Paschal Lamb. When the Lord Jesus had completed the sacrifice of the Paschal Lamb, he instituted a new sacrifice with himself as our Pasch to be offered. This he did saying, "This is my body which is given and broken for you. Do this in commemoration of me." It is as if he said explicitly that he was making a substitution: just as up to now you have kept the Pasch in commemoration of the exodus from Egypt, so from now on do this in commemoration of my offering. It is as if he spoke of the substitution of a new Pasch for the former and said, "You kept that Pasch by offering at a common supper; now do this by an offering at a common table in commemoration of me." The substitution of the new Pasch for the former shows that his words, "Do this in commemoration of me," refer to a doing in the manner of offering, since the former Pasch was carried out in the manner of offering.

Paul's narrative in 1 Corinthians 10[:16-21] also bears witness that this is the authentic meaning of Our Lord's command. Paul speaks of the sacred Bread and cup of the Blood of Christ among things offered, he refers to our table along with altars, and includes those who eat and drink at the table of the Lord with those who partake and drink of what was offered. Thus it is quite clear that the Apostles understood Christ's command, "Do this in commemoration of me," as referring to offering the Eucharist. In the time of the Apostles the Eucharist was understood in the Church of Christ to be not simply a sacrament but a sacrifice as well. The offering of the body and blood of Our Lord is in Scripture and not solely in Church usage and in later teachers. The Apostle's own words are as follows:

> Flee the worship of idols. I speak as to sensible men; judge youselves what I say. The cup of blessing which we bless, is it not a sharing in the blood of Christ? The bread which we break, is it not a sharing in the body of Christ? Because the bread is one, we though many are one body, since we all

share in the one bread. Consider Israel according to the flesh; are not those who eat the offerings sharers in the altar? What do I mean? That an idol is anything, or that an offering to an idol is anything? I mean, rather, that the offerings of the pagans are to demons and not to God. I do not want you to become sharers with demons. You cannot drink the cup of the Lord and the cup of demon$. You cannot share at the table of the Lord and at the table of the demons [1 Corinthians 10:14-21].

Thus far St. Paul.

Here the Apostle obviously lists the bread which we break and our cup of blessing along with what is sacrificed by Israel and with the offerings made to demons. He speaks of the table of the Lord along with the altar of Israel and the tables of demons. He mentions those who eat at the table of the Lord and who drink of his cup in the same breath with those who share in the victims of Israel's altar and those who partake of things offered to demons. From these parallels he argues that they cannot be sharers in what is offered to God and as well in what is offered to demons. The whole structure of Paul's argument from the offerings both to the true God and to demons would collapse, if the bread and cup of Christ were not offered to God. This is such clear evidence that the bread and cup of Christ were offered in Paul's time that our explanation is unnecessary.

4

CHRIST'S INSTITUTION OF THE EUCHARIST FOR THE FORGIVENESS OF SINS

By arguing in the same manner from Our Lord's command one can easily demonstrate the error in the second point made by the Lutherans, namely the denial that the Mass contains an offering for the forgiveness of sins. According to Matthew 26[:27f] the Lord Jesus took the cup and not only said, "This is my blood which is shed for many," but added, "for the forgiveness of sins," and then went on to the precept, "Do this in commemoration of me." The precept, "Do this," embraces therefore the act of offering the blood of Christ contained in the cup, not only as shed, but as shed for many for the forgiveness of sins. The literal meaning is that there is a parallel between the shedding of blood for the forgiveness of sins by the bloody victim for our sins and making present the cup of his blood shed for the forgiveness of sins. It is made present in an offering of the cup of blood precisely as shed for the forgiveness of sins, and as bringing about the forgiveness of sins, since being shed for the forgiveness of sins is to bring this about, at least objectively, whatever the actual effect might be.

Offering the body and blood of Christ under the form of bread and wine in commemoration of Our Lord Jesus Christ is therefore not a human invention but simply understanding and obeying the divine precept. That this offering is made for the expiation of sins is part of the same obedience, as is confirmed by constant and long-standing custom (the best interpreter of a law) in all the churches, not only the Latin and Greek, but those of the Armenians, Persians, and other spread over the whole world.

5

OBJECTIONS TO THE SACRIFICE OF THE MASS FROM THE EPISTLE TO THE HEBREWS

The Lutherans raise objections to these two doctrines from many statements in chapters 7 to 10 of the Epistle to the Hebrews. Three arguments are brought against the daily offering of the Eucharist.

The first argument proceeds from the multitude of priests. For the Epistle distinguishes between Christ, the priest of the new covenant, and the priest of the old covenant on this basis, namely, that while Christ is the sole priest, the others were many, and while Christ is an eternal priest, they were priests only for a time [Hebrews 7:23f]. It is therefore wrong to say that the new covenant includes an offering of such a kind that Christ, the unique priest, does not suffice. It is wrong for priests to be succeeding one another with the passage of time, as we see is required for the sacrifice of the Mass.

Second, they argue from the repetition of offerings. The Epistle distinguishes between the sacrifice of the old covenant and that of the new covenant on this basis, namely, that, the former was repeated daily by ordinary priests and annually by the High Priest, while the latter is repeated neither daily nor annually, since it was offered once and for all [Hebrews 7:27; 9:25]. It is wrong therefore to teach that the new covenant has a sacrifice that is to be frequently repeated.

Third, an argument is urged concerning what is offered. The Epistle distinguishes between the sacrifice of the old covenant and that of the new covenant on the basis that while previously the priest brought in the blood of goats, and the like, now Christ has offered himself once and for all through his own blood [Hebrews 9:12-14.19-26]. It is therefore wrong for us to offer under the form of bread and wine the same Christ who offered himself once and for all to suffice for all.[7]

Against the Eucharist being a sacrifice for sins the Lutherans also bring three arguments.

First, there is the question of repetition. In the old covenant the inability of its sacrifice to destroy sins is given as the reason for the repetition of sacrifice. If it cleansed from sin it would no longer be offered. Because the sacrifice of the new covenant does take away sins, it is not repeated [Hebrews 10:11-18]. Hence it is wrong to assert that the new covenant includes a sacrifice for sins that must be repeated, as is the case with the Mass.

Second, they urge the complete sufficiency of the single offering of Christ's sacrifice when he offered himself on the cross. By this he has made perfect all who draw near to himself [Hebrews 10:1-2.12-14]. Consequently it is detrimental to the complete sufficiency of Christ's sacrifice for the sins of the whole world to add another new covenant sacrifice for sins.

Third, an argument is made from the destruction of sins. The Epistle says that where no more sins remain to be expiated there is no need of an offering for sins. But all sins have been destroyed by the grace of the new covenant ratified by the death of Christ [Hebrews 9:15-17.26f; 10:18]. There is therefore no place in the new covenant for another offering for sins.[8]

6

RESPONSE TO OBJECTIONS

The basis for a true and understandable account of the different texts of Scripture on the sacrifice and priesthood of the new covenant lies in the oneness of the sacrifice offered simply, absolutely, and once and for all on the cross by Christ himself alone, and offered derivatively each day by the same Christ through ministers in his Church.

As the new covenant has a bloody offering, so it has an unbloody offering. We confess that Jesus Christ was the bloody offering offered once on the altar of the cross for the sins of the whole world. We also confess that the unbloody offering was instituted by Christ, that is, his body and blood under the form of bread and wine, as described in the Scripture passages treated above. But the bloody offering and the unbloody offering are not two offerings, but one and the same. What is offered is the same, since the body of Christ on our altar is none other than the body of Christ offered on the cross. The blood of Christ on our altar is none other than the blood of Christ shed on the cross. But the way in which this identical victim is offered is different. The unique, original, and basic way of offering was in a bloody manner, when in its own proper form the body was broken on the cross and the blood shed. But the daily, representative, and derived manner is unbloody, under the form of bread and wine, as Christ once offered on the cross is present again in the mode of an offering.

The bloody and unbloody offering therefore of the new covenant is one and the same as to what is offered and even as to the manner of offering in spite of the noted diversity. For even the unbloody manner of offering was not in itself instituted to be a disparate way of offering, but solely to refer to the bloody offering on the cross. Consequently, men of wisdom and understanding say that where one reality exists wholly for the sake of another there is in fact only one reality.[9] Strictly speaking, one cannot say there are in the new covenant two sacrifices, two victims, two offerings or immolations, and the like. For Christ is the bloody victim on the cross and the unbloody victim is Christ on the altar. The single victim offered once on the cross continues to be present in the manner of an offering in the Eucharist instituted by Christ and daily repeated.

We meet on our altar the continuation of the victim offered on the cross. Because of the identity of what is offered on the cross and on the altar, since it is one and the same body of Christ, we conclude that the offering on the cross and our offering on the altar are obviously not offerings of different victims. The victim of the cross and of the altar is the same, offered once on the cross but continuing in another manner on the altar by the mediation of Christ who said, "Do this in commemoration of me." When you join these two, namely, "Do this," and, "in commemoration of me," you can consider how one and the same thing that was done then we do in commemoration of Christ. The identical things broken and shed in the past continue under the form of bread and wine in commemoration of Chirst.

On this basis we can proceed to refute each of the six objections. Concerning the first, on the oneness of the priest, we answer that in the new covenant there is one priest, Christ. He is priest at our altar, since the ministers do not consecrate the body and blood of Christ in their own persons but in the person of Christ, as the words of consecration clearly show. They offer, acting in Christ's place. The priest does not say, "This is the body of Christ," but, "This is my body." In Christ's person he makes present the body of Christ under the form of bread, following the precept of Christ, "Do this." They conclude it is wrong to say the new covenant includes an offering, because this implies that Christ is not sufficient but must be succeeded by ministers. I answer that it is one thing to speak of disparate offerings requiring a succession of priests and something quite different to speak of the continuation of the offering made on the cross in a manner requiring a succession of ministers. The former is inappropriate in the new covenant, but the latter is proper in this covenant, to the end that the one victim offered once and for all might continually exercise influence.

To the second argument, on the repetition of offerings, I say that in the new covenant the sacrifice or offering is not repeated, but rather there continues in the manner of an offering the unique sacrifice offered once and for all. In the manner of its continuance a repetition does occur, but not in what is offered. Nor does the manner that is repeated constitute a sacrifice for itself but for the unbloody commemoration of the offering made on the cross. Such a repetition is not contrary to the teaching of the Epistle to the Hebrews. Evidence for this lies in the text where it is argued that if the sacrifice of the new covenant were repeated, Christ would have to suffer repeatedly [Hebrews 9:25f]. Manifestly the Epistle is speaking of repeating a sacrifice, and not of a repetition like that instituted by Our Lord Jesus Christ.

To the third argument, concerning what is offered, we respond that Christ's abundant and all-sufficient shedding of his own blood once and for all on the cross fits quite well with the continuation of that unique and all-sufficient shedding of blood on the cross in the Eucharist in the manner of an offering.

In response to the first argument against the Eucharist being an offering for sins, I grant that it was because of the inability of old covenant sacrifices to destroy sins that the repetition of this offering was prescribed. When they conclude it is wrong to assert that the new covenant includes a sacrifice for sins that must be repeated, I fully grant this in the strict sense. In the Mass the sacrifice is not repeated; rather, the sacrifice offered on the cross continues in the manner of an offering and is recalled in each Mass.

In response to the second argument, I say that the faithful should never consider for a moment that Mass is celebrated in order to supplement the effectiveness of the sacrifice offered on the cross. Mass is celebrated as a vehicle of the forgiveness of sins brought about by Christ on the cross. As the offering is not different, so the remission of sins offered is not different. As Christ entered heaven by his own blood to continue as an eternal priest interceding for us (as we read in the same Epistle [7:24f; 9:12.24]), so he continues with us in the manner of an offering interceding for us in the Eucharist. Just as the effectiveness and sufficiency of the supreme sacrifice on the altar of the cross does not exclude Christ's continuing in heaven in the work of interceding for us, neither does it exclude his continuing with us in the mode of an offering to intercede for us. Just as the continual intercession of Christ on our behalf in heaven does not derogate from the unique intercession of his death, no less is there a derogation in his continuing in the mode of an offering to intercede for us so we might be sharers in the forgiveness of sins brought about on the altar of the cross. This latter intercession occurs in mystery under the form of bread and wine, while the former occurs in heaven by Christ under his own proper form, the same under which he was crucified. If there is any derogation then it is in Christ's intercession under his own proper form after the unique intercession of his death. This derogates more from his death than intercession under an alien form. The former intercession would appear to be a supplementary intercession, but the latter appears to be a liturgical manner of intercession most appropriate to our condition.

Answering the third argument, we say that the saying, Christ's death forgives our sins, must be understood with the qualification that this is applied to us from Christ's death through the sacraments he instituted. We all agree on this as Christians. Among the sacraments Christ instituted is the sacrament of the Eucharist instituted by Christ himself in the manner of an offering, as we explained on the basis of the words of Christ and Paul. If therefore Christians come to need the forgiveness of sins after Baptism, the sacrifice of the Eucharist will profit them toward the forgiveness of sins by applying to them the effectiveness of the death of Christ. For those not needing forgiveness of sins, the Eucharist profits toward the sustenance of the soul, just as corporeal food and drink give sustenance to the body. Although the sacrament of the Eucharist was instituted in the manner of an offering in order to apply to its participants the expiation of sins brought about by the cross of Christ, it was not instituted solely for this purpose but as well for other benefits to the soul.

The sacrifice of the Mass celebrated by the Catholic Church in accord with the teaching of Christ and the Apostles stands therefore in agreement with all that is written in the Epistle to the Hebrews. This is said, admittedly, extending what is written there to touch on the Eucharistic offering. I know that according to the literal sense the author of this Epistle is speaking of bloody sacrifices, to show the excellence over all sacrifices of the old covenant of the bloody sacrifice offered by Christ in founding the new covenant. But admitting an extension of this kind appears to aid in clarifying Catholic truth, so that, to God's glory, no ground for any doubt might be left.

Rome, May 3, 1531.

VIII

GUIDELINES FOR CONCESSIONS TO THE LUTHERANS 1531

In this accord one must first be mindful of the distinction between matters of faith and matters of religious practice. There can be no concessions on matters of faith because they are of divine institution.[1] The Lutherans must believe and profess their faith in each and every article which the universal Church believes. This is what their forebears believed and what they themselves believed before the coming of the Lutheran innovations.

Nonetheless, two things should be avoided. First, the Lutheran teachers need not be required to retract what they have been saying and writing, but it can suffice that they simply refrain from this. Second, their princes and others need not be required to make the profession of faith with the ceremonies, but it can suffice for them to say they believe, etc. The reason for such a precaution is that if anything like this were demanded the whole accord would collapse, since they can never be brought to perform these public acts. After all, one tolerates the bandage applied to a wound.

Regarding matters of religious practice, the Lutheran demands come down to five points, which we will now take up individually.[2]

First, in the matter of clerical marriage, they can henceforth be allowed to follow the law of the Greek Church. Thus, for priests in Germany such marriages would be allowed as are permitted to the Greeks.[3]

Second, regarding marriages already contracted which are not allowed by Greek practice, we should lay down no policy, but should rather feign ignorance of them.[4]

Third, communion under both forms can be allowed, in accord with the terms of the bull of the Council of Basle for the Bohemians.[5]

Fourth, regarding the mass, one must in no way allow the exclusive use of another canon, but they must use both. To grant this point would cause great scandal.[6]

Fifth, there should be no specific changes in ecclesiastical laws governing the sacraments and other matters.[7] Instead, the following general accomodation can be applied to all precepts of human origin. Where we ascertain that the Lutherans have objections of any kind, this accomodation makes a general revocation. This is possible since the point at issue will be of either divine or human law. If it is of divine law, then the Church cannot take away what is prescribed. But if the objection concerns a precept laid down by human authority, then this accomodation will remove every misgiving that could trouble the conscience. Therefore, if one considers this step carefully, all problems of conscience will be solved, since this decree does not swerve from the truth of the Gospel and yet meets the wishes of all nations of the world.

The first points laid down special privileges for Germany, but this decree would apply universally to the Church of Christ.

Draft of a Decree

We define and declare that human precepts of all kinds, both those enacted by universal or local law and those imposed by superiors, even precepts binding under excommunication *latae sententiae*, henceforth bind the conscience in the following manner. If on any occasion a person does not obey such a precept and has an adequate reason for so doing, he is not guilty of sin. If he disobeys because of human weakness, his sin is slight, grave, or very grave in proportion to his sinful intention. But outside cases of contempt, such disobedience is not a mortal sin. Those guilty of contempt for law cannot, however, be excused from mortal sin.

No one should, however, conclude for himself or lead others to conclude that this salutary decree opens the way for him to marry a close kinswoman and thereby, as long as he acts without contempt, to avoid mortal sin. Neither should one conclude it is henceforth not a mortal sin to take over another's benefice as long as one acts without contempt. It should not be argued that marriage between close relatives is forbidden by positive law and that benefices are granted by ecclesiastical appointment. No one who knowingly does such acts, or others like them, can be considered free of mortal sin. The source of an impediment to marriage is irrelevant, since living with a woman who is not one's wife is clearly a mortal sin under divine law. Hence, as long as she is not your legitimate wife you continue to sin mortally by living with her. In the same way, it is irrelevant whence one legitimately receives a benefice, since one holding what belongs to another is obviously sinning against divine law. What we have said by way of example on these cases should be understood to apply in similar matters.[8]

IX

FOUR LUTHERAN ERRORS
1531

To the Supreme Pontiff, Clement VII:

I feel called to write by the stubbornness the Lutherans show, on alleged grounds of conscience, concerning reception by the people of both forms of the Eucharist, confession of less than all one's sins, the denial of satisfaction for sin, and rejection of the invocation of the saints.[1] I do not plan to treat these points comprehensively, but only regarding their derivation from Holy Scripture, since the Lutherans accept only the authority of Holy Scripture and profess to stand on this. What I write will not profit the stubborn, but I hope it will be of some use in restraining others from imitating them. It should also be of consolation and of no little comfort to the hearts of the faithful to have shown from Scripture the erroneous views the heretics teach while boasting how they hold to the holy Gospel. Even though I have written this on behalf of the Catholic Church, I submit it to the judgment of your Holiness no less than all my other writings.

1

COMMUNION UNDER BOTH FORMS

It is not enough for the Lutherans to receive Communion under both forms; they cannot indeed be persuaded to admit that

Communion under one form alone is allowable. They hold that both Christ's practice and command require reception under both forms.[2] We must therefore take up both points in the light of Holy Scripture and demonstrate that reception under one form alone by the people is prohibited neither by Christ's practice nor by his commands. When we have shown this, it will be evident that the people are not obligated by divine law to receive Communion under both forms.

Because at the Last Supper when Our Savior instituted the sacrament of the Eucharist he gave Communion to the Apostles under both forms, as the Evangelists bear witness, they conclude that a priest should give Communion only under both forms. Priests must distribute the Eucharist in the manner in which Christ distributed it, and we should all receive Communion in the manner the Apostles received.

We can easily show, however, that the practice of Christ and the Apostles does not have the force of a law obligating us to distribute the Eucharist to the people in a manner similar to theirs. For if Christ's practice had the force of law we would not be obligated to observe just certain parts of his way of distributing, while not observing other parts, but we would be obligated to follow every aspect of his practice. But we are obviously not obliged to follow every aspect of Christ's manner of distribution, and so we are not obliged in distributing the Eucharist to follow this one aspect of the two forms.

The fact that we are not obliged to observe every aspect is clear. Christ broke the bread and gave this broken form of bread, but it would be silly to say that a priest is bound to give a broken Host. As Christ distributed, he did not place the Eucharist in the mouths of the Apostles, but said, "Take and eat." But it would be inane to say a priest is prohibited from placing the Eucharist in the mouths of communicants but must place it in their hand so they can give it to themselves. Christ gave this sacrament to the Apostles after supper, but it would be quite ridiculous to say we are obliged to receive Communion after supper and it is forbidden to give the Eucharist to people who are fasting. Finally, Christ gave the Eucharist under the form of unleavened bread, but yet the whole Church admits there is no binding law requiring either unleavened or leavened bread. All these examples make it evident that Christ's practice in distributing the Eucharist does not have the force of law determining that we should distribute in a similar manner.

If one would argue that Christ's manner of distribution must be imitated in this one aspect of giving the Eucharist under both forms, then he should take note that Christ gave under both forms only to the Apostles, not to the seventy disciples nor to the multitudes who believed in him. All that one can therefore conclude from Christ's example is that the successors of the Apostles should be given the Eucharist under both forms. No more can be concluded from Christ's distribution, and so one cannot conclude that the Eucharist should be given all Christians under both forms.   It is evident that one cannot conclude from the practice of Christ that communion for the people under only one form is prohibited. Much less can one conclude this from the practice of the church at Corinth, about which Paul speaks in 1 Corinthians. The practice of one local church does not establish a law for other churches. — So much on Christ's practice.

We must now turn to the commands Christ gave both before the institution of the Eucharist and in the institution itself. A first command was at one time seen by the Bohemians in the words of Our Lord in John 6[:53], "Unless you eat the flesh of the Son of Man and drink his blood, you will not have life in you." What, they ask, could be more evident? The necessity of receiving Communion under both forms is enunciated in the same manner as was the necessity of baptism.[3] In the same manner as he spoke about baptism in John 3[:5], "Unless one is reborn of water and the Spirit, he cannot enter the kingdom of God," so he spoke of the Eucharist: "Unless you eat the flesh of the Son of Man and drink his blood you will not have life in you."

We answer, however, that in their authentic sense these words of Christ should not be interpreted as referring to the practice of the Eucharist, nor can they be so understood in the context of what we believe as Christians concerning sacramental food and drink.[4] This can be demonstrated quite easily, since if they were understood of the Eucharist this would undermine the sufficiency of Baptism for salvation. The necessity appears to be the same in both cases: concerning eating the flesh and drinking the blood of the Son of Man, and concerning the necessity of rebirth of water and the Spirit. Therefore it evidently follows that if the former words of Christ point to a necessity of receiving the Eucharist, then baptism is not sufficient for salvation. For one to have life, he would have both to be baptized and to receive the Eucharist.

Now we not only profess the contrary of this in the Creed, as we confess "one baptism for the forgiveness of sins", but Our Lord also said in the Gospel, "Whoever believes and is baptized will be saved" (Mark 16:16). Paul the Apostle wrote in Titus 3[:5], "He saved us ... by the washing of regeneration." Since, therefore, interpreting Christ's words in John 6[:53]˙ as referring to food and drink in the sacrament of the Eucharist would entail denying the sufficiency of baptism for salvation, it becomes evident that those words cannot be interpreted as referring to food and drink in the Eucharist. The text, consequently, does not issue a command obligating to reception of the Eucharist under both forms. Arriving at the authentic sense of those words of Christ is not part of our present undertaking; for the present question, one only needs to know that there Our Lord was not speaking of sacramental food and drink.

We can now take up the command Christ issued as he instituted the sacrament of the Eucharist. Look through all the gospels, and the only command you will find about the Eucharist is in Luke, immediately after the Eucharist was given under the form of bread: "Do this in commemoration of me" [22:19]. In Paul the Apostle, in 1 Corinthians 11[:24f], there are two commands recorded as given by Christ in the institution of the Eucharist: one immediately after giving the Eucharist under the form of bread, "Do this in commemoration of me," and the other immediately after giving the Eucharist under the form of wine, "Do this, as often as you drink it, in commemoration of me."

If each of these commands is examined carefully, it will become evident that none of them entails a command obligating to communion under both forms. The context itself shows that the command given immediately after the form of bread in both Luke and Paul obviously pertains to the Eucharist under the form of bread. The command recorded by Paul concerning the imitation of Christ in the Eucharist under the form of wine is, however, patently restricted to the times that we do drink in commemoration of Christ. It is not an absolute command, but one based on a supposition, namely, that if we drink in commemoration of Christ, we should do what Christ did. He did not command that we should drink in commemoration of him, but that whenever we do drink in his memory we should do what he did. As often as you use the chalice of the Eucharist, you should offer it in sacrifice. "To drink" manifestly refers to the use of the chalice, and consequently to doing a distinct action. "To drink" refers to consecrating it, and what is literally commanded is that we associate the use of the chalice with the sacrifice of the chalice.

By not commanding a similar association concerning use of the Eucharist under the form of bread, he suggests that use of the chalice outside of the sacrifice is forbidden, while use under the form of bread is allowed. The rite of the Church follows this rule, not reserving the Eucharist under the form of drink but only under the form of bread for the sick and for those who receive Communion outside solemn masses.

Someone could argue that because this command directly obligates priests, it binds the people as by a further consequence. Those who drink in commemoration of Christ are commanded, "Do this," from which evidently follows that priests celebrating masses (they clearly drink in commemoration of Christ) are commanded, "Do this," a command including as well the giving of the chalice to others. The command would embrace all that Christ did with the chalice, and so by this command a priest would be bound, whenever he drinks, to give the chalice to others and they are thereby bound to take and drink.

The person arguing this way should first take note of the words of the verse, since his interpretation does not fit with the verse's context. In the verse, "Do this" is distinguished from the drinking. Thus confecting the sacrament is distinguished from the use of the sacrament, and consequently "Do this" in this verse is not all-inclusive, but by the context is limited to indicating the sacrament itself, in distinction from the use of the sacrament, since it is distinguished from the use of the chalice. Whatever therefore refers to the use of the chalice is included here in the reference to drinking, while whatever refers to the sacrament itself is included under "Do this," in full accord with the meaning of the context. But it is evident that giving others the chalice refers to the use of the chalice and not to the sacrament itself. Consequently giving others the chalice is not included in this verse under "Do this."

One should finally take note that the Lutherans' practice is not consistent with what they say, since the argument obviously leads to obligating the celebrating priest to give the chalice to all present. This follows if "Do this" enjoins giving the sacrament in the manner in which Christ gave it. Christ gave it to all present, but the Lutherans do not observe this. Therefore the Christian people are not obligated to drink of the sacrament of the Eucharist by reason of this command of Christ, if the interpretation is to rest on the plain sense of the text and fit smoothly with it.

Since no command concerning eucharistic Communion is had in Holy Scripture except in the verses cited, it is evident that Christians are not obliged to receive Communion under both forms by a written command of divine right. It is therefore arbitrary and not grounded in Scripture when they proclaim that communion under the form of bread alone is forbidden. This is sufficient answer to the Lutherans who recognize only the authority of the Holy Scripture.[5]

This is what we have to say about communion under one form alone.

2

INTEGRAL CONFESSION OF SIN

The Lutherans not only deny that one must confess all the mortal sins he has committed, but they say that to do it would be contrary to Holy Scripture and is impossible, since it stands written [Psalm 18:13], "Who knows his offenses?"[6]

We say in response that, first, confession of all one's mortal sins rests on the Gospel; and, second, that it is not against the view cited from the prophet. The first can be shown from the form of administering the sacrament of Penance that Christ handed on when he instituted the sacrament in John 20[:22f]. Christ said to the Apostles, "Whose sins you forgive, they are forgiven, and whose sins you retain, they are retained." With these words Christ empowered the minister of the sacrament for two actions, either forgiving or retaining the sins of all men. Since the minister is empowered to discern whether the sins of each penitent are to be forgiven or retained, it evidently follows that the minister must know — unless he wants to administer blindly — whether any sins of the penitent are to be retained. This is the same as knowing whether anything in the penitent hinders forgiveness, since any retained sin would hinder the forgiveness of every sin of the person confessing.

One sin cannot be forgiven while another is retained, since all the mortal sins of the same person are evidently connected, both in regard to forgiveness and to retention, in relation both to God and to the minister of Christ. This clearly holds in relation to God, since a person whose sins God forgives is made a friend of God, according to the text, "Blessed is he to whom God imputes no sin" [Psalm 31:2]. But the person whose sin is retained remains in that one sin and is the enemy of God, since he is guilty of all, according to James 2[:10], "One who offends in one matter becomes guilty of all." Since both God's forgiveness and retention embrace all one's mortal sins, both the forgiveness and retention by the minister of Christ must consequently embrace not just some of the mortal sins of the penitent but all of them. For the forgiveness and retention by the minister should be such that his forgiveness is accompanied by divine forgiveness and his retention accompanied by divine retention. Otherwise Christ's words would not be verified, "Whose sins you forgive, they are forgiven, and whose sins you retain, they are retained." The forgiveness by the minister could not claim the accompaniment of divine forgiveness, if it were in discord with this divine forgiveness. But it would be in discord with the divine forgiveness if while God forgave all or retained all, the minister did not forgive all or retain all. So that the minister can either forgive all or retain all, he must have knowledge of all, unless he is to be a blind and rash minister of forgiveness and retention. Since the minister of Christ gains knowledge of the sins of the penitent through the latter's confession, the penitent must consequently confess all his mortal sins.

Let the knowledgeable reader examine, ponder, and weigh what I have said, and you will conclude that the confession of all one's sins derives from the very form of institution recorded in the Gospel.

It remains for us to refute the objections put forward by the Lutherans. We do this by distinguishing between confession taken absolutely and taken as a human act. To confess all one's sins absolutely is to leave no sin unconfessed. But to confess all, in so far as confession is a human act, is to confess all that by human power can be confessed.

Now since no one knows his offenses fully, it is impossible for one to confess all his sins absolutely, since unknown sins would remain unconfessed. Still, it does not thereby follow that one cannot humanly speaking confess all his sins, since an integral human confession does not include all sins absolutely speaking, but only those that are known and remembered. The confession of forgotten and unknown sins is beyond human ability. Since divine and human law obviously require of a person no action beyond his power, and since we have it from the Gospel that the confession of all sins is required for the sacrament of Penance, the confession of all sins absolutely cannot be meant, but rather the confession of all sins as that lies within human abilities. This is to say that the penitent is to confess all his sins, but not unknown or forgotten sins.

This is what needs to be said on confession of all sins.

3

SATISFACTION FOR SIN

The Lutherans reject satisfaction for sin, which is the third part of the sacrament of penance. They say satisfaction has no basis in Holy Scripture, since our works are neither meritorious nor satisfactory.[7]

We answer that Sacred Scripture teaches that satisfaction for sin is at times necessary after forgiveness and that it can be carried out through our words. The fact that satisfaction or punishment for sin can at times remain after sin is forgiven is witnessed by the twofold way God forgives sin. Sometimes God forgives both the guilt for sin and the punishment due, as in the case of the good thief, to whom Christ said, "Today you will be with me in Paradise" [Luke 23:43]. This is also the manner in which baptism forgives sin, since the baptismal grace alone suffices for eternal salvation, if before he dies the newly baptized person poses no further obstacle through sin. The ultimate effect of baptism is eternal life, and with forgiveness granted in this manner, there is evidently no need of satisfaction.

We also read, however, that in other cases God forgives sin without removing all need of punishment, as in 2 Samuel 12, where, after the prophet Nathan had accused David of adultery and murder, and after David had confessed, "I have sinned against the Lord" [12:13], Nathan answered, "The Lord also has put away your sin and you will not die. Nevertheless, the child born to you shall die" [12:13f]. God evidently forgave the sin as to the guilt and as to some of the punishment due, but he did not remit the punishment inflicted through the death of David's son, nor that suffered by his own son openly violating his wives (as recorded in Chapter 16), nor the punishment through that propensity to evil lodged in his own house. Because of his sin, David had to suffer much from his son Absalom. The prophet Nathan threatened David on behalf of God with all these punishments for that one sin. Since therefore God at times forgives sin while leaving an obligation of punishment after forgiveness, we must consequently say that God at times forgives sin without removing the full debt of punishment due for the sin. Thus the need arises to complete the remaining punishment not remitted when God forgave the sin.

This remaining punishment can be completed in two ways, either by suffering endured or by satisfaction rendered. David completed his satisfaction by suffering endured, since he did not inflict on himself the punishments due. Instead, God inflicted them on him. What remains is for us to show from Scripture that we can ourselves complete the remaining punishment by rendering satisfaction. If you read Chapter 3 of the Gospel of Matthew, you will see that John the Baptist preached two things: first, "Do penance" [3:2], and, second, "Bring forth fruit befitting penance" [3:8]. In the first, the Greek word indicated simply the act of repentance, obviously referring to the sin itself. But the second part of the words witness to our works following repentance, since the "fruits of penance" are works arising from penance as from a root or stock. He did not say, "Bring forth fruit befitting innocence," or, ". . . fruit befitting righteousness or goodness," but, ". . . fruit befitting penance." Consequently, he clearly meant quite specifically the fruit of penance as such, that is, a fitting product derived from interior repentance as its root. Since repentance pertains to previous sins, evidently the fruit befitting penance consists of works restoring that of which one repents. This is to repair what we repent of having neglected or done. This we call rendering satisfaction for our sins, since this entails the removal of all the evil left in the penitent from his sin, part of which is the debt of remaining punishment for his sin. If repentance does not yield fruit leading to the full restoration of all that the sinner lost through his sin, then it does not attain to the fruits befitting itself. Repentance tends by its own nature toward the completion of what it has begun, and it is clearly not complete as long as any debt remains to be paid from the sin.

Consequently we have it on the authority of Holy Scripture that at times one must make satisfaction after sin is forgiven, and this can be through works which are the fruits befitting repentance.

I think there is no need for futher discussion of the objection that our works are neither meritorious nor satisfactory. Scripture abounds with statements on both sides, with some denying that our works are meritorious and others affirming this. But these two views are obviously not contrary to each other. The meaning is that in so far as our works proceed from ourselves they are not meritorious and consequently not of satisfactory value; but in so far as they proceed from the divine grace that precedes, accompanies, and completes them, our works are meritorious and consequently of satisfactory value.[8] Both aspects are so obvious in myriad passages of Scripture as to be grasped with noonday clarity by those well grounded in the sacred text. We can therefore omit further treatment.

This answers the error on satisfaction for sin.

4

INVOCATION OF THE SAINTS

The Lutherans claim that invocation of the saints is not derived from Scripture.[9] Although I suspect they are not referring to the invocation of the holy angels, but of sainted men and women, we will stay on safe ground by first treating in summary fashion the holy angels, and then sainted men and women, showing what Scripture says about their invocation.

The fact that angels intercede for us is evident in the prophet Zechariah, where an angel says to God, "Lord of hosts, how long will you have no mercy on Jerusalem and the cities of Judah, against which your anger has continued seventy years?" [1:12]. And in Matthew 18[:10], Our Lord says that the angels plead on behalf of little ones who are despised: "See that you do not despise one of these little ones; I tell you their angels in heaven continually behold the face of my Father," doubtless to gain protection for the little ones who are despised.

We are taught to invoke the holy angels in Genesis 32[:26], where Jacob asked the angel to bless him, saying, "I will not let you go, unless you bless me." Then in Daniel 7[:16] the prophet related of himself, "I approached one of those standing there and sought from him the truth." No doubt he was referring to one of the holy assisting angels. Hebrews 1[:14] also refers to the holy angels, saying, "they are all ministering spirits, sent to serve for the sake of those who will attain the inheritance of salvation." Since God has arranged to govern us through intermediary angels, not for his own sake, but for the sake of us, the heirs of eternal life, we understand that he has ordained that we should invoke the holy angels as intermediaries between ourselves and God. Or are we to be so stupid as to say that once a prince or a court assigns an advocate to aid a pilgrim or orphan, the pilgrim or orphan is not to invoke the protection of the advocate assigned?

Since Holy Scripture is clear on the subject of the invocation of the holy angels, we can leave this topic and move to the invocation of sainted men and women. There are two manners in which we ordinarily invoke the saints, either by asking them directly, as in, "Saint Peter, pray for us," or by asking God through the merits of the saints, as the Church is accustomed to pray in the Canon of the Mass, saying, "By their merits and prayers may you grant . . . ." We hold that both manners are derived from Holy Scripture.

The fact that the souls of the saints intercede for us is attested in Revelation 6[:9f], "I saw under the altar the souls of those who had been killed for the word of God . . . and they cried out with a loud voice, saying, 'How long, O Lord holy and true, before you will judge and avenge our blood upon those who dwell on the earth?'" Now if the souls of the saints pray to God against evil persons dwelling on earth, how much the more will they pray for the salvation of the elect. The will of the saints is turned much more toward our benefit than toward evil for us. Again, in Luke 16 Our Lord revealed that the rich man in hell interceded for his brothers still in this life [16:27f]. This revelation suggests how much more the saints will intercede for the salvation of their own. For when the rich man was in this life he showed no interest in the salvation of his brothers; but once he was in torment, he prayed urgently for their salvation. How much more will sainted men and women, whose efforts in this life were for the salvation of their brethren, once they have put off the flesh and come to blessedness, continue the work done out of charity and intercede for the salvation of their brethren.

Matthew 27[:52f] indicates that we are to invoke the saints. It is written there that many bodies of the saints who had died rose, came into the holy city, and appeared to many. This shows that after the resurrection of Christ God rules and instructs us not only through the holy angels but through sainted men and women. They did not without purpose appear to many, but instructed them about the true Messiah and about his resurrection. Since up to that time God ruled us through the holy angels and not through sainted men and women, the beginning then of rule through sainted men and women suggests he had new intermediaries for ruling the elect. God wanted to show forth the sainted men and women who were now, through the merits of Christ's passion and resurrection, associated with the order of divine rule over us. Otherwise he would have sent angels into Jerusalem to appear to many and instruct them. The fact God revealed the resurrection of Christ not only through the angels who appeared to the women at the tomb, but also through the sainted men and women appearing to many in Jerusalem, indicates that God has now joined to the angels' ministry for our eternal salvation the ministry of sainted men and women.

It thus follows from the very order of divine rule, in which he rules us also through sainted men and women, that we are to have recourse to the saints. Otherwise we would fall into the same absurdity noted above, that is, if we are not to invoke the holy angels, for the apparitions cited from Revelation 6 and Matthew 26 bear witness that the saints have been appointed for our benefit as intermediaries between God and ourselves. So it is obvious that we may have recourse to these divinely given intermediaries. It would be no less absurd than before if God arranged to rule us through the intercession of sainted men and women (as our Scripture texts show he has done), and then we were not permitted to have recourse to these our intercessors.

Finally, Exodus 32 teaches that we are to pray to God through the merits of the saints. In Moses' prayer of petition to God, he said, "Remember Abraham, Isaac, and Israel, your servants" [32:13]. This is nothing other than asking through the merits of Abraham, Isaac, and Israel. If you join to this what was said above about the saints' intercession for us, you will evidently conclude that according to Scripture we are to supplicate God not only through the merits but through the prayers of the saints as well. You should add to this that praying to God through the merits and prayers of the saints comes down to the same thing as praying to the saints to offer their merits and prayers to God. The thing itself is the same, though the manner is different, but in both cases there is an invocation of the saints in one manner or another. Thus you may easily conclude that in every aspect the invocation of the saints is derived from Scripture.

Now that these answers have been given on the issues raised, let the reader recall that it is uneducated persons who demand the certitude of mathematical proof in matters of morality and the wider fields of our human actions.[10]

Rome, August 25, 1531.

X

FAITH AND WORKS —
AGAINST THE LUTHERANS
1532

To the Supreme Pontiff, Clement VII:

Obedience to the commands of Your Holiness is always due, but now it is for me a delight since I was wanting to refute the poisonous Lutheran views on faith and works. Fearing these were infecting even the hearts of the faithful, I had shortly before receiving Your Holiness' command felt called to write this treatise. This is consequently an agreeable act of obedience which I hope proves fruitful for Christ's faithful and pleasing to Your Holiness, whose office it is also to judge this short work.

1

THE LUTHERAN DOCTRINE OF FAITH

The Lutherans exalt the evangelical doctrine of man's eternal salvation through faith in Jesus Christ, our human Mediator between God and man. They teach that men attain the forgiveness of sins through faith in Jesus Christ, but they enlarge the term "faith" so as to include that conviction by which the sinner approaching the sacrament believes he is justified by the divine mercy through the intercession of Jesus Christ. They assign such great value to this conviction that they say it attains the forgiveness of sins through the divine promise.[1] They affirm that unless one has this firm conviction about the Word of God, one is despising the divine Word by not believing the divine promise.[2] But if in receiving the sacrament one firmly believes he is justified, then he is truly justified. Otherwise the divine promise would not be true and effective.

Some Lutherans so extol this kind of faith that they teach it attains the forgiveness of sins before the sinner has charity.[3] They base this on extended texts of the Apostle Paul which distinguish justifying faith from the law. Charity, they hold, is included under the law, since the first and greatest commandment of the law is to love God with one's whole heart, and so on, as Our Lord said in the Gospel, in Matthew 22[:37].[4] – These views make up the heart of Lutheran teaching concerning faith.

2

A FIRST ERROR:
EQUIVOCAL USE OF THE TERM "FAITH"

"Faith" means one thing when Holy Scripture refers to that which justifies men, and means something else when it refers to that conviction by which one believes he is justified by Christ and the sacraments. Justifying faith is that which Hebrews 11[:1] defines: "Faith is the substance of things hoped for, and the conviction of things not seen." Taken in this sense, faith is one of the three theological virtues referred to by Paul, "Now faith, hope, and charity remain" [1 Corinthians 13:13]. Taken in this sense faith is the gift of God, as written in Ephesians 2[:8], by which we are saved and without which it is impossible to please God. By such faith we believe all the articles of faith and whatever is to be believed as necessary to salvation.

But faith, taken as a conviction by which a person believes he is justified as he here and now receives this sacrament by the merit of Christ, is much different from faith taken in the first way. As a first indication of this, consider what is believed. Now faith cannot hold to something false, but this conviction can be deceived, since it concerns a particular effect here and now. This conviction arises in part from the faith that is necessary for salvation and in part from human conjecture. Concerning the merit of Christ and the sacraments, it is faith that calls for such a conviction; but concerning the effect here and now in one's own case, it is human conjecture that gives rise to the conviction.

It is a matter of Christian faith that anyone trusting in the merit of Christ and inwardly and outwardly receiving the sacrament correctly is justified by divine grace. But Christian faith does not extend to the belief that I am at this moment inwardly and outwardly receiving the sacrament correctly. Similarly I am held by Christian faith to believe that the true body of Christ is in a correctly consecrated host, but Christian faith does not extend to the belief that the host consecrated at this moment by this particular celebrant on this altar is the body of Christ, since this latter can for various reasons be false.

A second consideration is that all Christians share in one and the same faith, according to Ephesians 4[:5], "One Lord, one faith." Obviously, my own faith does not entail believing that this man who is receiving the sacrament is here and now justified or that the body of Christ is in a particular host. Consequently no one's "faith" entails believing this particular effect of this sacrament in the case of this individual. Therefore, the unity of faith brings to light the second difference between faith and the conviction described.

Hence the first error of the Lutherans in this matter is that they attribute to this conviction what Holy Scripture attributes to faith. When they teach this conviction they constantly cite texts of Holy Scripture on faith, such as, "As justified by faith, we have peace with God" [Romans 5:1], and "by faith purifying their hearts" [Acts 15:9] and countless texts like these.[5]

3

THE SECOND ERROR:
TEACHING THAT THIS CONVICTION ATTAINS FORGIVENESS OF SINS

Their assertion that a conviction of this type attains the forgiveness of sins can be said and understood both rightly and wrongly. If it is said and understood that this conviction informed by faith and charity attains forgiveness of sins, this is true. But if the informing influence of charity is excluded, then it is false. As Augustine says in *De Trinitate*, Book XV, Chapter 18, there is no more excellent gift of God than charity, which alone distinguishes the sons of the eternal kingdom from the sons of eternal perdition.[6]

One should know that this conviction is in fact shared by all who devoutly approach the sacraments. A person devoutly approaching any sacrament does believe that by receiving it he is justified by the merits of the passion and death of Christ, or else he would not so approach. But this conviction is not the same in all, since one person may believe more than another that he is justified. Generally the devout join to this conviction a doubt, namely, that the contrary may be the case. They do this since no text of Scripture and no document of the Church teaches us that we must hold this conviction against all doubt. The reason for doubt is that generally no one knows whether on his part something impedes reception of the gift of forgiveness of sins. Generally, one does not know whether he is lacking the grace of God.[7] Hence such a doubt entails no despising of the divine promise. One is not doubting about God, not about the merit of Christ, and not about the sacrament, but one is doubting about himself. It is written [Psalm 18:13], "Who understands his own sins?" Further evidence for this ordinary doubt about a particular effect of the divine mercy, that is, the forgiveness of sins of an individual now devoutly turning to God, is found in chapter 2 of the prophet Joel. After speaking of those who had turned to God with their whole heart in fasting, weeping, and lament, and after referring to the greatness of God's mercy toward sinners, the prophet added [Joel 2:14], "Who knows whether God will turn and forgive?" Thus no one among those who were converted was certain, but each had some doubt whether God forgave them.

A confirmation of this lies in the fact that the doubt affecting this conviction would only be justifiably removed by one of three causes. First, divine revelation could bring this about, but this is not to the point here, since although God has revealed that all do attain forgiveness who inwardly and outwardly trust correctly that they attain this, he has not revealed that this person is now correctly turning to God inwardly and outwardly. This particular effect is not included in the revelation on which Christian faith is based. Second, a sufficient number of testimonies can motivate one to believe in a particular fact. For instance, a sufficient number of testimonies can bring one who has never left Rome to believe that the island of Calicut or Taproban does exist. But obviously in the case of the conviction by which one believes he is justified there do not occur any testimonies that bring the mind to be convinced about this effect now in oneself. Third, the special competence of witnesses could remove the doubt, for instance, if they were beyond all objection, as in Romans 8[:16] where the Apostle writes that the Holy Spirit bears witness to our spirit that we are sons of God. This witness presupposes that the forgiveness of sins has been conferred, because it presupposes that the one about whom witness is given is in fact a son of God, as the text clearly indicates.[8] But the conviction asserted by the Lutherans does not presuppose in one the forgiveness of sins, but is itself the way of attaining this, as a prior reality attains what follows.

Hence it is to posit an arbitrary dogma to say that this sort of conviction about the word of Christ, based on the merit of his passion, and so on, infallibly attains the forgiveness of sins. Consequently Leo X included the following among the condemned articles of Luther:

Sins are not forgiven unless when the priest forgives one believes they are forgiven; in fact, sins remain unless one believes he is forgiven. It is not sufficient that sins be forgiven and grace be given; one must also believe he is forgiven.[9]

You should in no wise trust you are absolved because of your contrition, but because of the words of Christ, "Whatever you loose . . ." Rely on these if you receive the priest's absolution; firmly believe you are absolved, and you will truly be absolved, however it might be with your contrition.[10]

If perchance, as could not occur, one is not contrite when he confesses, or if the priest gives absolution in jest and not seriously, still if one believes he is absolved, he is in fact truly absolved.[11]

4

THE THIRD ERROR: FORGIVENESS OF SINS
PRECEDING CHARITY

It is intolerable that one's sins would be forgiven before charity is infused in the person forgiven, as the following will convincingly show. An enemy cannot be made a friend unless he have the attitude of friendship. A friend devoid of the quality of friendship would be incomprehensible, just as something white is incomprehensible without whiteness. But when the unrighteous man is made righteous through Christ, an enemy of God is transformed into a friend of God, as the Apostle says in Romans 5[:10], "When we were enemies we were reconciled to God by the death of his Son." Reconciliation makes the reconciled person a friend. Hence it is impossible and incomprehensible that a sinner be justified in the absence of friendship toward God. Charity is this friendship between man and God, being both man's love of friendship toward God and God's love toward man. "God is love, and he who abides in love abides in God, and God in him" [1 John 4:16]. We read in the same Epistle, "We love God, because he first loved us" [4:19].

Since friendship consists in mutual love, the forgiveness of sins takes place essentially through charity. Hence what we call the righteousness of faith is identical with charity. We speak of the righteousness of faith, since by it a person is righteous before God, conformable to the divine realities and deeds in which we believe. The sense appetites are subject to the will, the will to right reason, and right reason is subject to God in conformity to what we accept in faith about him and about our heavenly homeland. We call the same thing charity since it also involves the love of friendship toward the God who is granting us citizenship in the heavenly homeland. Philippians 3[:20] says, "Our citizenship is in heaven." And Ephesians 2[:19], "You are no longer guests and strangers, but citizens with the saints and members of God's household." Also, in the Canticle, "My beloved is mine, and I am his" [2:16].

This reasoning suffices in itself to convince the mind, but it is further supported by the authority of Christ, and of Peter, John, and Paul, all of whom attribute the forgiveness of sins to both faith and charity. In Luke 7[:50], Christ said to the sinful woman, "Your faith has saved you." But he also said about her: "Many sins are forgiven her, because she has loved much" [7:47]. In this text the conjunction "because" shows that love is the proximate cause of the forgiveness of sins, that is, "because she has loved." Faith is the cause inchoatively, but charity is the cause completing the forgiveness of sins.

Peter the Apostle said in Acts 10[:43], "To him all the Prophets bear witness that everyone receives forgiveness of sins who believes in his name." Then in his first Epistle, chapter 4[:8], he wrote, "Charity covers a multitude of sins."

In a similar way the Apostle John wrote in chapter 5 of his first Epistle, "Everyone who believes that Jesus is the Christ is born of God" [5:1]. And in chapter 3, "We know that we have passed from death to life, because we love the brethren. One who does not love remains in death" [3:14]. Granted that John wrote specifically about love of the neighbor, but this does not disprove our point, since obviously the charity by which we love God for his own sake is identical with that by which we love the neighbor for the sake of God. John's first Epistle says this in chapter 4[:7-12] and finds evidence for the passage from death to life only in such love of the neighbor [3:14].

Finally, the Apostle Paul, in Romans 5[:1], wrote, "Justified by faith, we have peace with God." But in First Corinthians 13[:2], "If I have all faith, so as to move mountains, but have not charity, I am nothing," nothing, that is, in the spiritual realm where we are made children of God. In Galatians 5[:6] he wrote, "In Christ Jesus neither circumcision nor uncircumcision avails anything, but rather faith working through love." What avails in Christ is evidently not just any kind of faith but that working through love.

It is evident therefore that the ordinary teaching of the Chruch is true that the forgiveness of sins occurs not by uninformed faith but by faith informed by charity. The normative texts teaching that we are made righteous by faith are consequently to be understood in the precise sense of faith informed by that friendship toward God, which we call charity.

Now it was objected that faith is made distinct from and opposed to the law, and that charity is included under the law. We answer that when Christ spoke of the first and greatest commandment of the law, he used "law" in a different sense than did the Apostle in distinguishing faith from the law [Matthew 22:37f]. Christ used "law" to indicate all the divine commandments written in the books of Moses. But the Apostle spoke of "law" in a narrower sense, as embracing moral, ceremonial, and juridical precepts.

I have not invented this distinction, but have taken it from Scripture itself, so that even the adversaries should accept it. The fact that Christ used "law" in a broad sense is proven by the text of Deuteronomy 6 from which he cited the precept concerning love of God [6:5]. Immediately before this, there is a precept concerning faith, where it says, "Hear O Israel: the Lord our God is one Lord" [6:4]. In the same passage of the law there is laid down a precept of faith, believing God is only one, and a precept of loving the same God. We are to understand that a precept concerning charity is no less included in the law than a precept concerning faith, when we take "law" in a broad sense. Hence it is also clear that just as the Apostle distinguishes faith from the law, one can equally well distinguish charity from the same law.

But the fact that the Apostle speaks of the law in a manner excluding the elements of faith and charity is obvious when he calls it the "law of works" [Romans 3:27, Vulgate], and says that the gentiles observe it by nature, as in Romans 2[:14], "the gentiles who do not have the law do by nature what the law requires." It is certain that they do not do by nature what charity requires.

Since this objection equivocates in speaking of "law", it consequently is of no worth. Love of God is not embraced by the law of works which is distinguished against faith, but is under the same law that includes faith, as in Deuteronomy 6 where precepts of faith and love of God occur together. Answers to the other objections of the Lutherans are obvious from what has been said. — This is sufficient treatment of faith.

5

THE LUTHERAN TEACHING ON WORKS

The Lutherans teach that our works are neither meritorious of grace and eternal life, nor do these works make satisfaction for sins.[12] They argue that since Christ has superabundantly merited for us both the grace of forgiveness of sins and eternal life, and since he satisfied superabundantly for all, it is consequently perverse to attribute to our works the merit of grace (or of forgiveness of sins) and of eternal life, and to say our works satisfy for our sins. Such teaching is said to insult Christ, since it is blasphemy to attribute to ourselves what is Christ's own work. If there is need of our merits and satisfaction, this detracts from the merit and satisfaction of Christ, implying they are inadequate.[13]

These denials are made on the basis of many texts of Scripture, beginning with those asserting that we do not merit by our works the forgiveness of sins. This is proven by Paul's demonstration in Romans and Galatians that we are justified not by works but by faith. He cited Habacuc 2[:4], "The man righteous by faith will live" [Romans 1:17, Galatians 3:11]. Paul wrote to Titus, "Not by works of righteousness that we did, but through his mercy, he saved us" [3:5]. Also, in Ephesians 2[:8f], "By grace you have been saved through faith, not of your own doing, but by the gift of God, not because of works, lest one should boast."[14]

The fact that we do not merit eternal life through works, but attain it by the gift of God, is shown in Romans 6[:23], "The wages of sin is death, but the gift of God is eternal life."[15] Luke 17[:10] is cited to prove the same point and at the same time to demonstrate that no matter how righteous we may be, our works do not make satisfaction for sins: "When you have done all that I command you, say, 'We have done what we ought, we are unworthy servants.'"[16] If they are unworthy servants who have kept all the commandments of Christ, then clearly the reward is not merited. Those then who have not kept all the commandments, and so need to make satisfaction, are much more unworthy and incapable of making satisfaction.

I can omit the texts proving the sufficiency of Christ's merit and satisfaction on our behalf. About this there is no controversy.

The Lutherans therefore teach that good works are to be done, because they are commanded by God as the fruit of justifying faith, but not because they are meritorious of eternal life and satisfactory for sins.[17]

6

THE MEANING OF MERIT IN THIS CONTEXT

Before determining whether our works are meritorious or not, we must first briefly examine what is meant by merit and how theologians understand it in this context concerning our works.

Merit is said of a voluntary work, whether interior or external, to
which by right a payment or reward is due. The Apostle says in
Romans 4[:4], "To one who works payment is not accounted as a
grace, but as his due." Hence four elements go together to constitute
merit: the person meriting, the voluntary work of merit, the
payment due for the merit, and the person rendering payment. The
last is essential, since it would be pointless to merit unless it be from
some person rendering one payment.

Since we are discussing our merit before God, we must explain
how men can merit from God a reward for their works. It appears
problematical that God would by right render payment for our
work, since between ourselves and God there is no right, strictly and
absolutely speaking. Scripture says, "Enter not in judgment with
your servant, Lord" [Psalm 142:2]. There is only a derived kind of
right, which is much less than the right of a son toward his father
and of a slave toward his master. How much less are we in relation to
God than a man who is slave in relation to the man who is his
master, and than a son in relation to the earthly father who begot
him. So, if as is written in Book V of the *Ethics*,[18] there is no right
strictly and absolutely speaking, but only a derivative kind of right
between slave and master and between father and son, then much
less is there a right between ourselves and God.

All that the slave is belongs to the master. A son cannot render
as much to his father as he received. Hence a right, strictly and
absolutely considered, cannot exist between master and slave and
between father and son. It is true to a much greater extent that all
that a man is belongs to God and that man cannot render as much to
God as he received. Hence man cannot merit something from God
that would be due him by right, unless this be a right so weakened
that it be far less than the right between master and slave and father
and son. Even such a weakened right is not, absolutely speaking,
found between man and God, because absolutely speaking man's
every voluntary good action is due to God. In fact, the more and the
better a man's interior and outward works, so much more does he
owe to God, since it is God who works in us both to will and to
complete our every action [Philippians 2:13]. This weakened right is
found between man and God by reason of the divine ordination by
which God ordained our works to be meritorious before himself.

When man merits anything before God, God never becomes man's
debtor, but rather his own. If even this weakened debt were given in

an absolute sense between man and God, then God would owe man the payment he earned. But it is obvious that God is in debt to no one, as Paul says in Romans 12[=11:35], "He who has given the gift, shall he then reward this?" God is therefore indebted to himself alone, that he should carry out his own will by which he granted that human works would be meritorious so he would render to man the reward for his work.

This is undoubtedly true about the simple and absolute sense of merit. In other cases, an agreement is presupposed between God and man on some matter, as among men when a master makes a pact of some kind with his slave. In this case a right can arise between master and slave. Thus if God deigns to make a pact with man, a right can arise between man and God with reference to the matter of the agreement. We often read in the Old Testament that God deigned to enter covenants with men. Genesis 9[:9-16] records God's covenant to never again permit a flood over the whole world. Genesis 15[:18-21] describes God's covenant with Abraham concerning the land of Canaan which was to be given to his offspring. Genesis 17[:1-11] tells of the covenant of circumcision. In Exodus 24[:8] Moses says, "This is the blood of the covenant . . ." In Jeremiah 31[:31-34] God speaks explicitly of the covenants of the old and new law. In the New Testament Our Savior reveals God under the form of the householder hiring workmen for his vineyard for a day's wages, in Matthew 20[:1-16]. "After making an agreement for a denarius a day, he sent them into his vineyard" [20:2]. Further on [20:13], "Did you not enter into an agreement with me?"

These texts make it clear that there can be in our works an element of merit even by right, with reference to the reward concerning which an agreement has been made with God.

Keep in mind though that to whatever extent there is a pact between God and man concerning a reward, still God never falls into our debt, but is only in debt to himself. For in view of the agreement made, there is due to our works the reward on which was agreed. God does not thereby become indebted to us regarding this reward, but rather indebted to his own prior determination by which he deigned to enter a pact with us. Consequently we profess in full truth that God is indebted to no one but to himself. One can therefore ascertain a double aspect of merit before God in our works. There is first the weakened right, and second the agreement. But never is God indebted to us. — These, then, are the initial considerations for a right understanding of the terms used in treating our merits before God.

7

HUMAN WORKS MERIT SOMETHING FROM GOD

God has revealed in Holy Scripture that human works have some merit with himself. To avoid becoming occupied in explaining each text of Holy Scripture on this point, we should realize that whenever God promises man a reward, merit is to be understood as entailed, since reward and merit are correlative to each other. Merit is merit of a reward and a reward is reward for merit.

Consequently, whenever you read in Holy Scripture that God promises man a reward, no further explanation is required for you to conclude that man can have merit with respect to the reward God will render. But in both testaments God openly promises men rewards. In Genesis 15[:1] he said to Abraham, "I shall be your own great reward." Isaiah 40[:10] says, "Behold, the Lord will come; behold, his reward is with him." In Ezechiel 29[:18] God says, "Son of man, Nebuchadnezzar, king of Babylon, made his army labor greatly against Tyre . . . but no payment was given him." Then he added, "The land of Egypt shall be his army's payment" [29:20]. In Matthew 20[:8] God says, "Call the workmen and pay them their wages." Also, in Revelation 22[:12], "Behold, I am coming soon, bringing my reward, to render to each one according to his works."

In these texts there is clear evidence that not only the works of the saints are meritorious of some benefit from God, but also the works of evil men and even of pagans such as the King of Babylon and his army. The latter besieged Tyre without any intention of serving God, but nonetheless God bore witness that they have merited a reward as he decreed that Egypt shall be given them as this reward. Hence we are to understand that the divine goodness is so generous as even to bring the wars of mankind into his service and to rejoice in admitting even evil actions as meritorious of some benefit from himself. From this we have impressive evidence that God is by far more willing to admit the good deeds of men as meritorious of some reward from himself.

8

ETERNAL LIFE MERITED BY LIVING MEMBERS OF CHRIST

Many agree that human works are meritorious of some benefit from God, but not of eternal life. Therefore we must show specifically that the works of the living members of Christ are meritorious of eternal life. Our Savior said in Matthew 5[:12], "Rejoice and be glad for your reward is great in heaven." Thus the heavenly reward of those who suffer for Christ's sake entails first of all beatitude, or eternal life. When Matthew 20[:9f] describes the payment given the workmen, saying they received a denarius, it is obvious that the payment given to all the workers in the Lord's vineyard is eternal life.

Paul wrote in Timothy 4[:7f], "I have fought the good fight, completed the course, and have kept faith. For the rest, there is laid up for me a crown of righteousness which the Lord, the just judge, will grant me." Clearly the crown given Paul is first of all beatitude. Also, unless the reward was due by reason of his previous works, it would not be true that God is giving him the crown precisely as the just judge. Paul obviously teaches that eternal life is due to him by right because of the works he referred to. Our Lord made the same thing clear in describing how in judging the world he will give eternal life in return for the works of mercy. "I was hungry and you fed me . . ." [Matthew 25:35]. This scene ends: "These go away for eternal punishment, but the righteous enter eternal life" [25:46]. The judge determines this by reason of the diversity of works, as the works merit; otherwise, he would not have given the reasons on each side.

According to Holy Scripture, therefore, the works of some men are clearly meritorious of eternal life. What is more, according to Matthew 20, the workmen merit this by reason of an agreement. Origen, Jerome, Augustine, Gregory, and Chrysostom all explain the denarius given to each as the beatitude in which the blessed share.[19]

9

HOW OUR WORKS MERIT ETERNAL LIFE

Theologians say that our works are meritorious of eternal life, because they arise from charity, from sanctifying grace, and from the Holy Spirit dwelling within us. Human works, as proceeding from our free choice, are not meritorious of eternal life, except by a certain kind of fittingness, by which it would be proper for God to reward out of the abundance of his grace a man who uses his free choice rightly in the things pertaining to God. However, in so far as these works stem from the Spirit dwelling in a person through grace and charity, they are meritorious of eternal life.

Grace, or charity, is comparable to the seed of God mentioned in 1 John 3[:9], whose power extends to producing fruit, so that just as the fruit is due by natural right to the action of the seed, so the fruit of eternal life is due to the actions of divine grace in the soul. Also, divine grace, as Our Lord said in John 4[:14], becomes in the man having it a spring of water welling up unto eternal life. This clearly indicates the efficacy of grace in us to attain to eternal life. By saying that the grace given wells up unto eternal life, he teaches that the attaining takes place by an intervening activity, since what occurs in me after accepting grace occurs with my cooperation. Especially, the power of the Holy Spirit dwelling in a person is adequate for attaining eternal life and for bringing it about that eternal life is due to his works in us.

A more manifest and convincing reason for merit of this kind can be seen in the fact that meriting eternal life is less our own action than the action of Christ who is head in us and through us. When we begin with the Apostle's teaching, in Romans 12[:4f], Ephesians 4[:15f], and Colossians 2[:19], then persons in grace are living members of Christ the head. Christ the head and the persons who are his living members do not make up a body of a political type, like the body of citizens in a well-governed state. Rather they constitute a body like a single natural body, since Christ the head gives life to his members by his own Spirit. As is clear in Paul's texts, he unites the members of the body by spiritual bonds and ligaments. Going on from this, we find that Holy Scripture also teaches that the sufferings and deeds of Christ's living members are the sufferings and deeds of Christ the head. Christ himself gives evidence concerning the sufferings in Acts 9[:4], "Saul, Saul, why are you persecuting me." But Saul was persecuting his members. In Galatians 4[=3:1, Vulgate] Paul reminds the Galatians that Christ had been crucified in them, no doubt referring to the sufferings they had undergone for Christ. Concerning actions, Paul said in 2 Corinthians 13[:3], "Do you desire proof of him who speaks in me, that is, Christ?" He said in an all-embracing manner in Galatians 2[:20], "I live, now not I, but Christ lives in me." Hence I can most truly say, "I merit, now not I, but Christ merits in me; I fast, now not I, but Christ fasts in me," and so on, about the other voluntary actions carried out for God by Christ's living members. In this way the merit of eternal life is not so much attributed to our works as to the works of Christ the head in us and through us.

Consequently we discern a difference between the merit of eternal life by baptized infants and by adults advancing in God's grace. Eternal life is due the infants solely by the merit Christ gained as he lived, suffered, and died in this mortal life. But to adults progressing in grace eternal life is due in a two-fold manner, first by right of the merit Christ gained in his own person and then by right of the merit of Christ working meritoriously as the head in and through this adult person. It is appropriate to the divine munificence to grant the merit of eternal life in both manners to adults who are God's sons and daughters. As we read in Romans 8[:29], "He predestined them to be conformed to the image of his son." Those however are more conformed to Christ who have merit of eternal life in both manners rather than only in the first. Christ's own glory was due him by a two-fold right. First it was his by right of the grace of personal union by which the Word was made flesh, a right devolving on Christ without his meriting. Second, the same glory was due Christ by the merit of his obedience unto death, as Paul says in Philippians 2[:8f], "He became obedient unto death, death on the cross. Therefore God has exalted him . . ." Hence Christ has glory by a two-fold right, and we are made conformed to him by attaining eternal life by a two-fold right, namely without our own meriting but through the merit of Christ in his own person, and with our meriting through the merit of Christ the head in and through us.

As it pertained to Christ's excellence also to gain eternal life for his body, glory for his name, and the like, by his own merit, so it belongs to the dignity of a member of Christ to cooperate with his Head in attaining eternal life. "The most divine thing of all is to become a cooperator with God," says Dionysius in the *Heavenly Hierarchies*, chapter 3.[20] Thus, you see it is not superfluous for us to merit eternal life, for this is to make eternal life our due in another manner or by an additional right, just as Christ merited his exaltation, making it due to himself by an additional right. — We will respond below to the objections urged against this.

10

WORKS PERFORMED IN MORTAL SIN

We agree that the works performed by persons in mortal sin are neither meritorious of eternal life nor of the forgiveness of sins. Nonetheless they are of considerable importance for a man caught in mortal sin, since Holy Scripture says they lead to attaining forgiveness of sins. Although these works have no power to merit forgiveness of sins, they do have power to impetrate this forgiveness, since in the manner of a supplication they are of great value in attaining from the divine goodness the forgiveness of sins. Our Savior bears witness that prayer is of considerable importance toward gaining forgiveness of sins, when in Luke 18[:13] he described the Publican as praying, "God, be merciful to me a sinner." Thereby he obtained mercy. Joel witnesses to the value of fasting when he speaks in God's stead, "Turn to me with all your heart, in fasting, weeping and lament" [2:12]. The remark follows [2:14], "Who knows whether God will turn and forgive?" The value of alms is shown by Daniel in Chapter 4[:24], where he counsels King Nebuchadnezzar, "Redeem your sins by alms." Hebrews 13[:16] says, "Forget not giving aid and sharing what you have; by such offerings God is appeased." The same can be affirmed concerning pilgrimages, hardships, continence and other acts of this kind.

Over and above this power of supplication, Holy Scripture points to a greater power of impetration in the observance of all the commandments of God. Ezechiel 18 teaches us that the conversion of the sinner to keeping the commandments of the law leads eventually to the forgiveness of sins. The text reads,

> You say, 'the way of the Lord is not just.' But hear now, House of Israel. Is my way not just? Is it not your ways that are not just? When a righteous person turns from his righteousness and commits sin, he shall die in the sin he committed. When an evil person turns away from the sin he committed and lives righteously, he will gain life for his soul. Because he took thought and turned away from all the sins he committed, he shall live and not die [Ezechiel 18:25-28].

This text indicates that the justice of God's ways consists in this, that just as the turning of a righteous person from righteousness to sinful deeds leads to the death of the soul, so the conversion of a sinner to good deeds leads to life for his soul. It was revealed to the prophet that the conversion of a sinner with regard to works (that is, from evil works to good works for God's sake) is so pleasing to God that he no longer considers all his previous sins. This is the same as granting forgiveness of sins and the life of grace.

God revealed a yet greater power of impetration in works of this kind by men caught in sin in a passage of Isaiah:

> Wash yourselves, make yourselves clean, remove the evil of your thoughts from my sight, cease to act wickedly; learn to do good and seek what is right, aiding the oppressed, defending the orphan, and taking the part of the widow, and we can reason together, says the Lord. If your sins are like scarlet, they will become white like snow; if red like crimson, they will become like white wool [Isaiah 1:16-18].

From this we learn that God's largess is so great that to those converted from wickedness to works of righteousness and mercy God presents himself as arguing their case if he has not forgiven their past sins.

We have therefore gained this from divine revelation: the good works of sinners are not only of importance toward the forgiveness of sins, but when they stem from the heart of one turning to God, God's generous love so accompanies them that they do lead to forgiveness of sins and impetrate this as if an agreement had been made. God is truly generous toward us, arranging that in spite of our inability in the state of sin to merit the forgiveness of sins, we are capable of impetrating this by prayer, fasting, alms, and other good works.

God's immense love for sinners and desire of their salvation is shown in his deigning to grant the power of impetrating forgiveness of sins to our good works even done in sin. In addition, as we showed in Chapter 7 from the text of Ezechiel, these works are meritorious of certain temporal benefits from God. Consequently sinners should be urged to perform good works, since they are in fact of value in impetrating and attaining the forgiveness of sins, when done devoutly.

11

WORKS SATISFYING FOR SIN

Since the Lutherans deny any element of satisfaction in our works, we must indicate the mind of the Church on this topic. One must first distinguish according to the state in which the works are performed, whether in mortal sin or in the state of grace. Also one must distinguish concerning satisfaction for sins between guilt and punishment.

We say first that none of our works satisfy for the guilt of our sins, since no deed done in the state of mortal sin satisfies God for our offenses, as is clear. Our deeds in the state of grace presuppose the removal of the guilt or the offense by divine grace through the satisfaction Christ made to God for our offenses against God, when he offered up his life to God on the altar of the cross.

We say secondly that none of our works done in mortal sin satisfy God for the punishment due for our sins, even if these were forgiven previously in the sacrament of penance. The reason for this is quite clear, since when God forgives the offense of sin, the sinner is changed from being an enemy to being a friend of God. Consequently he is no longer subject to punishment in a hostile manner as in the punishment of hell. But if with forgiveness of guilt the gift of grace is not given so abundantly that all punishment is remitted, one remains bound to fulfilling the rest of the punishment in a loving manner. If one in this latter condition falls back into sin and again becomes an enemy of God before he has completed the rest of the punishment, his works are then done in a state of hostility, not a state of friendship, and so they cannot satisfy for the previous punishment.

We say thirdly that the works of one continuing to love God are in no way prevented from being satisfactory for the punishment that may remain. On this point the Lutherans err in a two-fold way. They first teach that when the guilt of sin is forgiven all punishment is remitted as well. One who has attained mercy from God upon his sin is no longer bound to any punishment.[21] This is patently contrary to Holy Scripture, which teaches in 2 Samuel 12 that even though David gained the forgiveness of sins when he said, "I have sinned against the Lord" [12:13], still he did not attain remission of all punishment but remained bound to many punishments, as Scripture bears witness. The second Lutheran error is denying the satisfactory power of the works of Christ's living members regarding punishments not yet remitted.[22] This is contrary to the effectiveness in us of Christ the head, since "I satisfy, now not I, but Christ satisfies in me." It is also against the practice of the Catholic Church by which salutary acts of satisfaction are customarily imposed through the ministry of priests upon those who truly repent and confess.

12

RESPONSE TO OBJECTIONS

It remains for us to answer the objections.[23] The first arose from the sufficiency of the merit and satisfaction of Christ. We answer that the merit of Christ was completely and utterly sufficient, and that his satisfaction was more than adequate for our sins and for the sins of the whole world, including original sin, mortal sins, and venial sins, as 1 John 2[:2] teaches. Therefore it is not because of an inadequacy in the merit and satisfaction of Christ that we attribute merit and satisfaction to the works of Christ's living members, but rather because of the excessive riches of Christ's merit which he shares with his living members so that their works as well may be meritorious and satisfactory.[24] A greater grace is conferred on us by Christ, when he our head merits and satisfies in and through us his members than if we were only to share in the merit Christ gained in his own person.

To the objection that what is proper to Christ must not be attributed to us, we answer that it should not be attributed to us in the manner in which it is proper to Christ. It can be attributed to us in another manner, namely by participation. Something proper to God can be attributed to no one in that manner proper to God, but it can be shared by others by participation. For instance, the vision of the divine essence is proper to God, and no creature can see God as he is, since he alone by his own nature sees himself. But God can by grace grant a share in the vision of God, and this he does to all the blessed. In the present case merit of eternal life is proper to Christ, when this is understood as merit by one's own power. But this can be granted to his living members, not that they merit by their own power, but that they merit by the power of Christ the head. The same thing can be understood concerning satisfaction.

There is no need to respond concerning the forgiveness of sins, since we already said that this is not granted to Christ's living members, because their good works presuppose that their sins have been forgiven. No one merits that which he already has. Merit is gained concerning something not had. For this reason Christ apportions to his members the merit of an increase in grace and of heavenly beatitude. He does not apportion to them merit of forgiveness of sins. Eternal beatitude is something lacking to Christ's members in this life, while they do have forgiveness of sins by the very fact of becoming members of Christ. No one merits what he has but what he hopes to attain. This makes it clear that our merits and satisfactions in no way detract from the merit and satisfaction of Christ, but rather that the grace of merit and satisfaction Christ gained in his own person is extended to himself as head working in and through his members.

All the texts cited as showing that we do not by our works merit the forgiveness of sins require no answer, since we agree with this conclusion. But we must respond to the texts cited to prove that we do not merit eternal life by our works. To the text of the Apostle from Romans, "The gift of God is eternal life" [6:23], we answer that we indeed say and teach this, since it is by God's gift of sanctifying grace that we are members of Christ, and by the power in us of Christ the head that we merit eternal life. We do not say that we merit eternal life through our works specifically as ours, but in so far as they are in us and through us from Christ.

We propose the same distinction in answer to the objection raised from Christ's words, "Say, 'we are unworthy servants'" [Luke 17:10]. However much we might fulfill all the commandments of Christ, to the extent we fulfill them by our own free choice, we are unworthy servants regarding our Father's heavenly household. We are unworthy of our homeland in heaven and whatever concerns it, such as the forgiveness of sins, the grace of the Holy Spirit, charity, and other things proper to God's children. The reason is obvious, since when we act on our own we are too weak to reach the higher order in which are conferred the proper goods of God's children. This goes together with the other truth, namely, that in so far as our deeds proceed from the influence in us of Christ the head in his living members, we can contribute much through our works to gaining the heavenly homeland and our Father's household. As his members, we are raised to the order of God's children, not to be unworthy servants, but worthy members of our Father's household and the heavenly homeland.

As argument can be made from these words of Christ against the capability of good works done in the state of mortal sin to impetrate the forgiveness of sins, as above in Chapter 10. If the argument is made that our good works have no usefulness in impetrating the forgiveness of sins, we answer that in so far as prayer, fasting, alms, and other good works arise from them as sinners they are not capable of impetrating forgiveness of sins. But in so far as the divine goodness orders them to impetrating forgiveness of sins, they are highly effective for impetrating this. Consequently, in Ezechiel these works are called "the ways of God" and not "our ways" [18:29]. The divine goodness has arranged that we impetrate many things we never merit. As Christ, Isaiah, Ezechiel, and the Apostle (in Hebrews) bear witness, the divine goodness has conferred on the good works of persons returning to God the power of impetrating the forgiveness of sins from the divine mercy through the merit of Christ. Because of this, the fasting, prayers, alms, and other righteous works of sinners are beneficial, not for meriting, nor for satisfying, but for impetrating forgiveness of their sins.

This, I believe will suffice to explain these questions about faith and works. May it bring glory to Almighty God and consolation to the devout.

Rome, May 13, 1532.

XI

MARRIAGE WITH A BROTHER'S WIDOW — A POSITION 1534

To Henry VIII, King of England, Defender of the Faith:

I have rejoiced over what I have heard about Your Majesty's dissolution of his former marriage and taking of a new wife, for it is related that you did not act on the basis of your exalted power, but were motivated by the teaching of Holy Scripture. You do not claim to have learned of the liceity of your act by taking the advice of theologians, but by using your own mind and exercising your own gifts of shrewdness. We must give thanks to God for ornamenting our age with a King so proficient in theology.

Because you acted on such motivation, I have judged it part of Christian charity to beg the learned King to read the following, to ponder it, and to compare it with the views that swayed the mind of Your Majesty. Perhaps two pairs of eyes will see more than one. Since I address a King adept in theology, I treat only the deeper foundations of true theology.

Your Highness knows quite well where lies the nub of the whole question at issue. It is whether it is by divine moral law that marriage between a man and his brother's widow is forbidden. The affirmative position for such a prohibition rests on the law recorded in Leviticus 18[:16] and 20[:21], and on the words of John the Baptist given in Matthew 14[:4] and Mark 6[:18]. Consequently, if it be ascertained that none of these texts involve a moral prohibition of this kind, then such a marriage will be shown not to be against the moral law of God.

Now it can be demonstrated from two sources that the law of Leviticus is not forbidding a moral offense when it says, "You shall not uncover the nakedness of your brother's wife, for she is your brother's nakedness" [18:16].

First, another verse in the same chapter allows a man to marry the sister of his deceased wife: "You shall not take the sister of your wife into concubinage, nor shall you uncover his nakedness while her sister is yet alive" [Leviticus 18:18]. According to the Hebrew original, "concubinage" means "indigence". Still the fact that the prohibition of marriage with a sister-in-law is restricted to the wife's lifetime makes it evident that the prohibition does not touch a marriage with the sister of a deceased wife. "While she is yet alive" was added as a limitation, showing one is free to marry the sister of a deceased wife. In the same way that marriages within any degree of affinity or consanguinity not forbidden by the law of Moses are reckoned as permitted, so also marriage with the sister of one's deceased wife, since it is not forbidden by the law of Moses, must be judged as permitted.

If we then compare this law with the previous one, the relationships obtaining are of the same degree of affinity: first between a woman and two brothers, and then between a man and two sisters. Obviously the ground of impropriety is the same in each case. If there is any moral offense in a marriage with a brother's widow, then also marriage with a surviving sister of one's wife is also a moral offense. But if marriage with this surviving sister entails no moral offense, then also marriage with the widow of one's brother entails no moral offense. Since, however, the law of Leviticus shows there is no moral offense in marriage with this surviving sister, since it does not forbid it, we consequently learn from the very same chapter of Leviticus that there is no moral offense entailed in marriage with the widow of one's brother. Hence the latter is not forbidden because it is morally wrong, but is instead wrong because forbidden. If it were forbidden as morally offensive, then marriage with the sister of one's deceased wife would not have been permitted, since it would entail the same kind of moral offense.

We do not need to prove that the bond of obligation is equally binding in each case. The fact that the ground of impropriety is the same in both is evident: first, uncovering the nakedness of one's sister-in-law is prohibited because it is the nakedness of one's deceased brother, that is, because one's brother and sister-in-law were one flesh; similarly, uncovering the nakedness of one's wife's sister is prohibited because it is the nakedness of her deceased sister, since the sister-in-law and the deceased were made one flesh. Since however the divine law forbids the former and allows the latter, the reason for forbidding the former is not some moral offense, but lies in the authority of the law-giver, who deemed it right to so legislate.

The second source of proof is a comparison of the law of Leviticus with the uprightness of a marriage between a man and his brother's widow when the brother dies without offspring. Prior to the law of Moses, such a marriage, in these circumstances, was not only allowed but was prescribed either by custom or by the authority of the Patriarchs. The story of Tamar in Genesis 38[:8-11] suggests this, and the law of Moses, in Deuteronomy 25[:5-10], then made it a command. Thus, while marriage between a man and his brother's widow was ordinarily illicit, when the brother died without offspring, it was allowed. The conclusion is that if a marriage between a man and his brother's widow were in itself morally evil it would be allowed in no circumstances. But since when the brother died without offspring, it was allowed both prior to the law and in the time of the law, such a marriage must not be in itself morally evil. Let us demonstrate and prove the premise assumed. It is clear that blasphemy, perjury, lying, adultery, rape, theft, and sins of this kind are intrinsically evil and in no circumstances are they allowed. What pertains to something intrinsically is never absent from it but is present whenever it occurs, for it is a necessary aspect of the thing. A thing can never be without the aspects pertaining to it intrinsically. If then marriage between a man and the widow of his brother is intrinsically evil, it will always and in every circumstance be evil. Its evil character will always accompany it.

Consequently, because marriage between a man and his brother's widow is at times not evil, we hold that it is not intrinsically evil and that it was not forbidden as being intrinsically evil. Rather it became evil by the authority of the law-giver who laid down the prohibition. — This is sufficient treatment of the law of Leviticus.

John the Baptist said to Herod, Tetrarch of Galilee, "It is not lawful for you to have your brother's wife" [Mark 6:18]. But this is not to the point here. First, John was speaking of the wife of a brother still alive, as Josephus related in *The Antiquities of the Jews*, Book XVIII, Chapter 14. He clearly says that Herodias left her husband while he was still alive.[1] Hegesippus, in Book II, Chapter 4, of

The Fall of Jerusalem, narrates that Herod carried away his brother's wife while he was still alive and she was pregnant by him.[2]

It is one thing for a marriage with a brother's widow to be forbidden, and another thing for this marriage to be forbidden because moral evil is intrinsically involved in such a marriage. It is fallacious to judge one specific case from a plurality of cases, since a prohibition can derive from a number of sources. In the present case the obvious source was the law of Leviticus, since Herod professed to follow the law of the Jews. Thus if Herodias were his brother's widow, John would be right in saying, "It is not lawful for you to have your brother's wife," since the law forbade this. It was evident that he did not marry her in order to beget offspring for his brother. But one cannot therefore conclude that such a marriage was intrinsically evil. The moral evil derived from the law's prohibition, and this evil was certain and evident to all.

If my opinion is valid, most learned King, and if it appears adequate, then you must set right what you have done. If you judge it insufficient, please show what is lacking. I trust in the abundance of divine grace that he who began this work will complete it. If you judge these points only probable, you, the Defender of the Faith, should conduct yourself as one who cannot decide between probabilities. Your Majesty knows quite well how one is to act in doubtful cases, that is, how the law of Deuteronomy 17 determines one is to act when doubts arise.[3] If, finally, you judge my view to be wrong, then may the most learned Prince be pleased to refute it. I am ready to learn and to change my opinion.

I beg you to remove the cause of scandal to such vast numbers of Christians in Europe. It is affecting the common people as well as religious and learned men. Remove it, by a public deed of righteousness, so that scandal be not given but rather removed. I offer myself to serve as herald of Your Majesty's righteousness, which, I pray, may abound and prosper.

Rome, January 27, 1534.

BIBLIOGRAPHY

1. Cajetan's Works of Controversial Theology

The first published product of Cajetan's work against the Reformation was *De divina institutione pontificatus Romani Pontificis*, which appeared in Rome, Cologne, and Milan, in 1521, the year of its composition.

Cajetan's three anti-Lutheran works of 1531-32 were published in the following octavo editions: *De sacrificio missae et ritu adversus Lutheranos* (Rome 1531, Paris 1531, Cologne 1532); *De quattour Lutheranorum erroribus tractatus de communione sub utraque specie* ... (Rome 1531, Paris 1531, Cologne 1532, Venice 1534, Lyons 1536 — on each occasion together with the preceding or subsequent work); *De fide et operibus contra Lutheranos* (Rome 1532, Venice 1534, Lyons 1536).

Cajetan's two works in defense of the validity of the marriage of Henry VIII and Catharine of Aragon were both printed together with works of biblical commentary: *De coniugio regis Angliae cum relicta fratris sui* (written 1530, published with Cajetan's commentaries on Proverbs, Ecclesiastes, and Isaiah 1-3, Paris 1545 and Lyons 1545); *De coniugio cum relicta fratris sententia* (written 1534, published with Cajetan's commentary on Job, Rome 1535).

Cajetan's controversial works began to appear in collections of his treatises, *quaestiones,* orations, etc., in 1529 (Monza 1529, Paris 1530, Venice 1531). The present editor was not able to inspect personally the first two of these editions. Friedrich Lauchert reported (*Die italienischen literarischen Gegner Luthers,* 137, 161) that *Quaestiones quodlibetales* (Paris 1530) contained Cajetan's 1518 Augsburg treatises, the 1519 *quaestio* on the abuse of Scripture, and the 1521 defense of five articles of *Exsurge Domine.* It did not, however, contain *De divina institutione pontificatus Romani Pontificis.* The *Opuscula quaestiones et quodlibeta* (Venice 1531) printed the Augsburg treatises, the *quaestio* on the abuse of Scripture, *De divina institutione pontificatus Romani pontificis,* the defense of five articles of *Exsurge Domine, Instructio Nuntii circa Errores Libelli de Cena Domini* (1525: Chapter V, above), and *De sacrificio missae.*

Larger editions of Cajetan's *Opuscula* incorporating most or all of his works in response to the Reformation began appearing in 1541 and were reprinted with considerable frequency down to 1612. A number of these editions published Cajetan's *Opuscula omnia* together with Aquinas' *Summa* and/or Cajetan's commentary on the *Summa.* The following are the editions of the *Opuscula omnia* of which the present editor has become aware:

Lyons 1541, 1552, 1554, 1558, 1562, 1568, 1575, 1580, 1581, 1588;

Venice 1542, 1588, 1594, 1596;

Antwerp 1567, 1576, 1612;

Turin 1582;

Bergamo 1590.

Three of Cajetan's controversial works have appeared in the twentieth century. W. Friedensburg published the 1531 work we have entitled *Guidelines for Concessions to the Lutherans* in "Aktenstücke über das Verhalten der römischen Kurie zur Reformation 1524 und 1531," *Quellen und Forschungen aus italienischen Archiven und Bibliotheken* 3 (1900), 16-18. Friedrich Lauchert's critical edition of *De divina institutione pontificatus Romani Pontificis* appeared as *Corpus Catholicorum* 10 (Münster 1925). F. A. von Gunten brought out a fully annotated edition of *Instructio Nuntii circa Errores Libelli de Cena Domini* (Rome 1962), with a text based on *Opuscula Quaestiones et quodlibeta* (Venice 1531).

2. Studies of Cajetan and the Reformation

Alfaro, J., *Lo Natural y lo Sobrenatural: Estudio historico desde Santo Tomas hasta Cayetano* (Matriti 1952).

Allgeier, A., "Les commentaires de Cajétan sur les Psaumes," *Revue Thomiste* 17 (n. 86/87, 1934-35) 410-443.

Anderson, M. W., "Thomas Cajetan's Scientia Christi," *Theologische Zeitschrift* 26 (1970) 99-108.

Bauer, R., *Gotteserkenntnis und Gottesbeweis bei Kardinal Cajetan* (Regensburg 1955).

Baum, W., *The Teaching of Cardinal Cajetan on the Sacrifice of the Mass* (Rome 1958).

Bäumer, R., "Das Kirchenverständnis Albert Pigges," *Volk Gottes* (Festschrift J. Hofer), ed., R. Bäumer and H. Dolch (Freiburg/B. 1967) 306-322.

—————, "Der Lutherprozess," *Lutherprozess und Lutherbann,* ed., R. Bäumer (Münster 1972) 18-48.

—————, *Martin Luther und der Papst* (Münster 1970).

—————, *Nachwirkungen des konziliaren Gedankens in der Theologie und Kanonistik des frühen 16. Jahrhunderts* (Münster 1971).

Beumer, J., "Suffizienz und Insuffizienz der Hl. Schrift nach Kardinal Thomas de Vio Cajetan," *Gregorianum* 45 (1964) 816-824.

Bodem, A., *Das Wesen der Kirche nach Kardinal Cajetan* (Trier 1971).

Borth, W., *Die Luthersache* (Lübeck und Hamburg 1970).

Bourke, V., "Cajetan, Cardinal," *Encyclopedia of Philosophy,* ed., P. Edwards (New York 1967), II, 5-6.

Brosse, O. de la, *Le Pape et le Concile. La comparaison de leurs pouvoirs à la veille de la Réform* (Paris 1965).

—————, J. Lecler, et al., *Latran V et Trente* [Histoire des conciles oecumeniques 10] (Paris 1975).

Brotto, A. G., and G. Zonta, *La facolta teologica dell' universita di Padova* (Padua 1922).

Collins, T. A., "The Cajetan Controversy," *American Ecclesiastical Review* 128 (1953) 90-100.

—————, "Cardinal Cajetan's Fundamental Biblical Principles," *Catholic Biblical Quarterly* 17 (1955) 363-378.

Colunga, A., "El Cardenal Cayetano y los problemas de introducción biblica," *Ciencia Tomistica* 18 (1918) 21-32, 20 (1919) 43-50.

Congar, M. -J., "Bio-Bibliographie de Cajétan," *Revue Thomiste* 17 (n. 86/87, 1934-35) 1-49.

—————, "Le date de mort du Cardenal Cajétan (10 Aout 1534)," *Angelicum* 11 (1934) 603-608.

Cossio, A., *Il Cardinale Gaetano e la Riforma* (Cividale 1902).

Delius, W., "Der Augustiner Eremitenorden im Prozess Luthers," *Archiv für Reformationsgeschichte* 63 (1972) 22-42.

Doherty, D., *The Sexual Doctrine of Cardinal Cajetan* (Regensburg 1966).

Fabro, C., "L'obscurcissement de l'esse dans l'école thomiste," *Revue Thomiste* 58 (1958) 443-472.

Gargan, L., *Lo studio teologico e la biblioteca dei Domenicani a Padova nel tre e quattrocento* (Padua 1971).

Garrigou-Lagrange, R., "Le sens du mystère chez Cajétan," *Angelicum* 12 (1935) 3-18.

Giers, J., *Gerechtigkeit und Liebe. Die Grundpfeiler gesellschaftlicher Ordnung in der Sozialethik des Kardinal Cajetans* (Düsseldorf 1941).

Gilson, E., "Autour de Pomponazzi. Problematique de l'immortalité de l'âme en Italie au debut du XVIe Siecle," *Archives d'historie doctrinale et littéraire du Moyen Age* 36 (1961) 163-279.

————, "Cajétan et l'existence," *Tijdschrift voor Philosophie* 15 (1963) 267-286.

————, "Cajétan et l'humanisme theologique," *Archives d'historie doctrinale et littéraire du Moyen Age* 22 (1955) 113-136.

Gleason, E. G., "Sixteenth Century Italian Interpreters of Luther," *Archiv für Reformationsgeschichte* 60 (1969) 160-173.

Grabmann, M., "Die Stellung des Kardinals Cajetan in der Geschichte des Thomismus," *Angelicum* 11 (1934) 547-560.

Groner, J. F., *Kardinal Cajetan, eine Gestalt aus der Reformationszeit* (Fribourg and Louvain 1951).

Gunten, F. A. von, "La doctrine de Cajétan sur l'indissolubilité du mariage," *Angelicum* 43 (1966) 62-72.

Halmer, N. M., "Die Messopferspekulation von Kardinal Cajetan und Ruard Tapper," *Divus Thomas* 21 (Fribourg 1943) 187-212.

Harrison, F. R., "The Cajetan Tradition of Analogy," *Franciscan Studies* 23 (1963) 179-202.

Hefele, C. -J., and J. Hergenroether, *Historie des Conciles*, ed., H. Leclercq, Volume VIII/1 (Paris 1917).

Hennig, G., *Cajetan und Luther* (Stuttgart 1966).

Hillman, E., "Polygamy and the Council of Trent," *The Jurist* 33 (1973) 358-376.

Hoffman, L., "Die Zugehörigkeit zur Kirche nach der Lehre des Kardinals Thomas de Vio Cajetan," *Ekklesia* (Festschrift M. Wehr) (Trier 1972) 221-233.

Horst, U., "Der Streit um die Heilige Schrift zwischen Kardinal Cajetan und Ambrosius Catharinus," *Wahrheit und Verkündigung* (Festschrift M. Schmaus), ed., L. Scheffczyk et al. (Munich 1967) I, 551-577.

Hoyer, T., "An Anniversary We Forgot," *Concordia Theological Monthly* 6 (1935) 349-356.

Hurter, H., *Nomenclator Litterarius Theologiae Catholicae,* Volume II (Innsbruck 1906).

Iserloh, E., *Der Kampf um die Messe* (Münster 1952).

————, "Das tridentinische Messopferdekret in seiner Beziehungen zu der Kontroverstheologie der Zeit." *Il Concilio di Trento et la Reforma Tridentina* (Rome 1965) II, 401-439.

————, "Der Wert der Messe in der Diskussion der Theologen vom Mittelalter bis zum 16. Jahrhundert," *Zeitschrift für katholische Theologie* 83 (1961) 44-79.

Jager, C. F., "Cajetans Kampf gegen die lutherische Lehrreform," *Zeitschrift für die historische Theologie* 28 (1858) 431-479.

Jedin, H., *History of the Council of Trent,* Volume I (London 1957).

————, *Papal Legate at the Council of Trent,* trans., F. C. Eckhoff (St. Louis and London 1947).

Jenkins, R. C., *Pre-Tridentine Doctrine. A Review of the Commentary on the Scriptures of Thomas de Vio ... Cajetan* (London 1891).

Kalkoff, P., "Der Briefwechsel zwischen dem Kurfursten Friedrich und Cajetan," *Zeitschrift für Kirchengeschichte* 27 (1906) 322-333

————, *Forschungen zu Luthers römischen Prozess* (Rome 1905).

————, "G. B. Flavio als Biograph Kajetans und sein Bericht über Luthers Verhör in Augsburg," *Zeitschrift für Kirchengeschichte* 33 (1912) 240-267.

————, "Kardinal Cajetan auf dem Augsburger Reichstage von 1518," *Quellen und Forschungen aus italienischen Archiven und Bibliotheken* 10 (1907) 226-230.

————, *Luther und die Entscheidungsjahre der Reformation* (Leipzig 1917).

————, "Luther vor dem Generalkapitel zu Heidelberg," *Zeitschrift für Kirchengeschichte* 27 (1906) 319-323.

————, "Luthers Antwort auf Cajetans Ablassdekretale (30. Mai 1519)," *Archiv für Reformationsgeschichte* 11 (1914) 161-175.

————, "Die von Kajetan verfasste Ablassdekretale und seine Verhandlugen mit dem Kurfursten von Sachsen in Weimar," *Archiv für Reformationgeschichte* 9 (1911) 142-171.

————, "Zu Luthers römischem Prozess," *Zeitschrift für Kirchengeschichte* 25 (1904) 91-147, 273-290, 399-459, 501-603, 33 (1912) 1-71.

Kelly, H. A., *The Matrimonial Trials of Henry VIII* (Stanford 1976).

Klubertanz, G. P., *St. Thomas Aquinas on Analogy* (Chicago 1960).

Köhler, W., *Zwingli und Luther*, Volume I (Leipzig 1924).

Kolde, T., "Cajetan," *Realencyclopädie für protestantische Theologie und Kirche*, Volume III (1897) 632-634.

Kristeller, P. O., *Renaissance Concepts of Man* (New York 1972).

————, *Le thomisme et la pensée italienne de la Renaissance* (Montreal-Paris 1967).

Lauchert, F., *Die italienischen literarischen Gegner Luthers* (Freiburg/B. 1912).

Laurent, M. -H., "La causalité sacramentaire d'aprés le commentaire de Cajétan sur les Sentences," *Revue des Sciences philosophiques et theologiques* 20 (1931) 77-82.

————, "Le Commentaire de Cajétan sur le *De anima*," Introduction to Cajetan's *Commentaria in De anima Aristotelis,* ed., I. Coquelle (Rome 1938), vii-lii.

————, "Quelques documents des Archives Vaticans," *Revue Thomiste* 17 (n. 86/87, 1934-35) 50-148.

Lindon, T., *Faith and Sacrament in Justification According to Cardinal Cajetan* (Rome 1969).

Löhr, G. M., "De Caietano reformatore Ordinis Praedicatorum," *Angelicum* 11 (1934) 593-602.

Lortz, J., *The Reformation in Germany* (London and New York 1968).

————, "Wert und Grenzen der katholischen Kontroverstheologie in der ersten Hälfte des 16. Jahrhunderts," *Um Reform und Reformation*, ed., A. Franzen (Münster 1968) 9-32.

Lubac, H. de, *The Mystery of the Supernatural* (London and New York 1966).

McCanles, M., "Univocalism in Cajetan's Doctrine of Analogy," *New Scholasticism* 42 (1968) 18-47.

McNally, R. E., "Pope Adrian VI (1522-23) and Church Reform," *Archivum Historiae Pontificiae,* 7 (1969) 253-285.

—————, "The Roman Process of Martin Luther: a Failure in Subsidiarity," in J. A. Coriden, ed., *The Once and Future Church* (Staten Island 1971) 111-128.

McSorley, H., "Some Forgotten Truths about the Petrine Ministry," *Journal of Ecumenical Studies* 11 (1974) 208-237.

Maes, J. D., "Le Pouvoir pontifical d'apres Cajétan," *Ephemerides theologicae Lovanienses* 12 (1935) 705-721.

Mancini, I., *Cardinale Caietanus et Montes Pietatis* (Jerusalem 1954).

Mandonnet, P., "Cajetan," *Dictionaire de Théologie Catholique,* II (1935) 1313-29.

Marenga, I. M., "Caietani vitae operumque brevis descriptio," Editor's Introduction to Cajetan's *Commentaria in Porphyrii Isagogen ad Praedicamenta Aristotelis* (Rome 1934) XI-LXIV.

Matheson, P., *Cardinal Contarini at Regensburg* (London 1972).

Maurer, A., "Cajetan's Notion of Being in his Commentary on the Sentences," *Medieval Studies* 28 (1966) 268-278.

Minnich, N. J., "Concepts of Reform Proposed at the Fifth Lateran Council," *Archivum Historiae Pontificiae* (1969) 163-251.

Mondello, V., *La dottrina de Gaetano sul Romano Pontifice* (Messina 1955).

Mortier, A., *Histoire des Maîtres généraux de l'ordre des Frères Prechêurs,* Volume V (Paris 1911).

Müller, G., "Die römische Kurie und die Anfänge der Reformation," *Zeitschrift für Religions— und Geistesgeschichte* 19 (1967) 1-32.

—————, *Die römische Kurie und die Reformation 1523-1534* (Gütersloh 1969).

Napoli, G., *L'immortalità dell'anima nel Rinascimento* (Turin 1963).

Nardi, B., *Saggi sull' aristotelismo padovano dal secolo XIV al XVI* (Florence 1958).

—————, *Studi su Pietro Pomponazzi* (Florence 1965).

O'Connell, Marvin, "Cardinal Cajetan: Intellectual and Activist," *New Scholasticism* 50 (1976) 310-322.

O'Malley, J.W., *Giles of Viterbo on Church and Reform* (Leiden 1968).

————, "Historical Thought and the Reform Crisis of the Early Sixteenth Century," *Theological Studies* 28 (1967) 531-548.

————, "Preaching for the Popes," *The Pursuit of Holiness,* ed., C. Trinkaus (Leiden 1974) 408-440.

Parmiter, G., *The King's Great Matter* (London 1967).

Pastor, Ludwig, *The History of the Popes,* Volumes VI-X, ed., F. I. Antrobus and R. F. Kerr (London and St. Louis 1938-1950).

Paulus, N., "Cajetan und Luther über die Polygamie," *Historisch-politische Blätter* 135 (1905) 81-100.

Pesch, O. H., "'Das Heisst eine neue Kirche bauen' Luther und Cajetan in Augsburg," *Begegnung* (Festschrift H. Fries), ed., M. Seckler et al. (Graz 1972) 645-661.

————, "Thomismus," *Lexikon für Theologie und Kirche,* II (1965) 157-167.

Pfnur, V., *Einig in der Rechtfertigungslehre?* (Wiesbaden 1970).

Polman, P., *L'element historique dans la controverse religieuse du XVI Siecle* (Gembloux 1932).

Pollet, V.-M., "La doctrine de Cajétan sur l'Église," *Angelicum* 11 (1934) 514-532, 12 (1935) 223-244.

Poppi, A., *Causalità e infinità nella scuola padovano dal 1480 al 1513* (Padua 1966).

Quetif, Jacques, and Jacques Echard, *Scriptores ordinis praedicatorum,* Volume II (Paris 1792).

Reilly, J. P., *Cajetan's Notion of Existence* (The Hague 1971).

Rivière, J., "Cajétan Defenseur de la Papauté contre Luther," *Revue Thomiste* 17 (n. 86/87, 1934-35) 246-265.

Scarisbrick, J. J., *Henry VIII* (London 1968).

Schmitt, Charles B., *Critical Survey and Bibliography of Studies on Renaissance Aristotelianism 1958-69* (Padua 1971).

Schwarz, H. T., "Analogy in St. Thomas and Cajetan," *New Scholasticism* 28 (1954) 127-144.

Selge, K.-V., "Die Augsburger Begegnung von Luther and Cajetan in Oktober 1518," *Jahrbuch der hessischen kirchengeschichtlichen Vereinigung* 20 (1969) 37-54.

————, review of G. Hennig, *Cajetan und Luther,* in *Archiv für Reformationsgeschichte* 60 (1969) 271-274.

Ullmann, W., "Julius II and the Schismatic Cardinals," *Schism, Heresy, and Religious Protest,* ed., Derek Baker (Cambridge 1972) 177-193.

Vaccari, A., "Cardinalis Cajetanus Sacrarum Litterarum studiosus," *Verbum Domini* 14 (1934) 321-472.

Vosté, J. M., "Cardinalis Cajetanus in Vetus Testamentum praecipue in Hexaemeron," *Angelicum* 12 (1935) 305-332.

————, "Cardinalis Cajetanus sacrae scripturae interpres," *Angelicum* 11 (1934) 445-513.

Walz, A., *I Domenicani al Concilio di Trento* (Rome 1961).

————, "Von Cajetans Gedanken über Kirche und Papst," *Volk Gottes* (Festschrift J. Hofer), ed., R. Baumer and H. Dolch (Freiburg/B. 1967) 336-360.

Weisheipl, J. A., "Cajetan (Tommaso de Vio)," *New Catholic Encyclopedia* (1967) II, 1053-55.

Wells, N. J., "On Last Looking into Cajetan's Metaphysics," *New Scholasticism* 42 (1968) 112-117.

Wicks, J., "Thomism Between Renaissance and Reformation: the Case of Cajetan," *Archive for Reformation History* 68 (1977) 9-32.

3. Unpublished Materials

Selge, K. -V., Normen der Christenheit im Streit um Ablass und Kirchenautoritat. Das Jahr 1518. Heidelberg Habilitationschrift, 1968.

ABBREVIATIONS

CC 10 — *Corpus Catholicorum*, Volume 10 = Cajetan, *De divina institutione pontificatus Romani Pontificis*, ed. F. Lauchert (Münster 1925).

CCL — *Corpus Christianorum. Series latina* (Turnholt 1953ff).

CIC — *Corpus Iuris Canonici*, ed. E. Friedberg, 2 Volumes (Leipzig 1879-81).

CR — *Corpus Reformatorum. Philippi Melanthonis Opera* (Halle 1834ff).

CSEL — *Corpus Scriptorum Ecclesiasticorum Latinorum* (Vienna 1866ff).

Concord — *The Book of Concord. The Confessions of the Evangelical Lutheran Church*, ed. and trans. T.G. Tappert et al. (Philadelphia 1959).

DB — H. Denzinger and C. Bannwart, eds., *Enchiridion Symbolorum*, editions 18-31 (Freiburg/B. 1932-57).

DS — H. Denzinger and A. Schönmetzer, eds., *Enchiridion Symbolorum*, editions 32ff (Barcelona 1963ff).

EA va — *D. Martin Luthers sämmtliche Werke, Varia argumenta* (Frankfurt/M. and Erlangen 1826-57).

LW — *Luther's Works (American Edition)*, eds. J. Pelikan and H. Lehmann (St. Louis and Philadelphia 1955ff).

PL — *Patrologiae cursus completus. Series latina*, ed. J.P. Migne (Paris 1844-64).

PG — *Patrologiae cursus completus. Series graeca*, ed. J.P. Migne (Paris 1857-1912).

ST — St. Thomas Aquinas, *Summa Theologiae*.

WA — *D. Martin Luthers Werke. Kritische Gesamtausgabe* (Weimar 1883ff). References indicate volume, page, and first line of passage.

WABr — *D. Martin Luthers Briefwechsel. Kritische Gesamtausgabe* (Weimar 1930ff). References indicate volume, number of letter, first line of passage, and, after a semi-colon, the page.

WATR — *D. Martin Luthers Tischreden. Kritische Gesamtausgabe* (Weimar 1912ff). References indicate volume, number of table-remark, and, after a semi-colon, the page and line.

Woolf — B.L. Woolf, editor, *Reformation Writings of Martin Luther*, 2 Volumes (London 1953-56).

Introduction

1. F. Lauchert, *Die italienischen literarischen Gegner Luthers* (Freiburg/B. 1912), 176; J. Lortz, *The Reformation in Germany* (London and New York 1968), II, 142; E. G. Gleason, "Sixteenth Century Italian Interpreters of Luther," *Archiv für Reformationgeschichte* 60 (1969), 161f.

2. Surveys of the Catholic literary effort against the early Reformation underscore the self-sacrificing spirit of the Catholic defenders, but relate no significant successes in counteracting the powerful influence of Luther's polemics. The defensive theology of these apologists suffered from the negative task thrust upon them, from having to fight on terrain chosen by the opponents, and from the writers' inexperience in using Scripture in the new critical manner so different from the methods of scholastic theology. Lortz, *Reformation in Germany*, II, 175-223; H. Jedin, *A History of the Council of Trent*, I (London and St. Louis 1957), 392-409. Lortz returned to this subject in a 1967 lecture, "Wert und Grenzen der katholischen Kontroverstheologie in der ersten Hälfte des 16. Jahrhunderts," in *Um Reform und Reformation,* ed. A. Franzen (Münster 1968), 9-32.

3. The studies underlying this biographical sketch are listed in the Bibliography (above, pages 247ff) under the names Congar, Cossio, Gargan, Groner, Hefele, Hennig, Hurter, Lauchert, Mandonnet, Marenga, and Quetif.

4. Paris, Bibliotheque Nationale, Lat. 3076. This early work has been studied by M.-H. Laurent, "La causalité sacramentaire d'après le commentaire de Cajétan sur les Sentences, *"Revue des Sciences philosophiques et théologiques* 20 (1931), 77-82, and A. Maurer, "Cajetan's Notion of Being in his Commentary on the Sentences," *Medieval Studies* 28 (1966), 268-278.—Complete catalogues of Cajetan's works are given by M.-J. Congar, "Bio-bibliographie de Cajétan." *Revue Thomiste* 19 (1934), 1-49, and J. F. Groner, *Kardinal Cajetan* (Fribourg-Louvain 1951), 66-73. We can be quite sure about the dates of Cajetan's works, since he habitually wrote the date and place of composition at the end of each treatise or commentary.

5. Modern editions and English translations have appeared in this century. *In De Ente et Essentia D. Thomae Aquinatis Commentaria,* ed. M.-H. Laurent (Turin 1934); *Commentary on Being and Essence,* trans. L. Kendzierski and F. C. Wade (Milwaukee 1964); *De Nominum Analogia,* ed. N. Zammit (Rome 1934); *The Analogy of Names and the Concept of Being,* trans. E. A. Bushinski and H. J. Koren (Pittsburgh ²1959).

6. H. T. Schwarz, "Analogy in St. Thomas and Cajetan," *New Scholasticism* 28 (1954), 127-144; G. P. Klubertanz, *St. Thomas Aquinas on Analogy* (Chicago 1960), 6-10, 14-16, 120-123; F. R. Harrison, "The Cajetan Tradition of Analogy," *Franciscan Studies* 23 (1963), 179-202; M. McCanles, "Univocalism in Cajetan's Doctrine of Analogy," *New Scholasticism* 42 (1968), 18-47.

7. E. Gilson, "Cajétan et l'existence," *Tijdschrift voor Philosophie* 15 (1953), 267-286, and "Cajétan et l'humanisme théologique," *Archives d'histoire doctrinale et littéraire du Moyen Age* 22 (1955), 113-136; C. Fabro, "L'obscurcissement de l'esse dans l'école thomiste," *Revue Thomiste* 58 (1958), 443-472.

8. M.-H Laurent, Introduction to Cajetan's *Commentaria in De Anima Aristotelis*, ed. I. Coquelle, I (Rome 1938), x-xxi; B. Nardi, *Saggi sull'aristotelismo padovano dal secolo XIV al XVI* (Florence 1958); G. di Napoli, *L'immortalità dell'anima nel Rinascimento* (Turin 1963), 81-84, 97-105, 179-275; P. O. Kristeller, *Renaissance Concepts of Man* (New York 1972), 22-42.

9. The context of this work is treated in A. Poppi, *Causalità e infinità nella scuola padovano dal 1480 nel 1513* (Padua 1966).

10. M.-H Laurent, Introduction to Cajetan's *Commentaria in De Anima Aristotelis*, I, xviii-xxi.

11. Books I and II were published as *Commentaria in De Anima Aristotelis*, ed. I Coquelle, 2 Vols. (Rome 1938-39), and the work has been completed by *Commentaria in libros Aristotelis De Anima Liber III*, ed. G. Picard and G. Pelland (Brouges-Paris 1965).

12. Cajetan's position has been treated with admirable thoroughness by M.-H Laurent in his Introduction to the Coquelle edition of the work and more recently by E. Gilson, "Autour de Pomponazzi. Problematique de l'immortalité de l'âme en Italie au debut du XVIe Siècle," *Archives d'histoire doctrinale et littéraire du Moyen Age* 36 (1961), 163-183. Note, however, Kristeller's reminder that Florentine Platonism was a significant factor in the discussion of the immortality of the soul in the late fifteenth and early sixteenth century. *Renaissance Concepts of Man*, 39.

13. Laurent and Gilson both speak of the likelihood of Cajetan's influence on Pomponazzi. Laurent, Introduction to Cajetan's *Commentaria in De Anima Aristotelis*, I, xlvii; Gilson, "Autour de Pomponazzi," 187, n. 2. B. Nardi looks on this influence as quite probable. *Studi su Pietro Pomponazzi* (Florence 1965), 194, 375f.

14. Spina's polemic against Cajetan is reviewed by Gilson, "Autour de Pomponazzi," 195-202.

15. H. de Lubac, *The Mystery of the Supernatural* (London and New York 1966), 8-14, 51, 90-93, 181-206. Cajetan's originality on this point has, however, been somewhat reduced through the work of Juan Alfaro, who showed that Cajetan was to a considerable extent echoing the views of a broad stream of late medieval thinkers. *Lo Natural y lo Sobrenatural* (Matriti 1952). O. H. Pesch has drawn up an instructive catalogue of the individuating characteristics of the Thomism created largely by Cajetan, including fifteen theological points of notable discrepancy between Aquinas and early modern Thomism. "Thomismus," *Lexikon für Theologie und Kirche*, X (Freiburg/B. 1965), 163-165.

16. John W. O'Malley has studied fifty-one of the sermons given in this setting. They are products of an asacramental religiosity, which is inspired more by the Incarnation than by the Redemption, is little concerned by sin, but still relies on grace and prayer for living up to the high ethical calling of a humanity dignified in Christ by assumption into union with God's eternal Word. "Preaching for the Popes," *The Pursuit of Holiness*, ed. C. Trinkaus (Leiden 1974), 408-440.

17. Cajetan's five "court sermons" are found in his *Opuscula omnia* (e.g., Lyons 1575, col. 181a-189b). The sermon for the First Sunday of Advent

1503, on the subject of human immortality, has recently been translated into English by James K. Sheridan, *Renaissance Philosophy*, ed. L. A. Kennedy (The Hague 1973), 41-54. For a fuller study of these sermons, see J. Wicks, "Thomism Between Renaissance and Reformation: the Case of Cajetan," *Archive for Reformation History* 68 (1977) 9-32.

18. P. L. Nyhus translated Cajetan's short treatise of 1501 on a priest's obligation to a person for whose intention he has agreed to offer mass. *Forerunners of the Reformation*, ed. H. A. Oberman (New York and London 1966), 256-264.

19. D. Doherty, *The Sexual Doctrine of Cardinal Cajetan* (Regensburg 1966), 29. Another modern study elaborated the basic principles of the social order in Cajetan's ethical works: J. Giers, *Gerechtigkeit und Liebe* (Düsseldorf 1941). The work by I. Mancini, *Cardinale Caietanus et Montes Pietatis* (Jerusalem 1954), was inaccessible.

20. The following paragraphs on Cajetan's Dominican generalate are greatly dependent on A. Mortier, O.P., *Histoire des Maîtres Généraux des Frères Precheurs*, V (Paris 1911), 141-230, and to G. M. Löhr, "De Cajetano Reformatore Ordinis Praedicatorum," *Angelicum* 11 (1934), 593-602.

21. *Monumenta Ordinis Fratrum Praedicatorum Historica*, IX, ed. B. Reichert (Rome-Stuttgart 1901), 93. John W. O'Malley has, however, pointed to the widespread pessimism of the first decades of the sixteenth century. A "rhetoric of reproach" affected the fabric of thought through which many perceived their own age. The evil condition of the time was proverbial in discussions about the Chruch and its religious orders. A more empirically oriented perception would most probably not be so readily convinced by the evidence of decline and decay. "Historical Thought and the Reform Crisis of the Early Sixteenth Century," *Theological Studies* 28 (1967), 531-548.

22. On the practical side of common life, there is the *ordinatio* Cajetan issued during a visitation in June 1513 to his old residence in Padua. Luciano Gargan cites a text in which the Master General commands under penalty of grave fault that all who have books belonging to the house library must return them to the librarian within three days so they might be properly replaced in the common library. *Lo studio teologico e la biblioteca dei Domenicani a Padova* (Padua 1971), 185, n. 1.

23. R. Bäumer, *Nachwirkungen des konziliaren Gedankens* (Münster 1971), gives a comprehensive treatment of the strains of conciliarist theology proposed in the first decades of the sixteenth century. Among his observations is the expression of surprise that Pisa gained so few episcopal adherents, in view both of the canonical principles justifying an assembly without a pope and of the valid charges made against Julius II, who had not fulfilled his oath to call a reform council. The canonical position underlying Pisa has been set forth by Walter Ullmann in "Julius II and the Schismatic Cardinals," in *Schism, Heresy and Religious Protest*, ed., Derek Baker (Cambridge 1972), 177-193. Ullmann characterizes Cajetan's theological response as a stale re-statement of medieval hierocratic ideas poorly suited to the situation of early-modern Europe. An opposed evaluation is offered by M. O'Connell in "Cardinal Cajetan: Intellectual and Activist," *New Scholasticism* 50 (1976), 315f.

24. *De comparatione auctoritatis Papae et Concilii,* published in Rome (1511) and Cologne (1512), and in a modern edition, ed. V. M. Pollet (Rome 1936), which also included the subsequent *Apologia de comparata autoritate Papae et Concilii* (original, Venice 1514). See O. de la Brosse, *Le pape et le concile* (Paris 1965), for a detailed and critical study of Cajetan's argumentation against the conciliarists. While showing how competently Cajetan stated the case for papal primacy, la Brosse does not hesitate to indicate elements of onesidedness in the resulting ecclesiology: insensitivity to the historical evolution of the papacy, neglect of the apostolic-pastoral responsibilities attendant on ecclesiastical office, and reduction of the episcopate to mere administrative assistance under the pope.

25. See the works in our Bibliography by Bodem, de la Brosse, Maes, Mondello, Pollet, Riviere, and Walz ("Von Cajetans Gedanken über Kirche und Papst").

26. *Acta et Decreta Sacrorum Conciliorum Recentorum,* VII (Freiburg/B. 1890), 391.

27. A. Bodem, *Das Wesen der Kirche nach Kardinal Cajetan* (Trier 1971).

28. Even this concession brought Cajetan under fire from the right. In February 1512, Angelus de Fondi, a Vallumbrosian monk, published a short *Epistola . . . contra Generalem Ordinis Praedicatorum* attacking Cajetan for subordinating an heretical pope to the ministerial authority of a council. Whatever the Pope's failures, even in doctrine, no human instance is to judge him, but God alone. Angelus assured Julius II that upon reading Cajetan's concession, "*meo stomacho nauseam inducit.*" Fol. 1v.

28a. Harry McSorley recently referred to this chapter on dissent and resistance in an instructive article, "Forgotten Truths about the Petrine Ministry," *Journal of Ecumenical Studies* 11 (1974), 208-237. A slightly revised version of this study appeared in the *Proceedings of the Catholic Theological Society of America* 29 (1974), 165-198.

29. *De Ecclesiae et Synodorum Differentia* (Rome 1512), included in later editions of Cajetan's *Opuscula omnia* (e.g. Turin 1582, 281a-285a). The oration has been synopsized and studied by Nelson H. Minnich, "Concepts of Reform Proposed at the Fifth Lateran Council," *Archivum Historiae Pontificiae* 7 (1969), 175-179. The work of the council has been recently described by O. de la Brosse in *Latran V et Trente* (Paris 1975), 13-114.

30. *Sacrorum conciliorum nova et amplissia collecio,* ed. J. D. Mansi et al. 32 (1901), 842-843, and *Concilium Oecumenicorum Decreta,* ed. J. Alberigo et al. (²1962), 581f.

31. *Sacrorum conciliorum,* ed. Mansi, 32, 843.

32. The following pages on the proceedings against Luther, on Cajetan's three meetings with Luther, and on the diplomatic efforts on Luther's behalf by Friedrich the Wise are heavily indebted to the detailed researches of Paul Kaikoff and Wilhelm Borth (see Bibliography). Verlag Aschendorff, Münster, allowed me to read R. Bäumer's critical essay, "Der Lutherprozess," in the page proofs of *Lutherprozess und Lutherbann.* Kurt-Victor Selge, Heidelberg, kindly provided me with a copy of Part I of his insightful dissertation, *Normen der Christenheit.* The most recent addition to our knowledge of the Luther-proceedings is Walter Delius, "Der Augustiner Eremetinenorden im

Prozess Luthers," *Archiv fur Reformationsgeschichte* 63 (1972), 22-42. R. E. McNally, S.J., gave a succinct but critical account of the proceedings in "The Roman Process of Martin Luther: a Failure in Subsidiarity," in J. A. Coriden, ed., *The Once and Future Church* (Staten Island 1971), 111-128. In spite of the remarkable industry of these researchers, my account of the "Luther case" must include some surmises and lack of complete precision, because the primary documentation is not complete. While being respectfully grateful for all the information passed on by past researchers, I must take responsibility for the tone and emphases in the following pages, since they are in fact an attempt to interpret the available documents from a perspective oriented especially to Cajetan's opinions and course of action.

33. On the events and non-events of Luther's intervention on indulgences, see E. Iserloh, *The Theses Were Not Posted* (Boston and London 1969). On the theological treatise, now given in WABr 12,n. 4212a; 2-10, see J. Wicks, "Martin Luther's Treatise on Indulgences," *Theological Studies* 28 (1967), 481-518.

34. *Tractatus de indulgentiis* (dated December 8, 1517). This treatise is found in all the later collections of Cajetan's shorter works, e.g., *Opuscula quaestiones et quodlibetales* (Venice 1531), 46v-49r.

35. R. Bäumer, "Der Lutherprozess," 19f, 23 n.21, refers to Tetzel's statement and shows that there is no evidence for his having taken steps against Luther.

36. The theses and proofs of Luthers arguments are found in WA 1, 353-374 (LW 31, 39-58).

37. See P. Kalkoff, "Luther vor dem Generalkapitel zu Heidelberg," *Zeitschrift für Kirchengeschichte* 27 (1906), 319-322, where he has indicated the reasons for seeing Luther's response in the "*Protestatio*" found in WA 2, 620.

38. Prierias' *Dialogus* is given in EA va 1, 341-377, and Luther's *Responsio* in WA 1, 647-686. Heiko Oberman set this dispute in its many-sided theological context in "Wittenbergs Zweifrontenkrieg gegen Prierias und Eck," *Zeitschrift für Kirchengeschichte* 80 (1969), 331-358.

39. WABr 1, n. 85; 188.

40. Ulrich von Hutten, "Febris prima," *Opera*, ed. E. Böcking, Vol. IV (reprinted, Aalen 1963), 29-41; "Inspicientes." *Ibid.*, 272-308. H. Holborn, *Ulrich von Hutten and the German Reformation*, trans. R. H. Bainton (New Haven 1937), 104-109.

41. EA va 2, 349f. There is a modern tradition ascribing the actual composition of this letter to Cajetan. But K. V. Selge has pointed out how key members of the imperial chancery could well have been behind the letter, since it evinces antipathies to Reuchlin's humanism as well as to Luther (*Normen der Christenheit*, 77f). I would also ask whether Cajetan had enough time to amass the information underlying the letter in the days before his address to the Diet. There is no evidence that he shared the anti-Reuchlin views of the Cologne Dominicans. In fact, his own approach to Scripture points directly in the opposite way.

42. WA 2, 23-25 (LW 31, 286-289).

43. EA va 2, 352-354.

44. The principal documentation of this meeting is Spalatin's letter to Luther, September 5, WABr 1, n 92. K. V. Selge has pieced together further evidence from widely scattered sources (*Normen der Christenheit*, 83-85). The present editor's judgment on Cajetan's behavior takes account of the fact that diplomacy has never been an activity ruled by the imperative of total disclosure – as Friedrich the Wise knew quite well.

45. Cited by Paul Kalkoff, *Forschungen zu Luthers römischen Prozess* (Rome 1905), 58-59.

46. On these letters see Kalkoff, *Forschungen,* 61, and Selge, *Normen der Christenheit,* 87.

47. Christoph Scheurl, a jurist in Nuremberg, formerly of Wittenberg, wrote this in letters to Otto Beckmann, October 21, 1518, and to Johann Eck, November 24, 1518. *Christoph Scheurl's Briefbuch*, eds. F. von Soden and J. K. F. Knaake, II, 51 and 62.

48. In important studies of Luther's development during the period 1518-21, K.-V Selge has focused carefully on this question of the norms of Christian teaching and judgment. The forthcoming publication of his *Normen der Christenheit* will be a significant addition to the literature on the genesis of the Reformation.

49. One can isolate six distinct sources that narrate the exchanges between Luther and Cajetan: Luther's letters written in Augsburg before, during, and after the three meetings with Cajetan (WABr 1, nn. 97-104); Cajetan's letter to Friedrich, October 25, 1518 (WABr 1, n.110; pp. 233-235); Luther's *Acta Augustana,* composed in Wittenberg in November (WA 2, 6-26; LW 31, 259-277); Luther's letter to Friedrich the Wise, late November, commenting on and responding to Cajetan's letter (WABr 1, n. 110; pp. 236-246); a "short narrative" probably prepared for Friedrich the Wise ("Kurtze Erzelung der Handelung mit D. Mart. Luth. ergangen zu Augsburg," *Der Neundte Teil der Bücher des Ehrnwirdigen Herrn D. Martin Lutheri* [Wittenberg 1557], fol. 35v-36r); a "longer report" also for Friedrich ("Lenger und weitleuffiger Bericht der Handlung D. Mart. Luth. fur Caietano," *Ibid.,* fol. 36r-39v). Although these sources are not stenographic records of what Luther and Cajetan said to each other, they do provide a full account of the substance of their exchanges. The main historical problem is that five of the six sources are decidedly favorable to Luther – although not in the sense of later confessional polemic – while only one is written from Cajetan's standpoint.

50. The date was most probably Thursday, October 14, since most of the reports speak of meetings on three consecutive days. The "Longer Report" indicates that there was a one day interval before Luther came to Cajetan with his written defense, that is, on Friday, October 15 ("Lenger und weitleuffiger Bericht," fol. 38r).

51. Luther gave the tenor of the document in the *Acta Augustana* (WA 2, 9-16; LW 31, 264-275).

52. WABr 1, n. 99 (to Georg Spalatin, for Friedrich) and n. 100 (to Andreas Carlstadt, of the Wittenberg theology faculty). Both letters were dated the feast of St. Callixtus (October 14), which confirms that the third meeting was in fact on Thursday, October 14.

53. This important information is given only by the "longer report"

("Lenger und weitleuffiger Bericht." *Der Neundte Teil,* fol. 38r). K.V. Selge called attention to it in his review of G. Hennig, *Cajetan und Luther,* in *Archiv für Reformationsgeschichte* 60 (1969), 273. At first glance, this seems remarkable in view of Cajetan's sharp rejection of Luther's notion of *fides sacramenti* in the second of the *Augsburg Treatises.* This was a requirement that Cajetan judged as tantamount to building a new Church (see above, p. 55). Two reasons would probably have swayed Cajetan to drop this objection for the present: his central point in rejecting it had been the "ordinary understanding of the Church" (*communis ecclesiae sensus*); also, a key point in his argument, the notional uncertainty of one's being in the state of grace, had been most fully articulated by Thomas Aquinas. Thus, it would have been very difficult to demonstrate in a manner adequate for a canonical *processus* that Luther had veered from the teaching (as distinct from the living piety) of the Church (as distinct from a leading theologian). The significance of this shift in Cajetan's demands is that it shows that his final word to Luther was clearly not a word from the leading Thomist of the day but a word of one serving as a papal-ecclesiastical diplomat in the framework of a canonical procedure aiming to guard the soundness of public teaching in the Church.

54. WABr 1, n. 103.

55. WABr 1, n. 104.

56. Excerpted, DS 1447-49 = DB 740a. Cajetan included the text of the bull in his commentary on *Summa* III, 48, 5.

57. WABr 1, n. 110; pp. 233-235.

58. Luther's comments on Cajetan's letter: WABr 1, n. 110; pp. 236-246. Friedrich's answer: *Ibid.,* pp. 250f.

59. WABr 1, n. 134,17ff; p. 300, and n. 136,37-60; p. 307f. In the second letter Luther adverts to the new critical spirit abroad in the land, especially now that the biblical and patristic sources are made available. In this new age, integrity demands that one know on what basis he is asked to accept the teachings and practices of the Church.

60. WABr 1, n. 178; pp. 402f.

61. *Acta Augustana:* WA 2, 18, 7-17 (LW 31, 277f). Letter to Friedrich the Wise, November 1518: WABr 1, n. 110, 71-85; p. 238.

62. A partial record of Cajetan's instructions and activity is found in *Deutsche Reichstagsakten, Jüngere Reihe,* Vol. 1 (Gotha, 1893; reprinted Göttingen, 1962), pp. 148, 224, 274f, 346f, 519, 569f, 656f, 832f.

63. P. Kalkoff, "Zu Luthers Römischem Prozess," *Zeitschrift für Kirchengeschichte* 25 (1904), 115, cites Cajetan's reaction to the censures against Luther issued by the Louvain and Cologne theological faculties: *"Sint errores, non haereses."*

64. Cajetan's role, and frustrations, in the preparation of *Exsurge Domine* are narrated by Kalkoff. *Ibid.,* 91-120.

65. The full texts are given in *Bullarum . . . Sanctorum Romanorum Pontificum,* Vol. V (Turin 1860), coll. 748ff and 761ff. The forty-one censured propositions of *Exsurge* are listed in DS 1451-92 = DB 741-781. Cajetan would not have been surprised to read Johann Eck's later memoradum, probably from 1523, telling of the ineffectiveness of *Exsurge,* which he had sought to promulgate in southern and eastern Germany. Eck

called for a new, more selective bull of condemnation that would give a biblical statement of Catholic doctrine. *"Totus enim orbis solidam scripturam audire desiderat."* Cited in *Acta Reformationis Catholicae,* ed. G. Pfeilschifter, Vol. I (Regensburg 1959), 143.

66. In a letter of August 13, 1521, Erasmus referred to Cajetan's *De divina institutione* while lamenting the frenzy of early Reformation argument. "Recently a book by the Reverend Cardinal of St. Sixtus has appeared, which completely refrains from attacking persons and avoids all insults. He treats his subject cleanly with arguments and texts of authorities, matching his astuteness with laborious effort. Would that Luther were attacked by six hundred books like this, which illuminate the subject without stirring riots. Then everyone would want to learn." *Opus Epistolarum,* ed. Allen, IV, 560.

67. In 1523, Cochlaeus chided Luther for failing to respond when Cajetan defended the divine origin of the Roman primacy with so many arguments and texts of Scripture. *Adversus cucullatum Minotaurum Wittenbergensem* (CC 3, 23).

68. *Concilium Tridentinum,* XII, 31.

69. *Ibid.,* 32-39, synopsized and studied by G. Hennig, *Cajetan und Luther,* 136f, and by Robert McNally in "Pope Adrian VI (1522-23) and Church Reform," *Archivum Historiae Pontificiae* 7 (1969), 253-285, at 275-277. McNally's study presents in detail Adrian's potential as a reformer of the Church.

70. On episcopal residence, Cajetan was among the principal authorities cited by those who argued at the Council of Trent that this was a duty of divine origin (A. Walz, *I Domenicani al Concilio di Trento* [Rome 1961], 147f, 300). The tensions generated by this argument in 1562 posed a threat to the successful completion of the Council (H. Jedin, *Crisis and Closure of the Council of Trent,* trans. N.D. Smith [London 1967], 88f, 113f).

71. R.C. Jenkins, *Pre-Tridentine Doctrine* (London 1891), x.

72. The following editions of Cajetan's *Summula* are known to the present editor: Rome 1525, Venice 1525, Paris 1526 and 1530, Lyons 1529 1530 1537 1538 1561 1565 1581 1596, Douai 1613 and 1627. Portugese translations appeared as well; Lisbon 1557, Coimbra 1566.

73. The editor knows of the following editions of the *Jentaculum:* Rome 1525, Cologne 1526, Paris 1526, Lyons 1529 1530 1533 1539 1550 1561 1565 and 1596, and Douai 1613.

74. This exchange with Zurich has been pieced together by W. Köhler, *Zwingli und Luther,* I (Leipzig 1924), 154-163, and then further refined by F.A. von Gunten, O.P., in the preface to his 1962 edition of the text of Cajetan's *Instructio Nuntii circa errores libelli de cena Domini* (English. *Errors on the Lord's Supper,* pages 153-173 above).

75. J.-V. Pollet referred to Cajetan's critique of Zwingli as being valuable over a wider area than simply eucharistic doctrine ("Zwinglianisme," *Dictionnaire de Théologie Catholique,* XV/2 [1950], 3841f). Another modern appreciation of this work was given by C. Journet, *La Messe* (Tournai 1957), 235f.

76. Surveys and appreciations of Cajetan's biblical work are listed in the Bibliography under the names Allgeier, Collins, Colunga, Hennig (*Cajetan und*

Luther, 117-132), Horst, Jenkins, and Vosté. It is often said that Cajetan's interest in Scripture arose from Luther's impact on him at the Augsburg meetings of 1518. In fact, Cajetan may well have been drawn to Scripture as he followed the path of his namesake, Thomas Aquinas, whose lectures on Scripture continued throughout his intellectual career. The renewal of Scholasticism pursued by Cajetan in his commentary on the *Summa* would also be served by the new access to the *sacra pagina* afforded by the biblical humanism of the early sixteenth century. Thomistic theology, after all, understood itself as a *scientia subalternativa* which did not generate the affirmations it sought to understand. On the role of scripture in the curriculum of high scholasticism, see M. D. Chenu, *Towards Understanding Saint Thomas* (Chicago 1964),Chapter 7.

77. *Epistolae Pauli et aliorum Apostolorum* (Venice 1531), 193, cited by U. Horst in "Der Streit um die Hl. Schrift," *Wahrheit und Verkündigung*, I, 557. Cajetan similarly refrained from commenting on an Old Testament book: *"Canticum canticorum iuxta germanum sensum fateor me non intelligere"* (Commentary on Ecclesiastes [Paris 1545] , 176 v.)

78. *Cajetan und Luther*, 120.

79. *Evangelia cum Commentariis* (Paris 1543), 15a and 174a.

80. J. Beumer, "Suffizienz und Insuffizienz der heiligen Schrift nach Kardinal Thomas de Vio Cajetan," *Gregorianum* 45 (1964), 816-824.

81. WATR 2, n. 2668; p. 596,14.

82. The course of this controversy has been narrated by U. Horst, "Der Streit um die Hl. Schrift," *Wahrheit und Verkündigung*, I, 551-577, and T. Collins, "The Cajetan Controversy," *American Ecclesiastical Review* 128 (1953) 90-100.

83. *Epistola Theologorum Parisiensium ad Cardinalem Cajetanum reprehensoria* (Wittenberg 1534). M.-H. Laurent gives a list of the twenty-four propositions submitted for censure at this stage of the dispute (*Revue Thomiste* 17 [n. 86/87, 1934-35] , 118-121).

84. Cajetan's independent view on divorce has been recently presented by F. A. von Gunten, "La doctrine de Cajétan sur l'indissolubilité du mariage," *Angelicum* 43 (1966), 62-72.

85. Commenting on Romans 9:21f, Cajetan listed immortality among the mysteries of faith, and on Ecclesiastes 3:21 he denied outright the cogency of all the rational proofs he had seen offered. Texts given by Laurent, Introduction to Cajetan's *Commentaria in De Anima Aristotelis*, xxxvf.

86. In the next paragraphs, the narrative is largely dependent on the accounts of G. Parmiter, *The King's Great Matter* (London 1967), and J. J. Scarisbrick, *Henry VIII* (London and Berkely 1968), Chapters 6-8. More recently, Henry A. Kelly has described in great detail the succession of canonical arguments in *The Matrimonial Trials of Henry VIII* (Stanford 1976).

87. When the two cardinals met, Wolsey held up the example of Cajetan's unhappy experience at Augsburg a decade earlier as a dire warning against Campeggio's opposing Henry's desires. Campeggio quoted Wolsey's words in a letter of October 28, 1528, "Take care, Reverend Lordship, lest just as the harsh inflexibility of one cardinal caused the fall of much of Germany from the Apostolic See and from the faith, you in like manner let it come to be said

that another cardinal provided the occasion for the same thing happening in
England." Given by S. Ehses, *Römische Dokumente zur Geschichte der
Ehescheidung Heinrichs* VIII (Paderborn 1893), 50.

88. Nicholas Paulus indicates that Clement may have consulted Cajetan in
1529 on "the King's great matter". Clement was considering whether as a last
resort he could grant Henry a unique dispensation, one allowing him to
practice polygamy. In mid-1529 Clement told an English agent that one "great
theologian" had told him that this was not an unthinkable solution. The
theologian was probably Cajetan, whose Old Testament studies had heightened
his awareness that some prominent biblical figures had a plurality of wives.
Cajetan did hold that monogamous marriage was not of natural or divine
positive law. Clement VII was not about to grant this, however, since the rest
of his advisors had vigorously denied the possibility of such a dispensation. On
this point, Cajetan's opinion brought him into close proximity with both
Luther and Melanchthon (WABr 6, n. 1861A, 26, p. 179 and CR 2, 526f).
N. Paulus, "Cajetan und Luther über die Polygamie," *Historisch-politische
Blätter* 135 (1905) 81-100. Cajetan's independent opinion looms large in E.
Hillman's article, "Polygamy and the Council of Trent," *The Jurist* 33 (1973),
358-376.

89. The recent biographer of Henry VIII, J. J. Scarisbrick, singles out
Cajetan's 1530 work, "The King's Marriage," as qualitatively superior to the
other writers who opposed Henry's case against the dispensation of Julius II:
"When Henry challenged that dispensation, [Cajetan] delivered himself of a
quick retort that is a model of well-mannered, economical destructiveness."
Henry VIII (London and Berkely 1968), 167.

90. The text of the letter is given by A. Theiner, *Vetera Monumenta
Historiam Hibernorum et Scotorum Illustrantia* (Rome 1864), 590.

91. Cajetan voiced his view in an instruction written for the Legate
Gambara in December 1530. *Concilium Tridentinum,* IV, LIII.

92. On the context of these discussions, see G. Müller, *Die römische Kurie
und die Reformation 1523-1534* (Gütersloh 1969), 150-158. It must be kept
in mind, however, that the Reformation movement did not receive the
sustained attention of Pope Clement VII and his curia. Müller speaks of
Clement as never reaching clarity on the theological issues, and as having no
strong and abiding interest in developing policies to contain or throw back
the Reformation. While Pope and curia tended to expend their energies on
Medici dynastic affairs and on countering imperial influence in Italy,
the Reformation was given time to spread and consolidate itself in sections of
Germany, Scandanavia, and Switzerland. This is the general thesis of Müller's
book on Clement's pontificate (1523-1534), and has been stated in digested
form in "Die römische Kurie und die Anfänge der Reformation," *Zeitschrift für
Religions- und Geistesgeschichte* 19 (1967), 1-32.

93. M. de la Taille gave a long excerpt from *De sacrificio missae* in
Mysterium Fidei, 2nd edition (Paris 1924), 267f. M. Lepin cited it in *L'Idée
du Sacrifice de la Messe* (Paris 1926), 260, 265, 280, 283f. N. Halmer studied
Cajetan's views on eucharistic sacrifice in "Die Messopferspekulation von
Kardinal Cajetan und Ruard Tapper," *Divus Thomas* (Fribourg) 21 (1943),
187-212. Charles Journet referred to *De sacrificio missae* in *La Messe* (Tournai

1957), 49, 90, 115-120 (extensive translation from chapter 6), and 135. The historical works of E. Iserloh have singled out *De sacrificio missae* as one of the few works of its time that mastered the problem of the unity of Christ's and the Church's sacrifice. "Der Wert der Messe," *Zeitschrift für katholische Theologie* 83 (1961), 74ff; "Das tridentinische Messopferdekret," in *Il Concilio de Trento et la Riforma Tridentina* (Rome 1965), II 409f.

94. H. Jedin offered this reaction to Cajetan's memorandum: "It was impossible to go further in an endeavor to facilitate their return to the Church, the uttermost limit of what was possible had been reached, it may even have been crossed" (*History of the Council of Trent*, I, 275). Jedin adds that such a conciliatory approach was in fact a decade too late to hinder the development of Lutheranism into a separate confessional community. In the sixteenth century, Cardinal Sadoleto reported a conversation between L. Campeggio, Giles of Viterbo, and Cajetan, in which Cajetan appears to have maintained that the Church's laws of fasting did not bind under pain of serious sin. See John W. O'Malley, *Giles of Viterbo on Church and Reform* (Leiden 1968), 154, n. 2.

95. Erasmus wrote from Freiburg on March 5, 1532, referring to Cajetan's books on the Eucharist, confession, and the invocation of the saints: "In them I am delighted by the erudition, conciseness, and restraint in argumentation. Most writers today carry on defense with loud shouting and only make our tumultous times more disturbed. But these works I found very readable. I have passed them on to learned friends and finally I gave them to a printer for publication." *Opus Epistolarum*, ed. Allen, IX, 460. There was an edition in Cologne in 1532, which could have been instigated by Erasmus.

96. In the last stages of argument over the formulation of Trent's *Decree on Justification*, the Augustinian Father General, G. Seripando, cited extensively from chapter 9 of Cajetan's *De fide et operibus* on the root of merit being the work and influence of Christ the head in his members (intervention of November 26-27, 1546; *Concilium Tridentinum*, V, 672f). H. Jedin indicates the notable influence of Cajetan's works on Seripando's thought (*Papal Legate at the Council of Trent*, trans. F. C. Eckhoff [St. Louis 1947], 257f, 328f, 400f, 407, 666ff).

97. G. Mattingly, *Catherine of Aragon* (London 1942), 13.

98. See above, pages 21 and 24f, with note 53.

99. P. Kalkoff, "Zu Luthers römischem Prozess," *Zeitschrift für Kirchengeschichte* 25 (1904), 570; G. Hennig, *Luther und Cajetan*, 61; K.-V. Selge, "Die Augsburger Begegnung," *Jahrbuch der hessischen kirchengeschichtlichen Vereinigung* 20 (1969), 40f.

100. See above, page 27f. Also page 268, note 17, below.

101. K.-V. Selge, "Die Augsburger Begegnung," 42; O. H. Pesch, "'Das heisst eine neue Kirche bauen.' Luther und Cajetan in Augsburg," *Begegnung* (1972), 655ff.

102. *"In eius intelligentia adhuc laboro"* (WA 1, 539,36; LW 31, 98). O. Bayer's detailed studies have reached the same conclusion *(Promissio, Geschichte der reformatorischen Wende Luthers* [Göttingen 1971], 166, 182, 346).

103. *Ein Sermon von dem Sakrament der Busse* (WA 2, 709-723; LW 35, 9-22).

104. "Wert und Grenzen der katholischen Kontroverstheologie," *Um Reform und Reformation,* 18.

105. In the opening pages of *The Babylonian Captivity of the Church* (1520), Luther spoke of his earliest adversaries: "Since I see that they have an abundance of leisure and writing paper, I shall furnish them with ample matter to write about. For I shall keep ahead of them, so that while they are triumphantly celebrating a glorious victory over one of my heresies (as it seems to them) I shall meanwhile be devising a new one." LW 36, 17 (original at WA 6, 501,6).

106. M.-H. Laurent observed over thirty years ago that Cajetan's last days would have been saddened by the realization that he had made little impact by his efforts to renew scholasticism by the introduction of humanist methods of textual criticism. Introduction to Cajetan's *Commentaria in De Anima Aristotelis,* li-lii.

I. AUGSBURG TREATISES, 1518

The occasion for the writing of these treatises is related in the Introduction, pages 18-21, above. Translations and synopses were made from texts in Cajetan's *Opuscula omnia* (Lyons 1562), 97a-118b, and have been emended where a more accurate reading was given in *Opuscula quaestiones et quodlibeta* (Venice 1531), 49vb-60va. Titles of the individual treatises have been adapted and abbreviated from those given in the *Opuscula* of Lyons, 1562.

1. Luther, *Explanations of the Ninety-five Theses,* Thesis 19 (WA 1, 565, 1; LW 31, 141). Also, on Thesis 19 Luther had developed the argument that fear and dread constitute the worst pain endured in purgatory (WA 1, 565,27; LW 31, 142). On Thesis 18 Luther argued that one's purification in purgatory consisted in gradually replacing this fear by love (WA 1, 562-564; LW 31, 136-140).

2. *Ibid.* (WA 1, 565,27; LW 31, 142).

3. Luther did not develop this point, but did imply it in the wording of Thesis 19, "Nor does it seem proved that souls in purgatory . . . are certain and assured of their own salvation" (WA 1, 234,13; LW 31, 140).

4. This and the following four arguments are taken nearly verbatim from Luther's *Sermo de poenitentia* of early 1518. The first argument is now found at WA 1, 323, 23. See also Luther's similar argument in the *Explanations,* Thesis 7 (WA 1, 540,41; LW 31, 100f.).

5. Luther, *Sermo de poenitentia* (WA 1, 232,32); also *Explanations,* Thesis 7 (WA 1, 543,35; LW 31, 105).

6. Luther, *Sermo de poenitentia* (WA 1, 324,16). In 1518, Luther frequently cited the axiom used here, "*Non sacramentum, sed fides sacramenti quia creditur,*" from *Tractatus in Johannis Evangelium* 80, 3 (PL 35, 1840). See, for example, Luther's exposition of Hebrews 5:1 (WA 57 III, 170,1;LW

29, 172); the *Asterisci* against John Eck, where the former axiom is called *"dictum illud communissimum"* (WA 1, 286,18); thesis 10 in a disputation of mid-1518 (WA 1, 631,7); *Explanations,* Thesis 7 (WA 1, 544,40; LW 31, 107); and the *Acta Augustana* (WA 2, 15, 32; LW 31, 274). L. Villette gives further references in *Foi et Sacrement,* II (Paris 1964), 111. An indirect source of Luther's axiom was Pope Innocent III, whose two affirmations of the salvific effects of *fides sacramenti* in the absence of *sacramentum fidei* were passed on in the decretalist tradition (*Decretalium Gregorii IX Compilatio,* Liber III, T. XLII, cap. 4, and T. XLIII, cap. 3[CIC II, 647 and 648]).

7. Luther, *Sermo de poenitentia* (WA 1, 324, 2). Luther also contrasted contrition with faith in Christ's forgiveness in *Explanations,* Thesis 7 (WA 1, 542, 30, LW 31, 103).

8. Luther, *Sermo de poenitentia* (WA 1, 324, 11). There is a similar argument on grace being cast out if one does not believe he is forgiven in *Explanations,* Thesis 7 (WA 1, 543, 20, LW 31, 104).

9. Cajetan most probably added this argument after he met Luther in mid-October, three weeks after writing this treatise. Luther had not used these texts prior to Cajetan's study of his works, but did argue from them in the written defense he submitted to Cajetan on October 14, 1518. See the *Acta Augustana* (WA 2, 14,30, 15,9; LW 31, 272, 273).

10. Luther, *Explanations,* Thesis 38 (WA 1, 595,29; LW 31, 194).

11. *Ibid.* (WA 1, 595,5; LW 31, 193).

12. Luther's *Explanations,* Thesis 38, was on the efficacy of the keys as grounded in the words of Christ, Matthew 16:19 (WA 1, 594-596; LW 31, 191-196); and on Thesis 7 Luther cited and argued from this verse six times (WA 1, 539-545; LW 31, 98-107).

13. Luther, *Explanations,* Thesis 7 (WA 1, 543, 16; LW 31, 104).

14. This "ordinary norm" had been enunciated by Aquinas in ST I-II, 112, 5. One could know he is in the state of grace by revelation (a special privilege granted rarely), by concluding from evident principles (impossible in this case, since our knowledge of God, the *principium gratiae,* is indirect), or by conjectural knowledge based on certain signs (a possible way to moral certainty of being in grace, for example, when one experiences delight in the things of God). Duns Scotus had not treated the question explicitly, but a group of Franciscan theologians at the Council of Trent were able to develop arguments from Scotus for a certitude of a higher order than Aquinas' conjectural knowledge. This was especially so, when one received the sacrament of penance, since Scotus did not think that a person had to doubt whether his disposition was sufficient for justification through the sacrament. See *In* IV *Sent.,* D. 17, Q. 1 (*Opera Omnia,* 18, 510f). The Scotist position at Trent was argued in a treastise of August 1546 by Antonio D́elphinus, O.F.M., *Pro certitudine gratiae praesentis* (*Concilium Tridentinum,* XII, 651-658). In 1518, however, Cajetan could feel justified in appealing to a scholastic consensus, since the most respected recent Nominalist, Gabriel Biel (died 1495), had not developed the Scotist view, but had sharply rejected any certitude of grace and had attenuated the conjectural knowledge Aquinas had thought possible (*Sent.,* II, D. 27, Q. 1). The scholastic background and the arguments at Trent have been presented by Adolph Stakemeier, *Das Konzil*

von Trient über die Heilsgewissheit (Heidelberg 1947). See also, page 269, note 36, below.

15. *"Tantum habes quantum credis."* Luther, *Explanations*, Thesis 38 (WA 1, 595,5; LW 31, 193); also in the form, *"Tantum. . . accipies quantum credis te accepturum,"* in the *Sermo de digna praeparatione cordis*, also of early 1518 (WA 1, 331,6).

16. *Decretum pro Armenis*, November 22, 1439 (DS 1310 = DB 695).

17. Above, page 267, n. 9, we surmised the later addition by Cajetan of the sixth argument taken from Luther's defense in the Augsburg meetings. If this is correct, then this dramatic conclusion to Cajetan's fifth answer was the final word in the original text of his preparatory treatise of September 26. One finds it in uncanny correspondence with Luther's evaluation, near the end of the *Acta Augustana*, of the importance of his teaching on *fides sacramenti*: "In the latter answer, however, lies the whole summary of salvation. You are not a bad Christian if knowledgeable or ignorant of the [indulgence decree in] *Extravagante*. You are a heretic, however, if you deny faith in Christ's word" (WA 2, 18,14; LW 31, 278). As he mailed copies of the *Acta Augustana* to friends in December, Luther indicated that his argument with Cajetan over *fides sacramenti* has given rise to the suspicion that the Antichrist is now reigning in Rome. See the letter to W. Link, December 22, 1518 (WABr 1, n. 121,11; p. 270). – Thus the charge Cajetan made in consequence of this treatise did in fact lead to construction of a new church – or, more precisely, to a new Christian confession outside the *communio catholica.*

18. In the *Explanations*, Thesis 5, Luther does not use the technical term, *"forum ecclesiasticum,"* but Cajetan's formulation is quite close to WA 1, 536,11; LW 31, 92.

19. Luther, *Explanations*, Thesis 5 (WA 1, 534,31; LW 31, 90), into which Cajetan inserted part of Luther's renowned first thesis on indulgences.

20. *Ibid.* (WA 1, 537,28; LW 31,95).

21. *Ibid.* (WA 1, 538,1; LW 31,95).

22. In the early sixteenth century, Jubilees, or Holy Years, were actually held every twenty-five years, as decreed by Pius II in 1470. H. Thurston, *The Holy Year of Jubilee* (London 1900), 72.

23. The bull *Unigenitus* was issued by Pope Clement VI on January 27, 1343 (CIC II, 1304-06). The discrepancy between Luther's teaching and *Unigenitus* was the first of the two errors Cajetan cited against Luther in their meetings in mid-October. Luther then treated *Unigenitus* in the *Acta Augustana* (WA 2, 9-13, 20-22; LW 31, 264-270, 282-284), where he defended his refusal to recant in the face of its teaching on the treasury of indulgences.

24. Aquinas developed his views on indulgences in commenting on Distinction 20 of Book IV of Lombard's *Sentences*, a section which was then repeated as questions 25-27 of the Supplement to the *Summa Theologiae* (English Dominican Fathers' translation, Vol. 18 [London 1928], 302-329). The most comprehensive survey of the scholastic theologians' teaching on indulgences is N. Paulus, *Geschichte des Ablasses im Mittelalter*, I (Paderborn 1922), Chapters VI, VIII (pages 291f on Aquinas), and X. See also, B. Poschmann, *Penance and the Anointing of the Sick* (London and New York 1964), 219-227.

25. Cajetan cited four arguments from Luther's *Sermo de poenitentia*: it is

impossible to know all one's mortal sins (WA 1, 322,22); in the primitive Church only manifest mortal sins were confessed (322,24); all our works, even if in some respects virtuous, are sins leading to damnation (322,39); wanting to confess all our sins is seeking security in our confession and not throwing ourselves on God's mercy (323,4).

26. IV Lateran Council, *Omnis utriusque sexus*, November 1215 (DS 812 = DB 437). The Council of Florence spoke of confession of all sins *"quorum memoriam habet,"* in the *Decretum pro Armenis* (DS 1323 = DB 699).

27. Cajetan returned to the topic of integral confession in 1531, when he took up four aspects of religious practice controverted at the Augsburg Diet of 1530. See above, pages 210-212. He treated merit of eternal life in 1532 in *Faith and Works,* above pages 231-233.

28. This was implied in Luther's *Explanations,* Thesis 8, from which Cajetan constructed two arguments from the sixteen Luther had offered in support of the view that the penitential canons apply exclusively to the living (WA 1, 545-547; LW 31, 107-112).

29. Luther, *Explanations,* Thesis 6 (WA 1 539,1; LW 31,97).

30. The second argument begins from the situation Luther described in the *Explanations,* Thesis 7 (WA 1, 540,30-40; LW 31, 100), but underscores the intention to confess by citing a proof-text on the significance of this intention. Aquinas had cited Psalm 31:5 in ST III, 88, 2c.

31. Peter Lombard, *Liber Sententiarum,* IV, 18, 9 (Quaracchi edition, II, 862-864). The fullest monographic treatment of the early scholastic interpretation of absolution is P. Anciaux, *La Théologie du Sacrement de Pénitence au XIIe siecle* (Louvain 1949). See also B. Poschmann, *Penance and the Anointing of the Sick,* 156-165.

32. In presenting this "new theory", Cajetan has woven together phrases and themes from Luther's *Explanations,* Thesis 7 (WA 1, 543,20ff; LW 31, 104).

33. *Commentarium in Evangelium Matthaei,* III, 16, 19 (CCL 77, 142), a text probably accessible to Cajetan from a glossed bible (e.g. *Biblia, quinta pars* [Lyons 1520] , 52va).

34. *Decretum pro Armenis* (DS 1323 = DB 699).

35. Aristotle, *Topics,* I, 11 (*Aristoteles Graece,* ed. E. Bekker, I, 104b,22), which Cajetan cited according to the Latin translation of Boethius. *Aristoteles Latinus,* ed. L. Minio-Paluello, V, 1-3 (Brussels 1969), 17.

36. See above, page 267, note 14. Johann Altenstaig had stated in his *Vocabularius theologiae* (Hagenau 1517), "Many other signs [of present grace] are given by different saints and theologians. But all these are not immediate evidence, since without revelation we cannot discern clearly whether the light, joy and peace we experience is merely apparent and deceptive, as in the case of those whom the devil leads astray. Neither can we know whether our distaste for sin is ultimately directed to God. Therefore the signs give rise only to a conjecture and not to evident knowledge. It is said, 'Man does not know whether he deserves love or hate' [Ecclesiastes 9:1] .... No one, no matter how righteous he be, can know with certainty that he is in the state of grace, except by a revelation." Translated from the later edition of Altensaig, *Lexikon theologicum* (Antwerp 1576), 127 vb.

37. Luther had indicated this in remarks scattered through the *Explana-*

tions. Cajetan framed four arguments for the position. (1) Indulgences are not meritorious, and therefore are imperfect (*Explanations,* Thesis 28 [WA 1, 585, 17, LW 31, 176], Thesis 40 [WA 1, 598, 1, LW 31, 198], and Thesis 42 [WA 1, 599, 19; LW 31, 201]; see also *Sermon on Indulgence and Grace,* n. 17 [WA 1, 246,15; Woolf I, 54]). (2) Better Christians long to bear the cross, not to be exempted from it (*Explanations,* Thesis 40 [WA 1, 579,9; LW 31, 197]; *Sermon on Indulgence and Grace,* n. 9 [WA 1, 244,36; Wolff I, 52]; early sermons by Luther [WA 1, 99,6, 141,30]). (3) Theologians agree it is better to do one's penance even if one has gained an indulgence (*Explanations,* Thesis 43 [WA 1, 600,4; LW 31, 202], Thesis 58 [WA 1, 609,9; LW 31, 218]). (4) Indulgences remit the canonical penances for notorious crimes, and so are useful for imperfect Christians *(Explanations,* Thesis 13 [WA 1, 552, 24, 553,5; LW 31, 120f], Thesis 58 [WA 1, 612,35; LW 31, 224]).

38. Luther, *Explanations,* Thesis 58 (WA 1, 606,1; LW 31, 212), and Thesis 26 (WA 1, 580,25; LW 31, 168). Cajetan filled out the first phrases of Luther's argument with words from the earlier treatment of the *thesaurus* in connection with indulgences for the departed.

39. Luther, *Explanations,* Thesis 26 (WA 1, 580,27, LW 31, 168).

40. *Ibid.,* Thesis 58 (WA 1, 606,4; LW 31, 212).

41. *Ibid.* (WA 1, 606,9; LW 31, 212).

42. *Ibid.* (WA 1, 606,12; LW 31, 213), slightly condensed from Luther's argumentation.

43. *Ibid* (WA 1, 606,30; LW 31, 213).

44. *Ibid.* (WA 1, 606,34; LW 31, 213f), where Luther referred to Augustine, *De natura et gratia,* 35, 41 (CSEL 60,263).

45. Luther, *Explanations,* Thesis 58 (WA 1, 606,38; LW 31, 214), giving Jerome's argument from *Dialogus adversus Pelagianos,* II, 4 (PL 23, 538).

46. Luther, *Explanations,* Thesis 58 (WA 1, 607,3; LW 31, 214), citing *Retractationum,* I, 18, 4 (CSEL 33, 90).

47. Luther, *Explanations,* Thesis 58 (WA 1, 607,6; LW 31, 214), referring to *Confessiones,* IX 13, 34 (CSEL 33, 223).

48. Luther, *Explanations,* Thesis 58 (WA 1, 607, 14; LW 31, 214f), where Luther related Augustine's argument in *De natura et gratia,* 36, 42 (CSEL 60, 264).

49. Luther, *Explanations,* Thesis 58 (WA 1, 608,7; LW 31, 216).

50. *Ibid.* (WA 1, 607,22; LW 31, 215), into which Cajetan appears to have inserted the argument from Romans 2.

51. *Ibid.* (WA 1, 608,22; LW 31, 216f).

52. *Ibid.* (WA 1, 608,36; LW 31, 217), where Luther refers to a decretal of Pope Innocent III, given in *Decretalium Gregorii IX Compilatio,* Liber V, T. XXVIII, cap. 14 (CIC II, 888f).

53. Luther, *Explanations,* Thesis 58 (WA 1, 609,4; LW 31, 217f).

54. *Ibid.* (WA 1, 609,9; LW 31, 218). Cajetan reduced Luther's argument from this consideration to its essential point.

55. *Ibid.* (WA 1, 610,8-611,5; LW 31, 220f). Cajetan shaped Luther's rambling passage into a tightly articulated argument. An example of the advice of theologians to continue penance after gaining an indulgence is in Aquinas, ST Supplement, 25, 1 ad 4.

56. Luther, *Explanations,* Thesis 58 (WA 1, 611,6; LW 31, 221).

57. *Ibid.* (WA 1, 612,27; LW 31,224).

58. This argument is not based on a specific text of *Explanations,* Thesis 58. Cajetan appears to have constructed it in order to give himself an opportunity in the response to make a systematic presentation of the work of Christ in countering the effects of original sin and personal sin.

59. *Explanations,* Thesis 61 (WA 1, 615,28; LW 31,229).

60. *Ibid.* (WA 1, 616,1; LW 31, 230).

61. *Extravagantes Decretales,* Liber V, T. IX, cap. 2 (CIC II, 1304-06).

62. Gratian, *Decretum,* Pars I, D. XIX, c. 6 (CIC I, 61f), which is an excerpt from Augustine's *De doctrina Christiana,* II, 12.

63. *Decretum,* Pars I, D. XIX, c. 1 (CIC I, 58f).

64. *Decretalium Gregorii IX Compilatio,* Liber V, T. VII, cap. 9 (CIC II, 780f).

65. *Ennarrationes in Psalmos,* LXI, 4 (CCL 39, 774), LXXXVI, 5 (CCL 39, 1202), CXLII, 3 (CCL 40, 2061).

66. Pelagius, *Libellus fidei,* 21 (PL 48,491). This work, although not this passage, was cited in Gratian's *Decretum* and attributed to Jerome under the title *Expositio symboli ad Damasum* (CIC I, 616, 970).

67. *De spiritu et littera,* 36, 64 (CSEL 60, 224f).

68. See page 279, note 64, below.

69. *De natura et gratia,* 36, 42 (CSEL 60, 264).

70. Pelagius, *Libellus fidei* (PL 48, 491), cited in Gratian, *Decretum,* Pars II, C. XXIV, Q. 1, c. 14 (CIC I, 970).

71. *Decretum pro Armenis* (DS 1328).

72. Cajetan digested the arguments Luther had given in the *Explanations,* Thesis 41 (WA 1, 598,21; LW 31, 199), and cited Luther's argument from 1 John 3:17 from *Explanations,* Thesis 45 (WA 1, 600,23; LW 31, 203). Luther argued for the priority of almsgiving over indulgences in the widely circulated German *Sermon on Indulgence and Grace,* nn. 16f (WA 1, 245,35; Woolf I, 53). Fourteen printings of this work appeared in 1518 alone (WA 1, 240f).

73. Luther had argued for this kind of reflection in his *Sermo de poenitentia* of early 1518 (WA 1, 321,7), since confession should be made out of love of righteousness and not because of custom and fear of transgressing a precept.

74. Luther argued in *Explanations,* Thesis 18, that the souls in purgatory were being cleansed of a sinfulness that consisted in fear of punishment and lack of love. Cajetan's treatise organized a section of Luther's argument into this thesis and three arguments (from WA 1, 562,13; LW 31, 136), and added a fourth argument from the treatment of Thesis 14 (WA 1, 555,14; LW 31, 124f) on lack of trust as the root of fear of punishment. In the *Sermo de poenitentia* Luther had excoriated an imperfect sorrow for sin that arises from fear of punishment and he said it makes one an even greater sinner (WA 1, 319,16).

75. Luther, *Explanations,* Thesis 14 (WA 1, 554,27; LW 31, 123f). Cajetan's question deals with the original fourteenth thesis and the first argument given for it in the *Explanations.*

76. Luther had argued for a negative answer to this question in the first

section of *Explanations,* Thesis 26 (WA 1, 574-580; LW 31, 158-166).

77. *Ibid.* (WA 1, 577,15; LW 31, 162).

78. *Ibid.* (WA 1, 576,41; LW 31, 162).

79. Luther had said this in a general way at the beginning of *Explanations,* Thesis 25 (WA 1, 572,33; LW 31, 154f).

80. *Decretalium Gregorii IX Compilatio,* Liber V, T. XXXVIII, cap. 4 (CIC II, 885).

81. Cajetan apparently sensed the need for some explanation of indulgences for the departed *per modum suffragii.* On November 20, 1519, he completed a *quaestio* of moderate length *(Opuscula* [Lyons 1562] , 103b-105a) on whether a plenary indulgence gained for a soul in purgatory actually frees the intended soul from all remaining punishments. Cajetan gives three arguments for the affirmative but responds that the answer must be negative, because it would then follow that by indulgences the Pope could empty purgatory. Luther had used this argument in Thesis 82 of the Ninety-five Theses (WA 1, 237,22; LW 31, 32) and in *Explanations,* Thesis 26 (WA 1, 574,30; LW 31, 158). Cajetan explains that the Church's *suffragium* is its earnest communal petition that God graciously accept what we offer for the benefit of the souls in purgatory and let it suffice for their release. We have no right to this before God, and the souls are outside the scope of the Church's power to absolve, but the Church nonetheless trusts in God's acceptance of what she grants the souls out of her treasury of satisfactory merits. God's acceptance is, however, not automatic and, in addition to this, the souls themselves are in varying degrees deserving of and disposed for receiving this help offered by the Church. In responding to the initial arguments for actual release of specific souls, Cajetan delivers a concise rebuke to preachers led by avarice to preach the automatic efficacy of indulgences gained for the departed. This is not Christ's and the Church's teaching, but the product of their own ignorance. P. Kalkoff, often the trenchant critic, wrote admiringly of this *quaestio,* which he saw as directed against Prierias and Tetzel ("Zu Luthers römischem Prozess," *Zeitschrift für Kirchengeschichte* 25 [1904] 429).

82. Luther held this as a disputation position, not as a doctrinal assertion, in the *Explanations,* Thesis 18, from which Cajetan framed five arguments: only by charity does dread diminish (WA 1, 562,16; LW 31, 136); the souls in purgatory are still *in via,* and so must be advancing or declining (WA 1, 563,3; LW 31, 137); in the weakness of purgatory virtue is made perfect, in accord with 1 Corinthians 12:9 (WA 1, 562,39; LW 31, 137); all things work together for the betterment of those who love God (WA 1, 562,33; LW 31, 137); no one can persevere in love unless he is receiving an outpouring of more and more love (WA 1, 563,6; LW 31, 138).

83. Council of Florence, *Laetentur Coeli,* decree of July 6, 1439 (DS 1304 = DB 693).

84. St. Augustine, *Enchiridion de fide spe et caritate,* 29, 110 (CCL 46, 108), a passage Luther had referred to in his ingenious exposition of the nature of indulgences for the departed in the treatise sent to Archbishop Albrecht, October 31, 1517 (WABr 12, n. 4212a,48; p. 6; Wicks, *Man Yearning for Grace,* 246).

85. The background of this treatise is recounted in the Introduction, above, pages 16 and 25f. Luther's printed sermon on excommunication is now given at WA 1, 638-643.

86. Luther, *Sermo de virtute excommunicationis* (WA 1, 639,2).

87. Cajetan constructed this argument from Luther's discussion of excommunication, if justly imposed (WA 1, 640,2.11). Cajetan supplied the argument from Gratian, *Decretum*, Pars II, C. XI, Q. 3, c. 1 (CIC I, 642), who was citing Gregory the Great, *Homilia XXVI in Evangelia*, 6 (PL 76, 1201).

88. Luther *Sermo de virtute excommunicationis* (WA 1, 639,19, 640,16).

89. Peter Lombard, *Liber Sententiarum*, IV 18, 6 (Quaracchi edition, II, 864).

90. St. Bernard of Clarivaux, *De gradibus humilitatis et superbiae*, 56 *(Opera*, ed. J. Leclercq et al., III [Rome 1963], 58).

91. St. Augustine, *Sermo* 82, 4 (PL 38, 509).

92. *"Vinculo anathematis."* *Glossa interlinearis*, on Matthew 18:18 (for example, in *Biblia sacra cum glossa ordinaria* [Antwerp 1617], V, 306, and in *Biblia, quinta pars* [Lyons 1520], 57r).

93. St. John Chrysostom, *Homila LX in Mattheum*, 2 (PG 58, 586).

94. Cajetan cites here from Gratian, *Decretum*, Pars II, C. XI, Q. 3, c. 32 (CIC I, 653), where the words are attributed to Augustine. According to F. Russo, the text is not found in Augustine ("Penitence et excommunication," *Recherches de science religieuse* 33 [1946], 267). Gratian had taken over the text and the erroneous reference to Augustine from the canonical collection of Ivo of Chartres (e.g. PL 161, 183).

95. Cajetan is probably alluding to *Contra epistolam Parmeniani*, III, 1, 1-3 (CSEL 51, 98-104), an extended treatment of the medicinal purpose of excommunication. Augustine explains 1 Corinthians 5:5 by reference to 2 Corinthians 2:4-11, which in the Vulgate ends with the words, *"ut non possideamur a Satana."*

96. Cajetan cites Gratian, *Decretum*, Pars II, C. XI, Q. 3, c. 33 (CIC I, 653), where the words were attributed to St. Jerome. F. Russo directs us to the canonical collection of Ivo of Chartres, who cited the text as a letter of Eutychian, writing to bishops in Sicily *(Recherches de science religieuse* 33 [1946], 433, referring to PL 161, 838).

97. Gratian, *Decretum*, Pars II, C. XI, Q. 3, cc. 32-33 (CIC I, 653).

98. St. Augustine, *Sermo* 82, 4 (PL 38, 509), cited by Gratian, *Decretum*, Pars II, C. XI, Q. 3, c. 48 (CIC I, 657).

99. See above, note 87.

100. Cajetan added concrete examples where the gloss had spoken generally of errors of law and fact. Gloss on Pars II, C. XI, Q. 3 (*Decretum Gratiani cum Glossis Dmni Johannis Theutonici* [Basle 1511], 193r).

101. *Liber Sextus Decretalium*, Liber V, T. XI, cap. 1 (CIC II, 1093).

II. MISUSE OF SCRIPTURE, 1519

Our Introduction describes the occasion for this work, pages 23f and 28, above. The translation was made from the text in Cajetan's *Opuscula quaestiones et quodlibeta* (Venice 1531), 63v-64r.

1. Luther, *Acta Augustana* (WA 2, 21,6; LW 31, 282). The bull, *Unigenitus,* of Pope Clement VI, issued January 27, 1343, was published in the (for Luther and Cajetan) most recent compilation of papal decretals, *Extravagantes Decretales* Liber V, T. IX, cap. 2 (CIC II, 1304).

2. Luther, *Acta Augustana* (WA 2, 19,27; LW 31, 280f). The text was from Pope Gelasius (d. 496), as given in Gratian's *Decretum*, Pars I, D. XXI, c. 3 (CIC I, 70). The final citation, "*Quod uni dicitur omnibus dicitur,*" (WA 2, 20,22) was accepted by Cajetan in this treatise as a word of Christ. Later, in the *Divine Institution of the Pontifical Office,* he dismissed it as a text not found in the New Testament (CC 10, 31). Luther's use of it (WA 2, 20,22; LW 31, 281) appears to be an attempt to cite Mark 13:37 from memory, a text which in the Vulgate of the time read, "*Quod autem vobis dico, omnibus dico: vigilate.*"

3. Luther, *Acta Augustana* (WA 2, 19,3; LW 31, 279). Hebrews 7:12 was cited in *Decretalium Gregorii IX Compilatio,* Liber I, T. II, cap. 3 (CIC II, 8).

4. Luther, *Acta Augustana* (WA 2, 21,9; LW 31, 282).

5. The following arguments are an adumbration of the full treatment of Matthew 16:18f which Cajetan will give in chapters 2-7 of *The Divine Institution of the Pontifical Office.* See above, pages 107-116.

6. St. John Chrysostom, *Homilia* 88 *in Iohannem,* 1 (PG 59, 487), which Cajetan most probably cited from Aquinas, *Catena aurea, In Ioannem,* XXI, 3 (Marietti edition, II, 590).

7. Gratian, *Decretum,* Pars I, D. XXII, c. 2 (CIC I, 73).

8. The *Glossa* commented on Matthew 16:17, "One answered, and then this one was addressed for the benefit of all, so that unity might be guarded in all things" (PL 114, 141). In the *Catena aurea, In Mattheum,* XVI 3, Aquinas cited a longer text attributed to the *Glossa* on Peter as the principal vicar of Christ in the Church, who was appointed to preserve unity (Marietti edition, I, 252).

9. Aquinas, *Catena aurea, In Mattheum,* XVI, 3 (Marietti edition, I, 252). Aquinas was dependent upon a booklet given him for examination by Pope Urban IV in which he found a series of statements on the fulness of authority Christ entrusted to Peter. The booklet claimed to be excerpting statements from Cyril of Alexandria's *Thesaurus de sancta et consubstantiali Trinitate.* These sentences are not found in Cyril's original, but Aquinas cited them in the *Catena* and more at length in *Contra errores Graecorum.* Cajetan took over five statements from the latter work in Chapter 14 of *The Divine Institution of the Pontifical Office* (CC 10, 90f). See our synopsis, pages 142f, above.

10. Luther, *Acta Augustana* (WA 2, 20,22; LW 31, 281). On this alleged text, see note 2, above.

12. Aquinas, *Catena aurea, In Mattheum* XVI, 3 (Marietti edition, I, 252). On the alleged work of Cyril, see note 9, above.

13. St. Gregory the Great, *Epistolae,* IX, 12 (PL 77, 959), cited in Pars I, D. XXII, c. 4 (CIC I, 75).

III. DIVINE INSTITUTION OF THE PONTIFICAL OFFICE, 1521

The Introduction, page 30, above, relates the circumstances surrounding Cajetan's composition of this work. Our translation and synopses are based on *De divina institutione pontificatus Romani Pontificis*, edited by Friedrich Lauchert, as Volume 10 of the series, *Corpus Catholicorum* (Munster: Aschendorff, 1925). Lauchert's text was based on the 1521 Roman edition of the work. The notes to our translation and synopses are dependent on Lauchert's notes, except where we add references to similar texts available in English translations of Luther's works. We have also added internal cross-references as well. Our chapter titles follow closely those given by Lauchert on the basis of the 1521 Roman edition.

1. Luther, *Resolutio Lutheriana super propositione XIII de potestate papae* (WA 2, 186,5). Luther had published this work shortly before his disputation in Leipzig against Johann Eck in June-July 1519. After the disputation he expanded it somewhat and brought it out again. In the passage referred to here, he begins by acknowledging that the papal supremacy is a fact under the providential will of God. Luther made a similar "concession" toward the end of his 1520 work, *On the Papacy in Rome* (LW 39, 101).

2. Luther, *Resolutio* (WA 2, 186,38). In this passage Luther also explained the *de facto* papal supremacy in terms of humbly acceding to one's accuser (Matthew 5:25), being subject to human institutions (1 Peter 3:15), and agreeing with the actual consensus of Christians at his time (WA 2, 186-187). These, Luther contended, are credible arguments by which the authority of the Pope could be defended, even against its heretical or schismatic opponents (WA 2, 185,36).

3. The main sections of Luther's *Resolutio* sought to demonstrate the inconclusiveness of arguments for the papal supremacy being of divine right, that is, being instituted by Christ. Luther treated Scripture (WA 2, 187-197), canons and decretals (198-235), and arguments from reason and history (235-239).

4. In Luther's *Resolutio*, the section on Scripture had first argued that Christ's words to Peter in Matthew 16 were irrelevant to papal claims (WA 2, 187-194), and then that it was wrong to interpret John 21 as referring to pontifical power (194-197). *On the Papacy in Rome* argued to similar conclusions on these two passages in its final major section (on Matthew 16, · LW 39, 86-94; on John 21, LW 39, 95-101). Also in 1520 Luther took up these two Petrine passages in *Defense and Explanation of all the Articles*, Article 25 (on Matthew 16, LW 32, 68-71; on John 21, LW 32, 71-77).

5. Cajetan gives his refutation of this restrictive view in Chapter 2, below.

6. Cajetan takes up the conferral of the keys on Peter personally in Chapter 3, below.

7. Cajetan responds in Chapter 4, below, that Christ was not addressing all the apostles in Matthew 16.

8. Cajetan treats the unique role of Peter in Chapter 5, below.

9. Cajetan offers his explanation in Chapter 6, below, of how the gift to

the whole Church is dependent on the gift conferred on Peter alone.

10. Cajetan does not cite Luther in this chapter, but appears to construct this argument from some brief remarks in Luther's *Resolutio*, for example (WA 2, 191,23), "Who could deny that the keys were handed on to the one who by the revelation of the Father confessed Christ? Because of this, the keys are necessarily found wherever there is the revelation of the Father and a confession of Christ. But this is present in every church, not in any individual and unreliable man."

11. The arguments and confirmations are cited, in the main, from the section of the *Resolutio* found at WA 2, 189-193. The second argument, for example, is given thus (citing the text now at WA 2, 191,27): "After the glorious commendation of Peter, then when Peter tried to restrain him from going to death, Christ rebuked Peter, 'Get behind me, Satan, you do not think the things of God' [Matthew 16:23]. This rebuke following the commendation makes it clear that the previous 'Peter', the one who received the keys, was not Peter the child of Bar-Jonah, but instead the Church, the child of God, which God's word begets and which hears and confesses the word of God to the end. It was not one who at times does not think the things of God, and never one told to get behind as Peter was." In *On the Papacy in Rome*, Luther argued to a similar conclusion (LW 39,86-89), and then explained that the keys are a gift for the consolation of the afflicted: "The words of Christ are nothing but gracious promises to the whole community, given to all of Christendom, . . . so that the poor sinful consciences are consoled when they are 'loosed' or absolved by a man." LW 39, 90.

12. Cajetan referred to two such arguments from the *Resolutio* (=WA 2, 189,29; 188,34) and two from the *Acta Augustana* (=WA 2, 20,18.22; LW 31, 281). For example: "Unless through Peter all the disciples responded, then they surely were not disciples, they did not hear the Teacher, nor did they satisfy their questioner—which is unthinkable of apostles. In addition, Christ accepted Peter's response not for Peter alone, but for the whole college of apostles and disciples; otherwise, he would have questioned the others further." From WA 2, 189,31, and condensed by Cajetan.

13. Luther had argued in the *Resolutio* from Matthew 18:18 in a passage now at WA 2, 191,1; from John 20:22f in words now at WA 2, 188,23; from Acts 8:14 and 15:8 in sections now at WA 2, 203,5 and 204,1; and from Galatians 2:7f in passages now at WA 2, 195,10, 235,29, and 239,3. See also *Defense and Explanation of all the Articles*, Article 25 (LW 32, 73f), for the argument from Acts 8:14, and *On the Papacy in Rome* (LW 39: 86-89) for the same basic argument from Matthew 18 and John 20. Luther gave patristic evidence in this section of the *Resolutio* quite briefly (WA 2, 188,29), but argued more at length from Cyprian, *De unitate ecclesiae*, chapter 4, in the 1519 work, *Contra malignum Iohannis Eccii iudicium* (WA 2, 636-637).

14. Luther questioned the compatibility of these in the *Resolutio* (WA 2, 191,4).

15. Luther had argued that every church, in so far it is Christ's, is built on the rock, and so no church had privilege of place. WA 2, 194,18; 206,30; 208,3.

16. The Council of Constance censured forty-five propositions taken from

the works of John Wyclif, May 4, 1415. References to *ecclesia Romana* in the wide sense occur in nn. 37 and 41 (DS 1187, 1191 = DB 617, 621).

17. Even though Gratian gave two canons excepting the departed from the ambit of the Church's power to bind and loose (*Decretum*, Pars II, C. XXIV, Q. 2, cc. 1 and 2 [CIC I, 984]), he added a canon on the crime of heresy, for which one can be accused and excommunicated even after death. The latter canon cited two texts in which St. Augustine declared himself ready to excommunicate the deceased Caecilian, if the latter was proven to have taught heresy (*Ibid.*, c. 5 [CIC I, 986f]).

18. "The key carried on his shoulder can be understood as the scepter of the kingdom and the trophy of victory, that is, as the cross Christ carried on his own shoulder." *Glossa ordinaria*, on Isaiah 22:22 (PL 113, 1265).

19. Luther had argued in the *Resolutio*, "Christ appointed Peter to feed the flock only after he declared his love. . . . Does it not follow then that if he no longer loves he should not be listened to?" WA 2, 195,29. Luther argued in a similar vein in *On the Papacy in Rome* (LW 39, 98-101), and in *Defense and Explanation of all the Articles*, Article 25 (LW 32, 71-73).

20. Cajetan listed arguments scattered over the pages of the *Resolutio* on John 21 (WA 2, 194-197), for example, that Peter was obviously not commissioned to feed all the sheep of Christ, since Galatians 2:7 speaks of him being entrusted only with the Gospel for the circumcised (195,10).

21. Luther, *Resolutio* (WA 2, 195,19). See also *Defense and Explanation of all the Articles*, Article 25 (LW 32, 72). The similar argument in *On the Papacy in Rome* concludes, "Do you not see that 'tending' must mean something different from having authority, and that 'being tended' must be something different from being externally subject to Roman power?" LW 39, 96.

22. Luther, *Resolutio* (WA 2, 196,5).

23. *Ibid.* (196,20).

24. St. Augustine, *In Iohannis Evangelium*, 124, 1(PL 35, 1969).

25. St. John Chrysostom, *Homilia* 88 *in Iohannem*, I (PG 59, 487).

26. *Glossa ordinaria*, on John 21:17 (*Biblia, quinta pars* [Lyons 1520], 243r). Cajetan cited this text in the form given by Aquinas, *Catena aurea, In Iohannem*, XXI, 3 (Marietti edition, II, 590).

27. St. Gregory the Great, *Epistolae*, V, 20 (PL 77, 784).

28. Cajetan, or his earliest editor, carelessly gave "perfection of the sheep" in the verse from 2 Timothy, where the Vulgate read, "the knowledge of the truth."

29. Luther, *Resolutio* (WA 2, 193,17).

30. *Ibid.* (192,9).

31. Cajetan appears to have constructed this and the subsequent argument as further applications of the principle Luther laid down in the first argument (193,17). Or he could have noted Luther's somewhat similar argument from Luke 23:32 and Matthew 17:42ff in the 1519 work, *Contra malignum Iohannis Eccii iudicium* (WA 2, 632,19 and 633,6).

32. The fourth difficulty does not appear as such in Luther's *Resolutio*, although it is implied by the fact that various Gospel passages referring to Peter have to be shown not to involve an implicit reference to successors in his

office or privileges, Isaiah 5:4 was cited by Aquinas to underscore the notion that Christ supplied his Church all it needed for survival (*Summa contra Gentiles*, IV, 76).

33. Luther, *Resolutio* (WA 2, 236,33).

34. *Ibid.* (192,7).

35. *Ibid.* (192,12).

36. *Ibid.* (208,20).

37. Luther cited St. Jerome's letter at length in the *Resolutio* (WA 2, 227,33-228,35), and then drove home the fact of its cogency by referring to its inclusion in the code of law accepted throughout the Church (229,17). The passage is found in the *Decretum*, Pars I, D. XCIII, c. 14 (CIC I, 327f).

38. Luther cited St. Jerome's commentary in the *Resolutio* (= WA 2, 229,29), and noted its inclusion in the *Decretum*, where it is Pars I, D. XCV, c. 5 (CIC I, 332f). The real force, however, of Jerome's point is, according to Luther, the fact that it rests solidly on Scripture.

39. Theophylact, *Ennaratio in Evangelium Lucae*, on Luke 22:32 (PG 123, 1073), cited by Cajetan from Aquinas' *Catena Aurea*, *In Lucam*, XXII, 9 (Marietti edition, II, 289).

40. Cyril of Alexandria, *Commentarium in Lucam*, on Luke 22:32 (PG 72, 916), cited by Cajetan from Aquinas' *Catena Aurea*, *In Lucam*, XXII, 9 (Marietti edition, II, 289).

41. The final phrase refers back to the three main arguments in the body of the chapter, above, pages 125f.

42. Cajetan's phrase, *"gubernare catholicam ecclesiam,"* has not been located among the works of Aquinas either by F. Lauchert or the present editor. However, these works are not wanting in statements affirming papal authority. In connection with the *thesaurus* of indulgences, the pope "presides over the whole church" (*Quaestiones quodlibetales*, II, 8, 2) and is said to have fulness of pontifical authority (*In IV Sent.*, Dist. 20, 4, ad 1 = ST, Supplement, 26, 3). In *Contra Gentiles*, IV, 76, the pope is the unique head of the whole Church and the pastor to whose care the universal Church is committed. *Contra errores Graecorum* refers to the fulness of power of the pope, who is first and greatest of all the bishops, the vicar of Christ, and the one who determines what is believed in the Church (ed. P. Glorieux [Tournai 1957] 167-171).

43. Luther, *Resolutio* (WA 2, 202,24).

44. *Ibid.* (192,30).

45. Cajetan developed the formulation of this difficulty from the principle laid down by Luther (WA 2, 193,17) that if the promise of the keys applies as well to Peter's successor then the other promises closely related to the keys must also apply to Peter's successors as well. But if one considers that some successors lacked faith (193,27), that the gates of hell prevailed against them (193,30), and that they are not protected from heresy (199,15), then the whole construction proves untenable.

46. Luther, *Resolutio* (WA 2, 195,29). See also *On the Papacy in Rome* (LW 39, 98).

47. Luther, *Resolutio* (WA 2, 196,22.30), which, however, did not draw the sharp contrast between *oves Christi* and *oves suas*.

48. Luther, *Acta Augustana* (WA 2, 20,8; LW 31, 281); *Resolutio* (WA 2, 201,15, 232,11). Luther refers to Gregory the Great's letters, for example, Book V, nn. 18, 20, 21, 43; Book VII, nn. 27, 31; Book VIII, n. 30 (PL 77, 738, 747, 749, 771, 882, 888, 893).

49. Luther, *Resolutio* (WA 2, 238,3), citing the passage of the *Ecclesiastical History* now found at PL 21, 463.

50. Luther, *Resolutio* (WA 2, 237,16).

51. *Ibid.* (236,11).

52. *Ibid.* (236,14).

53. *Ibid.* (236,22), where Luther cites Chapter 98 of Jerome's work (PL 23,699).

54. Luther, *Resolutio* (WA 2, 237,23, 203,33).

55. The Church sings of Peter's vision of Christ in Stanzas 4-5 of *Apostolorum passio,* a hymn often attributed to St. Ambrose, found in the Ambrosian, Cistercian, and Gothic breviaries on the feast of Saints Peter and Paul (text in Daniel, *Thesaurus Hymnologicus* [Halle 1841], 101, and PL 17, 1217). St. Ambrose's narrative is in *Sermo contra Auxientium* (PL 16, 1011).

56. PL 15, 2070.

57. Pope Boniface VIII, *Unam Sanctam,* November 18, 1302 (full text, CIC II, 1245f; excerpt, DS 870f = DB 468f).

58. *"Omnium ordinatores et iudices."* Glossa interlinearis on 1 Corinthians 12:28 (for example, in *Biblia sacra cum glossa ordinaria* [Antwerp 1617], VI, 309, and in *Biblia, sexta pars* [Lyons 1520], 53rb).

59. Cajetan had also argued in 1512, in his *Comparison of the Authority of Pope and Council,* Chapter IX, that an error in a papal definition would be tantamount to an error in faith by the whole Church (*De comparatione Auctoritatis Papae et Concilii,* ed. V.M. Pollet [Rome 1936], 67). Cajetan also treated the binding force of papal judgments in matters of faith in *Five Articles of Luther* (1521), pages 151f, above. Luther made no great issue of infallibility in the *Resolutio,* but simply dismissed it as untenable (WA 2, 199,15).

60. Gregory the Great, *Epistolae,* V, 20 (PL 77, 746).

61. Jerome, *De viris illustribus,* 98 (PL 23, 699).

62. Augustine, *Epistola* 53 (CSEL 34/1, 153).

63. CC 10, 89-99, gives detailed notes on the immediate sources of the links in Cajetan's chain of texts. A good number of these were cited in a manner indicating use of Aquinas' *Catena Aurea* and *Contra Errores Graecorum* and of Gratian's *Decretum.* But other texts were taken directly from the original sources, e.g. John Chrysostom's homilies on Matthew 16 and John 21, and five texts from letters and works of Bernard of Clairvaux.

64. Aristotle wrote, "It is the part of an educated man to look for precision in each class of things just so far as the nature of the subject admits; it is evidently equally foolish to accept probable reasoning from a mathematician and to demand from a rhetorician scientific proofs." *Nichomachean Ethics,* I, 3 (*Works of Aristotle,* IX [Oxford 1915], 1094b,25). Cajetan offered this caution in at least two other works of controversy (page 79, above, and page 217, above). This advice to heed the limits of human certitude can serve to highlight the crises experienced by the earliest adherents

of the Reformation. Luther and his early followers would surely not find helpful this bit of Aristotelian wisdom about the lesser degree of clarity and certainty attainable through rational pondering of moral and political realities. In both their personal and doctrinal quests, the earliest Protestants were convinced they had more than "moral certitude". In the event of sacramental absolution, Luther was sure Christians should be grasping an existential certitude of the forgiveness of sins, a certitude of considerable clarity and force under Christ's word. Faith apprehends a fully reliable word on which personal religiosity can then build. To secure this personal certitude, Luther undertook a reconstruction of doctrine (especially 1519-1521) which seemed necessary in view of the experienced bankrupcy of papal decrees and scholastic theology. Neither of the latter proved convincing as guarantors of Christian truth in the face of the new questions of the age. Luther turned to the plain text of Scripture, the earliest Councils, and the great themes of Augustine and the early Fathers. These normative sources, preeminently the Pauline letters and the Fourth Gospel, gave him a fresh hold on the central truths of Christianity with a far greater certitude than was afforded by decretals and recent theology. Cajetan, on the other hand, found his life and thought quite adequately secured by the classic theological system of Thomism and by an accentuated papalist ecclesiology. In Cajetan's own lifetime both had proven their adequacy in controversy. As the Reformation argument erupted they provided an unquestioned texture for thought and argument against the theses of those questioning the recent tradition. With the structural lines of theology and Church made certain by his Thomism and by the papal primacy, Cajetan could be content with cumulative, ultimately probable, arguments for points of detail.

IV. FIVE ARTICLES, 1521

On the occasion of this work, see the Introduction, page 31, above. Our translation is from Cajetan's *Opuscula omnia* (Turin 1582), 184a-186a, and has been slightly emended in accord with the text in *Opuscula quaestiones et quodlibeta* (Venice 1531), 64va-65rb. The Venice edition of 1531 gave no titles to the individual articles. We have considerably abbreviated those found in the Turin *Opuscula* edition of 1582.

1. *Exsurge Domine,* article 7 (DS 1457 = DB 747), taken from Luther's *Sermo de poenitentia* (early 1518), as now found at WA 1, 321,2f. Cajetan did not cite the bull verbatim, nor did he follow the precise text of the *Sermo* given by WA, which has the phrase we translated as "an excellent penance is to sin no more" in the German vernacular, *"Nymmer thun die hochste pusz."*

2. St. Augustine, *De nuptiis et concupiscentiis,* I, 26, 29 (CSEL 42, 241f).

3. Luther had said in his *Sermo von dem Ablass und Gnade* (February 1518) that the tripartite division of penance into acts of contrition, confession, and satisfaction was not based on Scripture or on the early Fathers (WA 1, 243,4; Wolff I, 50). This statement was then censured in *Exsurge Domine* (article 5, DS 1455 = DB 745). In *De captivitate Babylonica* (1520) Luther complained that this scholastic triad obscured the real heart of sacramental penance, namely, faith in God's promise of forgiveness (WA 6,

544,21; LW 36, 83f). In his response to *Exsurge,* Luther explained that his argument was with the notion of satisfaction taught by his opponents, that is, a satisfaction from which the Church could exempt by indulgences. Contrition and confession retain their importance for him, but *satisfactio* were better replaced by biblical terms like *disciplina Domini* or *correptio,* since God punishes sinners in a way which the Church cannot modify by indulgences. *Assertio omnium articulorum* (WA 7, 112-113) and *Defense and Explanation of all the Articles* (LW 32, 34; original at WA 7, 352,28).

4. *Exsurge Domine,* article 10 (DS 1460 = DB 750). Cajetan cited the first main clause, although not verbatim. The article was taken from Luther's *Resolutiones (Explanations of the Ninety-five Theses),* Thesis 7 (WA 1, 543, 15; LW 31, 104). Cajetan had treated this issue in the second and sixth of his *Augsburg Treatises* of 1518 (pages 49-55 and 63-67, above) and returned to it in Chapters 1-4 of *Faith and Works* in 1535 (pages 219-226, above).

5. *Exsurge Domine,* article 15 (DS 1465 = DB 755). Cajetan cited the first half of the article, which had been taken from Luther's *Instructio pro confessione peccatorum* (1518), now found at WA 1, 264,9f. Luther asserted the same thing in a German version of this *Instructio,* WA 1, 255,24f, and in a Latin work on worthy preparation for reception of Holy Communion, also in 1518 (WA 1, 330,36f).

6. *Exsurge Domine,* article 17 (DS 1467 = DB 757). The article, which adds, " . . . and of the saints," was taken from the ninety-five theses of October 1517, collating theses 56 and 58 to make a meaningful sentence. Cajetan cited this article exactly. He had made an extensive analysis of Luther's notion of the *thesaurus* in the eighth Augsburg treatise (pages 68-85 above).

7. Cajetan's compressed statement of the criticism appears to allude to the fact that the censure of Luther's article is overly reliant upon the bull of Pope Clement VI, *Unigenitus,* to which Leo X's decree *Cum postquam* (November 9, 1518) had been hurriedly added (DS 1447-49 = DB 740a). Cajetan played a major role in the drafting of the latter document, as G. Hennig showed (*Luther und Cajetan,* 90-92). But *Cum postquam* makes no effort at grounding its affirmations in either Scripture or Church tradition. Its aim is rather to assert clearly and normatively the teaching of the Church. Cajetan's present article may well have been conceived as supplying a succinct statement of the basis on which *Cum postquam* rests.

8. Luther argued from Romans 8:18 in the *Explanations,* Thesis 58 (WA 1, 606,9; LW 31, 212), drawing the conclusion that the saints were more than fully rewarded for what they suffered on earth and that consequently their works could not serve to aid others in gaining a heavenly reward. He repeated this in the *Acta Augustana* (WA 2, 10,29; LW 31, 266).

9. Luther had argued in early 1518 that indulgences could be given solely by the authority of the keys Christ had conferred on the Church in the words of Matthew 16:19. Luther stated this in thesis 61 of the Ninety-five Theses and expanded the notion in the corresponding *Explanation* (WA 1, 615f; LW 31, 229f). At this time Luther severely limited the effectiveness of such grants to the release from imposed ecclesial penances, as distinguished from the "life-penance" to which all persons remain obligated until the last infection of

sin is extirpated in death. Cajetan saw the two kinds of penance as interrelated, and so rejects the notion of remission by a pure act of authority.

10. *Exsurge Domine*, article 28 (DS 1478 = DB 768), taken from Luther's *Explanations*, Thesis 26 (WA 1, 583,5; LW 31, 172). Again, Cajetan does not give the article verbatim as found in Luther or *Exsurge*.

11. John IV, Patriarch of Antioch, *De comparatione maximi pontificis ad sacrosanctum concilium*, a work composed in 1434 at the Council of Basle (text in Mansi, *Sacrorum Conciliorum . . . collectio*, 29, 512-533). J. Almain had cited this conciliarist work against Cajetan in 1512 in his *Tractatus de authoritate ecclesiae*, VIII (*Johannis Gersonis Opera Omnia*, ed. L.E. du Pin, II [Antwerp 1706], 995f). An edition of the Patriarch's treatise was published in Paris in the early 16th Century (dated by the British Museum Catalog as *ca.* 1520).

12. Cajetan cites this text from Gratian's *Decretum*, Pars II, C. XXIV, Q. 1, c. 14 (CIC I, 970), where it is wrongly attributed to St. Jerome. In the critical edition of *The Divine Institution of the Pontifical Office*, F. Lauchert identified its source as Pelagius' *Libellus fidei*, a work of self-defense addressed to Pope Innocent I (CC 10, 95, n. 5).

V. ERRORS ON THE LORD'S SUPPER, 1525

The circumstances that gave rise to this work are described in the Introduction, pages 33-34, above. The translation is from *Instructio Nuntii circa Errores Libelli de Cena Domini*, edited by F.A. von Gunten, O.P. (Rome: Angelicum, 1962), which gives a text based on that found in Cajetan's *Opuscula quaestiones* (Venice 1531). Our notes include extensive borrowings from the notes in Fr. von Gunten's edition, especially for passages in Zwingli's *Commentarius* to which Cajetan took exception. We add references to similar texts available in English translations. Section headings have been composed by the Editor of this volume.

1. Zwingli, *De vera et falsa religione commentarius (Huldreich Zwinglis Sämtliche Werke*, ed. E. Egli et al., III [Leipzig 1914], 776,23.29, 780,41, 781,13; *The Latin Works of Huldreich Zwingli*, ed. and trans. S.M. Jackson et al., 3 [Philadelphia 1929], 201, 206, 207); *On the Lord's Supper (Zwingli and Bullinger*, ed. and trans. G.W. Bromiley [Philadelphia and London 1953], 199-207); *Exposition of the Faith (Ibid.*, 258-260). Cornelisz Hoen's "Most Christian Letter", which Zwingli had published, begins its argument on the presence of Christ from John 6:56 (*Forerunners of the Reformation*, ed. H.A. Oberman [New York and London 1967], 268).

2. Cajetan's arguments in favor of a Eucharistic interpretation of John 6 are not consistent with what he wrote in earlier and later works. In his extensive commentary on ST, III, 80, 12, Cajetan argued that John 6:53f is literally about belief in Christ and in his death for the life of the world. An argument in confirmation of the non-Eucharistic interpretation is that thereby John 6 provides no evidence against the Catholic rite of Communion under one form, as the Hussites had been contending, *Sancti Thomae Aquinatis Opera Omnia* (Leonine edition), XII (Rome 1906), 246-248. In his biblical

commentaries of the late 1520s, Cajetan returned to the view that Christ did not intend to speak about the Eucharist in John 6. See R.C. Jenkins, *Pre-Tridentine Doctrine* (London 1891), 53-56. In 1531, in responding to the Lutheran demand for Communion under both forms, Cajetan also denied that the *sensus genuinus* of John 6:53f was about the Eucharist, arguing that such an interpretation would undercut the unique necessity of baptism for salvation. See page 207, above. Later in the sixteenth century, Robert Bellarmine listed Cajetan among the handful of Catholic writers who, along with Luther, Zwingli, Oecolampadius, Chemnitz, and Calvin, said that John 6 contained no reference to sacramental eating. Bellarmine is convinced this view is wrong, but he excuses Cajetan of any fault, since he was among those who erred, *"optima intentione, ut videlicet facilius defenderunt veritatem,"* and because Cajetan subjected his views to the judgment of Councils and Roman Pontiffs, Bellarmine, *Controversarium de sacramento Eucharistiae, I,5* (*Opera omnia,* IV [Paris 1873], 16). In the response to Zwingli in 1525, Cajetan appears to have let the need of defense weaken his grasp on what he had once seen and will soon see again as the truth.

3. Zwingli, *Commentarius (Werke,* III, 782,16.23, 785,32; *Latin Works,* 3, 208f, 212); *On the Lord's Supper (Zwingli and Bullinger,* 205-210).

4. Zwingli, *Commentarius (Werke,* III, 783,16; *Latin Works,* 3, 210); *On the Lord's Supper (Zwingli and Bullinger,* 193-196). Berengar of Tours was forced to sign a massively realistic statent of the Eucharistic presence at the Roman synod of 1059, under Pope Nicholas II (DS 690). Berengar signed a second formula, which referred to a "substantial" presence, in 1079, under Pope Gregory VII (DS 700 = DB 355). Only the first formula was absorbed into the canonical tradition and thus made readily available to late medieval and early modern theologians. Zwingli cited the 1059 formula from Gratian, *Decretum,* Pars II, D. II, c. 16 (CIC I, 1328f). In contrast to Zwingli, Luther found the 1059 formula quite to his liking: "The fanatics [Carlstadt, Zwingli, Oecolampadius] are wrong . . . if they criticize Pope Nicholas for having Berengar to confess that the true body of Christ is crushed and ground with the teeth. Would to God that all popes had acted in so Christian a fashion in all other matters as this pope did with Berengar in forcing this confession" (LW 37, 300f, trans. R.H. Fischer, from WA 26, 442,39). The eleventh century controversy has been exhaustively portrayed by J. de Montclos, *Lanfranc et Berengar* (Louvain 1971).

5. Zwingli, *Commentarius (Werke,* III, 786,18; *Latin Works,* 3, 213).

6. *Ibid, (Werke,* III, 787,3; *Latin Works,* 3, 214).

7. *Ibid. (Werke,* III, 787,37; *Latin Works,* 3, 215).

8. *Ibid. (Werke,* III, 795,9; *Latin Works,* 3, 224); *On the Lord's Supper (Zwingli and Bullinger,* 223); Hoen, "Most Christian Letter" *(Forerunners,* 270).

9. Zwingli, *Commentarius (Werke,* III, 798,1; *Latin Works,* 3, 227).

10. *Ibid. (Werke,* III, 798,13; *Latin Works,* 3, 227) Here Zwingli refers back to a passage (*Werke,* III, 786,26; *Latin Works,* 3, 213) which Cajetan had treated in the second part of Chapter 4, above.

11. *Ibid. (Werke,* III, 798,24; *Latin Works,* 3, 227). In *On the Lord's Supper,* Zwingli's most forceful argument from the larger biblical context

focused on the Paschal Lamb *(Zwingli and Bullinger,* 225f), but he also argued from the commemorative aspect of the Eucharist *(Ibid.,* 229f).

12. Peter Lombard, *Liber Sententiarum,* IV, 8, 7 (Quaracchi edition, II, 791).

13. Zwingli, *Commentarius (Werke,* III, 803,28; *Latin Works,* 3, 233).

14. *Ibid. (Werke,* III, 803, 30, 804, 7, 805,11, *Latin Works,* 3, 233, 234, 235). In arguing from Hebrews against the aspect of sacrifice Zwingli cited from his own *Antibolon* of 1524 against Jerome Emser. In framing Zwingli's argument for this chapter, Cajetan appears to have himself added the citation of Hebrews 10:14.

15. Cajetan will treat at some length the fundamental unity of the sacrifice of the cross and each mass in *The Sacrifice of the Mass* in 1531 (above, pages 197-200).

16. The two canons are consecutive: *Decretum,* Pars III, D. I, cc. 47-48 (CIC I, 1306).

17. F. von Gunten gives as Cajetan's source for the story of Lawrence and Xistus (= Sixtus) the 1460 work of the Milanese humanist Boninus Mombritius, *Sanctuarium seu vitae sanctorum* (ed. F. Brunet [Paris 1911], II, 649).

18. Zwingli, *Commentarius (Werke,* III 808,12.27, 817,20; *Latin Works,* 3 239). Hoen had charged that adoration of the Eucharist was tantamount to idolatry in "Most Christian Letter" *(Forerunners,* 269).

19. Zwingli, *Commentarius (Werke,* III, 809-815, *Latin Works,* 3, 239-247), where a text from Jerome is also given. After the patristic texts, Zwingli concluded, "We have cited these renowned Fathers, not because we wish the support of human authority for a matter obvious of itself and solidly rooted in the Word of God, but rather to show the immature we are not the first to offer this interpretation." *Ibid. (Werke,* III, 816,1). In *On the Lord's Supper,* Zwingli gave texts from Jerome, Ambrose, and Augustine *(Zwingli and Bullinger,* 233), while referring the reader to the book of the Basle reformer, Oecolampadius, which had been translated into the German vernacular in early 1526, for a full treatment of the early Fathers' understanding of the Eucharistic presence.

20. Zwingli, *Commentarius (Werke,* III, 819,8; *Latin Works,* 3, 251).

VI. THE KING'S MARRIAGE, 1530

See the Introduction, pages 38-40, above, for an account of the occasion of this work. Our translation was made from the text given in Cajetan's *Opuscula omnia* (Turin 1582), 442a-446a, and was then emended in accord with the superior text printed as folios 193-199 with Cajetan's commentaries on Proverbs, Ecclesiastes, and Isaiah 1-3 (Paris 1545). A copy of the latter is held by the library of New College, London. Chapter titles in the translation slightly abbreviate those given in the two sixteenth century editions used.

1. There follows the text of the document of 1504 in which Pope Julius II dispensed Henry and Catharine from the impediment of affinity in the first degree. Cajetan abbreviated the text slightly by omitting in the body an elaborate listing of all conceivable canonical penalties from which the Pope —

by way of precaution – absolved Henry and Catharine. At the end of the citation, Cajetan omitted the standard warning issued by the Pope against anyone tampering with the document of dispensation.

2. Cajetan had used the services of two men knowledgeable in Hebrew for his translation and commentary on the Psalter (1527) and for the commentary on the books of the Old Testament on which he was working in 1530. See our Introduction, page 34, above. In writing this report on the King's marriage, Cajetan appears to have had a special consultation with his two resource men in order to test the cogency of arguments based on variants of the Hebrew original from the Vulgate.

3. Marriages between persons related by marriage were first prohibited by a series of ancient local councils, beginning in canon 2 of the Council of Neocaesara in 314 (Mansi, *Sacorum Conciliorum . . . Collectio*, II, 540). The prohibition was repeated in canons 9 and 11 of the Roman Synod of 402 (Mansi, III, 1137f), and by ten other councils of the sixth and seventh centuries. Certain expressions of patristic writers influenced considerably the understanding of the impediment. St. Basil (Letter 160 [PG 32, 627]), St. Augustine (*Contra Faustum*, XXII, 61 [CSEL 25, 656f]), and a letter which Bede attributed to Pope Gregory the Great (*Historia Ecclesiastica*, I, 27, 5 ed. Colgrave and Mynors [Oxford 1969], 84) referred to carnal union so uniting man and wife that a future union with a relative of one's spouse would be incestuous. This view was adopted by Popes and councils in the eighth and ninth centuries and came into Gratian's *Decretum* in the twelfth century (Pars II, C. XXXV, Q. 2-3, c. 15 and Q. 5, c. 3 [CIC I, 1267 and 1274f]). By the time of the Fourth Lateran Council (1215), there was need to contract the range of prohibitions, since these had been expanding to distant relatives of one's spouse. The council restricted the impediment to the fourth degree of the spouse's blood relatives, a stipulation taken up in the *Decretalium Gregorii IX Compilatio*, Liber IV, T. XIV, c. 8 (CIC II, 703f). This note has been based on the much fuller account by P. Dib, Affinité," *Dictionnaire du Droit Canonique*, I (1935), 264-285.

VII. THE SACRIFICE OF THE MASS, 1531

The context in which Cajetan wrote this work is related in the Introduction, page 40, above. Our translation is from the separate edition in octavo brought out by Gerald Bladus (Rome 1531). Our chapter titles follow closely the Bladus edition.

1. Cajetan is referring to *Errors on the Lord's Supper* (1525), translated on pages 153-173, above.

2. Most probably Cajetan is referring to the *Augsburg Confession*, submitted to Charles V on June 25, 1530. Article 10 is a concise statement of the Lutheran teaching "that the body and blood of Christ are truly present and distributed to those who eat in the Supper of the Lord" (*Concord*, 34). Article 24 explains the measures taken in Lutheran territories to rectify the abuses connected with the erroneous opinion that the mass involved an oblation making sacrifice for sins (*Concord*, 56-61). Cajetan may also have

studied Melanchthon's *Iudicium de missa* (CR 2, 208-215), composed in Augsburg in July 1530.

3. *Augsburg Confession*, Article 24, 30: "Christ commands us to do this in remembrance of him. Therefore the mass was instituted that faith . . . should remember what benefits are received through Christ and should cheer and comfort anxious consciences. For to remember Christ is to remember his benefits and realize they are truly offered to us" (*Concord*, 59). In *Iudicium de missa*, Melanchthon granted that this work of grateful remembrance could be called a sacrifice, but he was fearful that such a view would not fully exclude the practice of private masses and the notion that the mass is a meritorious good work (CR 2, 210f). In the *Apology of the Augsburg Confession* (May 1531), Melanchthon did include that the mass is a sacrifice of praise (Article 24, 74; *Concord*, 262f).

4. "Every sacrifice is something of ours which we present to God. But in the Lord's Supper the body of Christ is presented to us and grace is offered. Hence the Supper is not a sacrifice. The very words show that in the Supper there is no offering of the body [of Christ] to God, but the presenting of it to us: 'Take, eat . . . '" In explaining Luther's view, Melanchthon gives this concise definition: "the supper was instituted, not so that we would offer the body of Christ, but so that through the Supper something would be offered to us, namely a sacrament offering us grace, and we would be stirred to faith and terrified consciences would be consoled." *Iudicium de missa* (CR 2, 212).

5. "Human traditions which are instituted to propitiate God, merit grace, and make satisfaction for sins are opposed to the Gospel and the teaching about faith." *Augsburg Confession*, Article 10 (*Concord*, 37). The muliplication of private masses rests on the perverse theory "that Christ had by his passion made satisfaction for original sin, and had instituted the mass in which an oblation should be made for daily sins, mortal and venial. From this has come the common opinion that the Mass is a work which by its performance takes away the sins of the living and the dead." *Ibid.*, Article 24, 21f (*Concord*, 58). The *Iudicium de missa* attributed this theory to Thomas Aquinas (CR 2, 209).

6. "Concerning these opinions our teachers have warned that they depart from the Holy Scriptures and diminish the glory of Christ's passion, for the passion of Christ was an oblation and satisfaction not only for original guilt but also for other sins. So it is written in the Epistle to the Hebrews, 'We have been sanctified through the offering of the body of Jesus Christ once for all,' and again, 'By a single offering he has perfected for all time those who are sanctified'" [Hebrews 10:10.14]. *Augsburg Confession*, Article 24, 24-27 (*Concord*, 58f). Also: "This theory can be disposed of with great ease, once one understands the righteousness of faith. First, Christ satisfied once and for all for all sins, as Scripture gives witness, 'By a single offering he has perfected those who are sanctified' [Hebrews 10:14]. In the Church we must not tolerate the blasphemous notion that Christ's passion only satisfied for original sin." *Iudicium de missa* (CR 2, 208).

7. The origin of this very orderly presentation of Lutheran objections is not clear. Luther's *De abroganda missa privata* (1521) cited Hebrews 10:14 as part of his evidence against a special, visible priesthood in the New Testament

(WA 8, 415,21). His German work, *This Misuse of the Mass* (also 1521) expanded the argument, citing as well Hebrews 9:11f, 7:25, and 9:25f (LW 36, 145-147), to show that Christ is no longer sacrificed. The two Hebrews' citations against eucharistic sacrifice in the *Augsburg Confession* are given on page 286, note 6, above. It cannot be excluded that the threefold argument against a daily offering of the Eucharist has been constructed by Cajetan after he noted the use of various verses of Hebrews in Protestant writings. In Johann Eck's widely circulated *Enchiridion locorum communium adversus Lutheranos* (1525ff), the objections to the mass as sacrifice were given by a simple *catena* of verses from Hebrews: 10:14, 7:27, 9:12.26b, 10:10 (4th edition [Cologne 1527], fol. F1v).

8. The three arguments against an offering for sins are a more accentuated and systematic presentation of the argument of the *Augsburg Confession*, Article 24, 21-25 (cited on page 286, notes 5-6 above). Again Cajetan's own constructive reflection may well have contributed to the order and formulation.

9. Aristotle, *Topics*, III, 3 (*Aristoteles Graece*, ed. E. Bekker, I, 117a, 18).

VIII. GUIDELINES FOR CONCESSIONS, 1531

The background against which Cajetan composed this work is described in our Introduction, pages 40-41, above. The translation is from the text published by W. Friedensburg, "Aktenstücke über das Verhalten der römischen Kurie zur Reformation 1524 und 1531," *Quellen und Forschungen aus italienischen Archiven und Bibliotheken*, 3 (1900), 16-18.

1. According to the official position taken by Melanchthon and by the Lutheran estates at the Diet of Augsburg, this dogmatic principle laid down by Cajetan would have caused no great difficulty. After the twenty-one articles of faith stated in the Augsburg Confession, Melanchthon prepared the transition to topics of religious practice by declaring, "There is nothing here that departs from the Scriptures or the Catholic Church or the Church of Rome, in so far as the ancient Church is known to us from its writers. Since this is so, those who insist that our teachers are to be regarded as heretics judge too harshly. The whole dissention is concerned with a certain few abuses which have crept into the churches without proper authority." *Concord*, 47. The negotiations between Lutheran and Catholic theologians in August 1530 did bring wide-ranging agreements on the crucial doctrines of sin, grace, faith, and justification (V. Pfnür, *Einig in der Rechtfertigungslehre?* [Wiesbaden, 1971], 251-270).

2. The background of this analysis of the situation lay in the negotiations between Melanchthon and the Papal Legate, Lorenzo Campeggio, during the Diet of Augsburg (July 1530). An example of their exchange is Melanchthon's letter of July 7, stating that unity can be restored if the Lutherans be granted Communion under both forms and the option for clerical marriage. On their part, they would agree to the restoration of episcopal jurisdiction (CR 2, 173). See also the "conditions" Melanchthon submitted on August 4, 1530 (CR 2, 246-248). Shortly after his exchange with Melanchthon, Campeggio reported to Rome that the main Lutheran demands were four: communion under both forms, clerical marriage, modification of the canon of the Mass, and the calling

of a general council. *Nuntiaturberichte aus Deutschland,* 1. Erganzungsband, ed. G. Müller (Tübingen 1963), 70.

3. Melanchthon had argued that both preaching and good order would be aided if the law of clerical celibacy were relaxed. Many priests qualified to preach desired to marry. Greater scandal was being given by clerical unchastity than would be given of priests lived in lawful marriages. *Augsburg Confession,* Article 23 (*Concord,* 51-56); also CR 2, 292f. – Specific Roman acknowledgment of the non-celibate clergy of the East had been made by Popes Innocent III (letter of September 5, 1203) and Innocent IV (1245 bull, *Sub catholicae professione fidei*). Tacit acknowledgment was given by omitting the topic from *Laetentur coeli,* the bull of union with the Greek Church, issued at the Council of Florence, July 6, 1439. W. DeVries, *Rom und die Patriarchate des Ostens* (Freiburg-Munich 1963), 238.

4. Cajetan used the same word (*dissimulare*) that occurred in Melanchthon's appeals for a reasonable leniency in implementing measures that would have the effect of bringing the Protestants back under Roman obedience (CR 2, 170, 248).

5. The *Augsburg Confession,* Article 22 (*Concord,* 49f), called for the revocation of legislation making communion under one form obligatory. In his memorandum of August 4, 1530, Melanchthon assured Campeggio that the Lutherans did not condemn those receiving under one form and that they did profess the integral presence of Christ under each of the forms (CR 2, 246). – The "bull" Cajetan refers to would be the first of the four points of the *Compactata* promulgated in Bohemia by legates of the Council of Basle July 5, 1436, and ratified by the Council January 15, 1437. The text is given by E. Denis, *Huss et la guerre des Hussites* (Paris 1878 & 1930), 495-498. Cajetan is something less than the thoroughgoing papalist in recommending use of a measure Pope Eugenius IV did not recognize in 1437 and Pope Pius II formally annulled in 1462.

6. The *Augsburg Confession,* Article 24 (*Concord,* 56-61), had argued for tolerance of the suppression of private masses, the simplification of liturgical ceremony, and the downplaying of the notion of sacrifice in Lutheran worship. Cajetan's treatise, *The Sacrifice of the Mass* (above, pages 189-200), indicates he believed more was at stake than simply change of rite. Still, he does not call for prohibition of a liturgical formula incorporating the Eucharistic views of the Confession.

7. The *Augsburg Confession* treated ecclesiastical laws in Articles 26 and 28 (*Concord,* 63-70, 81-94). For example, "It is against Scripture to require the observance of traditions for the purpose of making satisfaction for sins or meriting justification, for the glory of Christ's merit is dishonored when we suppose that we are justified by such observances. It is also evident that as a result of this notion traditions have been multiplied in the Church almost beyond calculation, while the teaching concerning faith and the righteousness of faith has been suppressed, for from time to time more holy days were appointed, more fasts prescribed, and new ceremonies and new orders instituted because the authors of these things thought that they would merit grace by these works . . . . Where did the bishops get the right to impose such traditions on the churches and thus ensnare consciences . . . ?" Article 28,

35-37.42 (*Concord*, 86-88).

8. At first the curia rejected the concessions Cajetan recommended (*Nuntiaturberichte*, 80), but when Charles V urged the need of a council the curia shifted its ground in the hope of restoring unity by direct negotiation and possible concessions to the Lutherans. A letter of the imperial ambassador in Rome reported on June 26, 1531, that Clement VII agreed to the first, third, and fifth of Cajetan's concrete recommendations (G. Müller, *Die römische Kurie und die Reformation*, 151). But the instructions sent to the Nuncio in Germany, Girolamo Aleander, in later summer 1531 show that Pope and curia soon swerved back to a very reserved attitude contrasting sharply with Cajetan's openness to concessions (*Nuntiaturberichte*, 280-283, 287-290, 291, 310).

IX. FOUR LUTHERAN ERRORS, 1531

The Introduction, page 41, above, describes the circumstances in which Cajetan wrote this work. The translation is based on the text in a separate octavo edition by Antonius Bladus (Rome 1531), held by the British Museum. Our notes are largely dependent on the references given by G. Hennig, *Cajetan und Luther*, 154-161. The titles of the individual articles translate the titles found in the Baldus edition.

1. After stating twenty-one articles of belief, the *Augsburg Confession* turned to treat the changes introduced in Lutheran lands to counter abuses in the life of the Church. The plea is for the Emperor's tolerance in view of convictions of conscience: "We pray that Your Imperial Majesty will graciously hear both what has been changed and what our reasons for such changes are, in order that the people may not be compelled to observe these abuses against their conscience." Preface to Part 2 (*Concord*, 49). Article 22, 11, as cited in the following note, also appealed to conscience.

2. The *Confession* argued from Matthew 26:27 and 1 Corinthians 11:20ff in Article 22, 1-3, and said further, "It is not proper to burden the consciences of those who desire to observe the sacrament according to Christ's institution or to compel them to act contrary to the arrangement of our Lord Christ" (Article 22, 11). The passages are given in *Concord*, 49f.

3. Lutherans did not argue in this manner in Cajetan's day, since Luther had explained the whole of Christ's discourse in John 6 as a treatment of faith. In his commentary on the *Summa* (on III, 80, 12), Cajetan had also dealt with the Bohemian Utraquist argument from John 6 for reception under both forms.

4. See, however, Cajetan's argument for taking John 6 in a eucharistic sense in his 1525 refutation of Zwingli, pages 153ff, above, with note 2.

5. In the *Augsburg Confession*, however, Melanchthon had made a rudimentary argument for both forms on the basis of early tradition (Cyprian, Jerome, Pope Gelasius) and from the allegedly recent and quite obscure introduction of reception of Communion under one form. Article 22, 4-8 (*Concord*, 50).

6. *Augsburg Confession* Article 25, 7f (*Concord*, 62), given nearly

verbatim; also Article 11 (*Concord*, 34), where Psalm 18:13 is also cited. Cajetan had argued against Luther's statement of the same position in 1518 in the fourth of his *Augsburg Treatises* (synopsized, pages 62f, above). A comparison of Cajetan's arguments of 1518 and 1531 documents his growth in the understanding of the nature of Reformation controversy. Earlier his main evidence against Luther consisted in conciliar decrees from IV Lateran and Florence. But in 1531 he omitted any reference to such decrees, and instead guided his reader toward pondering the implications of the words of a Gospel passage.

7. *Augsburg Confession*, Article 12, 10: "Rejected are those who do not teach that remission of sins comes through faith but command us to merit grace through satisfactions of our own" (*Concord*, 35). Another passage, Article 20, 19-22, links the issue of satisfaction with the central religious message of the Reformation: "Consciences used to be plagued by the doctrine of works when consolation from the Gospel was not heard. Some persons were by their consciences driven into the desert, into monasteries, in the hope that there they might merit grace by monastic life. Others invented works of another kind to merit grace and make satisfaction for sins. Hence there was very great need to treat of and to restore this teaching concerning faith in Christ in order that anxious consciences should not be deprived of consolation but know that grace and forgiveness of sins are apprehended by faith in Christ" (*Concord*, 43f).

8. Cajetan will develop a biblical thesis on merit and satisfaction in Chapters 6-11 of *Faith and Works*, pages 227-237, above.

9. *Augsburg Confession*, Article 21, 2: "It cannot be proved from the Scriptures that we are to invoke saints or to seek help from them. 'For there is one mediator between God and men, Christ Jesus' (1 Timothy 2:5), who is the only savior, the only highpriest, advocate, and intercessor before God (Romans 8:34). He alone has promised to hear our prayers" (*Concord*, 47).

10. Aristotle, *Nichomachean Ethics*, I, 3. See page 279, note 64, above.

X. FAITH AND WORKS, 1532

Cajetan wrote this work as a counterpart to the Lutheran doctrine of justification as presented in Philip Melanchthon's *Apology of the Augsburg Confession* (1531). Our translation was made from the text in Cajetan's *Opuscula omnia* (Lyons 1562), and then emended to agree with the text given in the edition published by Iohannes Antionius (Venice 1534). Our chapter headings follow closely those given in both sixteenth century editions.

1. Melanchthon, *Apology*, IV, 44f, 76f, 80f, 264 (*Concord*, 113, 117, 118, 146); XII, 35-43, 72, 88 (*Concord*, 186f, 192, 195).

2. *Ibid.*, XII, 62 (*Concord*, 190). This had been more accentuated in Luther's works on *fides absolutionis* in 1518, e.g. *Sermo de poenitentia* (WA 1, 323,28), *Disputatio pro veritate inquirenda* (WA 1, 631,21), *Acta Augustana* (WA 2, 14,2; LW 31, 271).

3. Melanchthon, *Apology*, IV, 77, 111-114, 147-151 (*Concord*, 117, 123, 127); XII, 78, 87 (*Concord*, 193, 195).

4. *Ibid*, IV, 5-8, 145f, 159, 225-229 (*Concord*, 108, 127, 129, 138f); XII, 75 (*Concord*, 193), Matthew 22:27 was cited in IV, 226 (*Concord*, 138).

5. Romans 5:1 was cited in *Apology*, IV, 91, 195, 217, 304 (*Concord*, 120, 134, 137, 154), and XII, 36 (*Concord*, 186). Acts 15:9 occurred at IV, 99, 284 (*Concord*, 121, 150).

6. *De Trinitate*, XV, 18 (CCL 50A, 507).

7. See page 52, especially note 14, above.

8. In lecturing on Romans in 1516, Luther had explained Romans 8:16 in the sense of such a personal testimony of forgiveness (WA 56,369,27, *Lectures on Romans*, trans. W. Pauck [London and Philadelphia 1961], 234). See also *Acta Augustana* (WA 2, 16, 1; LW 31, 274). In both passages Luther's authority for such an understanding of the Spirit's witness was St. Bernard's *Sermo* 1 *In Annuntiatione Dominica*, 1-3 (*Opera*, ed. J. Leclercq et al., III [Rome 1968], 12-14). Melanchthon wrote in 1546 that Luther had once been helped greatly by an older member of the Erfurt Augustinian community who had instructed him in just this way on the authentic meaning of justifying faith (Preface to Volume II of Luther's collected Latin works, cited in CR 6, 159).

9. *Exsurge Domine*, Article 10 (DS 1460 = DB 750), taken from Luther's *Explanations of the Ninety-five Theses*, Thesis 7 (WA, 1, 543,14.22; LW 31, 104).

10. *Exsurge Domine*, Article 11 (DS 1461 = DB 751), taken from Luther's *Sermo de poenitentia* (WA 1, 323,23).

11. *Exsurge Domine*, Article 12 (DS 1462 = DB 752), taken from Luther's *Sermo de poenitentia* (WA 1, 323,32).

12. Melanchthon, *Apology*, IV, 196, 322f, 356-382 (*Concord*, 134, 157, 161-165); XII, 116 (*Concord*, 199).

13. *Ibid.*, IV, 204, 213, 215, 269, 324, 358, 361, 387 (*Concord*, 135, 136f, 147, 157, 162, 166); XII, 77 (*Concord*, 193).

14. The Habacuc verse was cited in *Ibid.*, IV, 100 (*Concord*, 121); Titus 3:5 was not cited in the *Apology*; Ephesians 2:8 was cited at IV, 87, 93 (*Concord*, 120).

15. *Ibid.*, IV, 356 (*Concord*, 161).

16. Cited at *Ibid.*, IV 334 (*Concord*, 158), but without specific development against the satisfactory value of the works of the righteous.

17. *Ibid.*, IV, 189, 214, 246 (*Concord*, 133, 136, 142); XII, 139, 174 (*Concord*, 203, 210).

18. Aristotle, *Nichomachean Ethics*, V, 6 (*Aristoteles Graece*, ed. E. Bekker II, 1134b,8).

19. Cajetan is most probably dependent on Aquinas' collection of patristic citations in *Catena aurea, In Mattheum*, XX, 1 (Marietti, edition, I, 292f). Origen interpreted the denarius as representing salvation in *Commentaria* in *Mattheum*, XV, 34 (PG 13, 1351). Jerome did not speak so clearly, but did explain that the denarius entailed a gift of the image and likeness of the King in *Commentarium in Evangelium S. Matthei*, III, 20 (CCL 77, 176). Augustine said the denarius stood for eternal life in *De sancta virginitate*, 26 (CSEL 41, 262). Gregory the Great agreed in *Homiliae XL in Evangelia*, XIX, 3 (PL 76, 1156). The final reference is to *Opus imperfectum in Mattheum*, 34 (PG 65,

819), which was incorrectly attributed to St. John Chrysostom throughout the Middle Ages.

20. Pseudo-Dionysius, *Heavenly Hierarchies*, III, 2 (PG 3, 166).

21. Melanchthon, *Apology*, XII, 116-121, 131-142, 172 (*Concord*, 199f, 202-204, 209).

22. *Ibid.*

23. See chapter 5, above, pp. 226f.

24. Cajetan's assertion that the *affluentia* of Christ's merit and satisfaction is the root of merit and satisfaction by Christ's members is an application of a basic Thomist conviction. In this view, the actions of created causes do not compete with God's causality. The human and divine agents are not a pair of near equals that divide the work, with each delimiting the ambit of the other's influence. The creature does not supplement where God is weak. Neither does God reduce secondary causes by the fact of his universal efficiency. Rather, *propter suam abundantiam* he confers on the creature an active, and, at times, a free, participation in His own causal activity (ST I, 22, 3).

XI. MARRIAGE WITH A BROTHER'S WIDOW, 1534

Our Introduction, pages 39f, above, relates the circumstances in which Cajetan wrote this work. It is a resume and continuation of the argument developed in *The Kings Marriage* (1530), pages 175-188, above. Our translation is from a text printed with Cajetan's commentary on the Book of Job by Antonius Bladus (Rome 1535), fol. 139-140.

1. Josephus, *Antiquities*, XVIII, 14 (*Opera Omnia*, ed. S. Naber, IV [Leipzig 1893], 160f).

2. Hegesippus, *Historiae*, II, 5 (CSEL 66/1, 140).

3. In difficult and disputed cases, "you shall arise and go up to the place which the Lord your God will choose, and coming to the Levitical priests, and to the judge who is in office in those days, you shall consult them, and they shall declare to you the decision. Then you shall do according to what they declare to you . . . and you shall be careful to do according to all that they direct you" (Deuteronomy 17:8-10). For Cajetan, the biblical law is prescribing recourse to a papal decision. See page 187, above.

Made in the USA
Monee, IL
26 September 2022